AS for AQA

success in
sociology

Peter Coving

© 2008 Folens Limited, on behalf of the author

United Kingdom: Folens Publishers, Waterslade House, Thame Road, Haddenham, Buckinghamshire, HP17 8NT

Email: folens@folens.com

Ireland: Folens Publishers, Greenhills Road, Tallaght, Dublin 24

Email: info@folens.ie

Editor: Joanne Murray

Project development: Mary James

Design and layout: eMC Design

Cover design: Jump To!

First published 2008 by Folens Limited

British Cataloguing in Publication Data. A catalogue record for this publication is available from the British Library.

ISBN 978-1-85008-260-6

Folens code: FD2606

Contents

Acknowledgements

The author wishes to personally thank his partner, Caroline, and children, Keir and Nye, for the support and love they have offered during the writing of this book.

Acknowledgement is made to the following for photographs and permission to reproduce copyright material:

'Dancing the night away' © iStockphoto.com / Jacob Wackerhausen
'Nightclub' © Corbis/Robert Wallis
'Sir Paul McCartney' © Robert Galbraith/ Reuters/Corbis
'High street takeaway shops' © Ashley Cooper/Corbis
'Parents interacting with young children' © Fotolia
'Person in wheelchair' © Fotolia
'Shopping' © iStock
'Genie the wild child' © Bettmann/Corbis
'Gang of Youths' © John Birdsall
'Morris dancers' © Adam Woolfitt/Corbis
'McDonald's in Russia' © Catherine Karnow/ Corbis
'Shakespeare' © iStock
'People shaking hands' © Fotolia
'Students in a school classroom' © Fotolia
'Children watching TV' © iStock
'Talcott Parsons' © The Granger Collection, New York
'Red London Bus' © iStock
'Karl Marx' © Michael Nicholson/Corbis
'Max Weber' © Condé Nast Archive/Corbis
'Woman carrying out domestic work' © Fotolia
'GP and patient' © Sebastian Pfuetze/zefa/ Corbis
'Howard Becker' © Bassouls Sophie/Corbis Sygma
'Maid' © Tim Pannell/Corbis
'Stelios Haji-Ioannou' © Eric Gaillard / Reuters/Corbis
'White-collar office workers' © Fotolia
'Chinese student' © John Birdsall
'Elderly person' © Fotolia
'Shopping centre' © Fotolia
'Factory worker' © William Taufic/Corbis
'George Ritzer' © George Ritzer
'Skyscrapers' © Fotolia
'Call centre' © iStock
'Businessman' © iStockphoto.com / TommL
'Run-down shops' © iStock
'Lakshmi Mittal' © Eloy Alonso/Reuters/ Corbis
'Pensioner in post office' © Rex Features/ Chat Magazine
'Smart Housing' © iStock
'Margaret Thatcher' © Peter Turnley/Corbis
'Nigel Lawson' © Hulton-Deutsch Collection/ Corbis
'Alistair Darling' © Yassukovich/Corbis/ Sygma
'Warehouse' © iStock
'Third World hunger' © Peter Turnley/Corbis
'Family watching colour TV' © Colourbox
'Run-down high rise flats' © iStock
'Mother with Child' © iStock
'Norman Tebbit' © Derek Hudson/Sygma/ Corbis
'Frank Field' © Getty Images
'Working in a hotel' © Corbis
'Baker carrying fresh bread' © Mika/zefa/ Corbis
'Earl Grey' © Hulton Archive/Stringer/Getty
'Care at home' © Photofusion Picture Library
'Private hospital room' © iStock
'University students studying' © iStock
'Happy child' © iStockphoto.com / Rosemarie Gearhart
'Family Unit' © iStock
'Nuclear family' © H. Armstrong Roberts/ Corbis
'Old-fashioned' family with servants' © Minnesota Historical Society/CORBIS
'Family at Christmas time' © Fotolia
'Family home and car' © Corbis

'Pre-industrial' © Stapleton Collection/Corbis
'Bangladeshi wedding' © Charles & Josette Lenars/CORBIS
'Couple just married' © Fotolia
'Couple with baby' © Gary Alvis /iStock
'Teenage mother' © iStock
'Extended family' © iStock
'Asian family' © Colourbox
'Single parent with children' © James Pauls/ iStock
'Man carrying out household tasks' © Colourbox
'Woman carrying out household tasks' © iStock
'Victim of domestic violence' © iStock
'Woman working out finances' © iStock
'Teenager' © Fotolia
'Working child in industrial times' © Horace Bristol/Corbis
'Children at school' © iStock
'Child using Internet' © Fotolia
'Fruit in Supermarket' © Fotolia
'At the lecture' © Dmitry Nikolaev. Image from BigStockPhoto.com
'Students in classroom' © Colourbox
'Old-fashioned classroom' © Frances Benjamin Johnston/Corbis
'Emile Durkheim' © Corbis/ Bettmann
'Students sitting an exam' © Will & Deni McIntyre/Corbis
'University students' © Peter Adams/Corbis
'Teacher giving instructions' © Corbis
'Paul Willis' © Paul Willis
'Schoolboys playing truant' © Image Source/ Corbis
'Children playing in East London urban adventure playground' © Janine Wiedel/ Photofusion
'Schoolchildren in early 1940s' © Hulton-Deutsch Collection/Corbis
'1950s schoolchildren sitting the 11 + exam' © Museum of London / Heritage-Images/ Imagestate
'Harold Wilson' © Bettmann/CORBIS
'James Callaghan' © Hulton-Deutsch Collection/Corbis
'City technology college' © John Walmsley/ Education Photos
'Tony Blair' © Brooks Kraft/Corbis
David Gillburn and Deborah Youdell © Robert Taylor Photography/Australian Education Union/Deborah Youdell
'Run-down housing estate' © iStock
'Pierre Bourdieu' © Nogues Alain/Corbis Sygma
'Diane Reay' © Diane Reay
'Mixed-race classroom' © iStock
'School teacher interacting with schoolchildren' © iStock
'Schoolgirl doing homework' © Colourbox
'Gang of schoolboys' © MM Productions/ Corbis
'Questionnaire sheets' © iStock
'Interviewer with school pupil' © Alamy/ ACE Stock
'Boys working together on a science experiment in a lab at at Haris School, South London' © Janine Wiedel/ Photofusion
'Operating room' © iStockphoto.com / Nathan Maxfield
'Doctor' © iStock
'Hospital' © iStock
'Active elderly people' © iStock
'GP and Patient' © Colourbox
'Arthur Kleinman' © Arthur Kleinman/ Harvard University
'Acupuncture' © iStock

'Anthony Giddens' © The London School of Economics/Lord Anthony Giddens
'Laboratory worker' © iStock
'Private hospital' © Colourbox
'Woman smoking' © iStock
'Men drinking' © Colourbox
'Elderly person in GP's surgery' © Frank Siteman Doctor Stock/Getty
'Washing hands' © iStock
'Michel Foucault' © AFP/Getty Images
'Woman carer' © iStock
'Students studying medicine' © David Joel/ Getty
'Emily Grundy' © Emily Grundy
'Pharmacist handing out prescriptions' © Colourbox
'Doctor discussing a patient with a senior nurse at Ealing General Hospital, London' © David Hoffman/Photofusion
'Interview' © iStockphoto.com / Nicholas Sutcliffe
'Spreadsheets' © iStock
'Academic Journals' © Bettmann/Corbis
'Questionnaire' © iStock
'Researcher' © Catherine Ledner/Getty Images
'Formal interview' © Fotolia
'Interview' © iStockphoto.com / Nicholas Sutcliffe
'Toddlers' © iStock
'Informal interview' © M. Thomsen/Zefa/ Corbis
'Group of people' © iStock
'Gang on the street' © Lisa Woollett/ Photofusion
'Old documents' © James L. Amos/Corbis
'Old Photographs' © Hulton-Deutsch Collection/Corbis
'Internet' © James Leynse/Corbis
'Auguste Comte' © Hulton Archive/Stringer
'Pile of questionnaires' © Simon Jarratt/ Corbis
'Tribe' © Jane Sweeney/Robert Harding World Imagery/Corbis
'Scientist carrying out experiments' © Jacky Chapman/Photofusion
'TV news reporter' © John Lund/Corbis
'Market researcher' © Digital Nation/ Photofusion

Department of Health for the graph "The proportion of working-age people who are deemed to be at a high risk of developing a mental illness is somewhat lower than a decade ago" source Health Survey for England, DH © Crown Copyright 2008; Department for Work and Pensions for the graphs "A half of all lone parents are in low income, two-and-a-half times the rate for couples with children" source *Households Below Average Income*, DWP, UK; "Infant mortality rate per 1,000 live births (England and Wales)" published by Office for National Statistics (data cover England and Wales); "Risk of income poverty by household characteristics, 2005/06" source *Households Below Average Income*, DWP; "The vast majority of people with very low incomes are either working age adults without children or couples with children. Relatively few are either lone parents or pensioners" source *Households Below Average Income*, DWP; and "Women are a bit – but only a bit – more likely to survive on low income households than men" source H*ouseholds below Average Income*, DWP© Crown Copyright 2007, 2008; Eurostat for "Graph showing proportion of children born outside of marriage in countries in the EU" copyright © Eurostat;

HM Revenue & Customs for the table "Share Of The Wealth 1% of population owns 21% of wealth" published by Inland Revenue Personal Wealth © Crown Copyright 2006; The Institute for Fiscal Studies for the figure "The Gini coefficient, 1979 to 2005/06 (GB)" copyright © Institute for Fiscal Studies, 2006; Joseph Rowntree Foundation for "Figure 1: From the Findings *Public attitudes to economic inequality* published in 2007"; "Table 1 From the Findings *Monitoring poverty and social exclusion in the UK 2006* published in 2006 by the Joseph Rowntree Foundation; and "Figure 3B From *Monitoring poverty and social exclusion in the UK 2006*, by Guy Palmer, Tom MacInnes and Peter Kenway, published in 2006 by the Joseph Rowntree Foundation. Reproduced by permission of the Joseph Rowntree Foundation; The King's Fund for the graph "spending on the NHS" 1983-2008 copyright © The King's Fund; Miniwatts Marketing Group for the table "Top 43 Countries with the Highest Internet Penetration Rate" 2007 www.internetworldstats.com copyright © 2008, Miniwatts Marketing Group. All rights reserved worldwide; The Newspaper Marketing Agency for the graph "Readership by Age and Social Class" from *NMA Marketplace Charts* November 2007 © NRS, Jan 07- June 07 copyright © The Newspaper Marketing Agency; Office for National Statistics for the graphs "Births & Deaths, Births to exceed deaths up to 2031 United Kingdom" source Office for National Statistics, General Register Office for Scotland, Northern Ireland Statistics and Research Agency, Central Statistics Office Ireland; "Children per woman"; "Distribution of Real Disposable Household Income in the UK" source *Social Trends* 36, 2006, "Fertility rate 1945-2020" source *Social Trends* 2002, "Average UK household size", "People in households by type of household" and "Households by type and family" sourced Census, Labour Force Survey, Office for National Statistics; "Divorces fall by 7 per cent in 2006, England and Wales" source Office for National Statistics; General Register Office for Scotland; Northern Ireland Statistics and Research Agency; "Gender Pay Gap Narrowest since records began" source Annual Survey of Hours and Earnings (ASHE); "Percentage of poverty levels by ethnic group"; "Projections for the future of people over the age of 50" source *National Statistics Population Projections*, Government Actuary's Department, 2001; "UK population 1901-2005" source *1901-71 British Historical Statistics*, Mitchell (1988) / 1981-2001 Office for National Statistics, Population Trends (1998); and "UK unemployment rate 1971-2006" © Crown Copyright 2001, 2006, 2007; PropertyInvesting.net for the graph "UK House Prices 1991 – 2004" from "Cornish Population Increase Drives Up Prices - will this last?" published on http://www.propertyinvesting.net/; and Scienceaid.co.uk for the graphs "exam results" and "people with flu" published on http://scienceaid.co.uk/psychology/approaches/representing.html.

There are instances where we have been unable to trace or contact the copyright holder. If notified the publisher will be pleased to rectify any errors or omissions at the earliest opportunity.

5

Introduction

Folens: Success in Sociology is the innovative product of many years teaching A level Sociology in a range of schools. It has been designed to meet the needs of students who are both new to sociology and those wanting to further extend their learning. Moreover, I wanted to develop a text that sociology teachers would want to use as their first point of call; that would meet the needs of experienced and new teachers alike, and also offer an integrated, thorough approach to learning.

The book covers the AS components of the A level Sociology AQA specification:

- Unit One (SCLY1): Culture and identity; families and households; and wealth, poverty and welfare.
- Unit Two (SCLY2): Education; health; and sociological methods.

In essence I have made sure that *Success in Sociology* does the following:

- Meets the needs of the new AQA sociology specification:

  The text guides teachers in teaching the new AQA A level Sociology specification. As with all new examinations, teachers have to interpret how they are going to teach the new material and how best to deliver it. As such, I hope this book and the accompanying Teacher Guide will prove to be of practical use to both students and teachers. Many textbooks on the market do not include exercises that can be used in the classroom and are only used by teachers rather than the students for who they are aimed! This textbook fuses the thoroughness of other key texts as well as offering student exercises. It is designed to support and be used alongside other traditional texts.

- Includes new studies to quote in examinations and in class:

  The book is full of recent and salient examples that can be used in essays and examinations. Of course, some older studies are still used, as many of these remain both influential and essential to students' understanding.

- Is contemporary, accessible and readable:

  The aim of this book is to be comprehensive, contemporary and easy to pick up and read; yet authoritative. My aim has been to make it as accessible as possible without trivialising the material with brevity. In its writing I have included many of the tips that I gained from the people I have been fortunate to learn the teaching trade from. As ever, teaching material is all about making the world relevant and interesting to the student. I hope this active approach motivates its readers as a result.

- Provides a consistent approach:

  Unusually for a sociology textbook, I have written all the modules; whereas most authors co-write. As a consequence there is a consistent approach to the text. Throughout it is designed to encourage the student to think about sociological concepts in a critical and thoughtful way. This is why, for instance, questions have been included to open up debate.

- Explains the changes in the new AQA specification:

  This book has been targeted very specifically for the AQA Sociology specification, primarily because this board has always dominated the assessment of sociology. However, I hope that it will also prove useful for those who are studying sociology with other examination boards. The new specification itself is more a reworking of an 'old friend'. Most of the newer bits of the specification have in fact been in previous specifications. Topic One, for instance, *Culture and identity*, used to be part of the 'old' pre-Curriculum 2000 A level. The most fundamental change is the move away from coursework.

The new AQA specification follows a very similar route to the last. *Integral elements* remain; specifically, sociological theories, perspectives and sociological methods. The core themes area of the specification is also remarkably similar: Socialization; culture and identity; and social differentiation, power and stratification. Within the specification itself, Unit One includes *culture and identity* which has been reintroduced. *Family and households* remains as before.

Much of the new specification uses words like *contemporary*. Students and teachers alike should be aware of the need to quote modern-day accounts of theory and method. The only really new area in *family and households* is the *demographic trends* section, with a 1900 starting point. And lastly, *wealth, poverty and welfare*, again is similar to what was required before. All of these need to be examined in relation to the two core themes as mentioned above.

Unit Two is where the real differences start to kick in. Although the two core themes remain, this topic adds applied methods into the mix. Candidates are expected to use examples of their own research when answering examination responses. I hope this allows both students and teachers to have more classroom time for mini projects similar to the old A level before Curriculum 2000. Unit Two specification follows the same format as Unit One, with old areas remaining as before. Within Assessment Objective 1 (AO1) students will be expected to have a good knowledge and understanding of sociological theories and know appropriate concepts, as well as needing to know about how sociologists do social research. Finally, within *knowledge and understanding*, the two core themes need to be integrated in each module. This is straightforward as it always was! AO2 is also similar to before, with pupils needing to show the skills of interpreting, applying and evaluating sociological material (this material can be the result of students' own investigation or of published research).

Key features of the text

I have designed the text to be user friendly. Therefore with each topic the following are provided:

- **What the AQA specification says:** The book is linked to what you need to know, allowing students and teachers the chance to get on with their learning effectively.

- **Skills required:** For each module area I explicitly explain what skills the examining board require from you. The book particularly focuses on a skill-based approach, encouraging students to think analytically about sociological theory and methods.

- **What it means to be studying:** Each topic introduces what is covered and how this can be contextualised for pupils and teachers.

- **Sociologists studied in each topic:** These are provided for each topic; with names, dates and key studies; enabling students to cross-reference key writers.

- **Learning objectives:** Each section has the expected outcomes explicitly outlined so students know exactly what they need to learn.

- **Research boxes:** Students will find contemporary research that offers an insight into how research is carried out, whilst providing examples that can be used in essays and project work.

- **Key terms:** Given the amount of jargon used by sociologists, key terms are provided to help develop knowledge and understanding, but also to help with revision. These are in bold throughout the book and also listed at the end of each topic so students can easily cross-reference them.

- **What do you know now?** These are diagnostic and self-assessment questions that students can use to check they have understood each section.

- **Section summaries:** Summary points are provided at the end of each section.

- **How to maximise your grade with AQA:** Practical tips are given on how to improve your grade.

- **Exam practice for AQA:** Sample questions in the same format as the new AQA AS Sociology examination are also provided.

Topic 1

Culture and identity

Learning objectives

What the AQA spec says	Section in this book	Page
Different conceptions of culture, including sub-culture, mass culture, high and low culture, popular culture and global culture.	Section One: What is culture and identity?	12
The socialization process and the role of agencies of socialization.	Section Two: Socialization and the role of agencies	18
Sources and different conceptions of the self, identity and difference.	Section Three: Self, identity and difference	24
The relationship of identity to age, disability, ethnicity, gender, nationality, sexuality and social class in contemporary society.	Section Four: The relationship of identity to different social groups	34
Leisure, consumption and identity.	Section Five: Leisure, consumption and identity	42

Exam skill focus

Skills required	
AO1 Knowledge and understanding of theories.	You should know about consensus and conflict, social structure, social action, postmodernism and feminism.
AO2 Demonstration of the skills of application, analysis, interpretation and evaluation.	You should be able to apply your knowledge of culture and be able to relate to different cultural products. Additionally, you should be able to evaluate theories.

What it means to be studying culture and identity with AQA

In this module, we will be introducing the concepts of 'culture' and 'identity'. We start off in **Section One** by looking at what is meant by culture; defining it, examining the differences and similarities between high and low culture, and the role of globalisation in the way we see our culture. Do we regard Paul McCartney as a purveyor of mass culture, high culture, or as the main songwriter alongside John Lennon? Or is he a classical choral music composer of such pieces as Ecce Cor Meum? Culture defines

who we are as people, our language, (Scouse, Cockney), our regional identity (Liverpudlian, Londoner). But of course we are increasingly influenced by other worldwide changes; for example, our penchant for Chinese or Indian takeaways.

Section Two explores the concept of socialization, how we develop similar norms and values, and the role of our parents and other influences in passing on culture. How, for example, we learn what is 'normal', natural and inevitable and why we learn not to question these ideas. Why, for instance, do must of us just accept that we will go to school, get a job, have a family and then slip into old age?

In **Section Three** we examine how different theories of culture suggest our behaviour is regulated. We look at the macro theories of functionalism and Marxism and contrast these with interactionist explanations.

Section Four looks at how age, disability, gender, nationality, sexuality and social class affect our identity. We examine if social class is still important – is there social mobility? And are some born to rule? Is disability becoming more socially acceptable, with disabled people being embraced within society rather than marginalised? We also look at the way society constructs ideas about different races, ages and those of differing sexuality. Finally, we explore how our shopping patterns divide our identity. Do we identify with people who have similar buying patterns as us? How and why have these patterns been changing in contemporary British society?

Culture and identity

Sociologists studied in this topic

Ken Auletta (1982)	American writer and journalist who first coined the phrase 'the underclass'.
Bates and Plog (1990)	Provided a useful definition of culture.
Jean Baudrillard	French philosopher and sociologist most associated with postmodernism.
Simone de Beauvoir	Her book, *The Second Sex*, is considered the catalyst for the 'second wave' of feminism. Famously married to Jean Paul Satre, much of her work was influenced by her 'open marriage' to Satre.
Howard Becker (b. 1928)	Developed his theory of labeling in his 1963 book, *Outsiders*. Becker found that societal reaction was key to how people perceived their deviance.
Harriet Bradley (1997)	Feminist who has charted the rise in female employment in Britain, whilst appraising how the media has responded to this change.
Alan Bryman (1999)	Professor of Organisational and Social Research at Leicester University. Although originally known for his work or research methods, his more recent research focus has centred on assessing the influence of McDonald's and Disney on contemporary society.
David Gauntlett (2002)	Sociologist who has specialised at looking at the study of contemporary media effects. He is highly critical of the media effects model so beloved of the British media.
Paul Gilroy (1987)	Paul Gilroy is professor of Sociology at the London School of Economics (LSE). He has concentrated especially on cultural studies. He is known as a pathbreaking scholar and historian of the music of the Black Atlantic diaspora, and as a commentator on the politics of race, nation and racism in the UK.
Erving Goffman (1922–82)	Symbolic interactionist famous for his study of inmates in an asylum in Washington, D.C. Found that there are 'no truths' and that people act and interpret the world in different ways.
Vivian Gornick	American essayist who wrote the *Village Voice* for many years. The following quote gives some indication of her radical feminist approach: 'Being a housewife is an illegitimate profession … The choice to serve and be protected and plan towards being a family-maker is a choice that shouldn't be. The heart of radical feminism is to change that.'
Himmelweit, Jaeger and Humphries	Proposed that the same principles hold in voting as in purchasing consumer goods. The electorate votes on the basis of policies that chime with the personal beliefs of the individual.
Arlie Hochschild (2003)	Feminist who noted that women perform a 'double shift': paid work and then housework.
Jary and Jary (1991)	Provided a useful definition for the term 'culture'.

Jean-François Lyotard (1924–98)	A famous postmodernist who examined the impact of postmodernism on the human condition.
Karl Marx (1818–83)	Considered the 'Father of Communism'. He argued that capitalism would end in a revolution when the proletariat realised their exploitation.
Bernard Meltzer (1978)	Symbolic interactionist who stresses the importance of the 'self' in determining how humans function in society and, in turn, how society functions.
Millet (1970)	American feminist best known for her 1970 book, *Sexual Politics*, in which she attacks the patriarchy inherent in western society.
Heidi Mirza (1992)	Known internationally for her work on ethnicity, gender and identity in education with best-selling books such as *Young, Female and Black*, and *Black British Feminism*.
Mike Oliver	Said to be the person who has done more than anyone else to put disability on the academic map in Britain. As Professor of Disability Studies at the University of Greenwich, he has written books and papers that set out what he calls the social model of disability – the idea that it's society which disables disabled people.
Talcott Parsons (1902–79)	Important writer associated with functionalism. Key concepts include 'value consensus' and 'universalistic judgement.'
George Ritzer (1996)	George Ritzer is a Professor of Sociology and author of the book *The McDonaldization of Society*. Ritzer's work has concentrated on globalisation and the study of consumption.
Dominic Strinati (1996)	Postmodernist writer, who neatly summed up key components of postmodernism. In particular, he believed that style or substance is a common feature of media and cultural products.
Max Weber (1864–1920)	One of the founding fathers of modern sociology. Developed social action theory in reaction to functionalism and Marxist views of culture.
Paul Willis (1977)	Studied 12 working-class lads in a Midlands school. He found that far from being passive and docile, as suggested by Bowles and Gintis, the lads gained status from their poor behaviour.

My mock examination for this topic is in ....

I will be examined on this topic in ....

What is culture and identity?

Learning objectives

By the end of this section, you should be able to:
- Explain what is meant by culture
- Explain what is meant by identity
- Understand how culture is learned

Culture

Culture and **customs** are learned through communication, – both verbal and non-verbal – from the day we are born. Without communication, human beings are at risk of not learning fundamental skills and remaining in a primitive state. In the 1970s, a 13 year-old-girl named Genie was discovered living in a state of social deprivation in Los Angeles, USA. Genie wasn't taught to speak and is one of a few cases of human beings who grew up without any real contact with other humans. As a result, Genie was unable to develop language or lead a normal life in society.

In contrast, most of us live and interact together in groups, forming diverse, complex and interesting societies. However, this diversity can sometimes be difficult for us to understand and can seem strange and alien to us. Culture and identity are joining points between society and the individual. Our identities are made up of expectations. For example, as a teacher there are societal expectations about how I should behave, alongside expectations of my subject knowledge and examination success.

Consequently, culture is seen as an important concept in sociology. Given there are over 200 definitions of culture it is clearly not easy to pinpoint a universal meaning. However, **Bates** and **Plog** (1990) offer a useful definition:

> *Culture is a system of shared beliefs, values, customs, behaviours and artefacts that the members of society use to cope with their world and with one another, and that are transmitted from generation to generation through learning.*

Ultimately then, culture allows us to share the same **values**. We obtain these values through learning our society's customs, norms of behaviour, our roles and our various statuses. According to sociologists, our status can be 'achieved', based upon personal skills, abilities and efforts (for example, being a teacher) and 'ascribed' (or given to us from birth); for instance, being born into the royal family.

Identity

Jary and **Jary** (1991) define identity as 'a sense of self that develops as the child differentiates from parents and the family, and takes a place in society.' This refers to who we see ourselves as. Some areas of identity will be highly significant. These areas crop up continuously in sociology and include gender, ethnicity, sexuality, nationality and social class. While our identities are related to our individuality they are also the product of social interaction. However, our own self-identity may not necessarily be confirmed by the social groups that we belong to. Old-style sociology suggested that our personal identities were fixed and unchanging; however, more recently postmodernist sociologists believe that our identity can change according to the situations in which we find ourselves, that personal identity may be very different from our social identity. Moreover, they suggest we can 'mix and match' our identities and join groups that change and alter our social identities to conform to others around us.

Sub-culture

As society has evolved, our human cultures have become far more diverse within that we experience as our own culture. As a result of this diversity, **sub-cultures** have developed, particularly amongst young people, who might, for instance, join gangs. We also see sub-cultures in different ethnic groups. Each group, or sub-culture, then manifests an individual way of life, with values different to that of mainstream society. Sub-cultures are useful to such groups as it enables them to share a common belief, problem or practice, which distinguishes them from the rest of society. Theorists are undecided on how to contextualise subcultures. Some, such as functionalists, stress the degree of commonality between all members of society. However, others stress the cultural pluralism that such groups bring and how these differences can lead to sources of strain in society.

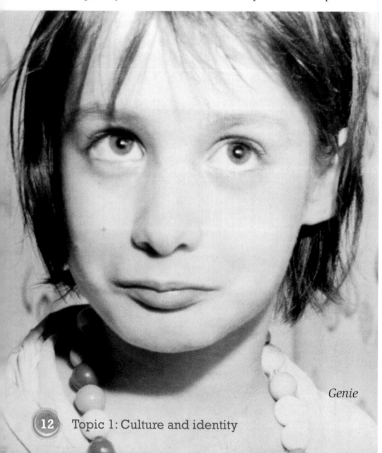

Genie

Focus on research

Northern Soul: Music, drugs and sub-cultural identity
Andrew Wilson (2007)

Wilson's ethnographic research explores how actions considered by the majority of society to be wrong; for example, drug use and burglary, become the norm for the members of a sub-cultural group.

Wilson believes that sub-cultural differences are the key to explaining this, with early-life experiences having an impact on social identity. He suggests that socialization, or rather, a lack of socialization by parents, leads to a culture of criminal activity; for example, a link between burglary of chemist shops, opiate use and fatalities from drug overdoses.

Folk culture

It is interesting to note that in pre-industrial times there was a rough and ready 'folk culture' that equates to today's **mass culture**. Although the majority of the population did not necessarily have the ability to write or engage in reading pieces of classic work such as Chaucer, folk culture did have its merits.

People were involved in activities that are still engaged in today, albeit on a more local scale. Festivals were an important source of culture, often based around the seasons, which allowed citizens to meet up and celebrate. Music and dancing, such as morris dancing, was an integral part of the gatherings. Food was also an important part of culture, with recipes being handed down for future generations. Although this culture was not exactly the same across Britain, it was a culture with which the majority felt happy and at ease. It was created by the people for the people on a self-ownership basis. As a consequence the masses enjoyed their cultural diversity and it went hand in hand with family life.

This folk culture was passed down through generations with little change occurring. However, with the advent of industrialisation and mass production, folk culture was slowly replaced by mass culture. Instead of people actively creating their own culture, their own entertainment, mass culture was created for them, with its primary aim to make as much money as possible. As a consequence much of the traditional folk culture was lost. So today, rather than people making their own food using recipes passed down from previous generations, they will eat in places like McDonald's. Or they go to the cinema rather than dancing at a village fête.

Marxists, who believe that working-class traditions should have been upheld and maintained as a way of encouraging people to be active and critical, suggest that this has alienated the working classes, with their discontent being manifested by strikes, crime and family breakdown. They suggest that these trends of being passive and accepting are a direct result of the plastic mass culture that has replaced the more authentic folk culture.

Mass culture

Mass culture, also known as popular culture, is the cultural products and experiences that appeal to the mass market. Many of these products are aimed towards entertainment, such as reality television shows that are currently so common globally. Although these programmes are watched in their millions, it is unlikely viewers will remember the winners, or indeed, the shows themselves, in years to come. Sociologists are keen to understand the differences, as well as the similarities, of modern mass culture to folk culture so they can comprehend why modern-day consumers of mass culture are so inert by comparison to those in the past.

High culture

High culture refers to what are considered to be the greatest artistic and literary achievements. It is considered by some to be a thing of the past, in terms of truly critical, artistic and intellectual cultural products; for instance, great works of music as produced by Beethoven, or Mozart, for example; literature such as that written by Dickens and Chaucer; operas like *The Magic Flute* and *Carmen*, and paintings by such greats as Picasso and Rembrandt.

Socially advantaged groups like to place a distance between their culture and that of the masses. Some fear that high class culture is being eroded by the spread of mass culture by the media, and that entertainment such as television will only lower the cultural knowledge of the general population, leading to the suffocation of more 'deserving' cultural pursuits.

Low culture

Low culture is a derogatory term for some forms of popular culture. It particularly applies to the parts of culture that are produced for commercial purposes, such as popular music or escapist fiction, which are for immediate consumption rather than for any lasting artistic merit.

Postmodern culture

Postmodern writers such as **Dominic Strinati** (2004) suggest that we are now witnessing the continuing emergence of a postmodern culture. Postmodernists originally rejected

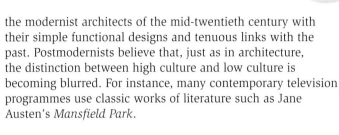

the modernist architects of the mid-twentieth century with their simple functional designs and tenuous links with the past. Postmodernists believe that, just as in architecture, the distinction between high culture and low culture is becoming blurred. For instance, many contemporary television programmes use classic works of literature such as Jane Austen's *Mansfield Park*.

Globalisation and culture

Some sociologists have connected the development of postmodern culture to **globalisation**. Globalisation refers to the process of increasing interdependence of societies on a worldwide basis. We see this in multinational corporations engulfing local economies, the consumption of large brands the world over, email being sent across the globe in mere seconds. This process implies that no culture will be left independent of the global culture. Even in parts of the undeveloped world it is predicted there will be consumption of global products such as Pepsi and Kentucky Fried Chicken, which are the same worldwide. Given this process, it is likely that culture as we know it will be further diversified as we mix other cultures with our own; which we already see today when we look at, for example, curry; originally an Asian food, and which is now the most popular takeaway in Britain.

What do you know now?

1 Using examples, describe what is meant by:
   - Culture
   - Values
   - Sub-culture
   - Folk culture
   - Mass culture
   - High culture
   - Low culture
   - Postmodern culture
   - Globalisation and culture

2 By which process do we learn our own culture?

3 What is the difference between 'achieved' status and 'ascribed' status? Give three examples of each.

4 Explain how folk culture is different to mass culture.

5 What is globalisation?

6 How will globalisation impact on a country's national culture?

7 Put the following under either popular, mass culture or high culture:

   - The *Sun*
   - The Archers
   - *The Da Vinci Code*
   - Beethoven
   - Paul McCartney
   - The *Guardian*
   - Coronation Street
   - Constable
   - Andy Warhol
   - Shakespeare
   - Dickens
   - Jeffrey Archer
   - Jean Michelle Jarre
   - Ballet

Key terms

Culture	Denotes the way of life of a society or social group. Includes aspects of society such as language, customs and dress.
Customs	Practices followed by people of a particular group or region.
Globalisation	Refers to the increasing connectivity, integration and interdependence in the economic, social, technological, cultural, political and ecological sphere.
High culture	The set of cultural products, mainly in the arts, that are held in high estimation by the cultural elite.
Low culture	Produced simply for money and for immediate consumption, not for lasting artistic value.
Mass culture	A set of cultural values and ideas that arise from common exposure of a population to the same cultural activities, communications media, music and art.
Sub-culture	The shared customs and beliefs of a smaller group within a larger dominant culture.

Section summary

- Culture is the way of life of a society or social group.
- Culture covers language, customs and dress, as well as symbols that give an idea of who we are in both professional and private life.
- Status is a person's position in society that is either achieved in a professional role or ascribed at birth.
- Sub-cultures develop mainly amongst the young; sub-cultures usually share some of the values of the host culture, but may also be opposed to it.
- Mass culture is the cultural products and experiences that appeal to the mass market. Many of these products are aimed towards entertainment.
- High culture refers to what are considered to be the greatest artistic and literary achievements of the time.
- Low culture is a derogatory term for some forms of popular culture, in particular those areas of culture that are made for commercial purposes and immediate consumption rather than for any lasting artistic merit.
- Globalisation is the process of increasing interdependence of societies and economies on a worldwide scale.

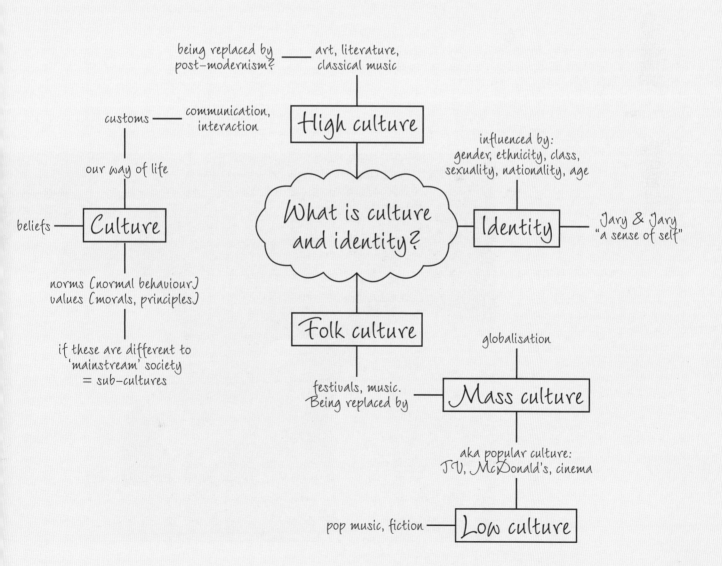

Socialization and the role of agencies

How we develop culture

Our culture is formed by a number of essential parts. These include our **values**, **norms**, **customs**, **statuses** and **roles**. As a result of the creativity of the human condition these vary between geographical regions.

Values

Values are widely accepted beliefs that are shared by societal members. For example, much of British culture tends to follow old-fashioned virtues of concern for individual rights, equality of opportunity, democracy, dress codes and Christian values of decency. However, these values are hugely individual to the culture they inhabit. These values impact on how certain groups are perceived. Why, for instance, does British society seem to value the skills of footballers such as David Beckham, whilst seeing academics as stuffy and boring?

Norms

Norms are certain rules that identify what is expected of people in certain settings. So whilst it might be acceptable to swear in this country, it is particularly inappropriate in some religiously devout countries of the world. These norms operate in lots of different circumstances ranging from table manners to how we meet and greet people. Norms also direct our gender behaviour, with women being expected to take what **Talcott Parsons** (1902–79) considers to be the 'expressive role' in society, whilst men act as the breadwinner. However, norms do change – as many as a third of women do not have children in Britain today, and increasingly the male partner is staying at home taking on the role of 'house-husband'.

There are three types of norm:

1. **Folkways:** These are generally seen as useful in helping us to assess our relationships with others. For instance, with routine casual interaction, when we first meet people we will often shake their hand. Violation or deviation from this norm however, is not considered to be that serious. So a refusal to shake hands would merely lead to a reassessment of the relationship.

2. **Mores:** These are norms that are considered vital for the continuing welfare of society. There are far stricter sanctions for the breaking of mores. So, for example, mores such as bigamy and incest carry custodial sentences if social infringement occurs. Therefore, it is not only within the family that mores are considered important, but within society too.

3. **Laws:** Laws are norms with strict and formal sanctions. Punishments are decided by a legal system and those who work within the system, such as the police and the judiciary with punishment varying in relation to the severity of the crime. At the lower end of the scale ASBOs and community orders can be served; however, for crime such as murder, life imprisonment (or capital punishment in some countries) may be applied. It should be noted that although laws are similar across the world, cultural relativism leads to different countries seeing each of the three types of norm in different ways, with one culture's mores being another culture's folkways, and another culture's laws.

Customs

Cultures and traditional patterns of behaviour are established. Many cultures have strict rules in formal settings; for example, at a wedding the bride traditionally wears a white dress, whilst at a funeral the mourners wear black in respect for the deceased. These customs help to fuse society.

Statuses

Our social status is the 'standing', honour or prestige attached to our position in society. Sociologists like to distinguish between statuses that are fixed at birth (ascribed statuses such as son or daughter) and achieved statuses that are the result of personal meritocratic attainment (such as being a teacher or doctor).

Roles

The roles we fulfil are the expected patterns of behaviour in certain circumstances, often governed by status. For instance, the role of a barrister is governed by rules of attire and conduct in the court room.

Sociobiology

Some sociologists believe that in the end all social behaviour is a consequence of natural instincts or inborn biological drives, such as the instinct for survival and to procreate. This is known as **sociobiology**. However, critics of this view argue that if this really was the case we would all tend to act in the same way. In the real world, people do not behave in a predictable manner.

How we develop culture: socialization

Because behaviour is directed by norms and values, children have a huge amount to learn from their carers – cultural norms and how people think and behave within the society that they are raised in. Children accept culture without thinking, and accept it as completely normal.

Parents and socialization – primary socialization

Parents play a crucial role in the development of their children, having a major influence on their development. Most children learn to use the toilet, eat at the table and develop language skills from their parents. The majority of children learn these skills in the first few years of their life within the family unit. This formative process is described by sociologists as **primary socialization** – a process that allows us to gain the basic attitudes and social skills to live successfully in society. However, socialising influences are now extending beyond the reach of the family as children spend more time watching television and on the Internet, making friends on social networking websites such as Facebook and MySpace.

Secondary socialization

Families provide most children with their main experience of primary socialization; however, many other social institutions and agencies play a role. These are sometimes referred to as agencies of **secondary socialization** and help to build skills in people for their future lives. Schools are one of the main agencies for secondary socialization, having a large input in preparing students with the necessary discipline and vocational and social skills that enable children to progress seamlessly from school into the workplace.

Schools

In some cultures schools do not exist and even in Britain compulsory schooling was introduced relatively late in 1870. Since then, however, schools have taken a major role in the transmission of values, preparing schoolchildren for the workplace, and transmitting culture. This is done through the teaching of a range of subjects that form part of the national curriculum. Cultural knowledge is also taught in a more disguised form, such as in PE, where the genders are segregated. Education also teaches a hidden curriculum, where norms and values are taught via the process of education rather than through the lesson themselves. Schoolchildren soon learn what is acceptable behaviour, what the school rules are and what uniform should be worn. However, although most follow these rules without question, it should be noted that not all accept them. Some turn these rules on their head and provoke opposition at school. For example, **Willis** (1977) found that the 'lads' he studied in *Learning to Labour* actively rejected rules. These young males resisted rules and formed their own sub-culture populated by those who detested school, as opposed to those outside of it who accepted school rules. However, Willis' methodology has been criticised, mainly for studying only 12 students, all male, to draw conclusions on the whole of the working class.

The mass media

Sociologists believe that the media has an increasingly important role in socialization. Many children regularly spend hours in front of the television and so the media has an increasing influence on them and their parents. Some suggest that watching violent programmes can itself lead to copycat re-enactment as purportedly was the position with Jon Venables and Richard Thompson in the Jamie Bulger murder case. On the other hand, others believe that we are sophisticated readers of the media and possess the 'media literacy' to understand the difference between fact and fiction.

The mass media offers a huge amount of information about the world and helps us rationalise what is happening around us, providing commentary and explanations in a complex world. In 2005 The Economic and Social Research Council (ESRC) found that the average person in Britain spent 157 minutes, or just over two-and-a-half hours, each day watching television, videos or DVDs, or listening to music. Whilst the Broadcasters' Audience Research Board (BARB)/Infosys (2007) found that children watched on average 135.64 minutes per day across the five terrestrial television stations. And although television viewing is decreasing in popularity because of increased competition from the Internet in particular, it still offers an important window into the world for adults and children alike with a huge and diverse diet of 416 channels specifically targeted at the British audience. We can watch channels dedicated to sports, soaps, history, music, news, adult entertainment, children's programmes and shopping, to name just a few.

Peer groups

Our peers are people with similar social status to us, such as friends, colleagues or school friends. They often exert a powerful influence on us, especially when we are young, and affect our norms and behaviour. Often peer groups exert a far greater influence on adolescents than their parents or teachers.

Later, in our professional lives, peer groups may influence how we act in the workplace, with professional associations directing what is considered to be the correct way to act with our colleagues and clients. Failure to comply to these expectations leaves us open to being belittled or ostracised by those around us.

Focus on research

The Formation of School Peer Groups: Pupils' Transition from Primary to Secondary School in England

Simon Burgess, Ron Johnston, Tomas Key, Carol Propper and Deborah Wilson

February 2007

The authors of this paper document the flow of pupils from primary schools to secondary schools in England's state education system. It finds that the way in which pupils are allocated across schools at the age of 11 has an impact on the make-up of secondary school peer groups, in turn potentially impacting both on pupils' educational experiences and their attainment.

They additionally found that socially disadvantaged pupils from high scoring primary schools tend to be more geographically dispersed with a greater likelihood of going to lower performing secondary schools. This leads to different levels of expectation for those from poorer backgrounds.

What do you know now?

1   Using examples, describe what is meant by:
- Values
- Norms
- Status
- Roles
- Peer group

2   Give a definition of primary socialization.

3   Give a definition of secondary socialization.

4   What values do schools instil in their students?

5   Why is the media so important in shaping our culture?

6   What role do peer groups play in shaping our behaviour?

Key terms

Customs	A collection of established and repeated pattern of behaviour.
Norms	Expectations of how people are meant to behave in certain situations.
Primary socialization	Socialization before we go to school, usually learnt from parents.
Roles	The characteristic and expected social behaviour of an individual, with a particular social status, shown under defined circumstances.
Secondary socialization	Socialization that is ongoing throughout life. Agencies that perform this function include the education system, the workplace and global media.
Socialization	The process of learning one's culture and how to live within it.
Sociobiology	An approach that argues that human behaviour can be explained by evolutionary biological forces such as the urge to reproduce the human species.
Status	A position in society relative to others. The position concerned may be associated with certain roles and duties.
Values	Ideas of what seems important in life.

Section summary

- Values are widely accepted beliefs shared by societal members.

- Norms are certain rules that identify what is expected of people in certain settings.

- There are three different types of norms: folkways, mores and laws.

- Customs are established and traditional patterns of behaviour.

- There are two types of socialization. Primary occurs within the family, whereas secondary socialization occurs outside of the family.

- The hidden curriculum is all the things that are learnt but not officially taught.

- The media also plays an important role in socialization given that the average person spends two and a half hours watching television every day.

- Peers are people of similar social status to us.

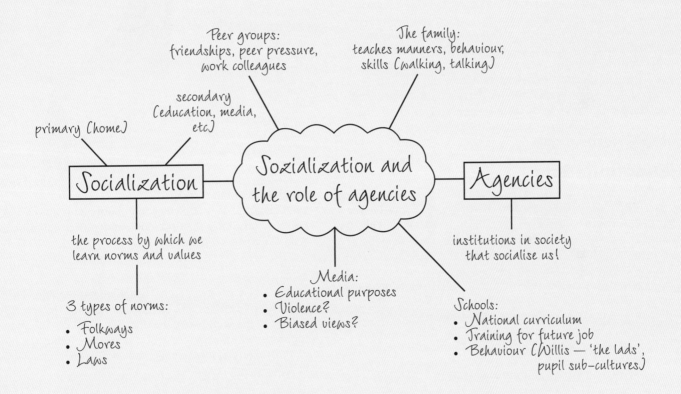

Self, identity and difference

Structural theories

Structural theorists believe that our behaviour is strongly influenced by the structure and working of society, suggesting that rules and regulations help to organise relationships between members of society. They argue that it is values that provide general guidelines in terms of behaviour regarding roles and norms. Institutions such as the family, education and the media play an important part in interconnecting roles and expectations between these institutions. So, the family teaches us how to behave at home, and the skills learned in the family unit are then carried on into the school environment. Interpretivist theorists concentrate upon small-scale interaction (**micro**), with culture being seen to be the result of social interaction.

Functionalism

Functionalism is the first of the structural theories. The theory asserts that we are all shaped by the structure of society. The word 'structures' is utilised in sociology to explain that society is made up not just of individuals, but also more permanent structures. So although individuals may die, these structures continue regardless. An example of such a structure is the family. Family is a structure because it consists of definable members and even when one of the family members dies it continues anyway. It therefore takes a **macro**, or wide, approach to looking at how we operate together. It suggests we are all influenced by the people and institutions around us, and these influences impact on who we become. Most importantly though, functionalists suggest that society is a far more powerful and enduring influence than any one person. It moulds us, and produces 'laws' of society. This belief suggests that we usually act in predictable and non-threatening ways that help society to agree about things. Functionalists therefore see **consensus** or agreement as an important factor in this functioning.

Consequently, functionalists like to look at the role of all the different institutions in society. By looking at each part of the structure of society they argue we can see how each shapes us by instilling norms and values that we all share. This helps to ensure ongoing stability and allows society to continue functioning just as it has done for thousands of years.

Functionalists stress the importance of shared values allowing society to achieve all of the above. These are instilled by the process of socialization. Socialization occurs first within the family (primary socialization) and then within the workplace and wider institutions (secondary socialization). In both arenas however, its role is similar. We learn what is important in society and we internalize this and make it part of us. For some writers, such as Talcott Parsons, this produces what he calls **value consensus**, where everyone agrees upon the most important values of society. For example, most accept that we live in a society where achievement is an important motivating force. Many accept or have internalized the idea that any achievement will be the result of a fair and unbiased system that allows the most talented to get to the top, regardless of their class, gender or ethnicity.

Talcott Parsons

This sharing of ideas allows us to bond together into a united whole and facilitates the development of social solidarity and a sense of universal identity.

From this, social order can be created, where each part of the system works seamlessly with the next. In the family, clear roles are taken by each parent, which allows the effective transmission of values and efficient working of society. Similarly in the workplace, the division of labour allows us to produce with greater efficiency, improving living standards and allowing us to function as parts of a harmonious whole.

Social identity is further enhanced by the role that institutions play within our lives. They teach us that we are part of something much bigger than just a set of individuals. We are the product of past culture, of a common language, and the norms and values that we are taught in school. Consequently, this allows us to replace workers with people who share similar goals and aims in life.

Functionalism and culture and identity

A functionalist idea is that we all put meanings to things, usually in a consistent way. This allows us to make sense of cultural images. So for example, we associate Beethoven and Constable with high art, whereas Gwen Stefani and Oasis are considered low or popular culture. Equally, we pick up other cultural cues just as easily. See an image of a red London bus and most people across the world will associate it with Great Britain. Talcott Parsons believes that individuals are predictable at picking up cultural associations.

This culture has to be picked up through institutions – the media, the family and education playing key roles in this process. From these organisations we absorb culture. This provides a cornerstone of our identity. However, although some of this process is passive (we just acquire it), it is also an active procedure. We actively discuss culture, get involved with it and purchase it. From this we influence those around us. For example, one member of a family will listen to, or purchase, a cultural product that will then lead to others also listening to or watching it and ultimately purchasing it.

An evaluation of functionalism

- The functionalism theory fails to explain why there is a lack of consensus in society. If society is so much in agreement then why is there crime? Why do some groups suffer discrimination? Why are some people more powerful than others?

- It is too deterministic. Other theories realise that people, far from being shaped by society, actually shape society. Rules are there to be broken, and often are by individuals making their own choices.

- Functionalism is sometimes called a 'march of progress' theory. Functionalists believe that society is getting better. Yet problems continue as before, for example, sexual abuse and criminality. Socialization cannot provide value consensus for all of us.

- From a cultural point of view it fails to explain why dominant groups perpetuate their cultural control through cultural products; for example, why does the national curriculum insist that students learn Shakespeare?

However, it does have its strengths:

- It understands how consensus has produced a stable society where we all perform a number of roles and functions.

- It realises that society does affect our culture. Our dress and speech are good examples of how we are influenced by those around us through socialization.

- It is an optimistic theory that looks for cultural and societal improvement and it respects cultural tradition.

Conflict theory and culture

The previous section looked at culture and the process of socialization from a functionalist point of view. Conflict theories reject the idea that society is based on consensus and instead argue that there are inequalities based on wealth and power. From a cultural point of view, these differences in power lead to less powerful groups developing sub-cultures in response to, and in resistance of, the dominant culture. To begin with we will look at Marxism and then the work of **Max Weber**.

Marxism

Developed by **Karl Marx** (1818–83) this theory believes that most societies are in conflict, revolving around two classes: the **bourgeoisie** and the **proletariat**. Marx saw the bourgeoisie as the ruling class, running society for their own benefit and ensuring that capitalism is served at all levels. Marxists argue that the bourgeoisie benefit at many levels whilst the proletariat, the working classes, must sell their labour to live. The proletariat accrue very few assets. In the workplace, the bourgeoisie pay in wages far less than they receive from the profits of production. Marxists call this 'surplus value'.

Similar to functionalism, Marxism is a structural theory that believes that we are a product of the structure of society. Most of this shaping of our personalities is done to benefit the needs of capitalism. Essentially, for Marxists, it is the owners of the factors of production (those who own factories, machinery, land, and possess entrepreneurial knowledge) who are the most powerful. The proletariat, by contrast, can merely sell their labour so have very limited power. Therein lies the problem: unequal power between two groups that results in conflict fuelled by inequalities in society, provoking the 'them versus us' attitude of the working classes. For Marx this provided a real puzzle: why weren't the working classes willing or able to have a revolution to overthrow those in power?

Ideology

Despite the inequalities, capitalism has remained dominant. Marxists believe that this will not continue: eventually the proletariat will realise they are being exploited and do something about it. However, it cannot go unnoticed that the revolution that Marx predicted 150 years ago has failed to materialise. Marx, however, explained the lack of a revolution through the concept of 'ideology'.

Marxists believe that the proletariat are controlled by their hearts and minds rather than merely force. This is done through the process of socialization, so the working classes accept their position within capitalism and see it as fair, natural and normal. Therefore, despite the educational system being skewed in favour of the upper classes, Marxists would claim that the working classes are socialised to see their immobility as a result of their own educational failure rather than their class position.

Marxists then link this to culture, arguing that the elite have the power to shape our culture or way of life for its own benefit. An example of this, Marxists claim, is how the dominant classes use culture to divert us away from what is really going on, that is, our exploitation. So we end up with a culture where the sports pages or the gossip magazines are deemed more important than the 'real' news. In the meantime, media companies try to sell their goods and we are distracted, the theory suggests, with watching trivial television programs.

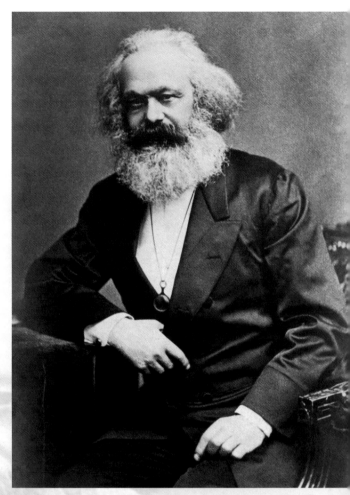

Karl Marx

Marxists also suggest that adverts create false needs, so instead of going to church on a Sunday, for example, people would rather visit shopping centres. By diverting our attention, Marxists believe that a general consensus is being encouraged through culture, asserting the commonality of cultural products. However, at the same time, culture is also used to encourage the working classes to see the middle classes as being dominant. So whilst a working class person might read the tabloids, for example, which only need an average reading age of 12, the middle classes are more likely to favour the broadsheets, which require a reading age of 18 and over. This dichotomy allows the working classes to think of those at the top of the hierarchy as more intelligent, more widely read and better able to rule.

Marxists have a phrase for people unaware that they are being exploited: **false consciousness**. They believe that with ongoing exploitation, workers will eventually wake up to their situation and gain **class consciousness**, realising that their class is exploited and that the only way to escape the shackles of this exploitation is through class struggle and a revolution.

Evaluation of Marxism

Marx's ideas have created considerable debate and helped spawn a new breed of Marxists (neo-Marxism). Nonetheless, a number of criticisms have been levelled at them.

Some critics feel that Marxists place too much store on the role of the economic system. Others, such as Weber, challenge this and suggest that people and religion can change the economic system.

Interactionists suggest that Marxism ignores the power of the individual to make sense of their world. We all have free choice to some degree and can refuse to accept capitalism.

- Marxism over-emphasises conflict. In reality concessions have been made by capitalists to the workforce; for instance, unemployment benefit ensures that those without paid employment have some income whilst they search for a new job.

- Marxism believes that all cultural conduct is related to class. However, as a consequence, Marxists tend to ignore other aspects of our culture such as how culture is affected by gender and race.

Max Weber

Max Weber: social action theory

So far we have focused on Karl Marx. However, other writers have also been keen to look at conflict. Perhaps the most influential of these writers was Max Weber (1864–1920). Although he agreed with Marx that class is important, he believed that other factors are also fundamental to inequality that sometimes have very little to do with class. Examples of these are found across the world: In South Africa during apartheid, class was not as important as a person's ethnic background, whilst in India the caste system still possesses real importance, again with class remaining relatively unimportant as to the status of individuals. Indeed, the caste system is completely 'closed' and based not on occupation but religious purity: how pure a life a person has led. Ultimately, however, Weber was concerned to show how individuals can affect society and how they are not necessarily the product of their socialization. Human beings can respond to the situations they find themselves in, and decide to accept this or to take social action against it. The ultimate expression of this for Weber was the Protestant ethic that showed the power of religiosity to create successful capitalism.

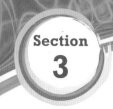

Feminism

Feminists suggest that gender is another source of inequality within society. They argue that we live in a patriarchy: a society dominated and run by men, for men's benefit. They point to a number of statistics that show the power men have over women; for example, only 20 per cent of MPs, 35 per cent of the Cabinet and 19 per cent of the House of Lords are female. Whilst in occupational roles, for instance, in 2006 women made up one per cent in senior ranks in the armed forces, 26 per cent in civil service top management, 18 per cent of trade union general secretaries or equivalent, and

only 21 per cent of local authority chief executives are women (*Uncovering Women's Inequality in the UK*, 2007). These inequalities are further enhanced by what is known as female 'double shift' (**Arlie Hochschild**, 2003), where women are expected to go to work full- or part-time whilst still performing most or all of the domestic duties at home.

Feminists are divided as to whether the situation is improving. Liberal feminists are keen on legislation. They believe that the position of women has improved over the last 30 years because of laws that have been introduced to address sexism; the Equal Pay Act (1975) and Sex Discrimination Act (1976)

were introduced to help. Although this has happened to an extent, inequality still exists. Marxist feminists are not as optimistic as liberal feminists. Marxist feminists argue that the root cause of oppression for women is capitalism. Female enslavement suits capitalism for many reasons. It offers the 'warm bath theory' as women look after the male workers, whilst additionally, through reproduction, the workforce is always renewed, Marxist feminists believe that female equality will only occur when capitalism is replaced with a system based on full equality.

Finally, radical feminists believe that female oppression is the result of patriarchal domination in society. They argue that this domination is instilled within women from an early age. Women are encouraged to see themselves as different to men and to accept different life goals to the men around them. Domination then occurs by means of marriage, the workforce, childcare and in family relationships. Men benefit from this society, but women don't. Indeed, some radical feminists believe that women should live in one hemisphere of the world and men on the other!

Within a cultural context writers such as **Millet** (1970) developed the idea that male domination was inherent at all levels of society, including the production of culture and identity. Millet believed that male domination within the family has been achieved by means of rape and domestic violence, encouraging women to believe their subordinate role within both the family and society. Feminists see this domination being culturally determined with male notions of women looking after and socialising children.

However, writers such as **David Gauntlett** (2002) detect a real change in gender identities. He believes the timid female of yesterday has been replaced by successful, feisty women who know exactly what they want. By contrast, he argues that men have been going through a period of self-reflection leading to them seeking advice and realising the limiting factors of their masculinity. Gauntlett believes that although gender stereotypes remain, a wider set of gender identities has developed.

Social action theory

Social action theorists believe that it is people who make choices. Children, in particular, watch and learn from those around them, observing what most people do in certain situations, and making decisions based on the actions of others.

This theory focuses not on the macro level – looking at the wider aspects of society – but looks at how the individuals affect each other – the micro level. Therefore we are a product of our interaction: people interact and consequently look to understand the links that develop between each other.

When we interact with people we constantly look for clues, looking for a variety of symbols that tell us how people are feeling, their status and how they feel about us. For example,

in a hospital setting, if a person is wearing a white coat and a stethoscope, this suggests to us that they are a doctor of status and importance. Or, in a nightclub, if a member of the opposite sex makes eye contact, we might conclude that the person is interested in us.

Symbolic interaction therefore helps us to make sense of the world. It takes out uncertainty as we learn what appropriate behaviour is in different situations. This ensures that we do not deviate from what is considered acceptable, thereby taking a degree of the strain out of our everyday interactions.

How do we learn this identity?

Social action theorists believe that we gain knowledge of what is expected of us in different social settings from the process of socialization and education. From this socialization individuals gain a personality or identity. A number of components make up our identity for social action theorists. Firstly, we develop our identity as we discover the ways that we are unique from each other, perhaps from the way our parents respond to us, and from more formal ways in which bureaucracy separates us; by the use of passports, driving licences, national insurance numbers, and so on.

Secondly, social action theorists suggest that we learn our social identity from looking at the roles that we are expected to perform, for example, parents' roles usually revolve around the need to provide money and stability for the family. As we go through life we soon discover what is expected from each of us in these different role situations.

Thirdly, we derive an 'internal' sense of who we are. This is the idea that the self is produced through interaction with two or more people; the self as a mother is a social self because a mother cannot be so without a child. However, we also develop this self as a result of our past experiences. The self therefore, is the internalisation of how we have met our societal role, compared to what is expected of us in that role.

The self consists of two parts, the 'I' and the 'me'. The 'I' is the impulsive tendency of the individual. It is the spontaneous, unorganised aspect of human existence. The 'me' is the incorporated other within the individual. For example, teachers react to those around them in the classroom. They will react in ways they think are appropriate by way of praise or admonishment. The 'me' is formed by the reactions of others – the way we react that will cause least embarrassment to those who we are interacting with. In contrast, the 'I' gives us our confidence, creativity and spontaneity.

Thus, the concept of self is a powerful and comprehensive understanding of how humans function in society and, in turn, how society functions (by both changing and remaining constant). The concept also depicts the relationship between the individual and society (**Meltzer** 1978). Writers such as **Erving Goffman** (1959) argue that we act out our lives in role play (this is sometimes called the **dramaturgical approach**

– literally like a drama). This role play occurs in a social and cultural environment; for example, the doctor's surgery is the stage in which we sit when consulting the medical profession and within the surgery there are rules. During the consultation the doctor sits at his desk and asks questions or examines the patient in order to make a diagnosis. The cultural script is often used; on entry to the surgery the doctor greets their patient and asks what the problem is. Within this interaction the professional will also want to offer a performance that offers you a positive impression designed

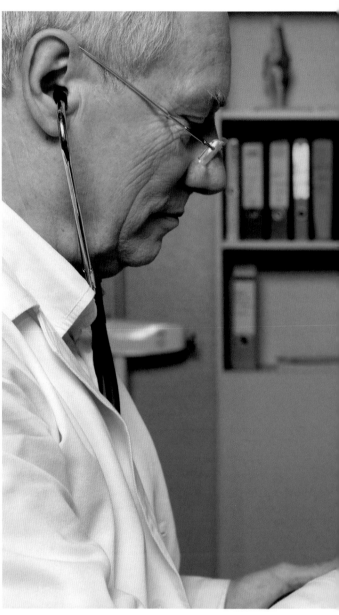

Howard Becker

to create confidence. As a result, we will offer different behaviours in differing contexts. With our doctor, because we want them to help us, we will show a degree of respect at their professional qualifications and their status. However, in other social situations these rules change. Additionally, within these contexts we will manage a picture of who we are. So, the doctor wears his white coat and stethoscope in hospital to distance themselves from the ordinary public. Social action theorists call this a 'front'.

Labeling theory

This theory is often associated with social action theory. As its name suggests, labeling theory understands how negative labels can have an impact on those who receive them. Writers associated with interactionism, such as **Howard Becker**

unlikely to be remembered. Becker calls this 'master status'. Moreover, as a result of this label Becker believes that the person labelled then faces the prospect of being stereotyped; any teacher found guilty of such a crime would never be allowed to teach again. This may lead to the teacher further immersing himself in the company of those who are similarly labelled as 'deviant'. This holds the likelihood that the initial labelling would lead to further deviance. Interactionists call this the self-fulfilling prophesy. However, not all sociologists are confident about how much labels may be responded to by the individual. Some sociologists believe that certain individuals work against the label they have been given and want to prove those who have labelled them wrong.

Erving Goffman's famous study of *Asylums* (1961) shows this process in action. He discovered that some inmates found their individuality was stripped away by uniform, routine and being given a number, and became institutionalised, dependent upon the institution, later finding it difficult to reintegrate into society. Goffman calls this process 'mortification'. However, some inmates actively fought this process, and although appearing to accept their situation, in reality they continued to fight against the system and celebrate their individuality.

Criticisms of social action theory

Social action theory has been subject to a number of criticisms. These include:

- Methodologically, the studies quoted are often far too small-scale and therefore lack validity. Generalisations are difficult to make when only a small group has been observed.

- Marxists believe that social action theory tends to exclusively peer into the lives of deviant groups who lack power. Marxists therefore assert that social action theory tends to ignore powerful groups, ones who shape and make rules in society.

(1963), found that, within schools, when teachers label pupils or lower their aspirations this tends to create an anti-school culture. This is further reinforced by structures within schools such as setting and banding. Once students feel that the system no longer values or wants to develop them, they have no stake in the system and therefore 'live up to' the label that they have been given.

Worryingly, such labels can also be applied later on in life. Indeed, many of the students who end up failing at school may additionally commit crime. In such an eventuality Becker believes that the label that is applied by the agents of social control can override all statuses that have been achieved before. For example, a previously respected teacher who is found guilty of paedophilia is likely to be known only by the negative label. All their hard work and good teaching is

What do you know now?

1. How do social action theorists see people differently from structural theories such as Marxism and functionalism?
2. How are people socialised according to social action theory?
3. Explain the concept of the 'I' and 'me'.
4. What is the self-fulfilling prophesy?
5. Describe a criticism of the self-fulfilling prophesy.
6. What is a 'deviant career'?
7. What is the result of this?
8. What is meant by social solidarity?
9. What are the key values of all societies according to Talcott Parsons?
10. What agencies are responsible for people acquiring norms and values?
11. How might these norms and values be further instilled by family, and by the education system?
12. What are the bourgeoisie and the proletariat?
13. What is the function of ideology in maintaining the status quo?
14. What are the strengths of Marxism?
15. What are the weaknesses of Marxism?
16. What other forms of inequality exist beyond occupation?

Key terms

Bourgeoisie	One of Marx's main two classes. This powerful group own the factors of production: land, labour, capital and entrepreneurship.
Class consciousness	Workers who are aware that they have a common interest with all other workers who are oppressed. Upon this realisation it will serve to bond the working classes together and encourage them ultimately to pursue revolutionary action to depose the bourgeoisie.
Consensus	Literally means agreement. Often used by functionalists to explain how similar norms and values allow a bond to be created amongst most members of society.
Dramaturgical approach	An approach which emphasises the sociology of co-presence. Our personality is shaped not merely by the self, it is also the product of our interactions with those around us.
False consciousness	Used by Marxists to explain how the working classes fail to recognise their oppressors, but merely accept the legitimacy of the power structures that oppress them.
Macro sociology	A focus on the large-scale, particularly the structures of society. Associated with structural theories such as functionalism and Marxism.
Micro sociology	Looking at the small-scale, particularly individuals in society and usually associated with the interactionist school of sociology such as social action theory.
Proletariat	The other of Marx's two main classes. The group that do not own the factors of production and who have to sell their labour in order to survive. Consequently, are often called the 'wage slaves'.
Value consensus	Shared culture, and general agreement on what is important in society.

Section summary

- Structural theorists believe that our behaviour is strongly influenced by the structure of society.
- Functionalists see society as made up of interdependent sections that work together to fulfil the functions necessary for the survival of society as a whole.
- For functionalism we all give meanings to objects, usually in a consistent way. This allows us to make sense of cultural images. Functionalism was a dominant explanation of society for a considerable time in sociology, being particularly influential in the 1960s. Recently, however, other theories have become more fashionable in response to the many criticisms that can be made of this theory.
- Marxism believes that most societies are in conflict. This conflict revolves around two classes: the bourgeoisie and the proletariat. Marx saw the bourgeoisie as the ruling class.
- Feminism is a perspective that examines the social world from the viewpoint of women. Feminists believe that culture tends to be created and dominated by men rather than women.
- Social action theory believes our actions are affected by the presence of others around us. We therefore need to understand the interpretation and motives of people to comprehend their behaviour. This of course, needs to be the case in the formation of our culture and identity.
- Labeling theory concentrates on the ways in which the agents of social control label particular groups and how those stigmatised changed their behaviour as a result of this label being imposed.

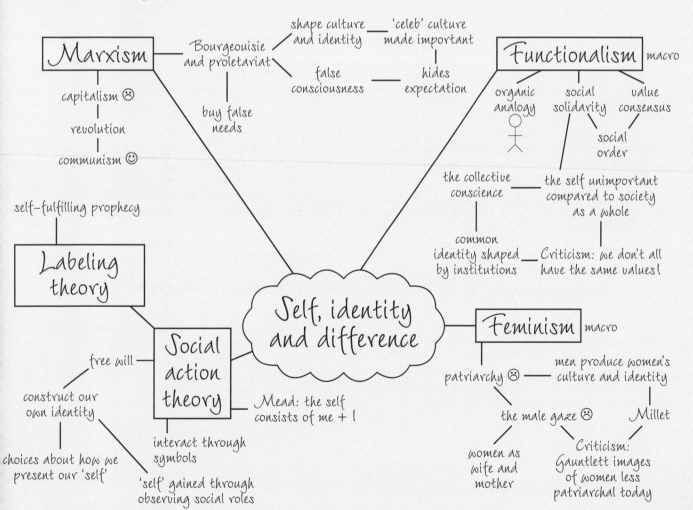

The relationship of identity to different social groups

> ## Learning objectives
>
> By the end of this section, you should be able to:
> - Explain the concept of class, and the varying ways to define this
> - Explain the different classes in contemporary Britain
> - Explain how other factors apart from class impact on identity and status

Social class

Our **social class** is a key part of our social identity and can have a significant impact on our life chances. For example, the Blair/Brown Labour government constantly promised to cut both child and adult poverty in Britain. This pledge is a reflection of the fact that, even in 2004, poverty for working-age adults remained unchanged despite many adjustments in the benefit system to address this. However, it is apparent from relevant data that British society is split up into different groups on the basis of our wealth. Sociologists call this 'social stratification'. There are a number of ways of ranking social status. These include the newest method known as the National Statistics: Socio-Economic Classification (NS-SEC), which was introduced in 2000. The NS-SEC is an occupational-based system that includes rules to cover the whole of the adult population. It is based on a rather complex set of criteria that measure authority in the workplace, income and economic security. Many are unhappy about this classification system, as it relies upon those who work and does not take into account those who are so wealthy they don't have to work at all.

Sociologists also point out that social class is merely one form of separating groups in society. For these groups, other processes similarly serve to divide them and lead to disadvantage. Feminists argue that gender is an important source of inequality; they note that women earn on average 87.4 per cent of men's hourly pay (2006). Again, ethnic inequalities disadvantage people from ethnic groups. This is demonstrated by statistics that show that one-third of all Pakistanis in Britain earned less than £6.50 per hour in 2006 (the Poverty Site).

Regardless of class it is apparent that the elite at the top of the system have advantages in terms of health, education and mortality that set them apart from the rest of society. Additionally, these elite can expect to have greater power to maintain the inequalities into the next generation.

Despite this, there are plenty of sociological writers that believe class is playing a declining role in the formation of our identity. **Harriet Bradley** (1997) found that although inequalities have actually increased between classes, fragmentation had occurred with 'classes being split by religion, public or private sector membership, gender or ethnic origins, amongst other things'.

Differentiation and stratification

Social class, although not as important as in previous times, still plays an important role in differentiating people. We give clues to others about our social class in many ways; the dress, language and customs of dominant groups are often very different from others. These differences are likely to show the wealth and political power of the group. In sociology this process of stratification is the hierarchical arrangements of social groups. This is a process that is not new, with some groups always having more power than others. An early example of this was feudalism. This is any system that resembles the one used in the middle ages, where the people provided labour and military service to a lord in return for the use of his land. At the very bottom of the system would be found the serfs who had little power; they were not allowed to leave the land under any circumstances.

More recently, domination was considered perfectly acceptable, leading to many either being designated as slaves or being 'in service' as maids and cooks to the wealthy landowners in major British cities. These variations also exist in other countries. One of the best known examples of this is the caste system used in India and by immigrant groups that have settled around the world. Although most associated with Hinduism, people of other faiths, such as Sikhs, also use it. This stratification system is also based on occupation and despite being outlawed in India 50 years ago still plays a powerful role in India today. Human Rights Watch (2007) paints a sorry picture, with millions of low caste Hindus being victims of crime every 20 minutes.

Social class in Britain

Social class continues to be the main form of stratification in Britain. However, some would argue that our system is becoming an 'open' system that allows **meritocracy** for all. Those who believe this give examples of working-class people who have moved up the social class system. Sociologists call this **social mobility**; this can be achieved by obtaining qualifications, by hard work, luck (for example, winning the lottery) or by marriage.

Some sociologists dismiss this idea of merit being the most important factor for success. They point to the continued domination of positions of power in the boardroom and in politics by, for example, Oxbridge-educated middle-class men.

It is generally agreed that there are four broad classes that exist in Britain. These are:

The upper classes

The **upper classes** are made up of three categories:

1. **The jet set:** This is a journalistic term used to describe the lives of people organising and participating in social activities around the world. The jet set has huge wealth and status and includes film stars, rock stars and top professionals from a wide range of disciplines including sport and business.

2. **Landowners:** This refers to people who have inherited land and property. For example, the Duke of Norfolk owns 30 000 acres in Sussex (The Land Registry, 2007).

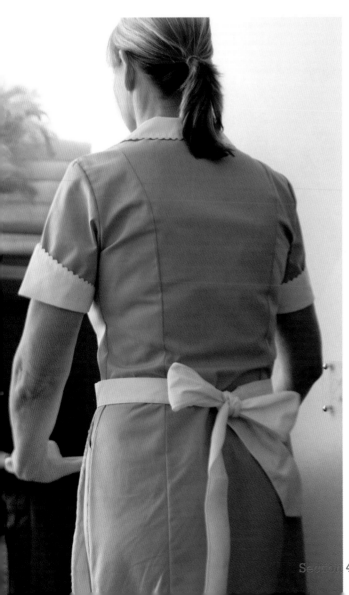

3. **The entrepreneurial rich:** These are people who have made their wealth from owning stocks and shares in companies they have often formed themselves or which they run. Some have inherited these, such as the Sainsbury family, whilst others are self-made millionaires; for example, Easyjet founder Stelios Haji-Ioannou.

Stelios Haji-Ioannou

The middle classes

The **middle classes** consist of those with economic independence. They are usually non-manual workers who often have a lot in common. However, the following different groups can be isolated:

Professionals: This group holds professional qualifications, are well educated and tend to pass on their attitudes to their children leading to 'cultural reproduction'. This is where the children of this group are likely to end up in similar or higher status jobs than their parents. Professional occupations include doctors, teachers, lawyers, and so on.

Managers: These consist of workers who have specific skills used by organisations. Additionally, they include workers who have proved successful on the shop floor and have thus been trained and moved up their company hierarchy.

White-collar workers: Traditionally referred to those workers who wear shirts with white collars. This group now includes office staff such as clerical, administrative and professional workers.

The petite bourgeoisie: A French term used for the lower-middle classes in eighteenth-century France, including the self-employed small businesspeople such as shopkeepers, who work alongside the staff they employ.

The middle classes have grown quicker than any other social class, with *The New Middle Britain Report* (William Nelson) indicating that there has been a 44 per cent increase in the numbers of the middle classes since the 1960s. Research shows that more people will see themselves as middle class than working class in twenty years. Research by The Future Foundation (2006) demonstrates that whilst only 30 per cent of people saw themselves as middle class in 1966, now 43 per cent do.

From an identity perspective the old class distinctions that pervaded British culture have become far more blurred,

with the above report indicating that 36 per cent of builders see themselves as 'middle class' whilst 29 per cent of bank managers consider themselves to be 'working class'. William Nelson believes that it is how we spend our money, or indeed save it, which is fundamental to class difference. So, just as we vote for the party that give us the best shopping experience (**Himmelweit**, **Jaeger** and **Humphries**), this leads to working-class voters tending to vote for the Conservative Party and middle or upper class voters tending to vote for Labour, resulting in working-class consumption of desired cultural products that confer an identity that may not chime with the social class of the individual.

The working classes

This term refers to skilled, semi-skilled and non-skilled workers. According to statistics 57 per cent of the workforce sees themselves as working class (National Centre for Social Research, 2007). This group however, is disadvantaged compared to others in Britain, with lower pay, fewer holidays and fewer opportunities for advancement at work. Additionally they are also more likely to suffer from heart disease, unemployment and poor housing compared to other classes. Sociologists also believe that an additional class has been created. This is known as the **underclass**.

Whilst the generally subscribed view is that we see ourselves as being more middle class and less working class, this ignores the complexities of our identity. Whilst income increases it is perhaps true that we could suggest a decline in the working classes, however, values and beliefs do not necessarily change with increased prosperity.

The underclasses

The underclass is a term that was first coined in the USA by **Ken Auletta**. This is the social class that is considered to be at the bottom of our class system. This group, according to some New Right writers, are 'work-shy', enjoy living off benefits, are criminally deviant, and see themselves as outside the rest of mainstream society. This group sees little point in voting and takes a dim view of authority figures such as the police and the judiciary.

Difference in social status

Although class remains an important reason for social difference, some argue that such differences are not solely the preserve of occupational status. Such differences can be due to factors such as where we are educated, our gender and ethnicity. This diversity of social difference has been explored

by sociologists who are keen to examine other statuses apart from occupation.

Gender

Gender inequality provides a common identity for women across Britain. However, this identity is far from clear-cut. With the move away from a single theory of feminism to the more complex definitions we use now, gender identity has become fragmented. Radical, Marxist and liberal feminists, although in general agreement about the existence of female oppression, clearly disagree as to the reasons for the oppression. Whilst radical feminists blame men (patriarchy), Marxist feminists believe that capitalism is the root cause of gender inequality.

Hegemonic Marxists go even further, arguing that men impose their idea of female identity on women. Writers such as **Simone de Beauvoir** and **Vivian Gornick** go as far as to call for the removal of women's choice to be homemakers. With this they believe the institution of marriage should be abolished and identity be formed by way of a chosen career, rather than through being a homemaker or child carer, for example.

Moreover, not all women are disadvantaged in the same way. Whilst some middle-class women appear to do well out of the present system, others, such as women from working class backgrounds or different ethnic groups, see the world very differently. Other gender identities are actually formed out of disadvantages; for example, black women may gain a great source of identity and support from the matrifocal family. A study by **Mirza** (1992) showed that black girls rejected the labels imposed on them by teachers. They often did this when being subject to racist attitudes. They responded, not by being fatalistic about educational failure, but wanting to prove the label applied to them was wrong by achieving the highest qualifications possible.

Equally gender inequality also provides a common identity for males. This has been particularly expressed by the Fathers for Justice movement formed in 2002 by Matt O'Connor.

Ethnicity

Stratified inequalities also exist within ethnicity with white groups tending to possess more power in British society than other ethnic groups. This is shown in the education system, where some ethnic groups, such as people of Chinese origin, obtain high GCSE grades (79 per cent of Chinese girls and 70 per cent of Chinese boys obtain five GCSEs or more [Department for Education and Skills, 2004]), whereas other ethnic groups, such as black boys, do particularly badly, with only 27 per cent of this group obtaining five GCSEs or more.

South Asians appear to be less resistant to British culture and have embraced the 'enterprising culture' (Chan, 1997) with vigour. Additionally, middle-class Asian parents use education and have been found to be not only highly motivated but also possess the economic, social and cultural capital to ensure successful selective school entry (Abbas, 2007).

Other areas, such as politics, betray ongoing inequalities; there are 15 black or Asian MPs in the House of Commons (2005 election); far less than expected, given that six per cent of the total population come from these ethnic groups (2001 census). Inequalities are also apparent within the criminal justice system. Home Office data also shows that white men form 95 per cent of drug users in England and Wales, though they make up only 70 per cent of people imprisoned for drugs (2006). The black community, on the other hand, makes up only two per cent of drug users but accounts for 16 per cent of those imprisoned. Consequently, this has led many to conclude that a range of institutions within Britain appear to be institutionally racist, particularly the police, with stereotypes and discrimination being an everyday and endemic part of these organisations.

Ethnicity has increasingly become an important source of differing social identity in contemporary Britain. Much of this stemmed from the mobilisation of 'Black Power' that developed at the end of the 1960s. This movement spawned a realisation amongst British blacks that they were oppressed and needed to bond with their 'brothers' to overcome this oppression. Amongst the sociologists keen to comment upon this was **Paul Gilroy**. In his book, *There Ain't No Black in the Union Jack* (1987), Gilroy comments that a new form of racism has developed in Britain: a cultural one. Thus, those who are born in Great Britain and personally see themselves as being British in cultural identity are seen as 'outsiders', and a 'threat' to British culture. Despite this, Gilroy generally takes an optimistic view of race in Britain believing that culture is far from unchanging; instead we are seeing a diaspora, or dispersal, of black culture, with it having a strong influence on white youth culture in Britain. For example, Jamaicans such as Bob Marley had a strong influence on the formation of ska music in cities like Birmingham and Coventry.

Disability

This has been a new area for sociologists to explore, with an increasing recognition that reaction to **disability** is a social creation rather than merely a reaction to a person's medical condition. **Mike Oliver** is a keen advocate of the social model of disability, believing that everyone is equal and that it is society that restricts their opportunities and erects barriers that prevent disabled people participating. Oliver wants to see 'the differently abled' being accommodated in a similar way to the rest of the population.

Unfortunately, despite new legislation such as the Disability Discrimination Act (1995), which came into full effect in 2004, discrimination against the disabled is still common. For example, disabled adults aged 25 to retirement age are twice as likely to live in low-income households as their non-disabled adult counterparts: 30 per cent compared with 15 per cent (the Poverty Site, 2007).

Sexual orientation

Sexual orientation offers us our final source of inequality, despite the new openness that has occurred since the Parliament Act in 1967, before which consenting homosexual sex between men was illegal. This has allowed gay and lesbian couples to be increasingly open about their sexuality. The age of consent for sex between consenting men has dropped in response to this; from 21 in 1967, 18 in 1994, and finally to 16 in 2000. It should be noted that the Parliament Act had to be forced through by the speaker for it to reach ascent.

Despite all of this, homophobia remains common in Britain, with attacks on gay people and discrimination still prevalent. Activists such as Peter Tatchell have campaigned for gay equality, 'outing' high-profile celebrities, and working with the African National Congress (ANC) in drawing up a non-discriminatory constitution, thereby protecting gay and lesbian people in post-apartheid South Africa.

Ageism

Although in some societies age is considered to produce attributes of wisdom and strength, within Britain it appears the elderly are often discriminated against. Indeed, many think they are being 'kind' when they treat the elderly in a different way from everybody else. Such views, however, are soon to be challenged with the Employment Equality (Age) Legislation (2006), which will make it unlawful to discriminate against workers under the age of 65 on the grounds of age. Moreover, evidence from OFCOM (2007) indicates that the elderly are far from passive, being the most active users of the Internet of all age groups (42 hrs per month), using it in particular to keep in touch with relatives, shopping and taking part in community based forums.

Of course **ageism** is not only a problem for the elderly. The young are still subject to many legal constraints that limit their participation in adult activities, despite the fact that we appear to physically mature earlier than ever before in contemporary society.

What do you know now?

1. Using examples, describe what is meant by:
   - Social class
   - NS-SEC
   - Hierarchy
   - Upper classes
   - Middle classes
   - Working classes
   - The petite bourgeoisie
   - The underclass
   - Globalisation and culture

2. Give a definition of stratification.

3. What do we mean by social mobility? Give an example.

4. Explain how radical feminists would explain the absence of the relative lack of power of women in general.

5. What do we mean by sexuality?

6. What do we mean by ethnicity?

7. What is ageism? Give an example.

Key terms

Ageism: Discrimination based on age, especially prejudice against the elderly.

Differentiation: Ways of distinguishing between social groups. For example, the NS-SEC system uses occupational status to achieve this.

Disability: The Disability Discrimination Act (DDA) defines a disabled person as someone who has a physical or mental impairment that has a substantial and long-term adverse effect on his or her ability to carry out normal day-to-day activities.

Meritocracy: A system in which advancement is based on individual ability or achievement.

Middle classes: The social group between the working classes and the upper classes. Includes professional people.

NS-SEC: Relatively new (2001) eight-point classification system used by the government to create a single-class classification system.

Patriarchy: A family, community or society, based on or governed by men.

Social class: The hierarchical divisions in capitalist society. Defining characteristics include wealth, income and occupation.

Social mobility: The way individuals or groups move upwards or downwards from one status or class position to another within the social hierarchy.

Underclass: Those belonging to the lowest and least privileged social stratum. Some see this group as disadvantaged by the economic system, whilst others believe they are a product of their own work-shy attitudes.

Upper classes: The classes of the highest socio-economic level. For example, royalty and those with inherited titles such as Lord and Lady.

Working classes: The class of people who are employed for wages, especially as manual workers.

Section summary

In this section, you have learned:

- Social class is a key part of social identity and can have a significant impact on life chances.

- Social class, although not as important as in early days, still plays an important role in differentiating people.

- There are a number of ways of ranking social status. These include the newest method known as the National Statistics: Socio-Economic Classification (NS-SEC), which was introduced in 2001. The NS-SEC is an occupational-based system that includes rules to cover the whole of the adult population.

- Social class continues to be the main form of stratification in Britain. However, some would argue that our system is becoming an 'open' system that allows meritocracy for all.

- Traditionally there are three classes: the upper class, middle class and working class.

- The upper classes are made up of the jet set, landowners and the entrepreneurial rich.

- The middle classes are non-manual workers consisting of professionals, managers, white-collar workers and the petite bourgeoisie.

- The working classes are skilled, semi-skilled and non-skilled workers.

- The 'underclass' is the social class that is considered to be at the bottom of the social-class system. It includes people who refuse to work for a living and those who choose not to take part in political participation.

- Some consider gender, sexuality and ethnicity as important reasons for differences in social status in Britain today.

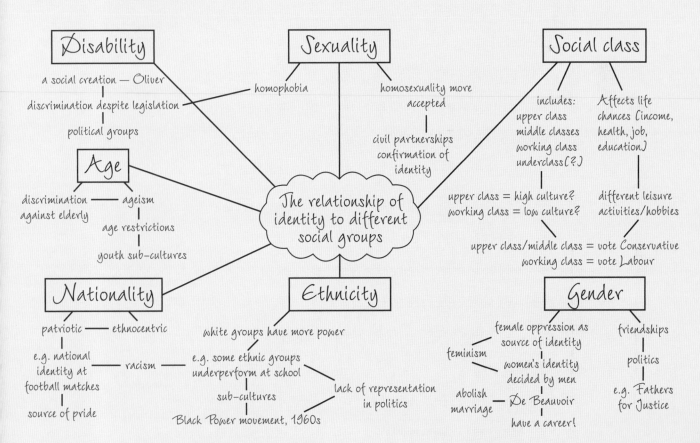

Leisure, consumption and identity

Learning objectives

By the end of this section, you should be able to:

- Explain the term postmodernism
- Be aware of the characteristics of modernity
- Explain the main aspects of postmodernity and culture
- Understand and be able to explain strengths and weaknesses of postmodernism

Leisure time

Our last section area explores how our leisure time is affected by our consumer-driven society. Are we defined by what we buy? Postmodernist writers, such as **Jean Baudrillard**, have argued that we increasingly buy signs, symbols and lifestyles when we go shopping. Products are chosen on the basis of how we would like to be seen rather than necessarily being bought for a more functional use. Leisure and our choices of how to spend our leisure time are made on the basis of buying into a lifestyle choice. These choices are offered to us through media advertising and the British obsession with shopping. It was once said that Britain is a nation of shopkeepers. However, it appears that we are now an obsessed nation of shoppers, with all social classes seemingly spending their leisure time at shopping centres such as Bluewater, the Trafford Centre and Meadowhall.

Postmodernism

Postmodern writers believe that in the late twentieth and early twenty-first centuries we are witnessing large changes, particularly in the world of work and the organisation of businesses. These changes have impacted greatly on the way we live our lives today. In the past, roles and expectations were clear cut, with women being expected to stay at home and look after children, whilst men were likely to go to work either in a factory or in an office. Postmodernists think that we are moving into a new era. They call this 'postmodernity'. Sociologists have long been interested in the way people respond to changes in society.

Responses to the human condition have frequently resulted in great changes and from these changes our lives become

different. Up until the time of the Industrial Revolution, in Britain most people had worked in the countryside. With the onset of industrialisation and the development of new industries, people's lifestyles, families and the way they saw themselves changed enormously. Suddenly, they were expected to turn punctually for work, be able to follow written orders and be paid for the work they did. Not surprisingly, people wanted to be able to make sense of these changes and looked for new academic ideas to explain what was happening and why. This new society has been called **modernity** by sociologists. Postmodernists have since wanted to look in detail at these changes, to explain them and to tell us about what they think will happen to society in the future.

The characteristics of modernity

A complex of economic institutions often interrelated

Industrial production is mechanised and the economic relationships are clear cut and easily identified. This has produced what has been called a 'McDonaldization of society'. **George Ritzer** (1996) argues

George Ritzer

that we are now sold a standardised product across the globe that additionally necessitates the formation of large multinationals such as Nike and McDonald's that have a corporate global identity. These corporations thus have the power to influence both production methods and the economics of nation states.

Postmodernists understand the hierarchies of control that have resulted from industrialisation: how the bosses control and own their businesses whilst workers are forced to sell their labour in order to make a good standard of living. Similar to Marxists, postmodernists realise that social class based on occupational role is an important source of dissimilarity and identity in modern day societies.

Industrialisation

As society has developed, one of the key changes has been the change from living and working in the countryside to working in the city. Modernity has gone hand in hand with development of new skyscrapers and the bright lights of the city. By contrast, rural life is considered to be rather boring in comparison to the 24/7 lifestyle of modern industrial cities in the western world. We live in an industrialised age where we live in a 'global village', where technology and high tech buildings allow us to believe that national and cultural barriers are being broken down. However, many critics believe that industrialisation is not necessarily a good thing. Although it may be 'exciting', they suggest the reality is that industrialisation takes advantage of the poor and desecrates the environment.

Additionally the workplace has seen huge changes with how production is organised. From the moment that Henry Ford installed his first production line to build the Model T Ford it has led to workers having to endure alienating, boring repetitive jobs – with the caveat that for this monotony they were rewarded with decent wages and falling prices for goods produced in this way. So, whilst a Nissan Micra built in 1991 was sold at the equivalent of £10 000, the modern corresponding model in the Nissan range offers far more equipment and safety at a similar or lower price. However, the fear is that these production methods are being extended across the economy, particularly in the retail sector to guarantee a homogeneous or standard product – be it a Burger King Whopper or a Skinny Latte from Starbucks.

The bureaucratic state

Many writers, such as Max Weber, have commented upon the notion that as states develop they become highly bureaucratic. Governments in particular have continued to extend their influence as modernity has increased; for example, the development of education, the welfare state and law and order have also resulted in the state moving into new areas of life. With each of these comes bureaucracy and justification.

Rationality

Until the development of industrialisation the world revolved around superstition, tradition and religion. With modernity, this way of thinking was replaced with a belief in scientific development and rationality, using logic and reason to help the development of individuals and of society. These new ideas and theories have competed against each other to explain the human condition. Postmodernists call these **metanarratives**. Each has surfaced to explain differences, with some calling for full-scale change socialism, whilst others have looked at other areas such as gender (feminism) and the environment.

The postmodern changes

Postmodernists believe that over the last couple of decades a number of new trends have emerged. They claim that modernity is changing and being replaced by new ideas. These ideas are challenging many concepts and ideas that we thought were important and unchanging. Postmodernists particularly point to some areas where change has been most profound. These include:

1. **The growth of the service sector**

This sector has seen a massive increase in importance. Gone are the days when factories employed the masses. Instead, jobs such as customer services and call centres have sprung up. Additionally, as wealth has been created this has encouraged the purchase of consumer durables, leading to the development of a mass army of workers to help sell and service them. Our perceptions about employment have also changed. No longer is it likely that workers will have one job during their lifetime. Instead, a new world of numerous job changes, part-time working, self employment, and job sharing is occurring. According to official government figures, the services sector accounted for 55 per cent of all jobs in Britain at the end of 2006. Although it perhaps should be mentioned that this has benefited women rather than men; women, for instance, show greater empathy, use attentive body language and are able to convey warmth and sincerity in a way that men often find difficult.

2. **The spread of globalisation**

Huge companies called Transnational Corporations (TNCs) have developed a worldwide, or global, appeal encouraging us to buy similar products across the world. This has resulted in products that are bought and recognised across the globe. Some of these brands are so powerful that many argue they can destroy local culture. **Alan Bryman** (1999) goes so far as to suggest that Disney theme parks dominate more and more sectors of society.

Bryman sees four aspects seeping into mainstream society. Firstly, theming; where previously unconnected elements within shopping centres have been combined with a corporate logo or colour scheme. Secondly, dedifferentiation of consumption; where organisations such as Disney theme

parks sell not only the ride experience, but also fast food and merchandise. Thirdly, merchandising; with goods being sold with copyrighted images of football players, or theme park characters to increase economic demand. And lastly, what Bryman calls emotional labour – the scripted friendliness that has to be displayed by service-sector employees in such parks, and encourages the tourists within them to ignore their artificiality and money-making purpose.

Ritzer sees similar processes at work in McDonaldization, which is the process by which the principles of the fast-food restaurant are coming to dominate more and more sectors of American society, as well as of the rest of the world (Ritzer, 1993). For Ritzer this has been achieved by rationalisation and organisational force. This organisational fervour has led to 31 000 McDonald's restaurants worldwide (2008), with the central concepts of efficiency and speed, quantification with the emphasis on size rather than quality (such as regular and large sizes), and predictability (being homogeneous throughout Britain).

It is hardly surprising that some nation states find global brands a threat too far; the French are becoming worried by the 'Americanization' of France. At the same time, many people in France and elsewhere fear that huge American corporations, such as the new giant, AOL Time Warner, will suppress their native culture and their languages by controlling the content of the Internet.

3. The end of metanarratives or truth

In a postmodern society truth is relative. Therefore, although in the past there appeared to be truths that we could hang on to: the rationality of scientific progress, the power of technology and the science of ideas such as Marxism, for postmodernists these no longer explain our condition. So, in our new postmodern society, diversity is the key. **Lyotard** (1979) suggests that we are developing a new 'language game' that does not make claims to absolute truth but rather celebrates a world of ever-changing relationships. We can effectively mix and match the things that we consume, not feeling the need to conform to old stereotypes of what we should be. Our identity is self-developed and symbolised by our choice of clothes, different ideas and lifestyles.

4. Culture

Postmodernism influences have also impacted on how we see ourselves. With the introduction of multi-channel television, we find ourselves being influenced on our appearance, lifestyle and relationships from a wide range of sources. Postmodernism allows us to dip into these ideas, define which ones are most relevant and apply them in any way we see fit. The act of consumption, purchasing from a wide range of goods, cultural and cultural influences, is the key for postmodernists. Teenagers will often mix modern cultural iconic brands such as Nike with styling cues taken from earlier times, for instance by wearing Levi 501s that hark back to the 1940s and 1950s. Significantly, these cultural products confirm our identity, as either 'fashion chick' or 'fashion disaster'.

Some sociologists explain this in terms of our power to shape our world: to take iconic images and to make them our own; for example, the Mona Lisa has famously been shown smoking a pipe and a spliff. Here we can see that the dividing line between high art and pop art (mass culture) is being blurred. This example shows the power of postmodernity to mix different images from different times to create a new order.

5. Style over substance

Postmodernists also believe that our cultural identities are influenced by the over-arching consumerism of capitalism. In the past, our identities were clearly fixed, often by our class, gender or ethnicity. However, these identities no longer have the same importance. Our new postmodern identities are made up of symbols. These symbols include designer clothes that indicate our taste, the make of our cars, the brands we use, and so on. For postmodernists style has become more important than substance. A good example of this is the growth in the number of reality programmes rather than expensive drama. These offer little in terms of script or intellectual integrity; however, they engage a sense of voyeurism rather than having any dramatic or literary objective. They are also far cheaper to produce and offer the prospect of huge spin-offs; hit records, websites, and so on.

However, some argue that some aspects of consumption remain firmly fixed by our old identities or social class and gender. The working classes, for instance, are still far more likely to play darts, and the upper class, to play polo.

6. Mixing up of time, space and narrative

In the past, narratives generally told a story using a well-worn method; for example, with a novel the writer spun a plot, developed characters and used time as the vehicle to further develop the storyline. Postmodernism, however, abandons the concept of consistent narrative and allows cultural producers to mix up two worlds at the same time. This idea has been used by modern film-makers, notably Quentin Tarantino in his film *Pulp Fiction* (1994) where the plot, in keeping with most other Tarantino works, runs in nonlinear order. The unconventional structure of the movie is an example of a so-called postmodernist film. It uses ideas that standard films don't usually use; the storyline is not arranged in chronological or time order, whilst the narrative is circular with the final scene overlapping and explaining the first scene.

Similarly, television news also offers an example of this confusion over time and space. 'Real-time' satellite broadcasts did not exist 20 years ago, therefore we were less aware of time differences across the world. However, with the advent of new technology, video phones, and live satellite links, presenters can talk to journalists from a variety of time periods, blurring the distinction of time and space, even within the relatively standard news settings.

Likewise, postmodernists would point to adverts' obsession with style rather than any meaningful message about a product; a recent Coca Cola advert taken from 2007 talks about the 'Coke side of life' (2007), taking the viewer into a world that gives no hint about the product or the taste of it. Instead, it builds two worlds that do not allow the viewer to be critical or well informed about the product being marketed.

7. The blurring of distinction between representation and reality

Pluralists believe that the media acts like a mirror, reflecting society's views. However, postmodernists argue that it is now the other way round; contemporary society increasingly reflects the media, and, to use Jean Baudrillard's analogy, that 'the surface image' becomes difficult to distinguish from reality. Baudrillard uses the Gulf War (1990) to exemplify his case. In his controversial book, *The Gulf War did not happen* (2001), he asserts that the war was so heavily edited when it was shown on television that what Americans saw wasn't even close to the real war. On this basis he believes that we could easily believe that the Gulf War had never occurred, given our obsession about a media-created reality of 'smart bombs', and non-collateral damage, rather than looking at the reality of war in the battlefield.

Criticisms of postmodernism

- The decline of social class, ethnicity and nationality can be over-played by postmodernists. Class for example, remains an important consideration in everyday life. We continue to vote and judge status in relation to our occupation. Class also continues to play a key role in consumption; without income, consumption is limited.

- Many claim that postmodernism is idealist. Postmodernists are particularly scathing about Marxists, but whilst there have been Marxist states there has never been a postmodern state.

- Although postmodernism claims to be against dominant and elitist cultural products, they could be accused of being hypocritical about this. Given the high degree of jargon used by postmodern writers it could hardly be said to be a theory that can be understood by all.

What do you know now?

1. Using examples, describe what is meant by:
   - Postmodernism
   - Industrialisation
   - Interdependence
   - Global village
   - Bureaucracy
   - Rationality
   - Service or tertiary sector

2. Give a definition of globalisation.

3. What do we mean by a metanarrative? Give an example.

4. Give an example of one image that explains how high and low culture has become blurred.

5. What do we mean by cultural symbols? Give an example.

6. Give an example of a postmodern film. Explain why it is considered to be a postmodern film.

7. Which war did Baudrillard consider it difficult to distinguish truth from media-created reality?

8. Look at the following sentences and work out whether they are an advantage or disadvantage of the concept under discussion:

- It is problematic or difficult to define culture.

- Not everyone conforms to what society wants to make them. On occasions people rebel by doing the reverse of what society expects them to do. This may lead to examples of adolescents joining sub-cultures alien to the rest of society.

- Functionalism reminds us of the fact that we are shaped by culture. Our accents, our appearance and values are all shaped by our culture.

- Functionalism tends to underplay the role of individuals in shaping our identity. We are not necessarily a product of society; we are also shaped by those individuals around us.

- Marxism correctly realises that culture often serves economic aims.

- Marxism is too economically deterministic. Some parts of culture are not shaped by economic forces.

- Social action theory reminds us of the importance of individuals in shaping their own cultural identity.

- However, it overstates the extent to which people are able to act and think without recourse to society. Culture remains a powerful force and whilst we might rebel in the short term, in the long term most conform again to societal expectations of parenthood and career.

- Postmodernism allows us to become more tolerant of other cultures as it champions diversity and differences, rather than an acceptance of normality.

- Many argue that because postmodernism sees no real truth and regards many arguments as invalid that it fails to move us forward.

Key terms

Industrialisation: A process of social and economic change whereby a human society is transformed from a preindustrial economy based upon agriculture to an industrial economy based upon industrial large-scale production.

Metanarratives: Or 'big story'. Phrase used by postmodernists for theories that attempt to explain how the world works such as Marxism, religion and science.

Modernity: Period of time beginning with the industrial age that was characterised by industrial production, living in the city, rational thought and strong government.

Postmodernism: A term used to describe the social and cultural implications of present day society that is characterised by globalisation, consumerism, media saturation and an uncertainty about knowledge

Section summary

- Postmodernists think that we are moving into a new era. They call this postmodernity.

- The McDonaldization of society suggests that we are sold standardised products across the globe.

- Postmodernists believe that with industrialisation new ways of production were introduced that have made products cheaper. However, the resultant jobs can be boring and repetitive.

- The state has become increasingly bureaucratic, having influence over people both through the education system and the workplace.

- The service sector has seen a massive rise in importance as income has risen.

- Huge companies called Transnational Corporations (TNCs) have developed a worldwide or global appeal encouraging us to buy similar products across the world.

- For postmodernists truth is relative. Those metanarratives that supposedly explain truth are no longer seen as important.

- Our new postmodern identities are made up of symbols; for example, designer clothing labels.

- Postmodernism notes confusion over time and space.

- Postmodernists suggest that that contemporary society increasingly reflects the media, and, to use Jean Baudrillard's analogy, that 'the surface image' becomes difficult to distinguish from reality.

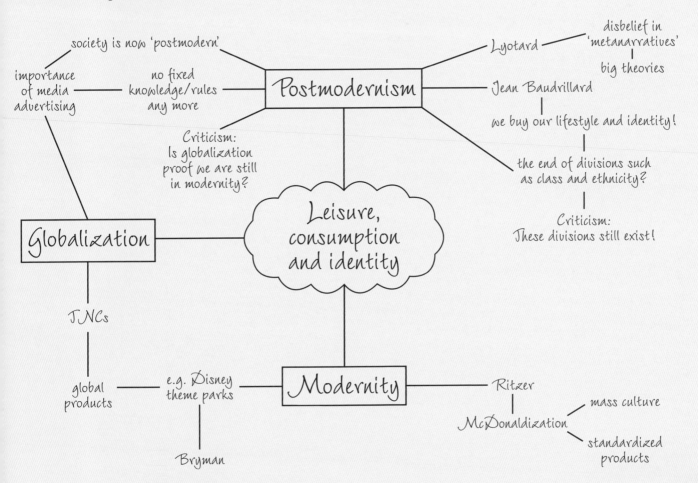

How to maximise your grade with AQA

Central to achieving a high grade in A level Sociology are the following two skills:

1. **Knowledge and understanding:**

You must understand the theories, methods and concepts contained in this module. Moreover, this understanding must be displayed within the examination where you are expected to communicate in a clear and effective manner. The best way to achieve this is to make sure that you regularly test yourself: know the key writers and their theories, and be aware of the methods that are used by sociologists to obtain the results that inform their research.

Please go to the companion CD-ROM where you will find a selection of crib sheets designed to facilitate your revision. These contain key writers along with their research and revision exercises designed to consolidate your learning. They should also provide a diagnostic test for you – allowing you to assess how successful your learning is. Please remember, however, that just knowing things doesn't necessarily mean that you will be successful in your examination. Far too often students think that just putting down all they know about a particular section means that they will receive good marks. This isn't the case. Of course it is important to know and revise material, but you must use this material in context.

2. **Demonstration of the skills of application, analysis, interpretation and evaluation:**

You must use your knowledge and relate it to the question asked within the exam. Moreover, you need to analyse, look at both sides of the arguments, apply your knowledge to the question and then evaluate it.

Evaluation is probably the most difficult of all of these skills. Many students merely assume it is knowing the weaknesses of theories; however, you should also look at the strengths of theories.

When writing essays and assignments the following tips are useful to promote analysis and evaluation:

- Within your essays ask challenging questions that relate to the set question.
- Whilst criticising theories and research also make sure that any strengths are also offered.

Exam practice for AQA

Item 2 A

Bradley does not see class as the strongest source of identity in contemporary Britain. She sees it as being mainly a source of passive identity. This is partly because class is less visible and obvious in the everyday world than age, race, ethnicity and gender. However, Bradley does not agree with the arguments of postmodernists who say that class is dying out or disappearing. Rather there is evidence of class both polarising and fragmenting.

Taken from *Themes and Perspectives* (Michael Haralambos, 2004).

Item 2 B

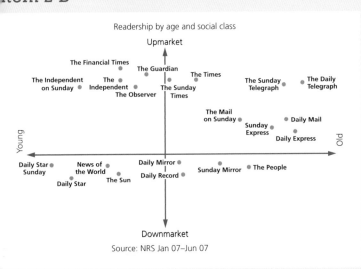

Readership by age and social class

a. Identity **two** consequences of poor or inadequate socialization. *(4 Marks)*

b. Suggest **two** ways in which globalisation has influenced culture. *(4 Marks)*

c. Suggest **two** ways in which class may be a stigmatised social identity. *(4 Marks)*

d. Drawing on material from **Items 2A** and **2B** and elsewhere, assess sociological explanations of differences in the consumption of cultural products between different social groups. *(24 Marks)*

e. Using material from **Item 2A** and elsewhere assess the extent to which modern industrial society has a single mainstream culture. *(24 Marks)*

Topic 2

Wealth, poverty and welfare

Learning objectives

What the AQA spec says	Section in this book	Page
Different definitions and ways of measuring poverty, wealth and income.	Section One: Defining and measuring poverty, wealth and income	56
The distribution of poverty, wealth and income between different social groups.	Section Two: Poverty among different social groups	72
Poverty in the UK in 2007.	Section Three: Sociological explanations of poverty	80
Different responses to poverty, with particular reference to the role of social policies since the 1940s.	Section Four: Solutions to poverty and the role of social policy	86
The nature and the role of the public, private, voluntary and informal welfare provision in contemporary society.	Section Five: Welfare pluralism	94

Exam skill focus

Skills required	
AO1 Knowledge and understanding of theories.	You will need to demonstrate knowledge of concepts, theories and studies throughout your written work.
AO2 Demonstration of the skills of application, analysis, interpretation and evaluation.	You should be able to apply these skills to the set question, utilising the material learned effectively, whilst also showing that you understand the strengths and weaknesses of the material being presented.

What it means to be studying wealth, poverty and welfare with AQA

We live in a country of contrasts, with the average wage in Britain being £447 (The Annual Survey of Hours and Earnings [ASHE], 2006), whilst others do not have to worry about money at all. For example, Indian steel magnate, Lakshmi Mittal, is worth £19 billion, with the richest person in the world (July 2007) being Carlos Slim, owner of a large telecoms corporation, who is worth £33.6 billon. With all this wealth floating around one might expect inequality to be reducing in Britain; however, *Poverty and Inequality in the UK* (Brewer, et al., 2007), has recently revealed that the number of people in relative poverty rose between 2004–5 and 2005–6 from 12.1 million to 12.7 million. Many will find this a shocking statistic given government pledges to 'abolish child poverty by 2020 and halve it by 2010' (Labour Party Manifesto, 2001) and has traditionally been a party of high taxation and high public spending.

Lakshmi Mittal

In this topic we examine how sociologists see this inequality. In **Section One** we look at definitions of terms such as 'wealth', 'poverty' and 'income', showing that definitions are in fact difficult and complex to apply universally. We also look at contemporary patterns of inequality in the UK, examining reasons why inequality has actually increased in recent times rather than fallen.

We look in a similar vein in **Sections Two**, **Three** and **Four** when it comes to poverty; again, trying to find appropriate definitions, examining patterns of poverty in the UK between the rich and poor, whilst looking at reasons for the persistence of poverty in the UK today, despite the huge amounts of wealth that is created in the economy.

Section Five takes a slightly different approach by examining social policy and its use in eradicating poverty. What policies have been used? Why have they not worked? Who is responsible for the eradication of poverty in this country: the public, private or voluntary sectors?

Topic 2

Wealth, poverty and welfare

Sociologists studied in this topic

Abel-Smith and Townsend (1965)	Conducted an important study that demonstrated poverty continued despite post-war welfare reforms.
Esping Anderson (1990)	First described the three welfare types that have developed over the last one hundred years.
Colin Barnes (2000)	A disability campaigner, writer and researcher with an international reputation in the field of disability studies and research.
Richard Berthoud (1998)	Research professor at the Institute for Social and Economic Research. His research concentrated upon deprivation within different disadvantaged groups, particularly those from ethic origins.
Cammack and Morrison (2004)	Critics of the third way, believing that it uses rhetoric to disguise a lack of substance.
Robert A. Dahl (1961)	Studied local politics in New Haven, US. He looked at a number of different decisions, such as the election of a major, land use and the structure of local education, and concluded that a number of different-interest groups, such as business and local pressure groups, had their say.
Mark Deal (2007)	PhD student who carried out studies that concluded that disabled people hold the same prejudices towards other disabled people as non-disabled people.
Anna Dixon and Julian Le Grand (2003)	Wrote a report, *Is the NHS Equitable*, which revealed that poor people make less use of NHS services than middle-income or richer people.
Danny Dorling (2007)	Examined geographical poverty in the UK.
Frank Field (1998)	MP for Birkenhead from 1997–8. Was Minister for Welfare Reform in Tony Blair's first cabinet and has written extensively on social security reform. He argued that Britain has a growing underclass consisting of the long-term unemployed, single-parent families and pensioners.
Gordon and Townsend (2003)	Provided the most convincing definition of absolute poverty.
Stuart Hall (2003)	Influential neo-Marxist sociologist who was Emeritus Professor for Sociology at the Open University from 1979–97.
Johanna Mack and Stewart Lansley (1985)	Used a method of deciding on a list of essentials for living and found 7.5 million people were living in poverty in UK. This list consisted of 22 items, including damp-free homes and outings for children.
Ralph Milliband (1969)	Socialist famous for *The State in Capitalist Society* (1969) in which he saw the state as being dominated by class interests.
James O'Connor (1984)	Marxist economist who had a major impact on the way contemporary Marxists see the world.

54   Topic 2: Wealth, poverty and welfare

Lucinda Platt (2007)	Summarised the findings of poverty and ethnicity research since 1991. In her report, *Poverty and Ethnicity in the UK* (2007), she describes the differences in poverty rates and experiences by ethnic group.
Rigg and Sefton (2006)	Looked at how age influences our understanding of income and poverty during our life cycle.
Benjamin Seebohm Rowntree (1899)	Investigated poverty in York, carrying out a wide-ranging survey into the living conditions endured by the working classes.
Westergaard and Resler (1976)	Argued that class inequalities generated by the capitalist system are the self-evident reasons for continuing poverty.

My mock examination for this topic is in ....

I will be examined on this topic in ....

Defining and measuring poverty, wealth and income (Part I)

Wealth: a definition

Sociologists find it very difficult to define the concept of **wealth**. Although there is an understanding that wealth includes possessions, assets and savings, sociologists are aware that there are difficulties in what to include. For example, do we include property? If we sold our house, a possible large amount of cash will increase our wealth. However, we all need to live somewhere; does it make any difference where? Some people, particularly those who have been widowed, find themselves in large houses and ostensibly wealthy, but may in fact be cash-poor and find it difficult to convert property into cash, and therefore wealth. Another issue is that of pensions: although these are savings, others argue that pensions are essential for day-to-day living and therefore should not be counted as wealth.

This problem with trying to define wealth has resulted in sociologists using a concept called marketable wealth. This is every kind of asset that can be bought and sold, such as personal property, shares, bank savings and housing (less the value of outstanding mortgages), but not including occupational pensions as these cannot be sold.

Problems in measuring wealth

It is very difficult to actually measure wealth as many people like to keep their financial affairs as private as possible. Given that the Inland Revenue does not undertake an annual assessment of wealth, researchers in this area have to use other data to help them find this information out. This can be done in two ways. Firstly, it can be achieved at death, as all wealth has to be declared to the tax authorities for will calculation. However, wills are not a great source of definitive judgement on wealth as wealthy people often try to avoid death duty by giving away 'wealth' when alive (each individual can give £3 000 per annum to any relative so they will have less tax liability at death), whilst there are other ways of avoiding this tax by using a 'discretionary will trust'. The other method of measuring wealth is to simply ask people what they are worth. With each of these methods however, there is a strong likelihood that the wealth of the very rich may be undervalued because of tax avoidance issues and because of a reluctance to reveal such personal data. It is perfectly legal to reduce tax liability: individual gifts can be given up to the value of £3 000 per year that is not taxable – this is called tax avoidance. Tax evasion, on the other hand, is a crime. Tax evasion typically involves failing to report **income**, or improperly claiming deductions that are not authorised.

Trends in wealth distribution over time in the UK

Despite the above difficulties, however, it is possible to present a clear picture of wealth in the UK. It is important to look at this problem from a historical point of view. In the 1920s, one per cent of the population owned over 60 per cent of the marketable wealth. This inequality started to improve in the 1970s, particularly with an agreement to increase top rate taxes, with the top one per cent owning 21 per cent of the wealth and the top five per cent owning 38 per cent. However, from 2000 inequality has again begun to increase. One might

argue that such diversity in wealth could lead us to conclude that **inheritance tax** is a good thing. Over the last couple of years the tax has been subject to considerable debate with some arguing that thresholds need to be raised to nearer £1 million, given the rise in property prices. Others are not so sure. Labour sees the tax as a way of paying for public expenditure. One interesting point is that the Conservative Party plans to pay for its pledge to increase the threshold to £1 million by charging 'non-domiciles' on profits made from property abroad.

Share of the wealth

1% of population owns 21% of wealth

United Kingdom Marketable wealth Percentage of wealth owned by:				Percentages				
	1976	1986	1996	1999	2000	2001	2002	2003
Most wealthy 1%	21	18	20	23	23	22	24	21
Most wealthy 5%	38	36	40	43	44	42	45	40
Most wealthy 10%	50	50	52	55	56	54	57	53
Most wealthy 25%	71	73	74	75	75	72	75	72
Most wealthy 50%	92	90	93	94	95	94	94	93
Total marketable wealth (£ billilon)	280	955	2,092	2,861	3,131	3,477	3,588	3,783
Marketable wealth less value of dwellings Percentage of wealth owned by:								
Most wealthy 1%	29	25	26	34	33	34	37	34
Most wealthy 5%	47	4	49	59	59	58	62	58
Most wealthy 10%	57	58	63	72	73	72	74	71
Most wealthy 25%	73	75	81	87	89	88	87	85
Most wealthy 50%	88	89	94	97	98	98	98	99

Distribution of wealth

The wealthiest 1 per cent owned approximately a fifth of the UK's marketable wealth in 2003. In contrast, half the population shared only 7 per cent of total wealth. The results are even more skewed if housing is excluded from the estimates, suggesting this form of wealth is more evenly distributed.

Wealth is considerably less evenly distributed than income, and life cycle effects mean that this will almost always be so. People build up assets during the course of their working lives and then draw them down during the years of retirement, with the residue passing to others at their death.

Source: Inland Revenue personal wealth

Notes:

Definition of wealth: the estimates of the distribution of people's marketable wealth relate to all adults in the United Kingdom. They are produced by combining Inland Revenue estimates derived from the estate multiplier method and ONS national accounts balance sheet estimates.

Estimates for individual years should be treated with caution as they are affected by sampling error and patterns of deaths in that year.

Adults aged 18 and over.

Published on 8 May 2006 at 9:30 am

Wealth today

The Joseph Rowntree Foundation (2007) found some contradictory trends in its recent report, *Poverty and Wealth across Britain 1968–2005*. They established that house ownership is central to wealth accumulation, with those who have been able to afford housing in the early twenty-first century seeing increases in their wealth. For example, Halifax Financial Services calculates that the value of housing assets inherited every year will more than double from £14 billion in 2002–3 to £32 billion in today's money by 2019–20. It also notes that those living in the south-east of England will account for 54 per cent (£17 billon) of the total value of residential housing by 2019–20. So there is a geographical inequality in relation to wealth, especially when it comes to wealth derived from housing.

Unfortunately the picture is not as rosy for those who have been left off the housing ladder. And although there are 23 per cent of households who are 'asset wealthy', research from Institute for Public Policy Research (*The Guardian*, 7 September 2002) found that the number of households without any assets doubled to one in ten.

Nonetheless, it should be added if only personal marketable wealth is considered, which includes property, shares and other savings and investments, the picture is rather different.

Margaret Thatcher

Much of this is to do with the increasing amount of stocks and shares that have been bought by many households. This was encouraged by the Thatcher government (1979–91), where utility shares, such as electricity and gas, were sold off at low cost to encourage short-term profit-making, whilst more recently building societies have demutualised, changing from non-profit-making organisations to ones that seek only to make profit and distribute these to their shareholders. This general encouragement to buy property and shares was coined by Margaret Thatcher as 'the property-owning democracy' – whether it was democratic or helped everyone is perhaps a moot point.

However, despite the increase in share ownership there is still a large amount of inequality in Great Britain, with 53 per cent of all the marketable wealth being owned by ten per cent of the population. However, it is perhaps interesting to note that despite the government's declared aim to eradicate child poverty, 23 per cent of children in Britain were living in households earning below 60 per cent of median income in 2001 (the median value divides income distribution into two equal parts: the first half of households earning less than the median household income and the other half earning more), compared to just five per cent in Denmark, ten per cent in Sweden and 14 per cent in Germany. It should also be noted that regional differences in wealth are also significant. So whilst some areas in London such as Kensington and Chelsea has an average income in excess of £100 000 per household (£101 600, Barclays, 2007) and the south-east has the highest average gross household income, other regions are not so fortunate: Wales; £32 600 and the north-east; £32 700 are revealed in comparison as areas with the lowest household incomes.

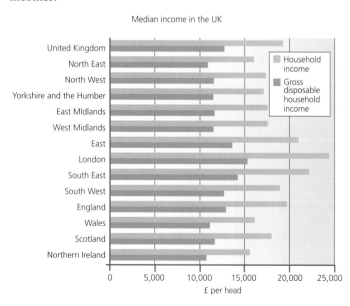

Median income in the UK

Income

It perhaps should not be difficult to define income as something like money received by a person during a period of time in exchange for labour or services. There are two types of income that can be received:

1. **Earned income:** usually received in payment for doing either a task or a job.

2. **Unearned income:** received from sources such as dividends from shares and bonds: income which has not been earned by working.

Just as finding out what people's true wealth is, looking at income also provides challenges. How do you measure it? Do you measure it by household or individually? Do you measure it before tax? Or after tax? And how do you measure income that is not put through the books, such as income that is cash in hand, that is not declared to the tax authorities? Other issues also arise, for example, how do you cope with welfare benefits such as bus passes?

Income distribution

In comparison to wealth, income is distributed more fairly; however, that is not to say that there is equality!

The most widely-used summary measure of the degree of inequality in household income distribution is the **Gini coefficient**. This represents an overall measure of the cumulative income share against the share of households in the population. The lower the value of the Gini coefficient, the more equally household income is distributed.

This followed a fall in income inequality between 2001–2 and 2004–5; there were faster earnings growth for those on lower incomes; in part due to increases in the minimum wage. Nonetheless in 2005–6, original income (before taxes and benefits) of the top fifth of households in the UK was 16 times greater than that for the bottom fifth (£68 700 per household per year compared with £4200) even after new benefits such as Child Tax Credit are taken into account. However, the IFS noted that income inequality remains historically high, with the large increases of inequality that occurred during Thatcher's reign in office during the 1980s not being curtailed as quickly as might be the case. The IFS believes the reasons for this large increase are as follows:

- The gap in wages between skilled workers and unskilled workers has increased. Reasons for this increased differential is due to reduced trade union power to increase the wages of unskilled workers and the introduction of skilled technology that has necessitated higher wages to attract workers with better technical and educational qualifications.

- Male participation in the labour market has declined, whilst female participation has increased. This had led to a change from the norm of having two-waged income earners in a household to having just the one.

- Finally, the IFS found that falls in top rate income tax that occurred in the late 1980s during Lawson's tenure as Chancellor of the Exchequer served to further enhance inequality, whilst increases in indirect taxation such as value added tax (VAT) and excise duty further exacerbated this problem for low-income earners, as these taxes are regressive. This is where the smaller the income of the earner, the higher the proportion of tax is taken. If, for example, a person earns £100 000, they will pay the same nominal tax when they buy a packet of cigarettes as someone who earns £10 000. Clearly, this is likely to take a much greater proportion of total income for the lower earner.

Nigel Lawson

The use of taxation to redistribute wealth

Britain has traditionally favoured direct income taxes, on the basis that this is a way of taxing those who earn the most, whilst those on lower income levels pay often low levels of income tax. The idea was that increased revenue would allow the government to spend money on public services and thereby increase living standards for all taxpayers. The British tax system uses two main methods. These are:

1. **Direct taxation:** These are taxes which are imposed directly on the individual paying them. Examples of direct taxation are income tax, capital gains tax and inheritance tax. Income tax is a progressive tax. This means that as income rises the proportion or percentage of income paid in taxation rises. In the UK, as of 2007, the lowest rate of income tax is ten per cent, the basic rate is 22 per cent and the highest is 40 per cent. Although this was a popular form of taxation 30 years ago, governments since then have increasingly tended to move towards indirect taxation. Some argue that taxing income provides a disincentive to work and high direct tax rates can lead to a 'brain drain' as highly self-motivated workers decide to go abroad rather than pay high marginal tax rates in the UK.

   Most of us pay tax through the Pay As You Earn (PAYE) system that allows us to pay our tax monthly, rather than having to save up for it when the end of the tax year occurs.

2. **Indirect taxation:** These are taxes which are levied in an indirect way rather than being charged directly on an individual's income or estate. The main example in the UK is VAT; charged on goods and services and paid by consumers. One of the main criticisms of indirect taxes is that they have a regressive impact on the overall distribution of income in the economy. A regressive tax bears down more heavily on lower income households: in effect the percentage rate of tax paid rises as average incomes fall. This is in contrast to the income tax system where the marginal and average rates of tax rise with income. VAT in particular is charged on a range of goods such as petrol and clothes that often cannot be avoided. However, some goods are 'zero rated', such as basic foodstuffs, books, newspapers and magazines, children's clothes, and equipment for disabled people.

Cash benefits

This has been the favoured system used by the Labour government of 1997. These include income support, pension credit, child benefit, incapacity benefit, and the state retirement pension, and play the largest part in reducing income inequality. These benefits tend to go to the lowest income earners in the UK and made up 61 per cent of gross income for the poorest fifth of households, 39 per cent for the next group, falling to two per cent for the top fifth of households.

Alastair Darling

Benefits in kind

In 2002 it was estimated by the Joseph Rowntree Foundation that the government spent the equivalent of £4000 per household on subsidised welfare services, including the National Health Service (NHS), state education and social housing. It is hardly surprising that the benefit of this is substantial, particularly for those on low incomes. The latest Labour government was strongly in favour of this kind of redistribution. This can be seen by the statistic that between 1996–7 and 2000–1 the value of the social wage increased by £260 per person for those in the poorest fifth, and by £50 for those in the richest fifth.

We will now look at how income is distributed across a range of social categories.

Social class

There is a strong correlation between high social class and income levels. For example, according to *Poverty and Inequality in Great Britain* (Brewer et al., 2007), income growth occurs faster for those on higher incomes than those on low ones, whilst they note that many indicators of income inequality rose in 2005–6 according to the most commonly used measure the Gini coefficient. On the other hand, other measures of inequality that do not take into account incomes at the very top and very bottom of the income distribution,

such as the 90:10 ratios, have fallen since 1996–7. The report further comments that without tax reforms the increasing amount of lower tax bands, the use of cash benefits and other benefit reforms, inequality would have increased even more between the richest and the poorest in society.

Age

Income levels tend to be lower for the young compared to the rest of the population, with only pensioners being worse off. This is probably to be expected as incomes tend to increase the longer employees stay in an organisation and may increase on top of any annual pay rises. Teachers, for example, in the early part of their career gain 'incremental points' that substantially increases income over and above any annual pay rise.

The Halifax (2006) has found that house prices have risen by 179 per cent over the last decade. Young, childless couples under 35 were much better off than their single counterparts. The trend towards having children later in life, if at all, will mean that couples in work will increasingly enjoy a financially fruitful time when incomes are high and outgoings are low. However, it also means that when women do decide to have children this has a major impact of 'income trajectories' according to Rigg and Sefton (2006).

UK House Prices 1991–2004

Recent research

Public attitudes to economic inequality

Michael Orton and Karen Rowlingson

Michael Orton and Karen Rowlingson have found that a large percentage (73 per cent) of the population consider the gap between the poor and the rich far too great in this country.

Generally people feel that although those on low incomes are not underpaid, those on high incomes by comparison are overpaid.

However, people have a contradictory view of this inequality. So, for example, although a small percentage of voters are in favour of income **redistribution** by means of higher direct taxes, 55 per cent of those asked in 2006 believed 'there was quite a lot of poverty in Britain'.

The report concludes that inequality should be given a lot more attention by the government. There is a need to educate the population about inequality, thereby increasing debate and thought on this important issue.

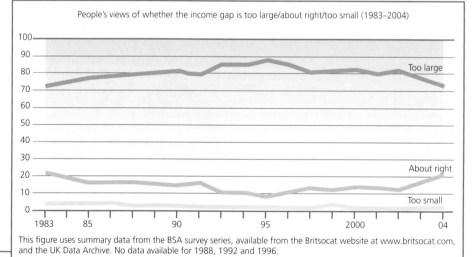

People's views of whether the income gap is too large/about right/too small (1983–2004)

This figure uses summary data from the BSA survey series, available from the Britsocat website at www.britsocat.com, and the UK Data Archive. No data available for 1988, 1992 and 1996.

Copyright © Joseph Rowntree Foundation

Gender

Women's wages have consistently been below those of men in the UK. Sociologists refer to this as the **gender pay-gap**. At present this gap, according to The Women and Equality Unit (2006) is 12.6 per cent, or, to put another way, this means that women working full-time are currently paid, on average, 87.4 per cent of men's hourly pay. Since 1975, when the Equal Pay Act came into effect, the full-time pay gap has closed considerably, from 29.5 per cent to 20.2 per cent in 1996 and from 20.7 per cent in 1997 to 17.2 per cent in 2006. As with all statistical averages this figure hides disparities along a number of different variables, such as race and social class. According to the government paper, *The Gender Pay Gap* (2001), the reasons for these differentials are as follows:

- **Part-time working:** The gap between men and women is particularly large because there are so many women who choose, primarily for childcare reasons, to work part-time. Part of the reason for this differential is due to the fact that part-time workers tend to have lower qualifications and less experience of the workplace.

- **Travel patterns:** Women, on average, are willing to commute less than men. The reason for this is that women tend to have to balance work with other factors such as childcare and house caring. This has an impact on potential earnings because subsequently women have a smaller selection of jobs for which to apply – the jobs that are available are often less well paid and part-time. For example, the Department for Transport found in *Travel to Work* (2007) that men, on average, spent 21 per cent more time commuting than women.

- **Occupational segregation:** Women tend to do relatively few occupational roles, with 60 per cent of women doing just ten jobs. The jobs they do tend to equate well with family and child care roles and invariably tend to be poorly paid in comparison with male jobs. This relates to the 'glass ceiling' as women still remain rare visitors to the top occupational positions in the UK job market. The UK Equalities Commission (2006) comments that 'Women will not make it to the top in significant numbers unless action is taken to remove the barriers that stand in their way, and Britain will continue to miss out on women's skills and talents for another generation.'

- **Workplace segregation:** At the level of individual workplaces, high concentrations of female employees are associated with relatively low rates of pay. And higher levels of part-time working are associated with lower rates of pay, even after other factors have been taken into account.

- **Human capital differences:** Differences in the past were often related to lower educational and experience levels of women. However, with the increasing trend towards girls achieving better qualifications than boys, one would expect this to become less of an issue. However, this still will not change the fact that women often tend to have breaks in their careers. These breaks tend to reduce experience levels and often necessitate women taking demotion to return to the career ladder.

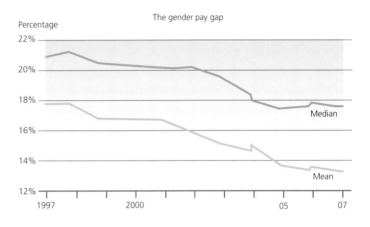

Ethnicity

Similarly there are wide differences between ethnic groups, with Bangladeshi, Pakistani and black people having the lowest income levels. Their low income, unfortunately, is likely to be the result of factors such as racial discrimination, especially where ethnic groups are overlooked for jobs because of the colour of their skin, despite educational qualifications and experience. Similar to women, who tend to be employed in a limited number of professions, this also impacts on ethnic income levels. For example, minority groups tend to be located in low-paid occupations such as in the NHS.

Geography

In sociological terminology wealth appears to have become more **geographically clustered**. This means that wealthy households are to be found in fewer and fewer areas of the UK. According to *Poverty and Wealth across Great Britain 1968–2005* (Dorling, et al., 2007) the poorest tend to be found in the inner cities whilst the affluent are concentrated around the outskirts and surrounds of major cities. In the report they found a trend for the 'exclusive rich' to live in and around London. By contrast poverty tends to be found in northern regions of England that have seen a decline in manufacturing, with only piecemeal replacement of jobs. The jobs that have been created are often low-paid service sector jobs that have low job security.

What other explanations can be offered for inequalities in wealth and income?

Other explanations tend to fall under two headings: recent trends and theoretical explanations.

Government policy

Recent trends in the last ten years have seen a move towards indirect taxation as opposed to direct taxation. This has led to lower top rate taxes for the rich and a switch to more unfair indirect taxation that actually makes the poor even poorer. This has been a conscious move by politicians as low income tax rates appear to be a vote winner for those in employment. However, it is bad news for those who are not. With a more punitive taxation system, wealth would be shared out by better public services and higher benefits. Given that this has not happened, despite huge wealth creation in the economy, inequality has continued to widen between the rich and poor.

Job Insecurity

The Poverty Site (2007) found that half of men and a third of women making a new claim for jobseeker's allowance were last claiming this benefit less than six months previously. This statistic indicates the short term and temporary nature of many of the jobs that are on offer in post-industrial Great Britain. This leads to many having unreliable income, so at times they have money, but when unemployed their savings are soon spent and they find themselves in debt again.

Globalisation

A recent trend has been the impact of globalisation. Strong links and the increasing ease with which goods and services can be transported across the globe have created a fierce global marketplace. One of those marketplaces is the labour market. So, whilst in the past the price of labour was merely a reflection of local supply and demand, it is now the result of global market pressures. This has led to a fall in real wages

for unskilled workers as they have to compete in a global market or face losing their jobs. For example, Dyson recently closed down their Malmesbury plant in Wiltshire to relocate to Malaysia (2005) and Peugeot closed down its Ryton plant in Coventry (2006) to relocate to Slovakia, claiming that wage costs were far lower in Slovakia in comparison with the UK. So decisions that are made in relation to location of Transnational Corporations are based upon worldwide considerations rather than just looking within one country.

Theoretical explanations of income and wealth inequality

Sociologists see wealth inequality as a product of ideology.

Functionalist view

Functionalists argue that inequality serves a function in society. It allows us to find the motivation to work hard to gain 'the American dream'. For example, they believe that we mostly aspire to wealth and fortune; therefore, so they argue, there will always be winners and losers. Moreover, functionalists suggest that for the economy to operate efficiently it needs to match the most able to the most academically-challenging jobs. To achieve this, rewards need to be given to those who are well educated and motivated through a system that they argue is based on merit (meritocractic). Thus, inequality is essential as a spur to this end. However, critics of functionalism argue that most of the top jobs in society seem to go to a small and unchanging elite; a group who tend to go to Oxford and Cambridge (Oxbridge), and who mostly go to top public schools such as Eton, Harrow and Westminster. Moreover, who decides which jobs are the most valuable to society? What makes a CEO worth millions of pounds, compared to a sociology teacher, for example, who would be lucky to earn that in their lifetime?

The Marxist view

Marxists argue that inequality is the consequence of a capitalist society; a society where some have vast wealth and riches because they own the factors of production and where others have to sell their labour in order to survive. The inequality of ownership allows capitalists to exploit their workers and give them only a small percentage of profits in the form of wages. It is argued that this inequality is persistent and ongoing given the power of the superstructure to protect the wealthy that always allow them to have the upper hand. However, Marxists don't recognise that inequality occurs for a multitude of reasons, not just from class, and as a theory it is too economically deterministic.

The Weberian view

Weberians use the phrase 'constant sum' to explain how they see some having more power than others. They believe that not everyone can be powerful; if one group of people has power then this means that another group does not. This competition between groups results in some wealthy groups and some poor groups. Weberians believe, as do Marxists, that the group who has this power will want to maintain it. However, for Weberians, class is not defined merely by the relationship to the means of production, but by the sharing of a common market position leading to shared life chances. For example, sociologists now look at council tenants and their common market position.

The New Right

The New Right take a similar view to functionalists; however, they tend to argue that inequalities are in fact a good thing in that they encourage citizens to be entrepreneurial and rational, and that the state is lumbering and inefficient. Wealth is created by competition and free markets that allow the individual to pursue their wealth goals. So the New Right see any organisations that stifle such competition, such as left wing governments, trade unions or the Civil Service, as distorting competition and reducing wealth creation. As a corollary of this, the New Right isn't that keen on the welfare state as they believe it leads to the creation of a 'dependency culture' that encourages the rational person to stay on benefits rather than having to work hard.

Defining and measuring poverty, wealth and income (Part II)

Introduction

When we consider the term 'poverty' it tends to bring to mind images of extreme hunger in the Third World or perhaps of children working long hours in extremely dangerous conditions during industrial times. Given that we take the widely accepted definition of poverty as having an income that is less than 60 per cent of the national average (excluding the wealthiest members of society), this means that one in five people in Great Britain are 'poor', and this figure has remained stubborn and resistant to government policies over the last 30 years.

Sociologists define poverty in two ways: absolute poverty and relative poverty.

Absolute poverty

First it is perhaps important to note that there is no complete agreement on what constitutes **absolute poverty**. Rowntree (1899) was the first to study poverty in the UK. In his study of York he calculated a minimum weekly sum of money which, in his opinion, was 'necessary to enable families to secure the necessities of a healthy life.' Those whose incomes fell below this mark were considered by Rowntree to be poor. Rowntree found in his study that 28 per cent of the working classes lived in such poverty; not having enough food, fuel and clothing to keep them in good health. Rowntree also went on to distinguish between:

- **Primary poverty:** which he considered not having enough money coming in each week to live a normal, healthy life, even if every penny was wisely spent.

- **Secondary poverty:** where people had earnings that were sufficient, but were spending some of that money on other things. Whilst some of these were necessary, others, such as expenditure on cigarettes and alcohol, were not.

Although this is useful, a more contemporary definition comes from **Gordon and Townsend** (2003) which sees absolute poverty as related to access to seven basic needs. If the household or individual does not have access to a particular basic need, they are defined as 'deprived'. Those who are deprived of two or more of the seven basic need indicators are defined as being in 'absolute poverty':

- Clean water
- Sanitation
- Shelter
- Education
- Information
- Food
- Health

Advantages and disadvantages of an absolute definition of poverty

The advantage of having a definition is that it potentially gives us a transparent idea of who is poor at any one moment in time, whilst we can use it to compare and contrast other societies with regard to poverty elsewhere in the world. For example, Rowntree's definition examining what is needed to be healthy is not particularly useful in today's society as almost all these needs will be met. Furthermore, it ignores the fact that what is seen as poverty changes with time. So, whilst 30 years ago a colour television was considered to be a luxury, today 99 per cent of the population has access to one. As a consequence, we need to decide what makes up a 'minimum' standard of clothes or diet. So although this definition works in relation to deciding if someone has nothing, it does not help us explain how people in our own country can be poor, yet still be able to feed themselves and wear adequate clothing.

Relative poverty

A different way to see poverty is to compare it with the everyday expectations of most of the population. As wealth increases, ideas of poverty differ too. So whilst ownership of a colour television is a good way to explain this perhaps ten years ago, a more modern way would be to look at the facilities most houses now possess. Access to a home computer and the Internet perhaps might be soon be seen as a measure of relative poverty given 62 per cent of people now have access to such technology (Internet World Statistics, 2007). So, relative poverty allows us to compare poverty with the expectations of the rest of the population. As a result the concept reflects that people look at 'the Joneses' to compare their standards of living with those around them.

Top countries with the highest Internet penetration rate

#	Country or Region	Penetration Latest Data (% Population)	Internet Users (2007 Est.)	Population	Source and Date of Latest Data
1	Norway	88.0 %	4,074,100	4,627,926	ITU - Sept/07
2	Netherlands	87.8 %	14,544,400	16,570,613	ITU - Sept/07
3	Iceland	85.4 %	258,000	301,931	ITU - Sept/06
4	New Zealand	77.7 %	3,200,000	4,115,771	ITU - Sept/05
5	Sweden	77.3 %	6,981,200	9,031,088	ITU - Sept/07
6	Antigua & Barbuda	76.3 %	53,000	69,481	ITU - Dec/07
7	Australia	75.9 %	15,504,532	20,434,176	Nielsen//NR - Dec/07
8	Portugal	73.1 %	7,782,760	10,642,836	IWS - Mar/06
9	United States	71.7 %	215,935,529	301,139,947	Nielsen//NR - Dec/07
10	Faroe Islands	71.6 %	34,000	47,511	ITU - Sept/07
11	Korea, South	71.2 %	34,910,000	49,044,790	ITU - Dec/07
12	Luxembourg	70.6 %	339,000	480,222	ITU - Aug/07
13	Hong Kong	69.9 %	5,230,351	7,554,661	Nielsen//NR - Sept/07
14	Falkland Islands	69.4 %	1,900	2,736	CIA - Dec/02
15	Switzerland	69.2 %	5,230,351	7,554,661	Nielsen//NR - Sept/07
16	Denmark	68.8 %	3,762,500	5,468,120	ITU - Sept/05
17	Japan	68.7 %	87,540,000	127,433,494	ITU - Sept/07
18	Taiwan	67.4 %	15,400,000	22,858,872	TWNIC - June/07
19	Greenland	67.4 %	38,000	56,344	ITU - Dec/05
20	United Kingdom	66.4 %	40,362,842	60,776,238	Nielsen//NR - Nov/07
21	Canada	65.9 %	22,000,000	33,390,141	ITU - Mar/07
22	Germany	64.6 %	53,240,128	82,400,996	Nielsen//NR - Dec/07
23	Liechtenstein	64.2 %	22,000	34,247	ITU - Mar/07
24	Bermuda	63.5 %	42,000	66,163	ITU - March/07
25	Finland	62.7 %	3,286,000	5,238,460	ITU - Sept/05
26	Slovenia	62.2 %	1,250,600	2,009,245	ITU - Sept/07
27	Monaco	61.2 %	20,000	32,671	ITU - Sept/07
28	Malaysia	60.0 %	14,904,000	24,821,286	MCMC - June/07
29	Estonia	57.8 %	760,000	1,315,912	ITU - Sept/07
30	Israel	57.6 %	3,700,000	6,426,679	TIM - July/06
31	Italy	57.0 %	33,143,152	58,147,733	Nielsen//NR - Nov/07
32	Barbados	57.0 %	160,000	280,946	ITU - Sept/06
33	Austria	56.7 %	4,650,000	8,199,783	C.I.Almanac - Mar/05
34	Spain	56.5 %	22,843,915	40,448,191	Nielsen//NR - Nov/07
35	Belarus	56.3 %	5,477,500	9,724,723	ITU - Sept/07
36	Guernsey & Alderney	54.9 %	36,000	65,573	ITU - Oct/05
37	France	54.7 %	34,851,835	63,718,187	Nielsen//NR - Nov/07
38	Singapore	53.2 %	2,421,800	4,553,009	ITU - Sept/05
39	Belgium	52.8 %	5,490,000	10,392,226	ITU - Dec/07
40	Niue	52.3 %	900	1,722	RockET - Sept/05
41	San Marino	52.0 %	15,400	29,615	ITU - Sept/07
42	Ireland	50.1 %	2,060,000	4,109,086	C.I.Almanac - Mar/05
43	Czeck Republic	50.0 %	5,100,000	10,228,744	ITU - Dec/05
	TOP 43 in Penetration	66.7 %	676,306,057	1,013,272,507	IWS - Feb/08
	Rest of the World	11.5 %	643,566,052	5,593,699,152	IWS - Feb/08
	World Total Users	20.0 %	1,319,872,109	6,606,971,659	IWS - Feb/08

The strengths of at least trying to define relative poverty include:

- Allows us to think about how poverty is socially constructed and may change at different times and places.
- Allows us to extend the debate, as this measure realises that poverty is a comparison with what the rest of society possesses.

However, the concept of relative poverty has a number of problems:

- It is impossible to apply equally across the world. What is considered important in one country may not be in another.
- There is the problem that the measure of relative poverty means that there will always be poverty as long as there is unequal wealth.
- Some argue that relative measures of poverty tend to overplay the problem.

How is relative poverty measured?

Sociologists use two ways of measuring relative poverty:

The relative income measure (Households Below Average Income [HBAI])

This method was originally formulated by **Abel-Smith and Townsend** (1965) who wanted to formulate a relative measure of poverty. Initially they set poverty at 140 per cent of 'household entitlement to Income Support, plus rent and housing costs.' However, since then a new method has been formulated.

The Department for Work and Pensions (DWP) *Family Resources Survey* uses a measure of household poverty to be those that receive less than 60 per cent of the average British income. The HBAI is published annually and is considered to be a high-profile figure for the government. It has become an important government publication because it reports on whether child poverty figures are being reached, as well as giving an indication of poverty for adults and pensioners in the UK.

The Townsend deprivation index

Peter Townsend has been the forefront of the trying to measure poverty. Initially, starting with his study of relative poverty in 1968–9 and then a questionnaire of 1208 households and 3950 people in 1979, Townsend used these pieces of work to formulate the 'Townsend scoring system' which has the specific advantage of being calculated directly from Census variables and therefore required no other data to be made available. The Townsend deprivation index is based on a range of 60 census-based indicators including unemployment, car ownership, housing density and overcrowded accommodation, and housing tenure. From this list he chose 12 that he thought were most characteristic of deprivation. The index was useful on a number of levels. Firstly, it allowed Townsend to identify people who were more disadvantaged than others. Secondly, he was able to make correlations from his data. For instance, he found that those on low incomes were more likely to have a high deprivation index, with those on benefits being particularly disadvantaged. In his initial survey he found that 12.64 million individuals were below the poverty line in 1968–9. Thirdly, it allowed a representative sample to be taken, thereby increasing validity as well as looking at relative factors.

The consensual model

Consensus is agreement. With this measure people are asked to identify items that are essential in everyday life. This is done by interviewing respondents and asking them to rank possessions in order of importance. From this list judgements can be made about who is and who is not in poverty. On their selection of 35 items 22 were considered vital by at least 50 per cent of the 1174 interviewees. From this **Mack and Lansley**, who pioneered this research, deemed that those who had three or less of these because they couldn't afford them should be regarded as in poverty. From this agreed definition Mack and Lansley estimated that up to 7.5 million people were living in relative poverty in the UK. In this earlier study, however, the list was produced by the two researchers. It could be argued that, as Mack and Lansley concocted this list, that they were suffering from ideological bias; in a sense, deciding before the research what was essential.

Mack and Lansley revisited this research some years later in conjunction with London Weekend Television and used a similar methodology with a set of items that were slightly modified to update the research concluded from their sample of 1319. From this list the amount of items considered to be 'necessities' by over 50 per cent of the interviewees rose from 22 to 32. This reflected the general increase in affluence of the UK population between the two study dates. However, even given this increase in living standards, Mack and Lansley found that the actual amount of people in poverty had increased from 7.5 million to 11 million people.

This interesting study reveals how, even in a short time, societal expectations of necessities change. This change also impacts on how we perceive who is in poverty and how many this affects. Methodologically it can be praised because the set of 'necessities' was not chosen by the researchers but was formulated by a cross-section of society.

Social exclusion

Some researchers, however, have been uneasy about seeing poverty just in terms of not having goods or money. More recent work by Gordon et al. on behalf of the Rowntree Trust has extended its research to investigate **social exclusion**. By social exclusion we mean the way that those in poverty are disadvantaged in many different ways. Gordon's research, for example, examined how poor groups were deprived of long-term paid employment. As a consequence of this their 'social relations' are damaged. What Gordon means by this is that jobs are not just essential for income but provide social networking opportunities to make friends, gain contacts and remain psychologically and physically healthy.

In his study Gordon found that 'due to caring responsibilities, often due to long hours at work or caring for the disabled or elderly', people were excluded from 'socially necessary activities'. He found that one in eight had no friends or outside contacts and therefore were socially and financially excluded. This tended to be a particular problem for men, with this group being more likely to suffer from poor personal support, especially in times of need. Whilst, in general, poor groups also were less likely to get involved in 'civic engagement', rarely voting in either local or national elections and rarely getting out by using public services such as libraries and community centres. Gordon additionally found that poor groups were also subject to 'service exclusion', being far more likely to be cut off from gas, electricity and water supplies, which are essential. And even when they were connected they were often discriminated against by being offered high-cost meters or having to moderate their use of gas or electricity in fear of the price. Gordon found that one out of 14 are excluded from four or more of essential public and private services and nearly one in four from two or more services because they are either unaffordable or unavailable.

The movement towards using other factors to measure poverty, apart from income alone, has been led by the work of Peter Townsend, and government research in tandem with the Joseph Rowntree Foundation. Their rationale has been simple: whilst some believe that poverty can be eradicated by merely increasing income, others reject this idea. Instead, they believe in social exclusion, which the New Policy Institute believes can be measured by looking at:

- Levels of income
- Employment
- The percentage of low-birth-weight babies born
- Those between the ages of 16 to 18 who are not in education or training and not working
- Mental and physical health, such as suicide statistics for 16–24-year-olds
- Housing and homelessness
- Living in disadvantaged neighbourhoods

The New Policy Institute (Howarth, et al., 1999) has produced a set of 46 key indicators, each capable of regular updating. It has done this to help create a 'baseline' set of indicators that can be monitored regularly to ensure that the government is focusing clearly on eradicating poverty and social exclusion.

Summary of the poverty and social exclusion indicators

Indicator	Trends over time	
	Over the medium term (last 5 years or so)	Over latest year of available data
Income		
1. Numbers in low income	Improved	Improved
2. Low income and housing costs	N/A	N/A
3. Low income by age group	Mixed	Improved
4. Income inequalities	N/A	N/A
5. Lacking essential items	N/A	N/A
6. Out-of-work benefit levels	Mixed	Mixed
7. Long-term recipients of out-of-work benefits	Steady	Steady
Children		
8. In low-income households	Improved	Improved
9. In receipt of tax credits	Mixed	Mixed
10. In workless households	Improved	Steady
11. Low birthweight babies	Steady	Steady
12. Child health Steady Steady		
13. Underage pregnancies	Improved	Improved
14. Low attainment at school - 11-year-olds	Improved	Improved
15. Low attainment at school - 16-year-olds	Steady	Steady
16. School exclusions	Steady	Steady
Young adults		
17. Without a basic qualification	Steady	Steady
18. School leavers	Steady	Steady
19. With a criminal record	Improved	Improved
20. Unemployment	Steady	Worsened
21. Low pay	Steady	Steady
22. Suicides	Improved	Improved
Adults aged 25 to retirement		
23. Low income and work	Worsened	Steady
24. Low income and disability	Steady	Steady
25. Low income and Council Tax	Worsened	Worsened
26. Concentrations of low income	N/A	N/A
27. Wanting paid work	Improved	Steady
28. Work and disadvantaged groups	Mixed	Mixed
29. Workless households	Steady	Steady
30. Low pay by gender	Improved	Improved
31. Low pay by industry	N/A	N/A
32. Pay inequalities	Mixed	Mixed
33. Disadvantaged at work	Steady	Steady
34. Support at work	Improved	Steady
36. Premature death	Improved	Improved
33. Limiting longstanding illness or disability	Improved	Steady
37. Mental health	Improved	Steady
Older people		
38. In low-income households	Improved	Improved
39. Benefit take-up	Worsened	Worsened
40. Excess winter deaths	Steady	Steady
41. Limiting longstanding illness or disability	Steady	Steady
42. Help from social services	Worsened	Steady
43. Anxiety Improved Improved		
Communities		
44. Without a bank account	Improved	Improved
45. Without home contents insurance	Improved	Improved
46. **Transport**	N/A	N/A
47. Polarisation by tenure	Steady	Steady
48. Without central heating	Improved	Improved
49. Homelessness	Steady	Improved
50. Mortgage arrears	Improved	Worsened

What these statistics show in 2006 The Blair legacy

The ninth edition of *Monitoring poverty and Social Exclusion* (Palmer, et al., 2006) is seen as giving a commentary of Tony Blair's time as Prime Minister (1997–2007). It reveals:

- **Child poverty:** This has improved substantially. However, the government target to reduce child poverty by a quarter compared with 1998–9 was not met, regardless of which income method is used. On the more commonly used 'after deducting housing costs' measure, the number of children in poverty in Britain fell by 700 000 or 17 per cent from 4.1 million in 1998–9 to 3.4 million in 2004–5. However, it is still some way short of the 25 per cent statistic required for the government to meet their avowed target.

- **Adult poverty:** Although there has been a reduction in pensioner poverty from 27 per cent in the late 1990s to 17 per cent in 2004–5, the poverty rate for working-age adults remains unchanged at 19 per cent. Nearly half of working-age adults in poverty live in households where someone is doing paid work. Other groups fare little better, with those who are disabled accounting for 30 per cent of all people who are in poverty.

- **Low pay and income inequalities:** With the introduction of the minimum wage the percentage of workers over the age of 22 who are low paid has fallen from 37 per cent in 2000 to 29 per cent in 2005. However, there has been little reduction in the gender pay-gap, and those on low incomes have received substantially lower pay increases than those on high incomes.

- **Health inequalities:** These remain widespread, with those from lower manual social classes being more at

Focus on research

The New Policy Institute has produced a number of annual research papers that seek to report on poverty and social exclusion. The idea is that these provide a comprehensive analysis of trends over time and differences between groups. The 2006 report provided an interesting analysis of the Blair administration, for the New Policy Institute's first report in 1997 coincided with Blair's election into office as Prime Minister. The 2006 report found that:

- Child poverty had been reduced but not enough to meet government targets
- Pensioner poverty had seen reductions, although poverty amongst working-age adults remained a big problem
- Three-quarters of the extra income created over the last decade has gone to richer households
- The gender pay-gap continues to be a problem, with women earning considerably less than men doing similar jobs

The researchers conclude that the overall picture is not so much a mixture of success and failure as one of success and neglect. Where government has acted, change has happened. Where it has not, previous trends have continued.

risk of infant death, high levels of tooth decay, teenage motherhood and poor mental health. Moreover, this group is more likely to suffer from premature death from lung cancer and heart disease. However, more encouragingly, long-standing illnesses for those over 75 where there are differences between social class appear to be reducing dramatically.

- **Educational outcomes:** Again there have been some positive developments. Namely, the proportion reaching level four at Key Stage Two (age 11) has continued to rise, whilst headline rates of A*–C grades at GCSE have also risen. On the other hand, the proportion of those failing to gain five GCSEs at any level has been stuck at 11 per cent since 1999–2000, whilst children from deprived backgrounds continue to fail to gain qualifications commensurate with other members of society at ages 11 and 16.

- **Exclusion by institution:** One area of success has been the proportion of low-income households without a bank account fell to ten per cent by 2004–5, down from well above 20 per cent in the late 1990s, with the proportion of those without central heating falling by a similar amount.

- **Income:** The number of people on relative low income is now lower than at any time since 1987, but it is still much higher than in the early 1980s. Although it should be noted that a third of all people in low-income households are working-age adults without dependent children, whilst the high cost of housing leads to a much higher proportion of people having low income in the south-east after having housing costs deducted.

Why we need to be careful about statistics

Most statistics can be misleading: phenomenologists comment that statistics are merely the interpretation of those collecting them. The majority of the statistics we have looked at are quantitative, but whilst these can be useful for looking at general trends of poverty in the UK, they do not uncover what it is like to be poor in modern-day Britain, and the statistics which are collected by the government can always be accused of 'putting a gloss' on poverty. Peter Townsend reiterates that there is no agreed definition of poverty, with the Child Poverty Action Group believing that figures on poverty lack clarity, and the wide range of indicators leaves it open for the government to highlight the indicators that show the most favourable results.

Marxists believe that governments give some idea of poverty, but will try to use statistics to blind the public with terminology. A further school of thought is produced by postmodernists, who argue that there has been a decline in metanarratives. There are no universal truths anymore and therefore truth is completely subjective. Whilst in the past people merely accepted universal definitions of poverty, nowadays the discerning voter will take on opinions from a range of data for television, Internet and newspapers. Ultimately then, definitions are limited, do not reveal the individual hardship that people have to undertake, and the statistics themselves often mask and underplay real problems because the government wants it that way. To understand this is to understand the complexities of this issue.

What do you know now?

1. Look at the following and decide which types of taxation (direct or indirect) they relate to:
   - Value added tax
   - Excise duty
   - Income tax
   - Incapacity benefit
   - High quality public services

2. Explain why it is problematic to define the concept 'wealth'.

3. Explain the reasons why statistics on wealth might not be wholly accurate.

4. Explain how Marxists, functionalists and Weberians describe income inequality.

5. Look at the seven basic needs. In pairs, have a go at ranking them from the most important to the least important. Compare notes with others around you.
   - Clean water
   - Sanitation
   - Shelter
   - Education
   - Information
   - Food
   - Health

6. Explain the differences between absolute and relative poverty.

7. What criticisms have been made of the absolute and relative measures of poverty?

8. Outline the strengths and weaknesses of different approaches to the definition and measurement of poverty.

Key terms

Absolute poverty: Where people lack the necessary food, clothing, or shelter to survive.

Gender pay-gap: The gap between male and female pay in the UK.

Geographically clustered: Found in only a few areas of the country.

Gini coefficient: A measure of inequality of a distribution of income. The lower the value of the Gini coefficient, the more equally household income is distributed.

Households below average income: Uses statistics derived from an analysis of the Family Resources Survey.

Income: Money received by a person during a period of time in exchange for labour or services.

Inheritance tax: The state tax levied upon the value of property received after inheritance.

Life cycle: Refers to how, during life, people's financial circumstances change.

Marketable wealth: Incorporates every kind of asset that can be bought and sold, with the exception of housing and pension.

Median income: The middle number present in a set of data when the incomes of all household are arranged in an order of highest to lowest.

Occupational segregation: The concentration of women in the workplace doing particular jobs.

Redistribution: A political policy intended to transfer wealth from the rich to the poor. These taxes are then used to improve public services, which particularly benefit the poor.

Relative poverty: Defines income or resources in relation to the average. It is concerned with the absence of the material needs to participate fully in accepted daily life.

Social exclusion: Defined by the UK government as what can happen when people or areas suffer from a combination of linked problems such as unemployment, poor skills, low incomes, poor housing, high crime, bad health and family breakdown.

Wealth: The accumulation of resources such as property, savings and other assets like stocks and shares.

Section summary

- Sociologists find it very hard to define the concept of wealth as it is difficult to decide what should and what shouldn't be included.

- Despite the increase in share and property ownership there is still a large amount of inequality in Great Britain.

- The most widely used summary measuring of the degree of inequality in household income distribution is the Gini coefficient. This represents an overall measure of the cumulative income share against the share of households in the population.

- The tax system is used as one way to redistribute income. Traditionally, direct taxes have been levied as these are progressive. However, over the last 20 years there has been a movement to the use of indirect taxation.

- Income levels tend to be lower for the young compared to the rest of the population, with only pensioners being worse off.

- Women's wages have consistently been below those of men in the UK. Sociologists like to refer to this as the 'gender pay-gap'.

- Similarly there are wide differences between ethnic groups, with Bangladeshi, Pakistani and black people having the lowest income levels.

- Absolute measures of poverty are difficult to define.

- Absolute poverty is defined as the lack of adequate resources with which to keep body and soul together.

- The advantage of having a definition is that it potentially gives us a transparent idea of who is poor at any one moment in time, whilst we can use it to compare and contrast other societies with regard to poverty elsewhere in the world.

- Relative poverty defines income or resources in relation to the average. It is concerned with the deficiency of the material needs to participate fully in accepted daily life. A number of measures have been used to measure relative poverty. These include the HBAI which is published annually and is considered to be a high profile figure for the government.

- More recent work has extended its research to investigate social exclusion.

- UK child poverty has improved substantially. However, the government target to reduce child poverty by a quarter compared with 1998–9 was not met.

- Adult poverty has shown a reduction in pensioner poverty; however, the poverty rate for working-age adults remains unchanged at 19 per cent.

- With the introduction of the minimum wage the percentage of workers over the age of 22 who are low-paid has fallen.

- Inequalities are still widespread in relation to health, educational outcome, exclusion by institution and income.

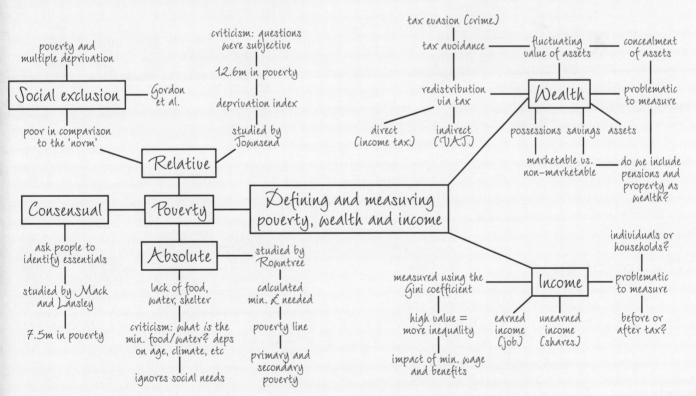

Poverty among different social groups

Introduction

As I have already explained, definitive measurements of who is poor in the UK depend upon which definition is used. The most common definition of low income is households earning 60 per cent or less of the average UK household income in a year after housing costs. Using this method as a yardstick, 22 per cent of the population is in poverty, or 13 million people in Britain are surviving on low incomes; this means a constant struggle for this group (The Poverty Site, 2006). This figure of 13 million represents an increase of three-quarters of a million compared with the previous year, 2004–5, and worryingly follows six uninterrupted years of decreases from 1998–9 to 2004–5. Poverty can therefore be said to be not uncommon in the UK and it touches a wide variety of people from differing backgrounds. In this section we will look at the groups most likely to suffer from poverty.

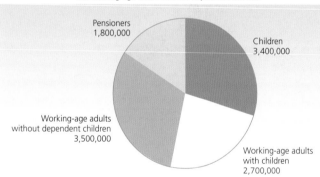

A third of all people in low income households are working-age adults without dependent children

Source: Households Below Average Income 2004/05, DWP; GB
Copyright © Joseph Rowntree Foundation

The number of people with relative low incomes is now lower than at any time since 1987, but it is still much higher than in the early 1980s.

Who are the poor?

Although this appears to be an easy question to answer, it isn't. It depends upon lots of variables. Sociologists need to make decisions about how to classify people, which statistical method to use, and so on. Nonetheless, a few trends can be isolated from income distribution. In 2004–5, 65 per cent of individuals had household incomes below the national average; however, although this figure is useful, we also need to decide either to measure poverty by household or **economic**

status. For example, household measurements might look at the nuclear family, whilst economic status might examine those in full-time employment.

Poverty by family group

The first way of looking at poverty is by looking at **family status**. The figure shows the numbers of the people in low-income households according to whether they are children, pensioners, working-age adults with dependent children or working-age adults without dependent children. From this you can see that half of lone parent families are on low income. This is two-and-a-half times the rate for couples with children. However, the good news is that in proportional terms low-income families have been falling at a faster rate than those with children. But in absolute figures the largest fall has been in families with children. This relates to the fact that the number of lone parent families has been increasing. It should be noted that the groups who are on very low income tend to be working-age adults without dependent children or couples with children. Relatively few are either lone parents or pensioners.

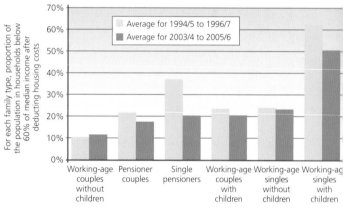

A half of all lone parents are on low income: two-and-a-half times the rate for couples with children

Source: Households Below Average Income, DWP; UK; updated June 2007

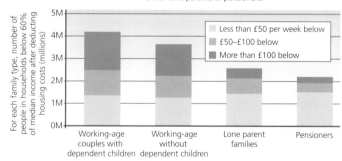

The vast majority of people with very low incomes are either working-age adults without children or couples with children. Relatively few are either lone parents or pensioners.

Poverty by economic status

Statistics on economic status

Those who are unemployed make up 29 per cent of the poor by economic status. The next group most likely to find themselves in poverty are the retired (16 per cent) and those in part-time work (13 per cent).

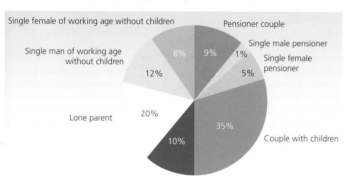

Make up of the poor population by household status, 2005/06

Looking at risk groups

The government uses the idea of groups who are at risk to compile their data on poverty. Again this is done by data showing household composition and economic status.

High-risk groups of living in poverty

The number of lone-parent families who tend to be headed by women (nine in ten) increased from 1.3 million in 1992 to 1.9 million in 2005, with children in the UK three times more likely to live in one-parent households than they were in 1972.

The reasons for this group's poverty are twofold. Firstly, as women from lower social classes are more likely to become single parents, they are already likely to be at risk of poverty before they become pregnant. Secondly, single-parent families have to pay a considerable amount of money for childcare. Moreover, because of their childcare duties, single parents often take low-paid part-time work rather than full-time employment, which further decreases their income. Yet it should be noted that single parents have become increasingly economically active with a rise in employment rates of 51 per cent in 2000 to 56.2 per cent in 2005, with 23 per cent working full-time and 28 per cent part-time, compared to 31 per cent who stay at home to look after family and home. This goes against the media image of single parents as 'people who live off the state'. As with all statistics it should be remembered that statistics hide disparities in wealth between single parents. Some, of course, are wealthy, but nonetheless, a significant majority remain in poverty.

Children

Despite government pledges to halve child poverty by 2010, figures for 2005–6 show that 3.8 million children were in poverty in homes on less than 60 per cent of average income including housing costs. This was a rise of 200 000 from the previous year. It was the first recorded increase in six years; since 1998–9. The proportion of children living in low-income households (using the low-income threshold of the 60 per cent of median income after deducting housing costs) fell from 34 per cent of all children in 1996–7 to 28 per cent in 2004–5, before rising to 30 per cent in 2005–6. Whilst 50 per cent of all lone-parent families are on low incomes compared to one in five couples with children. Two-fifths of all the children in low-income households are in lone-parent households. However, because of high levels of **structural unemployment**, it is also true that unless all adults in the household are working (and at least one of them full-time), the risks of being on low income are still substantial: 85 per cent for unemployed households, 75 per cent for other workless households and 30 per cent for those where the adults are part-time working.

The unemployed

Unemployment is a key factor in low income. In 2005–6 there were 1.8 million children living in workless families. Although this represents a reduction from 2.3 million ten years ago, it still equates to 16 per cent of all children living in such circumstances, with approximately 75 per cent of unemployed people living in poverty. Long-term unemployment leads to severe problems for those suffering it. As income levels fall families start to use savings on basic living costs that would otherwise be used to improve living standards through the replacement of furnishings and other general possessions. There is also evidence to suggest that jobs are important for mental health. For example, unemployed men are two to three times more at risk of suicide than the general population, and although no direct link has been shown between unemployment and young male suicide, there may be an indirect link from the effects of unemployment, such as poverty.

Global unemployment rate 1993–2007 (average of US, Europe and Japan, seasonally adjusted)

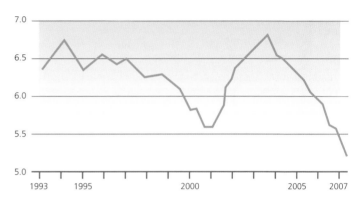

The low paid

Office for National Statistics (ONS) data for 2006 estimates that 4.5 million employees aged 22–65 were on wages of less than £6.50 per hour; two-thirds of these being women and one-third men. With such a low income it is hardly surprising that such individuals do not have enough money to live on. Those on these incomes invariably tend to have low human-capital skills. Unemployment is a particular problem in areas where traditional manufacturing has declined, leaving low-paid tertiary jobs in their place. Due to the high supply of labour and low demand for it, competition is fierce and consequently wages are depressed. Given women's gendered role, they are also highly affected by low income as they tend to have to take part-time jobs; 75 per cent of women in part-time jobs earn less than £6.50 an hour.

The sick and disabled

According to the *Labour Force Survey 2005*, nearly one in five people of working age (6.9 million, or 19 per cent) in Great Britain are disabled. The survey noted that there has been an increase in the number of working-age people reporting a disability from 6.2 million in Spring 1998 to 7 million in Spring 2005. Unemployment rates are high for the disabled, with only about half (45 per cent) being economically active. In relation to poverty, disabled adults aged 25 to retirement are twice as likely to live in low-income households as their non-disabled adult counterparts: 30 per cent compared with 15 per cent. There are a number of reasons why the **sick and disabled** tend to be on low incomes. Due to their disabilities they may be unable to work. Even if they are able to be economically active, they may be limited to certain occupations which allow them to work successfully. Furthermore, even after income has been earned, this group suffer from having to pay extra for their houses and cars to be modified, or pay for extra drugs or treatment. To look at more of these issues the following website is useful: www.disabilityalliance.org.

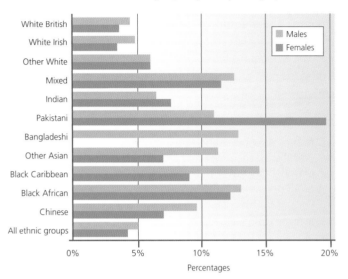

Percentage of poverty levels by ethnic group

The elderly

In 2006, 4.4 million men and 7.2 million women claimed the state pension: figures that are set to rise as the population continues to live longer. If we look at those over the age of 50 the figures are even greater, with 20.3 million claiming the state pension in 2005, representing a 26 per cent increase from 1961. Predictions for the future suggest that by 2031 there will be 27 million people over the age of 50 claiming the state pension. These figures represent the result of increased life expectancy and reductions in mortality for all age groups of the population. Potentially, this demographic trend has the potential to provide real problems for the UK economy as the 'baby boomers' of the 1960s reach retirement age. As this occurs, there will be fewer people who are economically active, whilst there will be a high level of **dependent population**. Some suggest that taxes will have to increase to pay for this group.

The good news is that due to government policies, such as the Winter Fuel Payment, increases on the basic state pension, substantial increases in means-tested benefits for pensioners – particularly younger pensioners – and the introduction of the Pension Credit in October 2003, there have been falls in poverty for pensioners. The proportion of pensioners living in low-income households has been falling since 1996–7, from 29 per cent of all pensioners in 1996–7 to 17 per cent in 2005–6. Poverty and age are linked because as we age we become limited to our pension funds, which tend to be fixed, and therefore don't increase in line with inflation or earnings. If inflation increases, pensioner poverty becomes worse. With more people living to an older age, those who have earned little during their lifetimes will find themselves unable to gain a decent standard of living.

Ethnic minorities

Those from ethnic-minority backgrounds are substantially more likely to suffer poverty than other groups in the UK, with around two-fifths enduring low income in their households: twice the rate of poverty compared with indigenous white groups in the UK. Within this figure there are disparities between different ethnic groups, with some groups far more likely to be in poverty. For example, 65 per cent of Bangladeshi people, 55 per cent of Pakistani people, and 45 per cent of black people live in low-income households (Kenway et al., *Poverty among ethnic groups: how and why does it differ?* 2007). Other groups are far less likely to live in poor households. The lowest rates are those of Indian descent with only 25 per cent, 'white other' at 25 per cent, and 'white British' at 20 per cent.

Poverty and ethnicity seem to strongly relate to unemployment. Unemployment rates for people from non-white ethnic groups were generally higher than those of the rest of the population. So although some groups have low levels of unemployment, such as Indian men (seven per cent), others such as Pakistani women had a 20 per cent chance of being unemployed. Lucinda Platt (2007) found that an **ethnic penalty** of low educational attainment tended to have an impact on income, whilst even high educational achievement groups, such as black people, did not obtain the jobs that their qualifications might lead us to think they could. Platt also found factors such as the extended family were substantially higher than average for Bangladeshi, Pakistani and Indian households, meaning there were higher demands on disposable income, whilst rates of disability and sickness were far higher for Bangladeshi households, leading to lower incomes for this group.

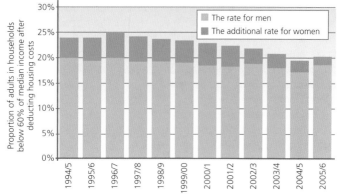

Women are a bit – but only a bit – more likely to live in low income households than men

Source: Households Below Average Income, DWP; UK; updated June 2007

Focus on research

Poverty and Inequality in the UK 2007

The Institute for Fiscal Studies (IFS)

Brewer, Goodman, Muriel and Subieta

This document provides an up-to-date commentary on trends in living standards, income inequality and poverty, using the same 'Households Below Average Income' data that is used by the government. Amongst its findings were:

- Half of the population had incomes above £363 per week, with the other half falling below this figure. This is considerably lower than the average or mean income of £445 per week.

- For the fourth year in a row both median and mean income rose, however, these rises have reduced with time.

- Rapid rises in household disposable income which occurred in the first half of Labour's tenure ended in 2001–2.

- Income growth since 2004–5 has been faster the higher a person's income is, with the 'high income' group's earnings rising by 1.5 per cent. By contrast the poorest fifth's income fell by 0.4 per cent.

- Overall income inequality, as calculated by the Gini coefficient, actually rose, with inequality being higher now than when the Labour government took control in 1997.

- However, other measures that do not take into account the extremes at the top and bottom, such as the 90:10 ratio, show income inequality falling since 1996–7.

Gender

Although women tend to be more likely to live in low-income households, the difference between male and female poverty (2007) remains insignificant, with 20 per cent of women living in low-income households compared to 19 per cent of men. This gap increases when looking at figures for single men and women, but again the disparities are relatively minor, with single men 24 per cent more likely to live in low-income families as opposed to 27 per cent for women. The main reason for this difference is the increased likelihood that women, both in employment and as pensioners, will be in low-income families. Another reason for the gap is that the majority of lone parents (90 per cent) are female: a group that has an increased chance of being on a low income. Again, there are differences between pensioner groups and poverty, with elderly women over 75 and older pensioner couples being more likely to live in a low-income household. These statistics reflect that as people become older they have to dip into savings over a longer period of time, and if they have been on low incomes throughout their adult lives this can have a substantial effect on poverty for the group concerned.

Poverty and locality

Poverty is also affected by geography, with some areas of the UK having higher levels of poverty than others. According to Dorling, et al in *Poverty, wealth and place in Britain 1968 to 2005* (2007), geographical poverty is one area that has been neglected by sociologists. Dorling found that using his measures for poverty, 'poor, rich and average households' were much less likely to reside in close proximity to each other. One group – what he calls the 'core poor' (people who are income-poor, materially deprived and subjectively poor) – in particular has remained geographically immobile, being unable to move to areas with lower unemployment that offer a better standard of living. Despite overall improvements in equality in the early part of the twenty-first century, Dorling believes that little progress has been made in reducing geographical polarisation. He found a general decline in 'average households' with wealthy households being concentrated in areas around major cities and the 'exclusive wealthy' tending to live within 50 to 100 miles around London. By contrast Dorling found what he calls 'poverty clusters' in inner-city London, South Wales, West Midlands, Northern England and Scotland. The differences in geographical wealth reflect unemployment and wage rates in these areas. These areas have remained stubbornly resistant to inward investment despite huge grants on offer from central government.

Social class and poverty

Class and poverty have always been strongly linked, so it is important to look at class in relation to poverty. Central to a discussion on class is the work of Karl Marx and his concept of 'class conflict'. Marx believed that there are two classes in society who are in constant opposition: The bourgeoisie who own the factors of production and who are able to extract surplus value out of the workers, selling goods at a higher price than it costs to make them, and the proletariat; the wage slaves who have to sell their labour for a relatively small amount in order to survive. This last point is central to our discussion. Low wages tend to lead to poverty, and, given Marx's analysis, the working classes by definition often have to accept low wages and, as such, exploitation.

A different view about class and poverty is provided by Max Weber. He believed that Marx's view was too simple, and, although he accepted that different classes do exist, he believed that status and privilege based upon a person's position in the labour market and educational qualifications was fundamental, rather than merely as a result of social class. Given this though, Weber believed that because the working classes lack marketable skills this leaves them towards the bottom of the class pyramid and as such is central to their working-class poverty.

Over the last decade The New Right in particular have highlighted another group who they call 'the underclasses'. According to writers such as Charles Murray, the underclasses consist of those who refuse to go to work, instead remaining on benefits. Murray sees this group as a drain on society's assets, with central government left to support them because of their refusal to move into the workplace. This debate has further fuelled the argument that differences between the 'haves' and 'have nots' is increasing. Evidence for this includes:

- In 2005–6, around 13 million people in the UK were living in households below the low-income threshold. This is around a fifth (22 per cent) of the population.

- The 13 million figure is an increase of three-quarters of a million compared with the previous year, 2004–5. It follows six uninterrupted years of decreases from 1998–9 to 2004–5.

- The UK has a higher proportion of its population in relative low income than most other EU countries. Of the 27 EU countries, only six have a higher rate than the UK. The proportion of people living in relative low income in the UK is twice that of the best country, Sweden.

1. Decide if the following are likely to be poor or rich in the UK:
   - Bangladeshi women
   - Lone-parent families
   - Those over the age of 76.5 years of age
   - Those who live on the outskirts of London
   - Those who live in a nuclear family structure
   - Single women
2. How many people lived in poverty in the UK in 2006?
3. State one criterion by which poverty is assessed.
4. Identify at least five groups who are considered to be in poverty.
5. Why do women tend to live in poverty?
6. Identify regions of the UK which are wealthy.
7. Explain the link between age and poverty.

Key terms

Dependent population: The part of the overall population who do not go to work.

Economic status: The way in which researchers classify people in relation to the method they gain income by.

Ethnic penalty: The sources of disadvantages that might lead an ethnic group to fare less well in the labour market than do similarly-qualified white people.

Family status: Used by researchers to classify those in poverty in relation to the family structure to which they belong (the same as 'household status').

Structural unemployment: The unemployment that arises when there is a decline in the number of jobs available in a particular region or industry. For example, the decline of the mining industry in the North of England resulted in unemployment.

The sick and disabled: The sick refer to those who are ill on an ongoing basis, whilst disability is defined by the Disability Act (1995) as someone who has a physical or mental impairment that has a substantial and long-term adverse effect on his or her ability to carry out normal day-to-day activities.

Section summary

- The most common definition of low income is households that earn 60 per cent or less of the average UK household income in a year after housing costs. Using this method as a yardstick, 22 per cent of the population is in poverty or, put another way, 13 million people in Britain are surviving on low incomes.

- The first way of looking at poverty is by looking at family status. Statistics on this show that one half of lone-parent families are on low income.

- We can also examine poverty by status. High-risk groups that include lone parents who tend to be headed by women (nine out of ten) increased from 1.3 million in 1992 to 1.9 million in 2005.

- Approximately 75 per cent of unemployed people live in poverty.

- ONS data for 2006 estimates that 4.5 million employees aged 22–65 were on wages of less than £6.50 per hour, with two-thirds of these being women, and one-third men.

- In relation to poverty, disabled adults aged 25 to retirement age are twice as likely to live in low-income households as their non-disabled adult counterparts.

- In 2006, 4.4 million men and 7.2 million women were claiming the state pension: a number set to rise as the population continues to live for longer.

- People from ethnic minority backgrounds are substantially more likely to suffer poverty than other groups in the UK, with around two-fifths of individuals from ethnic minority backgrounds enduring low income in their households.

- Wealthy households are concentrated around major cities and the 'exclusive wealthy' tend to live within 50 to 100 miles around London.

- Social class and poverty have always been strongly linked.

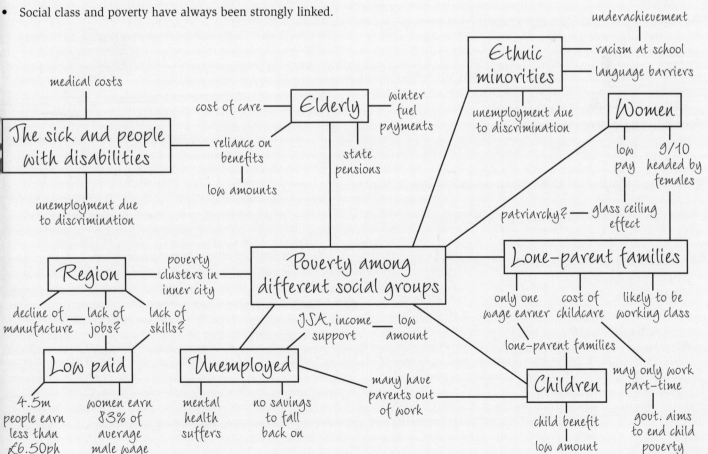

Sociological explanations of poverty

Learning objectives

By the end of this section you should be able to:

- Understand differences between cultural and structural explanations of poverty
- Understand New Right perceptions of culture and poverty
- Be able to describe and explain 'exclusion–based approaches' to poverty
- Describe how Marxists explain and perceive poverty

Cultural explanations of poverty

Cultural–based explanations of poverty seek to argue that poverty is partly the fault of the poor. This argument widens out to suggest how the poor need to modify their behaviour in order to escape from low income. In terms of chronology we will start with the work of Oscar Lewis (1959, 1961). Lewis, an anthropologist, studied the poor of Mexico and, later, Puerto Rico in the 1950s and 1960s, wanting to understand the cultural context of their poverty and, most importantly, how they coped with being poor. He identified what he called a **culture of poverty**; a set of behaviours or cultural values that stopped them from escaping poverty, even when opportunities existed for them to do so. These behaviours were not common amongst the affluent in society. Lewis refused to blame the poor themselves and realised that they were in that situation because they were deprived.

Lewis located some 70 behavioural characteristics that he argued remained continual barriers against escaping poverty. These cultural characteristics included:

- A feeling of hopelessness and fatalism
- The setting of only short-term goals rather than looking to the long term
- An inability to defer gratification, instead tending to 'live for today'
- The development of broken family structures
- A passive response to poverty
- Seeing children as an economic resource

He believed that these cultural ideas were constantly renewed and passed on from one generation to the next without question. He argued that the poor merely react to their condition; however, this reaction reduced their chances of escaping from poverty. His work implies that behaviour is also a key factor in poverty. Without a change in the perception of those in poverty about themselves, poverty will never disappear.

Strengths and weaknesses of Oscar Lewis's work

Lewis's work is useful because it explains the various ways of living that different groups adopt and why this occurs. However, critics of Lewis point out that the so-called culture of poverty is merely a pragmatic response to the deprivations suffered by the poor and the reality is that the poor really do understand their position: that there is no escape out of poverty for them or their children.

Other critics observe the low ecological validity of Lewis's work. Can the work of Lewis in the slums of Mexico and Puerto Rico really be compared to life the UK?

The New Right

The work of writers such as Oscar Lewis has been important in the formation of the ideas of the New Right. Writers such as American theorist Charles Murray strongly influenced the Conservative government of Margaret Thatcher (1979–90). Murray saw the underclass as a group of people who lived on the margins of British society; who saw no value in working but instead were more content to live off the state in unsocialised, criminal families. He was also concerned that the underclasses had the potential to reproduce itself at such a fast rate that British and American society would literally become less intelligent.

The New Right's influence led to ministers such as Norman Tebbit suggesting that the poor were in some way to blame for their own poverty, showing a belief that they should take responsibility rather than relying upon social welfare benefits to bail them out. Tebbit famously once said: "I grew up in the 1930s with an unemployed father. He did not riot. He got on his bike and looked for work, and he went on looking until he found it."

Although Murray is prepared to accept that poverty is not necessarily the fault of those affected, writers such as Mike O'Brien (1977) like to differentiate between poverty types.

The New Right differentiate the liberal distinction between:

- **The deserving poor:** Those who find themselves in poverty due to no fault of their own and who do everything in their power to get out of it, often working long hours in menial low-paid jobs.

- **The undeserving poor:** A group who are prepared to live on the margin of society, **voluntarily unemployed** and becoming involved in petty criminality. They tend to refuse to engage with the rest of society, for example, by not voting in general or local elections.

Norman Tebbit

The term 'underclass' was originally coined by the journalist Ken Auletta, although it was subsequently taken up by William J. Wilson who applied it in a rather different structural explanation of the failure of labour markets to create enough jobs. Wilson's work, which highlighted the position of urban black people, also underlines the racialised nature of the underclass debate in the US. However, Murray's analysis of the UK does not take this racialised approach. Instead he argues that the British underclass is characterised by the following beliefs:

- **Crime:** He argues that the underclasses are responsible for a large proportion of 'deplorable' crime, particularly property crime and violent crime. He suggests that they see crime as an acceptable and legitimate way to gain revenue.

- **High levels of illegitimacy:** Murray points out that in 1979 Britain had an illegitimacy rate of 10.6 per cent, but by 1988 this had risen to 25.6 per cent. This, he argues, indicates the result of casual sex, leading to children 'running wild' because they lack suitable role models of a two-parent family.

- **Joblessness:** Murray believes that the underclasses voluntarily 'drop out' of the labour market and have little interest in supporting either their children or partners. In essence, he believes they 'choose' to be unemployed. Figures show in the UK during the late 1990s there was low unemployment amongst young males, but this group has consistently remained economically inactive. Murray suggests they inhabit a 'seedy world' of the **hidden economy**, claiming benefits, yet often working for 'cash in hand' and therefore defrauding the state of money that could be going to the deserving poor.

Not surprisingly Murray's work has been robustly criticised. Empirical research shows that the unemployed are in fact more committed to the idea of work often than those in full employment.

Families from the underclasses often include cohabiting parents who take an active role in socialising with their children. One-parent families are not only found in the underclasses; they are present in all parts of the UK social structure and represent the changing nature of families in the UK, not necessarily an emergence of an underclass. As well as that, there is little evidence to suggest that crime and one-parent families go hand in hand.

Structural-based explanations of poverty

British writers such as **Frank Field,** who operate to the 'left' of British politics, argue that poverty is the result of powerful restriction of the poor. This approach takes a realistic approach to poverty, noting that some groups are much more likely to be represented within the poor. Field suggests groups such as ethnic minorities, the elderly, the young, women and children have been a victim of government policies.

He claims inequality and poverty is increasing in the UK as the underclasses are increasing in numbers. He believes the underclasses include:

- The long-term unemployed
- Single-parent families
- Elderly pensioners

Frank Field

These groups tend to be reliant upon state benefits which offer levels of assistance that are often too small to offer anything but a very low standard of living. They typically live in poor urban areas with a drug and crime culture, supplementing their income from the underground economy of 'cash in hand'. It is often said that such areas are so lawless that the emergency services refuse to go on 'shouts' within them. Moreover, because of the inherent meanness of benefits there is little prospect of escape from poverty.

Reasons the underclasses have suffered

- **Rising levels of unemployment**, particularly the development of long-term unemployment as opposed to merely moving between jobs. This has particularly affected the working classes, who are often unskilled or semi-skilled, with the structural changes that have occurred within the UK economy moving away from manufacturing towards a service-based economy.

Government economic policy has widened the gap between the poor and the rich. For example, Thatcher reducing the top band of income tax to 40 per cent is one example of a policy that has increased the polarisation between the rich and the poor in the UK today. Other polices that have had an impact on the poor include removing the link between pensions and average wages.

Changing attitudes to poverty: Field believes that the British public, after years of 'Thatcherism', have become too used to a 'blame' culture and see poverty as the fault of those who suffer it.

Field argues that it is now up to the government to reverse this. He advocates the following ideas:

Government policies that reduce poverty: Field believes that central government should take the initiative in relocating public sector jobs away from South East England, thereby encouraging the private sector to do the same. To further help the unemployed Field calls for effective training programmes that equip workers for the modern economy: 'training for a purpose'.

Subsidised childcare: Field believes the government should be involved in providing cheap childcare to allow the poor to go out to work. This in turn would help stop them getting stuck in the 'poverty trap', where childcare costs more than wages gained by employment.

Indefinite benefit payments for jobseekers: More controversially Field calls for benefits such as jobseeker's allowance to be paid indefinitely for those actively seeking work. In this Field is accepting that unemployment is not the fault of those who do not have jobs. Field was also a strong supporter for the introduction of the minimum wage which was introduced on 1 April 1999.

A further policy introduced by the latest Labour government was the development of the Social Exclusion Unit (SEU) in December 1997, with social **exclusion** and poverty becoming central to the social policies of the government. The Unit has since tackled a number of issues such as truancy and school exclusions; the developments of indicators of poverty. It has also created strategies to combat teenage pregnancy and sleeping rough, whilst making concerted efforts to reduce poverty in general. More recently, a new Social Exclusion Taskforce (2006) has been established with a brief to improve the early identification of the most at-risk households, raising the outcomes and aspirations of children in care, accelerating current progress in reducing the rate of teenage pregnancies and ensuring that people with mental health problems receive appropriate services.

Marxist perspectives on poverty

Marxists offer the most radical of all the perspectives on poverty, seeing poverty as a direct consequence of capitalism. They argue that whilst we have the bourgeoisie who own the factors of production and who continue to pay the proletariat low wages – and failing to share the wealth in the spirit of its production – poverty will always been an inherent part of the system. According to Marxists, poverty is a consequence of the following:

- Writers such as **Westergaard and Resler** (1976) believe that for capitalism to flourish it needs to have a continual source of labour – at the lowest possible wage. Once in employment workers realise that failure to produce or respond appropriately to their bosses offers the threat of poverty due to their position as 'wage slaves'.

- Capitalism is inherently unstable – national economies tend to go through cycles of boom and bust rather than stable growth. One upshot of this is that unemployment or the demand for labour varies dramatically. As the proletariat make up the majority of workers in unskilled and semi-skilled jobs, it is this group that suffers most because of these fluctuations; further exacerbating economic differences between the rich and the poor.

- **Ralph Milliband** (1969) is a key political thinker of the twentieth century. His work influenced a generation of left-wing thinkers in that he sought to define socialism and apply it to Great Britain. He believes that it is the proletariat's inability to use wealth and pressure groups to stand for their interests that creates a vicious circle of persistent and ongoing poverty for this group.

Marxists dislike the term 'poverty', instead preferring to use the term 'inequality'. They believe that society's obsession with small groups who are in poverty tends to distract from the macro- (wide) scale differences that occur right the way through the economic system. Marxists tend to see the welfare state as a useful way of suppressing opposition. It is useful to them as it provides the illusion that capitalists and the government cares for workers. Neo-Marxists call this idea 'relative autonomy' in that the state does play a limited independent role in the maintenance and stabilization of capitalist society. They believe cultural explanations offer a neat way to blame the poor for their situation, rather than locating the real reasons for inequality; namely, capitalism.

For Marxists the solution to poverty is monumentally simple: get rid of capitalism. Marxists believe that ultimately the proletariat will become so sick of their exploitation that eventually they will rise together as one group (this is known as gaining class consciousness) and create a new order (epoch) in which there are no social classes. Through industrial production, wealth would be so abundant that it could be shared equally. Moreover, production would not be subject to the vagaries of market conditions to insist on the manufacturing of things like wasteful packaging and plastic toys given out with fast food meals. Instead, manufacturing in the new epoch will be based upon human need.

What do you know now?

1. Explain the term 'the culture of poverty'.
2. Explain the social characteristics of the underclass according to Charles Murray.
3. Describe what 'social exclusion' means.
4. How does Frank Field believe that the poor have been disadvantaged?

Key terms

Culture of poverty:	First introduced by Oscar Lewis, this term refers to the set of attitudes and behaviour which is supposedly characteristic of the poor. These attitudes are passed on from generation to generation, leading to a vicious cycle of poverty that is very difficult to escape.
Exclusion:	The act of excluding people from the same rewards as the rest of society.
Hidden economy:	The part of the economy such as 'cash in hand' and 'casual work' which does not reach the attention of government agencies such as the Inland Revenue.
Underclass:	A term originally coined by Ken Auletta which refers to the group at the lowest part of the social class system. A group that New Right writers such as Charles Murray believe have developed a way of life which is reliant upon state benefits, criminality and unemployment.
Voluntarily unemployed:	Unemployment which is a deliberate choice of the person concerned.

Section summary

There are two arguments that seek to explain poverty. The first, cultural-based explanations, seek to argue that poverty is partly the fault of the poor.

The second, structural explanations, seek to explain poverty in the context of where it occurs.

New Right thinkers see poverty as being the fault of those who refuse to improve their circumstances and instead rely upon state benefits.

British writers such as Frank Field, who operate to the 'left' of British politics, argue that poverty is the result of the powerful restricting of the poor. This approach takes a realistic approach to poverty, noting that some groups are much more likely to be represented within the poor.

Marxists offer the most radical of all the perspectives on poverty, seeing poverty as a direct consequence of capitalism. They argue that whilst we have the bourgeoisie that own the factors of production and who continue to pay the workers (proletariat) low wages – failing to share the wealth in the spirit of its production – poverty will always be an inherent part of the system.

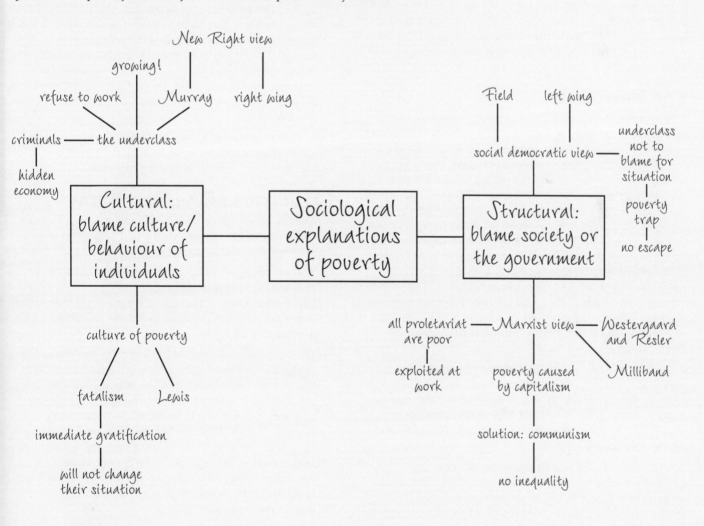

Solutions to poverty and the role of social policy

Learning objectives

By the end of this section you should be able to:

- Understand how the third way writers, Marxists, feminists, ethnic thinkers and disability thinkers believe social policy should tackle poverty
- Understand how the welfare state discriminates against some groups
- Comprehend which groups are most likely to suffer from income poverty

Introduction

It can be deduced from the earlier sections in this topic that poverty is a concept where there is little agreement with many competing approaches to the same problem. In this section we will examine the competing ideologies and their response to poverty and the welfare state.

The New Right

The New Right is usually associated with economic liberalism. By this we mean that for the New Right the most important people are not the poor but those who create wealth in the economy. Wealth creators, or **entrepreneurs**, play a central role by investing, innovating and taking economic risks. Without entrepreneurs jobs would not be created and, much more importantly, wealth would not be created for all of us. Given the importance of this group, the New Right believes that they should be rewarded for their creative entrepreneurial flair. The most appropriate way to achieve this is to allow businesspeople to be able to make money in any way they see fit, as long it occurs within free competition. So the state, although not a central theme within New Right thinking, needs to play the role of arbiter or referee, making sure that competition and business fairness, rather than criminality, should always flourish.

It therefore follows, so the New Right argue, that given the high degree of competition and the risks involved in such a system, that entrepreneurs should be rewarded. To encourage entrepreneurship the New Right believe that the state should take as little taxes from them as possible, as taxation discourages wealth creation.

Taxation can be kept to a minimum by ensuring that government expenditure is kept in check. Given that **social security** is the largest item of government expenditure, it is argued that if it can be avoided resources could be channelled towards keeping direct taxation as low as possible.

The New Right therefore see the solutions to poverty as follows:

- **The encouragement of free markets with only minimal state intervention:** Thatcher called this 'rolling back the state'; allowing easy set-up of small-business enterprises, and allowing these businesses to operate free of government regulation, especially in contrast to small companies in countries such as Germany who were hindered by the minimum wage.

- **Anti-welfarism:** For the New Right the welfare state is directly responsible for poverty. They believe it hinders initiative and makes it easy for people to choose to live on **welfare benefits**. Because of over-generous benefits, free health care and education the individual is stripped of the need to work, thus becoming a burden on the state, the result being that taxes have to rise and manufacturing income is lost. They argue that the solution is to stop universal provision of state benefits (that is, benefits given to all, such as child benefit), and instead to give benefits to the deserving poor who, for no fault of their own, and despite robust efforts to find a job, still find themselves unemployed.

Some degree of inequality for the New Right is considered essential. High wages act as an incentive for highly competitive jobs, thereby increasing inequality.

Criticisms of the New Right

- The theory seems very keen to blame the poor for their condition, rather than accepting that capitalism is an ideology prone to structural and international fluctuations.

- Will reducing welfare payments really be good for the majority of claimants? Some from the New Right believe that such a policy encourages the poor to get themselves out of poverty; however, others believe reducing welfare payments is uncaring.

- The New Right also ignore the social implications of their measures. Increased inequality breeds resentment and crime, and splits society into one where a few possess many riches and the rest don't. The group that do not have much may come to the conclusion that participating in such a society has little benefit for them. For example, in both the UK and America voter turn-out is particularly low amongst ethnic groups. In 2004 only 44 per cent of Asian and Pacific Islanders cast a vote in the presidential election, whilst in the UK, Black and Ethic minority (BME) was 48 per cent in the 2005 general election.

The social democratic approach to poverty

This is the model that dominated Britain from the post-war era up until Thatcher's election in 1979. Social democrats accept that there will always be some groups that hold a weak economic position when it comes to the labour market. Consequently, those who have few skills, or who are ill, disabled, retired, female or come from ethnic minorities are more likely to suffer from unemployment. Social democrats believe because these groups are often disadvantaged, both by lack of skills and by regional unemployment, this leaves them unable to move to areas such as the South East because of the high cost of housing, as well as worries about leaving friends and family. This problem is called 'geographical immobility'. Given these inherent problems social democrats argue that it is senseless to penalise the poor but rather they should be helped by means of welfare provision. It is argued that welfare provision allows basic standards of living to be maintained, whilst also ensuring that the group does not feel socially excluded, and therefore more likely to turn to crime and societal non-participation.

After the Second World War, this one-fits-all approach to welfare was in itself a completely new departure as before the war an integrated welfare system just did not exist. The social democratic model challenged this, allowing all to benefit regardless of how 'deserving' they were. And although this worked for many years because of increasing affluence, low unemployment and inflation, it did result in high income tax. Subsequently, by the early 1980s, Britain could no longer afford to take this approach, despite it being effective and humanitarian.

Criticisms of the social democratic approach

- The social democratic approach failed to respond to changes in economic and social conditions: it assumed that all claimants wanted to work. By the late twentieth century this clearly was not the case, with some taking the view that it was better to claim benefits than hold down a long-term job.

- As standards of living improved in the late twentieth century everyone's expectations moved with it, leading to the welfare system becoming linked to relative deprivation. Almost by definition welfare benefits became expensive and difficult to justify given the high levels of unemployment.

- It is argued, particularly by the New Right, that this welfare-based approach provides a disincentive to the workforce. This was true of certain groups such as the young and single mothers, who were caught in the **poverty trap**; a situation where an individual actually reduces their net income by taking a job.

The third way

The 'third way', as its name suggests, rejects the New Right ideas of individualism, and also sees the traditional social democrat approach as flawed and ineffectual. The third way has been championed by the Labour government, with their advisor, Anthony Giddens' (often referred to as Blair's guru), writings heavily influencing the Blair government. Giddens saw the old approaches as missing the point. For these thinkers a number of points are important. These include:

- A full set of policies needs to be introduced rather than just relying on the welfare state. This should be done by using government policies that are inclusive and enable all citizens to escape poverty. The Labour government believed that to effectively achieve this, specialised agencies should coordinate this task. Most recently this job has been undertaken by a new organisation: The Social Exclusion Task Force (2007). The role of this agency is, according to its mission statement, 'to coordinate the government's drive against social exclusion, ensuring that the cross-departmental approach delivers for those most in need. The task force will champion the needs of the most disadvantaged members of society within government, ensuring that as with the rest of the public service reform agenda, we put people first.' From this statement we get some idea of what the government has planned, with key words such as 'cross-departmental' giving an indication of the holistic approach it seeks to take, linking health, crime and family issues together to solve and improve poverty.

- Policies are needed to encourage workers to retrain so that workers' skills keep up with economic structural changes that occur. Giddens sees it as unlikely that workers will have just the one job during their working lifetime. As the economy changes Giddens believes that the state should encourage people to leave poverty rather than becoming dependent upon the benefit system through retraining and taxation policies. In addition regional policy has been used to encourage economic growth outside of the South East where wealth is highest.

- Giddens believes that encouraging a strong economy allows the state to secure greater social justice as all benefit. With greater wealth, greater provision can be made to improve public services and improve the lives of those on low incomes.

- Another important part of the third way revolves around the need to create a contract between individuals and the state. Government should provide resources to help people shape their own lives; but should in turn expect people to deliver their part of the bargain. For instance, in the past unemployment benefits have been an unconditional right, but this situation discourages personal responsibility and has the effect of locking workers out of jobs. Those who lose their jobs should have a responsibility actively to look for work, and should be given retraining opportunities should they need them.

Criticisms of the third way

- Some believe that the third way offers help to those in need only on the basis that they must in some way do something for the state. So whilst in the past benefits were universally given, the third way approach tends to involve limiting benefits for those who do not follow suggested government rules. For some this quid pro quo offers no respite from poverty for the most disadvantaged in society.

- The Old Left sees the third way as a betrayal of their old socialist ideals. They argue that the best way to redistribute income from the wealthy to the poor is by direct taxes such as income tax. And yet Gordon Brown has championed low marginal income tax rates. The neo-Marxist Stuart Hall (2003) offered a swipe at 'New Labour's lack of political will to reintroduce progressive taxation as the main way of redistributing wealth from the rich to the poor.' He saw this as a betrayal of the socialist ethos of the Labour Party.

- Others such as **Cammack** and **Morrison** (2004) believe that it makes a lot of use of rhetoric to disguise a lack of substance, or at least that its substance is other than that which it claims.

The Marxist view

Marxists believe that the huge inequality of wealth is the main reason for poverty in the UK. This inequality has in fact increased as we have moved towards the twenty-first century, regardless of which method is used to 'measure' poverty. Capitalism thrives on this inequality. Whilst the owners of the factors of production are able to secure huge wealth and the trappings of luxury, the workers who create this wealth have to exist on relatively meagre wages in comparison. So whilst low wages are paid to the 'wage slaves', high levels of surplus value (the difference between the wage paid to the 'wage slaves' and the profit gained for the capitalist) is created for those who own the factors of production. Ultimately, although this wealth is created in a cooperative environment by the workers, it is the bourgeoisie who keep the wealth for themselves.

For Marxists the welfare state is no solution to poverty. Instead, they believe that the welfare system merely helps to repel opposition to the unfairness of capitalism. So whilst it offers some degree of protection from unemployment with state benefits being offered, it does little to alter poverty for those on low incomes. Marxists argue it merely encourages them to think that the state does protect them, when the reality is that only fundamental changes to the system will alter the huge inequalities inherent in capitalism. The meagre amounts offered are given only on the basis that the state is able to peer into the lives of those claiming benefits. Marxists believe that the only solution to poverty is for there to be a fundamental upheaval in the political and economic system, best achieved by a revolution where private wealth is abolished and in its place common ownership

takes place. Society will then be based around social and economic equality. Thus the Marxist view on social policy offers a dramatic but simple solution to poverty: replace the old system with one based on complete equality, rather than patch up the present system with a welfare state that merely encourages acceptance of inequality rather than doing anything to solve it.

Criticisms of the Marxist view

- Critics believe that Marxism is too economically deterministic. Other factors apart from social class, such as race and gender, are also fundamental to causes of poverty and inequality.

- Although Marxists offer a simple solution, critics point out that when communism was introduced in states around the world after the Second World War, it was singularly unsuccessful. For example, the USSR, although subscribing to the ideas of communism, offered its citizens the prospect of poor living standards and continuing levels of inequality. Leonid Brezhnev (President of the USSR between 1977–82) was, for instance, said to have a fleet of 40 expensive western cars and lived in considerable luxury.

- Even if wealth were to be shared equally, critics believe the power of the bourgeoisie would simply result in accumulated wealth being moved away elsewhere.

Feminism

On a UK-level women are disadvantaged in a number of ways. *Uncovering Women's Inequality in the UK* (The Women's Resource Centre, 2007) splits up the inequality found into a number of sections. I will briefly cover each of these areas in turn:

- **Economic and social factors:** Figures from the Women and Equality Unit (2007) show that the gender pay gap, which shows the difference between men's and women's median full-time hourly earnings, presently stands at 12.6 per cent. This means that women working full time are currently paid, on average, 87.4 per cent of men's hourly pay. Since 1975, when the Equal Pay Act came into effect, the full-time pay gap has closed considerably, from 29.5 per cent to 20.2 per cent in 1996 and from 20.7 per cent in 1997 to 17.2 per cent in 2006, using the mean (there is discontinuity between 1996 and 1997 due to a difference in the methodology of data collection). Using the median, the full-time gender pay gap has closed from 17.4 per cent in 1997 to 12.6 per cent in 2006. Having said this, women still, in general, occupy lower-paid, lower-status jobs within the economy and are particularly over-represented in the secondary and tertiary sectors which offer lower wages and less job security than areas that men tend to be employed in.

The Equal Opportunities Commission's (EOC) report on gender equality (2007) notes that many workplaces,

institutions and services are still designed for an age when women stayed at home, creating a barrier to equality. The EOC believe the following is needed:

- Further increases in the minimum wage. The EOC comments that the UK is working with other countries 'towards a closing of the gender Pay Gap' (2003).

- The use of government strategic government agencies to set achievable targets for increasing female incomes.

- Improving support to families, particularly with the government offering subsidised child care and an improved level of childcare tax credits.

Family life

Men and women experience family life differently. With divorce being seen as far more acceptable these days, women are more likely to become single parents. *Breadline Britain* (2001) found that poverty rates were highest amongst single-parent families, with 54 per cent of single parents with two children reporting 'absolute poverty'. Women are also affected by their longevity. The Fawcett Society (2003) established that only 30 per cent of women say they are confident they have a good pension and are saving enough, compared to 46 per cent of men. Women's irregular work patterns, often lower pay and caring responsibilities put them at more risk of ending up in poverty in old age. Worryingly, the study revealed that married female pensioners receive just a third of the income of their

partner, whilst according to government figures, only 49 per cent of women qualify for the full state pension, compared with 92 per cent of men.

The Equal Opportunities Commission (2003) believes that the government needs to address the issue of pensions by being aware of the differing working patterns exhibited between the genders, with a general belief that women need to be included within employer pension schemes and be allowed to work flexibly within such a system.

The welfare system

At present the system is a complex mix of entitlements that generally result in women being penalised. Over the last 20 years benefits have become **means tested**, and although some universal benefits still remain, such as child benefit, the majority of government welfare is based upon income. Therefore the higher a person's income or the greater their savings, the less they will receive in government handouts. Because women often take time out to have children this leads to less women qualifying for insurance-type benefits such as jobseeker's allowance because they have not worked long enough to qualify for it. The Women's Resource Centre (2007) found that 17 per cent of working women in the UK do not earn enough to pay National Insurance compared to four per cent of men. This means that they are not entitled to certain benefits, such as the contribution-based jobseeker's allowance, incapacity benefit and state pensions. Furthermore, women are also failing to adequately provide for their retirement as broken careers, along with childcare responsibilities, lead to women being less likely to be able to contribute to the state pension. In 2006, 64 per cent of people living on state pensions were women, who are more likely to rely on their state pension as their sole source of income (2006). Social policies that could be introduced to improve the situation of women in general include:

- Extending and increasing state pension payments and, more importantly, linking increases in these to average earnings, rather than price increases. Average earnings will always be above the rate of inflation and this will ensure improved standards of living.

- An overhaul of the existing benefit system that takes into account the working patterns of women.

- Better childcare provision with subsidies being offered from central government.

Ethnicity and poverty

An additional social group that are marginalised and who suffer from deprivation and poverty are those from ethnic origins. Lucinda Platt in *Poverty and Ethnicity in the UK* (2007) notes the 'stark differences' in poverty rates by ethnic group. Platt argues that the high levels of unemployment are an indication that the welfare system is not combating poverty in ethnic minority groups. Due to the large number of people from ethnic minority groups employed in industries such as hotels and catering, distribution and transport and communications, incomes and job security in this group tend to be very low, further increasing the likelihood of poverty (Commission for Racial Equality factfile 2, 2004). **Berthoud** (1998) believes that there are three main issues for policy-makers to tackle in regards to ethnicity and poverty:

1. The extent of poverty amongst Bangladeshi and Pakistani groups needs to be tackled.

2. Berthoud's analysis reinforced the importance of means-tested benefits to minority groups, especially Pakistanis and Bangladeshis. Means-tested benefits accounted for a third of these groups' total income level. Whilst Berthoud acknowledges that means-tested benefits maintain a minimum level of income, they also create a dependence of welfare. This dependence may encourage long-term unemployment, whilst limited increases in benefits, due to them being based on inflation rather than income levels, lead to standards of living being lower for these two groups compared to other ethnic groups.

3. Lastly, Berthoud suggests that policymakers need to assess the needs of ethnic minorities independently to the rest of the population. Given this group's particular issues, Berthoud believes it unfair to apply cultural fixes that relate to the British population rather than the group that needs targeting.

Disability, welfare and poverty

The disabled are another group who suffer disproportionately from poverty. *Monitoring Poverty and Social Exclusion* (Kenway et al., 2005) comments that despite the UK having high employment rates that 800 000 disabled people aged 25 to retirement age are 'economically inactive but want work'; a much higher statistic than the 200 000 'unemployed' disabled people. In other words, the numbers of disabled adults who lack, but want, work is five times the number included in the official unemployment figures. They found that this leads to 30 per cent of disabled people living in poverty, a figure that has actually risen from 27 per cent a decade ago. This group have not been afforded similar policy initiatives to those the government have recently focused towards children and pensioners.

Interestingly, **Mark Deal** found from anonymous questionnaires in *Attitudes of disabled people toward other disabled people and impairment groups* (2007) that disabled groups use a hierarchy of disability to rank those with disabilities. Given this, it is hardly surprising that those without a disability can view the disabled as potentially being a liability. This perception hinders employment opportunities and access, particularly to the highest paid jobs in the UK economy. **Colin Barnes** (1999) believes that it could be argued that the barriers faced in accessing employment are a reflection of society's attitude towards disabled people as equal citizens.

In terms of social policy the government has set up the Disability Rights Commission headed by Trevor Philips; an independent body established in April 2000 by the Act of Parliament to stop discrimination and promote equality of opportunity for disabled people. The Commission has set its goal to 'create a society where all disabled people can participate fully as equal citizens'. However, given the problems of equality this may prove illusive. Additionally, many sociological commentators believe that the provisions of the Disability Discrimination Act, which cites: "to make it unlawful to discriminate against disabled persons in connection with employment, the provision of goods, facilities and services or the disposal or management of premises", offers too many exclusions. For instance, it only applies to organisations that employ more than 20 people. Moreover, it is a weak piece of legislation in comparison to parallel laws being introduced in the USA (**Goss** et al, 2000).

What do you know now?

1. Explain how the New Right see welfare benefits.
2. Explain how they believe poverty should be conquered.
3. Which welfare approach dominated in the 1960s up until the advent of Thatcher in the 1980s?
4. Explain the role of the welfare state as Marxists perceive it.
5. Explain one way the welfare state discriminates against women.
6. Why are ethnic groups more likely to suffer from income poverty?
7. Which organisation protects the rights of the disabled in the UK?

Key terms

Entrepreneur: One who recognises business opportunities and organises economic resources to take advantage of the opportunity presented.

Jobseeker's allowance: Unemployment benefit that is paid by the government to people who are unemployed and seeking work. It is part of the social security benefits system and is meant to cover the cost of living expenses in periods where the claimant is out of work.

Means tested: A system of assessment that offers benefits only when 'need' is confirmed. Such need is subject to social security definitions.

Poverty trap: A situation in which an individual in reality reduces their net income by taking a job.

Social security: A system of welfare support provided by the government. Relies upon citizens contributing by means of taxation through which unemployment benefits, pensions and sickness benefit are paid for. Additionally includes a non-contributory element, which provides for a basic safety net for those in dire need.

Welfare benefits: A system of financial aid and services provided by central or local government.

Section summary

- The New Right is usually associated with economic liberalism. By this we mean that for this group the most important people are not the poor but those who create wealth in the economy.

- Given the inherent problems of cyclical capitalism, social democrats argue that it is senseless to penalise the poor but they should be helped through welfare provision.

- The third way writers, which include the influential 'Blair Guru', Antony Giddens, see the need for a full set of policies to be introduced, rather than just relying upon the welfare state.

- Marxists believe that the only solution to poverty is for there to be a fundamental upheaval in the political and economic system, best achieved by a revolution.

- Liberal feminists are optimistic of improvement by legislation citing the improvements brought about by The Equal Pay Act and The Sex Discrimination Act. Marxist feminists assert that improvements to female emancipation will only occur with the defeat of capitalism. Finally, radical feminists believe that men remain the main source of oppression for women, ultimately suggesting that our patriarchal society should be replaced by a matriarchy.

- Ethnic writers see social policy as doing little to tackle poverty amongst ethnic groups.

- Disability thinkers believe that social policy has not gone far enough to counteract the deprivations suffered by this group. They point to the strength of legislation introduced in other major countries such as the USA, and contrast this with the weak and ineffectual laws coming onto the statute book in the UK.

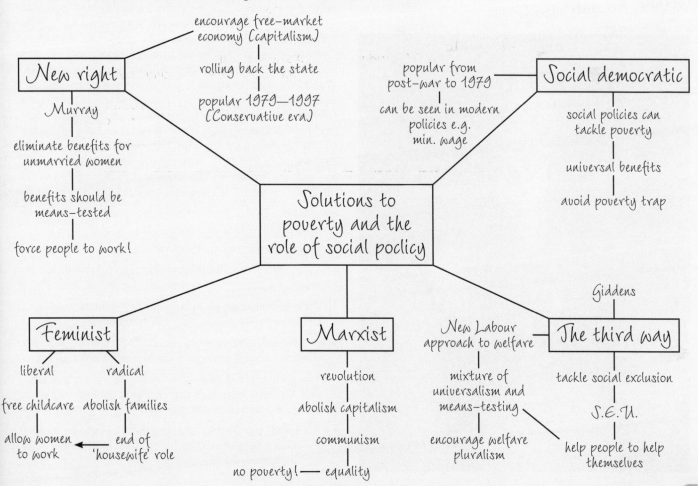

Section 4: Solutions to poverty and the role of social policy 93

Welfare pluralism

What was the situation before we had the welfare state?

Many assume that the welfare state is a recent phenomenon; however, the reality is rather different. Poverty has long been a problem and the state has at various times felt the need to intervene to combat it, even as far back as 1601 with the introduction of the Elizabethan Poor Law Act which offered a basic amount of money to paupers. By 1834 The Poor Law Amendment Act (1834) was introduced by Earl Grey, establishing the workhouse system, where each parish had to set up a workhouse.

Initially, inmates were free to enter and leave as they liked and received free food and accommodation. However, the concern was that too liberal a regime would lead to many people who could take it easy in the workhouse, leading not only to an excessive dent on charitable funds but also a dilution of the work ethic. To counter this, the principle of less eligibility was

Earl Grey

developed. Workhouse life was deliberately made as harsh and degrading as possible so that only the truly poor would apply. In the workhouse, men, women and children all lived separately from each other; in many ways it was similar to a prison.

Towards the end of the century, attitudes towards the ways in which the poorest people in society were treated at last started to change, and conditions slowly improved. However, workhouses remained open until 1928 and were only phased out after the Liberal government reforms of 1908 and 1912 that introduced sickness benefits and a rudimentary old-age pension.

Health care in the 1920s and 1930s, especially for the poor, was provided by charity or by taking out 'insurance' with local doctors to allow access to medical care. Nevertheless, poor housing and continued pollution still meant that many suffered miserable housing conditions and poor health. Some government intervention was acted upon, with the Liberals introducing labour exchanges in 1905 (the equivalent to today's job centres), and in 1906 introducing policies that form much of what we consider to be the welfare state today. Some of the policies introduced included school meals, school medicals for children and an old-age pension for those lucky enough to survive until they were 70 years old.

By the late 1920s economic **recession** and increasing unemployment meant for the first time that many more people needed assistance. As a consequence of this, and in response to a general awareness that poverty was not the fault of those suffering it, the *Beveridge Report* was published in 1942. Commissioned in 1941 by the then coalition government, it set out the ways that Britain should be rebuilt after the Second World War. The *Beveridge Report* was designed to counter illness, ignorance, disease, squalor and want. It considered the whole question of social insurance, arguing that want could be abolished by a system of social security organised for the individual by the state. Beveridge recommended the establishment of a NHS, national insurance and assistance, and family allowances, and stressed the importance of full-time employment. This scheme was named the 'welfare state'.

Specifically, Beveridge believed:

- Free health care would help banish disease. All health care should be paid for by the state.

- Compulsory contributions would help pay for the system, thereby allowing it to be free at the point of use.

- Free schooling for all in state-funded schools, colleges and university would ensure an end to ignorance.

- A national programme of council-built housing would produce 'homes for heroes' for the returning soldiers.

- The system could be paid for in two ways: income tax and National Insurance contributions paid for in part by employers and in part by employees.

- A bureaucratic system of department agencies offered the most effective method for implementation and administration for the welfare state.

Theoretical explanations for the implementation of the welfare state

Pluralism

This explanation emphasises that there was consensus amongst all the parties about how to deal with poverty in the UK. This consensus is sometimes known as *Butskellism*. The harmony revolved around the idea that it was only fair to provide a safety net for those in need. Agreement, however, did not alter the state's position that inequality was, and is, an essential part of British society. **Pluralism** stresses the ongoing bargaining between agencies, whilst accepting that some groups have more power than others. The pluralist approach suggests that the modern democratic state's actions are the result of pressures applied by a variety of organized interests. The sociologist, **Robert Dahl,** called this kind of state a **polyarchy**. Dahl carried out a study of New Haven in America. This was important as it confirmed the pluralist assumption that many interest groups compete in the political sphere, and the government's role is to act as the mediator between these groups.

Marxism

For Marxists, the welfare state and its provision is seen as a way to manipulate the working classes. They believe that although the welfare state did offer a range of benefits which helped the working classes escape the extremes of poverty, it was only offered to appease the working classes into thinking that such consideration would indicate that the working classes had a stake in capitalism. By offering 'titbits' to the working classes, Marxists believe that they are less likely to be revolutionary and will merely accept the inherent unfairness apparent within capitalism. Writers such as **O'Connor** (1984) believe in the inherent contradictions of capitalism: that the welfare state is created by the capitalist state, yet it is this very system that leads to exploitation and the need for welfare in the first place.

The welfare regimes across the world

Different countries have taken various approaches to dealing with the issues of poverty and welfare benefits. These, according to **Esping Anderson** (1990), can be summarised into three main typologies:

Liberal welfare states

These countries offer the minimum of amount of welfare support. Those who are in poverty, are sick or are disabled have to rely upon their families, charities and religious organisations for support. Those who are lucky enough to be employed by contrast are expected to pay into insurance policies to ensure that they receive benefits when or if they become unemployed, sick or retire. For those not able to afford insurance policies the state offers minimum standards of support that is assessed by a means-tested system. Only those who can demonstrate real financial need, such as those without savings and property, are approved to receive state help. Countries which use the liberal welfare typology include the United States, the UK and Spain.

Corporatist welfare states

Provision in these countries is excellent, with good-quality education and health care being offered by the state. Funding is obtained from a wide range of sources, ranging from government expenditure and employee contribution schemes. Additionally, other NGOs (Non-Government Organisations, which are either national or regional organisations whose members are not employed by the government) are also expected to play a role in assisting those in poverty. So, organisations such as trade unions, religious organisations and employee organisations, such as the CBI, are also expected to help out. The corporatist welfare state system often has the word 'conservative' placed in front of it. This is because corporatist welfare states tend to be conservative with a small 'c', supporting those only who exist in traditional groupings whilst providing less assistance for those who do not conform to the status quo. For example, gay and lesbian couples tend to be treated differently from heterosexual couples when it comes to welfare provision. As with the liberal welfare state, any support is means tested to make certain that only the neediest in society receive any assistance. This system is popular in mainland Europe with France, Germany and Belgium all being adherents to the corporatist welfare state model.

The social democratic welfare states

This is the most generous of the systems on offer, emphasising the need for all to receive good services, regardless of their class or ethnicity. To pay for such high-quality provision, high income tax has usually gone hand in hand with the social democratic welfare system. However, the high levels of revenue that the high income tax affords means that education, health and social security are all of a high overall standard and are free at point of use. As a result of the good quality of provision there is little need for private provision to be made, so things like private education and private health care are not used extensively as there is little need for them. However, such a system relies upon high levels of employment More recently though, erratic economic performance along with ideological changes have resulted in voters being less willing to sanction the high cost of this system. Nevertheless, it is used by many of the Scandinavian states, especially Sweden.

Welfare debates

As we have seen, welfare systems vary across the world and these differences indicate how differing approaches are taken about:

- Who the beneficiaries of benefits should be
- Which organisations should provide this assistance, whether it is the state or a mix of private and **voluntary organisations**

So who should receive benefits?

Central to this debate is how benefits should be provided. In one camp are the supporters of **universalism** who believe that benefits should be made available to all, regardless of their income. They suggest high-quality health care, education and pensions should be the preserve of all citizens. It is argued that the benefit of such a system is that it bonds society together, increasing social solidarity and reducing crime and marginalisation.

However, those who support **selectivism** believe that benefits should be targeted primarily by means-testing, to those who most need them most. Additionally, they remain sceptical about universalism. Does the prospect of the state intervening when people are in trouble reduce motivation and drive?

Practical considerations

The advantage of universalism is that everyone in society has the opportunity to receive the same benefits regardless of their background. Whilst many in society never need to use the welfare system, it is still a comfort to all that it is there to protect them if the worst happens. Additionally, because it is there for all, people feel less inhibited about applying for benefits when they need to. However, those in favour of selectivism point out that universal benefits fail to target those most in need. A good example of this is child benefit, which is a cheap benefit as it is universal, however, it might be thought to be more appropriate to target this money to those who really need it, rather than blindly giving it to those on low incomes and high incomes alike.

Contemporary changes in organisations that provide welfare

The UK has, over recent years, moved from a welfare state to a more market-oriented system of welfare. This has meant that whilst in the past the state had a monopoly of the supply of welfare services such as health, nowadays there is a plurality of organisations that provide welfare. For example:

- Private organisations that need to be profit-making
- Charitable organisations
- **Informal care** provided by family and friends

In Victorian times health care was provided by a mixture of philanthropic benefactors who donated money over a period of time, and by profit-making organisations. Whilst these organisations became less prevalent as the welfare state was introduced from the 1930s onwards, there are signs that such bodies are making a comeback. Much of this stems from the influence of the Conservative government (1979–97) which introduced marketisation within the welfare state, encouraging public services to be 'opted out' of local authority control, thereby making it more efficient and more responsive to the requirements of its customers.

This ideology has continued to be accepted as an essential component of the third way ideology embraced by the latest Labour government. General acceptance of these arguments has resulted in:

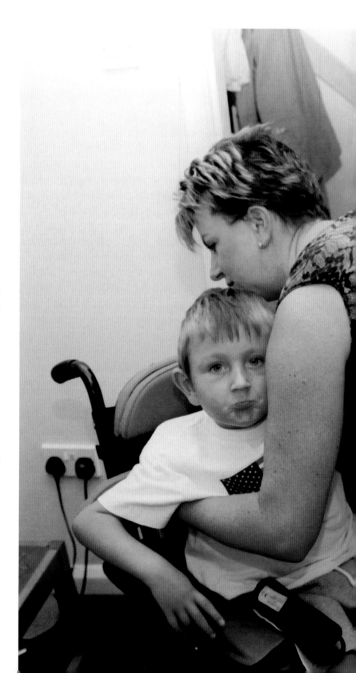

- The voluntary sector being handed some areas of welfare and care provision. This has particularly been the case in the provision of care to the elderly in care homes.

- The Private Financing Initiative (PFI) allowing hospitals to be built by private companies, with NHS trusts repaying them over a period of around 25 or 30 years.

- The further expansion of use of the private sector to carry out non-urgent operations. This has led to private operations being paid for by the public sector, rising from five per cent in 2005 to nearer ten per cent in 2008.

All health trusts are required to prepare an annual budget and ensure that customer standards are monitored and acted upon in accordance with the NHS (complaints) regulations 2004.

Disadvantages of using a private and public sector of welfare

As with all systems some inherent problems have been identified by critics. These include:

- The system encourages the development of 'dualism', allowing the wealthy to have immediate access to the best services at short notice, often to the detriment of NHS patients, as it uses the same doctors and often even the same hospitals.

- Voluntary organisations often cannot afford the best staff and therefore may offer standards that are lower than is acceptable.

- Some believe the system encourages care to be undertaken by families and friends. Almost invariably this burden falls upon women and female children within households.

Which groups have benefited from the welfare state?

If we are to believe the New Right, the welfare state benefits those who do not work for a living, whilst penalising the middle and upper classes who pay the taxes that provide the welfare state. To best answer this question it is important to look at a range of welfare services and assess the beneficiaries.

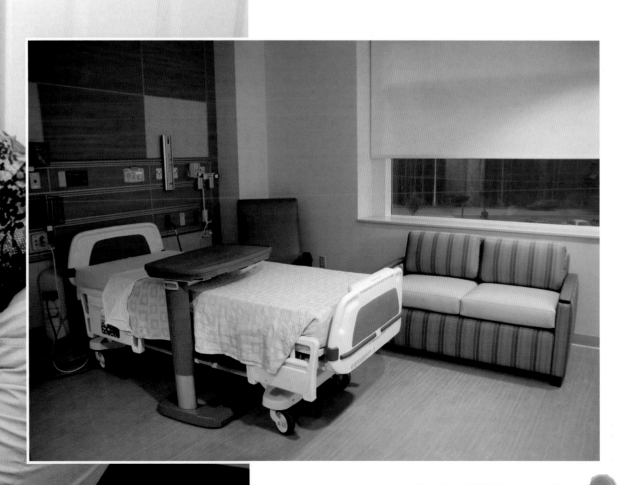

The National Health Service

Anna Dixon and Julian Le Grand in *Is the NHS Equitable* (2003) believe we live in a 'Tax Welfare State', noting that:

- The middle classes benefit from the system

- Deprived individuals and families use the health service less than their levels of need would indicate they should

- There are inequalities in gaining access to a range of NHS services. This is particularly true of surgery such as hip replacements, with a study in Yorkshire finding that lower socio-economic classes have a 30 per cent higher need for this type of intervention.

- Health care is more difficult to access for lower socio-economic classes. By contrast, the middle classes remain unintimiated by the system and know how to access care effectively and quickly.

- The use of private transport was another source of inequality, with the middle classes being able to use car travel to access better medical services.

- Nevertheless, Le Grand and John Hills (Director of the Centre for Analysis of Social Exclusion [CASE], which has analysed the policy decisions made by the Labour government with particular reference to health inequalities) generally believe the system particularly helps those from lower social class backgrounds.

Education

Generally there is a belief that the education system favours those from the higher social classes. Over the past few years reports produced by the Higher Education Funding Council for England and Graduate Prospects paint a depressing picture, showing that:

- The percentage of higher education students who come from poor backgrounds is decreasing rather than increasing. Students who come from managerial or professional families are now six times more likely to participate in higher education than those from disadvantaged families.

- The Higher Education Policy Institute (2005) has recently concluded that, unless something dramatic is done, the government will not reach its target of 50 per cent of young people taking part in some form of higher education by 2010.

- A study conducted by the London School of Economics (LSE) found that British children from disadvantaged backgrounds have less chance of moving up the social ladder today than they did 20 years ago. One reason for this is that working-class children are much more likely to leave school at 16, with dropout rates in the UK being one of the highest in the Organisation for Economic Cooperation and Development (OECD).

Welfare payments in general

John Hills, Professor of Social Policy and Director of Economic and Social Research Council (ESRC) Research Centre for Analysis of Social Exclusion (CASE) at the London School of Economics, believes that those earning less than the median income level benefit disproportionately more than those who

re working and who receive less benefits. Data from the Office for National Statistics (ONS) showed that without the redistributive measures Mr Brown has introduced, the UK would be a more unequal society. However, the abyss that opened up under Mrs Thatcher remains almost the same as when she left office at the end of 1990.

"Inequality still remains high by historical standards – the large increase which took place in the second half of the 1980s has not been reversed," commented the ONS in its annual study (2005–6).

According to the ONS (2007), the original incomes of the richest fifth of households in the UK were 16 times greater than those in the poorest fifth: £68 700 compared with £4200. After redistribution through taxes and benefits, however, the ratio between the top and bottom of the income scale was reduced to four-to-one: £49 300 against £13 500. However, it should be noted that redistributive patterns change within a lifetime. The ONS, for example, comments that some types of households gained more than others from redistribution. Retired households paid less in tax than they received in benefits and gained overall. Among non-retired households, single-parent families were winners from the tax and benefits system but all other households paid more in tax than they received in benefits. However, families with children did better than those without children due both to direct payments such as child benefit and benefits in kind such as hospitals and schools. The amount received from benefits in kind fell gradually as incomes increased.

Attitudes to redistribution

Case Annual Report
Tom Sefton and Tania Burcharat, 2005

Sefton looked at public attitudes towards redistribution and discovered that:

- The public is still concerned about the level of inequality in Britain but explicit support for redistribution as a means to reduce inequality has declined
- Nearly three-quarters of people questioned agreed that the gap between high and low incomes is too great but, when asked directly, less than one-third said they wanted the government to redistribute incomes from one group to another
- More detailed questioning revealed that most people are in favour of tax and spending policies that would involve a substantial redistribution of incomes from rich to poor and the most popular way to achieve this was through direct tax and universal benefits
- There is general agreement about the benefit of the welfare state
- Thirty per cent took the view that people have a responsibility to help others in need, regardless of whether or not they have paid their 'dues'
- Forty-five per cent took the view that an element of redistribution is necessary but their support was more conditional because of concerns about people abusing the system
- The last group took the view that people should look after themselves rather than relying upon the state to do so

What do you know now?

1. What is universalism? Give an example.
2. Explain the term 'selectivism'. Give an example.
3. Name the three types of welfare regimes used across the world.
4. Explain how the New Right criticises the ideas of the welfare state.
5. Explain the term 'informal care'. Who is most likely to provide this care?

Key terms

Beveridge Report:	Report by Sir William Beveridge that looked at ways of helping the poor in Great Britain. Published in December 1942, it proposed that all people of working age should pay a weekly contribution. In return, benefits would be paid to people who were sick, unemployed, retired or widowed. Beveridge argued that this system would provide a minimum standard of living 'below which no one should be allowed to fall'. These measures were eventually introduced by Atlee's government (1945–50).
Informal care:	Composed of family, friend or neighbour care which is unregulated or unlicensed.
Pluralism:	Sociological view that believes that power is distributed amongst many differing groups and individuals who are in competition. The groups are then mediated by the state.
Polyarchy:	Term introduced by Robert A. Dahl to describe the form of government where each person in a community is given equal consideration.
Selectivism:	A system of welfare where those most at need are selected for assistance before other groups.
Recession:	The decline in an economy's output for two successive quarters.
Universalism:	The belief that all should be entitled to welfare payments.
Voluntary organisations:	Self-governing bodies that provide welfare services whilst remaining non-profit making.

Section summary

- Poverty is difficult to measure with rates depending upon which methodology is employed.

- Whilst income and wealth inequality decreased between 1945 and 1970, it has since started to increase again.

- The UK is one of the few countries where this trend has been apparent.

- Even with the election of 'New Labour' in 1997 this trend has continued, with Blair and Brown's governments being seemingly more concerned with business efficiency and their pro-corporation stance than reducing inequality.

- A number of groups are most likely to suffer from poverty. Women, for example, are more likely to live in a low-income household than men.

- The elderly are another group most likely to suffer from poverty.

- Functionalists believe that inequality is good for society as it provides motivation and encourages the most talented people into suitable roles and jobs.

- Marxists blame capitalism for inequalities in wealth and income. They suggest that capitalism thrives on inequality of income, as without exploitation the profits needed by capitalism would not be made.

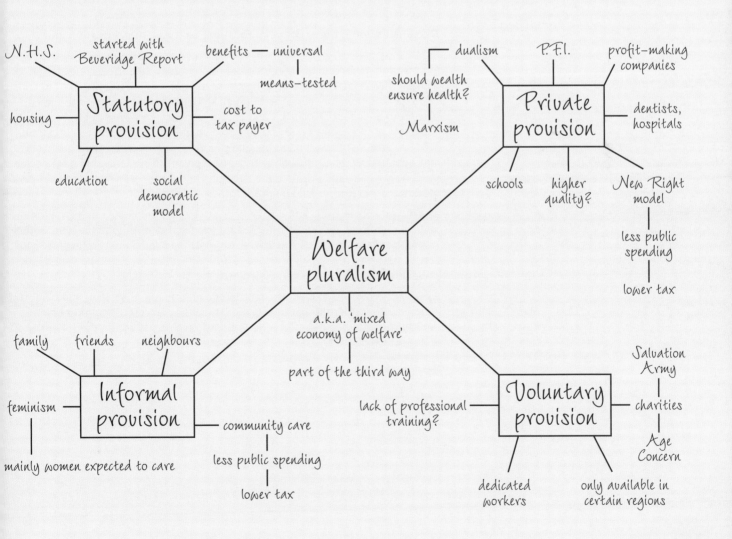

Topic summary

How to maximise your grade with AQA

Central to achieving a high grade in A level Sociology are the following two skills:

1. **Knowledge and understanding:**

   Students are expected to know definitions of poverty and how it is measured. Additionally examiners want to see a wide range of knowledge on a particular section with specific reference to the UK. It is therefore sensible for any student of A level Sociology to regularly read newspapers and keep an eye out for articles relating to poverty and wealth. Students are expected to know the names of specific writers and be able to quote these with the appropriate theory they developed. Within the new specification students must also know the range of methods used by sociologists and understand the relationship between theory and methods in relation to poverty and wealth. Finally, AS students are required to study two themes: Socialization, culture and identity; and social differentiation, power and stratification. The most relevant to poverty and wealth is social differentiation with reference to poverty and wealth.

2. **Demonstration of the skills of application, analysis, interpretation and evaluation:**

   This is probably the most difficult of all the required skills. You are expected to analyse the design of social investigations and assess the methods used to collect the data. It is therefore suggested that all students ensure that their teachers give them the chance to design and collect evidence on poverty and wealth. Secondly, AS candidates must be able to distinguish between facts and opinions, select a range of relevant concepts and theorists, and interpret both qualitative and quantitative data. Evaluation must be a given, so students will be expected to identity trends and evaluate the strengths and weakness of explanations on wealth and poverty in contemporary British society.

   As with all subjects this knowledge needs to be communicated in a structured and coherent manner whilst students are expected to use theory to achieve this. Appropriate evidence must be used to support the candidates' arguments, with conclusions based on good knowledge and understanding, and the well-honed skills of being able to apply knowledge to the question set.

   Answers need to be legible, use appropriate grammar and spelling and be coherent. It is expected that the style of students' answers are appropriate to their purpose and employ the expected vocabulary used within the sphere of A level Sociology.

Exam practice for AQA

Item A

Although there is an understanding that wealth includes possessions, assets and savings, sociologists find it very difficult to define the concept of wealth. What wealth should be included within this calculation?

Item B

Marxism offers the most radical approach to poverty. Marxists believe there will always be a conflict of interests between the two opposing groups in capitalist society: the bourgeoisie and the proletariat, with the bourgeoisie attempting to extract as much surplus value from workers as possible, leading to poverty.

a. Explain the difference between marketable and non-marketable wealth. *(4 Marks)*

b. Suggest **two** reasons why wealth is hard to measure. *(4 Marks)*

c. Explain the difference between direct and non-direct taxation. *(4 Marks)*

d. Examine the reason why some groups are more likely to be in poverty than others.

e. Using material from *items A* and *B* and elsewhere, assess Marxist arguments on how poverty is best eradicated.

Topic 3

Families and households

Learning objectives

What the AQA spec says	Section in this book	Page
The relationship of the family to the social structure and social change, with particular reference to the economy and to state policies.	Section One: The family in contemporary society	108
Changing patterns of: marriage, cohabitation, separation, divorce, childbearing and the life-course, the diversity of contemporary family and household structures.	Section Two: The extent of family diversity	116
The nature and extent of changes in the family: gender roles, domestic labour and power relationships.	Section Three: Domestic labour and gender roles in the family	126
The nature of childhood, changes in the status of children in the family and society.	Section Four: Childhood	132
Demographic trends in the UK since 1900; reasons for changes in birth rates, death rates and family size.	Section Five: Demographic trends since 1900	140

Exam skill focus

Skills required	
AO1 Knowledge and understanding of theories.	You will be expected to know writers and theories that pertain to the study of the family.
AO2 Demonstration of the skills of application, analysis, interpretation and evaluation.	You must apply these studies appropriately and in context. Additionally, you must be evaluative, outlining the strengths and weaknesses of the studies mentioned.

What it means to be studying families and households with AQA

Most of us have lived within a family unit at some stage in our lives and so we tend to think we know about families and may assume that our experiences are similar to those around us. Given our preconceptions about family life, it is hardly surprising that we may find it unusual that other people do not live their lives in a similar way to us.

Given the emotionally-charged nature of our family relationships, sociologists must be careful to examine this structure in a systematic and objective manner by setting aside their own experiences, looking at the available evidence and drawing conclusions on this basis. We start off in **Section One** by looking at definitions of the family, and how some theoretical perspectives view the family as a positive institution, whilst for others it is considered to be a damaging one. **Section Two** explores the relationship of the family to social change, particularly in reference to the economy and industrialisation, assessing in particular the theoretical perspectives of functionalism and Marxism and their views of the family. **Section Three** examines the changing patterns of marriage within the UK, focusing on the change in structure of the modern day family, divorce and new family structures that have developed to replace the traditional nuclear family. **Section Four** looks at the socially constructed concept of childhood, assessing the theory that 'childhood' appears to be based merely on age in society, with the reality being that definitions of childhood are different across the globe, and even within our own country. Finally, in **Section Five**, we look at overall population trends in the family that have occurred since 1900. This section is new and reflects the need for students to understand families and their development from a historical background. (Please note that you only need to know information from the start of the twentieth century.)

Families and households

Sociologists studied in this topic

Michael Anderson	Critic of Talcott Parsons who suggests that the nuclear family did not replace the extended family after industrialisation.
Ulrich Beck and **Elisabeth Beck Gernsheim** (1995)	Argue that the nature of love is changing, creating opportunities for democracy or chaos in personal life.
Norman W Bell and **Ezra F. Vogel** (1968)	Writers who, despite being functionalists, recognise that the family can be a dysfunctional place, particularly for children.
Ann Berrington and **Ian Diamond** (2000)	Add considerably to our understanding of the patterns of cohabitation in contemporary Great Britain.
Margaret Benston (1972)	Marxist feminist who asserted that women are exploited by capitalism as a source of unpaid labour in the home.
Mary Chamberlain and **Harry Goulbourne** (1999)	Writers who looked at how migration impacted on Caribbean identity.
Helene Couprie (2006)	Labour economist who found that employed women living with their employed partner spend more time doing housework than single women.
Christine Delphy (1992)	Compared rural and urban families and how labour and consumption differ between these diverse settings.
Norman Dennis and **George Erdos** (2000)	Supporters of New Labour who believe that the one-parent family is not as successful as the traditional nuclear family in instilling morals and a responsible attitude in their children.
Friedrich Engels (1820–95)	Studied the relationship between the development of the family and how capitalism negatively affects families.
Janet Foster (1990)	Conducted extensive research on crime, community and policing issues.
Diana Gittens (1998)	Describes how the notion of childhood innocence was important to alleviate the fear of a rapidly changing world.
Harry Hendrick (1992)	Criticised Ariès for using data that was unrepresentative or unreliable, whilst his work takes evidence out of context.
John Holmwood (2005)	Found that Parsons did in fact describe the situations where tensions and conflict existed or were about to take place, even if those conflicts weren't articulated.
Ronald David Laing (1964)	Radical psychiatrist who wrote extensively on how the family could lead to an emotional overload for its members.
Peter Laslett (1915–2001)	Questioned assumptions about the nature of the family and households in early modern Western Europe through the use of parish records.
Edmund Leach (1968)	Radical psychiatrist who suggested that we need to move away from the nuclear family and reintegrate with the rest of society.

Patricia Leighton (1992)	Found that when the male of the household becomes unemployed, the working wife tends to takes control over spending and regulating debt.
Stephen McKeown (1979)	Judged that mortality rates were reduced due to less air pollutants.
Patricia Morgan (2006)	Compared the state of the family in secular Sweden, Catholic Italy and Britain and found that in Britain government policies undermine the traditional family.
Jan Pahl (1993)	Examined which gender controlled money within family relationships and the affects of this on couples' happiness.
Ken Pease and Gary Farrell (2007)	Estimated that domestic violence statistics are 140 per cent higher than those stated in the British Crime Survey, which only records a maximum of five crimes per person.
Neil Postman (1985)	Argued that 'childhood' is ending, inferring that television is instrumental in this blurring between adulthood and childhood.
Carole Smart (1976)	Found that 'cohabitation' can mean very different things to different couples, with some cohabiting because of ideological objections to marriage and others doing so as a result of pregnancy.
John Hood Williams (1990)	Claimed childhood has removed children from being productive contributors to consumers.
Chris Wilson and Andrew Oswald (2005)	Emphasised that although both men and women benefit from marriage. Some investigators found that men gain more.

My mock examination for this topic is in ....

I will be examined on this topic in ....

The family in contemporary society

What is the family?

The family is a notoriously difficult institution to define. Let's start off with George Peter Murdock's classic definition. Before reading this chapter have a go at defining what a family is and what (if any) its purpose is.

Compare your answer to George Peter Murdock's definition of the family:

The family is a social group characterised by common residence, economic cooperation and reproduction. It includes adults of both sexes, at least two of whom maintain a socially-approved sexual relationship, and one or more children, own or adopted, of the sexually cohabiting adults.

It is interesting to know where the term 'family' comes from. The word itself comes from the Latin 'Familia' which means household or servant. During the fourteenth century, when this term was first used, the household consisted of servants and blood relations, whilst the adjective 'familiar' also gives us a clue about what kind of relations would exist with a group of people who were not necessarily blood related.

Without doubt the family is one of the most important social institutions and is found in many different forms across the globe. The major types are summarised in the following table.

Types of family	Forms of marriage and household
Nuclear family	A pair of biological parents and their children.
Extended family	A family that includes three or more generations. Usually includes grandparents, their sons and daughters, and their children.
Polygamy	A type of marriage where there is more than one spouse at a time.
Polygyny	A marriage structure where a man has more than one wife at a time.
Polyandry	A rare marriage structure where a woman has more than one husband at one time

The family also plays an important role in instilling norms and values into children and socialising them into the prevailing culture which surrounds them.

Many sociologists try to avoid using a definition and want to refer to 'families' rather than 'the family'. This suggests that it is almost impossible to define the family that fits with all the diverse domestic arrangements that are seen. Family then, means different things to different people.

Murdock's definition gives us a useful starting point of the characteristics and functions of families. The first part of his definition stresses the social relations of the family: essentially the family involves relationships between social beings. These relationships do not necessarily mean that the people concerned are married.

Additionally, other functional factors muddy the waters of this social relationship. Can the family contain only one spouse? Are both partners exclusive to each other? Does the family have to include children? Are both partners heterosexual? What is economic cooperation? What about families who have adopted their children or have been formed after a previous family break-up?

However, at least Murdock's definition allows us to rule out some **households** from his definition of the family.

In conclusion, we find that historically the family has evolved from a large group of servants and family members. However, by industrial times this had changed to the much smaller and exclusive nuclear family structure that we recognise today. Some argue that kinship is a more useful concept to use when looking at the family and defining it. Kinship refers to the special relationships we have with people who we feel responsible for and have an obligation towards.

Theories of the family

We can all conjure images of the family. Some are powerfully strong: images of parents, sisters, brothers, cousins meeting at family occasions, eating, drinking, Christmas and so on. For some the family is idyllic, comforting and supportive. For these the family can be a supportive place to flourish and perform functions that are useful for both the individual and society. Some theories tend to focus on the more positive aspects of the family and the role it performs; for example, looking at how families socialise which in turn allows society to run smoothly. However, other theories are more sceptical about the family, seeing it in particular as an exploitative place for women and children.

The functionalist view of the family

Functionalists have an optimistic view of the family. As with all structural theories they believe that the family plays an important role for the rest of society. They argue that it is beneficial for both those who are members of families and for the rest of society. Functionalists claim that every social institution plays an important role in relation to society's smooth functioning: the family is no different. Functionalists such as Talcott Parsons argued that the family meets a number of societal and personal needs. Functionalists like to see the family and other aspects of society as constantly evolving. Some sociologists call functionalists 'March of Progress

Theorists'. They believe that the nuclear family has evolved to meet the needs of modern day contemporary society. Specifically these functions for Parsons include the following which he believed cannot be reduced any further.

> **Focus on research**
>
> *Talcott Parsons*
>
> Family and Social Structure: The Changing Functions of the Family (blacksacademy.net)
>
> According to Talcott Parsons the family is losing many of its traditional functions. "It [the family] does not itself, except here and there, engage in much economic production; it is not a significant unit in the political power system; it is not a major direct agency of integration of the larger society."
>
> However, Parsons maintained that the family is still very important, its role becoming more specialised. Its main contemporary function is the structuring of the personalities of young people and their stabilization as adults: "the family is more specialized than before, but not in any general sense less important, because society is dependent more exclusively on it for the performance of certain of its vital functions."

Primary socialization

Primary socialization occurs within the family before school. There are two basic processes in primary socialization for Parsons. The family needs to mould the child's personality to fit the needs of society. This is achieved by internalisation of the society's culture and the structuring of the personality. This first stage, he believed, cannot be replaced. As a result of this socialization shared norms and values are established, and the central values of society are instilled in the child.

The stabilization of human adult personalities

Once the personality is established, adults need emotional security and a source of release from the stresses and strains of modern life. The emotional support of partners and the chance for parents to indulge in childlike behaviour with their children help to provide this security and release. It helps to prevent stress from overwhelming the individual and threatening the stability of society. This is sometimes called the 'Warm Bath Theory', where the strains and stresses of everyday life are eased by the warmth and love a person receives from their spouse. However, functionalists point to other functions that the family also fulfils.

Economic function

Families provide economic support for its members, particularly when they are young and paying for expensive items such as childcare. Increasingly this financial support has been extended beyond infanthood, with extra costs such as private education and university. Additionally, functionalists argue that the family also allows the economy to function successfully. The family achieves this by instilling attitudes and values suitable for the workplace, as well as helping to reproduce enough workers to allow for efficient production, whilst families are the ideal consumptive units in a capitalist society. Adverts of the 'cereal packet family' indicate that families are ideal units to help sell products, with major purchases being influenced by the family: houses, cars, consumer durables are all bought with the family in mind.

Agents of social control

Families teach us about stable relationships behaviour. Most of this occurs during socialization where children are taught the differences between right and wrong, helping ensure that society functions correctly. This is particularly the case with sexual relations, for example, if it were the norm for people to have multiple relationships this could be a source of conflict. So, through the family, 'rules' about sexual partners are established; from early teenage dating and curfews, to marital sex and extra-marital sex. Additionally, much evidence suggests that men, in particular, benefit considerably from a long-term marriage. Gallagher and Waite quote a 1990 article in the Journal of Marriage and the Family that concludes, "Compared to married people, the non married … have higher rates of mortality than the married: about 50 per cent higher among women and 250 per cent higher among men."

Reproduction

Family also provides an arena for reproduction as children are seen to be the logical outcome of a stable and loving relationship. Monogamy also eases the potential problems of patrilineal descent as paternity is usually certain, so each partner can be reasonably assured that inheritance will go to one of their children. Reproduction is also vital in order to keep the human race going.

Other functions of the family

Families tend to provide economic and emotional support when a member of the group is ill, disabled or in poverty. Indeed, this was one reason for the development of the extended family in early industrial times. Government statistics from 2001 show that around six million people (11 per cent of the population aged five years and over) provided unpaid care in the UK in April 2001. Of those, 45 per cent of carers were aged between 45 and 64; however, a number of the very young and very old also provided care.

Families offer us the economic, cultural and social support that allows status and the prospect of social mobility for its members. Those who live in one-parent families are significantly disadvantaged in modern-day society. As of Spring 2005 there were 1.9 million one-parent parents with dependent children living in the UK. The *Labour Market Review* (ONS, 2006) states that 60 per cent of lone-parent families are living in poverty. Those in traditional nuclear families, however, can offer financial help for educational resources and housing, thereby increasing the social status of those within the family.

Functionalists stress the positive functions of the family and, in particular, that of the nuclear family structure. They believe that this type of family structure offers the best 'fit' for a post-industrial country. They note that nuclear families offer **geographical mobility** and a positive sense of self reliance. However, many are highly critical of functionalist views, which we shall look at next.

Criticisms of functionalist view of the family

Critics argue that functionalists overplay the harmonious nature of the family: the family isn't that idyllic. For example, each week one child will be killed by their parent or carer in England and Wales (NSPCC, 2004), whilst one per cent of children experience sexual abuse by a parent or carer and another three per cent by another relative during childhood (One Plus One).

Critics also cite the high divorce rates in the UK. In 2005, 13 out of 1000 marriages ended in divorce (ONS, 2006). Men and women in their twenties have the highest divorce rates of all, with 27.1 divorces per 1000 couples. These statistics suggest that families are not a stabilising influence. One Plus One has shown that divorced adults have a greatly increased chance of heart disease, cancer, alcoholism and suicide compared to those who remain married (1995). **Bell** and **Vogel**, in their research, *The Emotionally Disturbed Child as a Family Scapegoat* (1968), highlight some dysfunctional aspects of the family. They believe that in a nuclear family, a child can often be an emotional scapegoat for the tension of unresolved conflicts between the parents, turning problems in the marriage onto the child. Bell and Vogel acknowledge that although this is dysfunctional for the individual child, it is a stabilising influence for the family

as a whole, and therefore society. Their work reinforces the notion that functionalism is a macro-sociological theory that is mainly concerned with the whole of society.

Feminists also attack the idea that the family is functional for all its members. They point to evidence to suggest that the family exploits women, such as figures that show two women are murdered each week by their partner (Home Office, 2006), whilst domestic violence alone contributes to 16 per cent of all violent crime in England and Wales (British Crime Survey).

Holmwood (2005) found that Parsons did in fact describe the situations where tensions and conflict existed or about to take place, even if he didn't articulate those conflicts. Marxist feminists do not believe that the nuclear family benefits all members equally and suggest that capitalism is the main beneficiary of the nuclear family structure. Writers such as **Margaret Benston** (1972) offers a Marxist analysis of the family. She suggests that the family helps capitalism replace or reproduce the workforce, with women assisting their husbands and the state by dispelling revolutionary anger by way of their tempering role within the family. Finally, Marxist feminists suggest that women act as a reserve army of labour. So, during times of high unemployment this reserve army disappears into the bosom of its family. However, when economic activity is high women reappear to help capitalism's drive for further profits. Radical feminists take a different view, believing that it is not capitalism that benefits from the nuclear family but men. Women, they suggest, have been socialised into accepting the female role that allows men to continue to dominate the highest positions in public life, whilst women support their successful men and children. Radical feminists believe that men have created an ideology that propagates and encourages this pattern as 'natural', thereby allowing men their continued dominance in society This is known as **patriarchy**.

A general criticism that has been aimed at functionalism is that Parsons tried to apply his studies of the US to the rest of the world. As such, many claim that it lacks ecological validity. Can we apply the middle-class families Parsons studied in America to the British version of the family with its different social classes, ethnicity and religious orientation?

Interactionists believe that we need to look at the individual person and how they interact with each other. They argue that how people interact with others impacts upon the way they perceive themselves and those around them.

The Marxist view of the family

Friedrich Engels, Marx's friend and financial supporter, offers an historical account of the development of the family in *The Origin of the Family, Private Property, and the State*. He considers that for capitalism to thrive the family is ideal for the reproduction of labour and as a way of confirming patrilineal descent. For Engels, the main purpose of monogamy is to ensure the systematic transfer of a father's

private property to his own sons. It is in this way he believes that men took control of the household, reducing women to mere instruments for their production of children.

The main difference between the two theories is that Marxism, far from seeing the family as functionally 'universal', sees it as an institution that serves capitalism. Marxists see the infrastructure, or the economic base, as being all-powerful and shaping all aspects of society, including the family. Marxists see the family as performing the following roles: firstly, by the process of Socialization, it mimics power relations within the workplace and encourages its members to see their failure as individuals rather than because of capitalism. Marxists call this 'False Consciousness'. Secondly, Engels sees the family as acting as a sanctuary from the exploitative wages and conditions that can be found in the workplace. The family comforts and de-stresses the so-called exploited male worker. However, in performing this function, Engels sees women being exploited by their domestic role which remains unpaid and undervalued by society. Lastly, the family offers the prospect of profit for capitalists as it buys consumer goods and services from them.

Criticisms of Marxism

There have been a number of criticisms levelled at Marxism.

- Anthropologists have suggested that the appearance of the nuclear family didn't correspond with the emergence of capitalism.

- As the Marxist view of the family is that of it only being shaped by the infrastructure and the needs of capitalism, it thereby ignores that often the family can be moulded by other factors, such as ethnicity.

- The Marxist view suggests a lack of free will that ignores the capacity of the human to actively create their own world.

- The Marxist view is economically deterministic, concentrating upon notions of class rather than looking at gender or ethnicity, for example.

The family and industrialisation

Functionalist writers have developed a 'best fit' thesis to explain that the family has adapted to fit the requirements of industrialisation. They argue that the nuclear family structure has developed into the main family structure in industrialised capitalist countries. Before this dominant family structure the extended family was the main family grouping.

The pre-industrial family

This family was based on extended kinship networks or a wide family network. The reality of this was that often many generations would live in the same household with other members of the extended family, such as aunts, uncles and cousins. This often meant that large family groups would cooperate economically, for example, in agriculture, and other small-scale industries such as textiles, baking, barrel making, and so on. Extended families would then trade their products with other local families ensuring the family was fully self-sufficient. In essence home was work and vice versa. Status was therefore ascribed and occupation was not based upon intelligence but upon the occupation of a person's family. This had a number of benefits for the family members. Firstly, without an education system, the family trained its members to be good workers through 'on-the-job training'. Secondly, in the absence of a welfare system the family looked after its own members; feeding them, looking after the young and the elderly, and making sure that those who were ill did not go without food and accommodation. This was done with the expectation that all family members cooperate both economically and socially, protecting each other in times of need and ensuring that all members came to no harm from other families in the locality. So, for example, childcare was undertaken by all members who were not economically active. The family was a multifunctional unit.

The industrialised family

After the industrial revolution, which occurred in Great Britain towards the end of the seventeenth century, changes in economic production and the way that society was organised led to drastic changes in family structure.

These changes in structure included a move towards a family that had to be much more geographically mobile. Whereas in preindustrial times jobs were located locally within the family, workers had to move to areas that had factories and therefore jobs. Instead of **nepotism** and local ties being important, achievement was based on education and intelligence. As a consequence, families tended to move towards towns that offered higher incomes and better prospects for those who had the requisite skills.

Writers such as Parsons believed that the extended family saw industrialisation stripping the family of many of its functions. Parsons refers to this process as 'structural differentiation'. For example, factories developed to provide consumer goods, whilst the government began to take on roles that had previously been the domain of the extended family, for example, education, welfare and health. The consequence of this was that work and home life became separate. People did not work at home but instead went to work, clocked in, and often worked for long hours. For Parsons this left the nuclear family to 'specialise' in what he called the two irreducible functions: the primary socialization of children and the stabilisation of adult personalities.

This resulted in a very different family structure: the nuclear family that included husband and wife and their children. Additionally, new roles started to emerge for those in the nuclear family. For Parsons the male was left with the **instrumental role** of providing economically for the family. By contrast, women took on the **expressive role**, being responsible for bringing up the children and teaching them the norms and values of society. Contentiously, functionalists believe that sexual division of labour is 'natural', thus allowing a specialisation of labour that ensures the emotional well-being of the children and their spouses.

However, Marxists see things rather differently, believing that the 'best fit' thesis allows the family to perform functions that are useful to the capitalist system: to literally reproduce in the family similar conditions and expectations that occur within the workplace.

Similarly, radical feminists do not see the family providing wellbeing for women. Instead, they see the family as a source of oppression, citing many incidences of the power of patriarchy over women's lives, for example, women's domestic role that assists capitalism, male violence within the family, and their reproductive role that limits career progression.

Criticisms of Parsons' view of industrialisation

Peter Laslett, an eminent Cambridge Historian, used historical parish records, wills and church records to examine whether Parsons was right to suggest that the most common form of family structure prior to industrialisation was indeed the extended family. These records helped him to scrutinise a number of variables such as birth and death rates, population size and household composition. From these Laslett observed that it was far too simplistic to see one predominant family structure before industrialisation. In reality, household composition depended upon social class. The upper classes, for instance, were often grouped in extended families as they had the room to house these family members. By contrast, lower-class groups, due to the high mortality rates of elder members of the family group, were often nuclear.

Such small families were probably the result of the prevailing economic and cultural times. Mortality rates were extremely high with average life expectancy being between 35 and 40 for the working classes. It was also common for families

to send their children into 'service' and become maids for the upper classes, whilst boys often gained apprenticeships. Additionally, families often 'lent' their children to childless relatives. Nonetheless, Laslett has been criticised for use of parish records that were often collated incorrectly. Interactionists comment that statistics such as Peter Laslett's give no qualitative idea of what life was really like at this time. Nonetheless, Laslett provides data that at the very least questions assumptions that Parsons makes about the composition of families in pre-industrial times.

The extended family provided shared income and extra support for those who were ill or disabled. It also provided assistance when it came to employment with those in work, nominating relatives for positions at their place of work. Finally, the extended family helped with childcare. With birth rates still high, childcare was often an arduous and thankless task. With parents increasingly having to go out to work in order to survive, older and younger members of the extended family helped with childcare so others in the group could secure full-time employment.

Michael Anderson also used historical data in his book, *Approaches to the History of the Western Family* (1971). His work cast doubt on the 'best fit thesis' that the nuclear family became preeminent to meet the needs of industrialisation. Although he was prepared to accept that the pre-industrial family tended to be extended, the reality was that a variety of family types existed. Anderson, in evaluating the census of 1851, was able to establish that extended family actually became more popular after industrialisation. This, he suggested, was particularly the case for those without market power, such as the working classes. His analysis of the rise in average household composition in Preston is that this occurred due to deprivation and poverty that existed in the mills. Anderson suggests that the move towards extended families was a response to this poverty, and by grouping like this families were able to mitigate hardship by looking after each other when they were unemployed, sick and suffering from very low income.

Willmott and **Young**, in their book, *Family and Kinship in East London* (1957), although agreeing with Parsons that the nuclear family best fitted the needs of an industrial society, disagreed with him over the speed of this change towards the nuclear family. They believed that this change was gradual rather than sudden, noting that extended families were common long after industrialisation. They found, in Bethnal Green in the East End of London, that the extended family was common because it provided many of the functions of self-support outlined by writers such as Anderson.

What do you know now?

1. Working individually, complete the following:

   - Try to define the family.

   - Write down five facts about **your** family.

   - List the main aspects of your family and compare them to your definition of the family.

2. Look at the following statements and assess whether each is a strength or a weakness of the best fit thesis.

   - Much of the artwork of pre-industrial times showed children as 'miniature adults'.

   - Peter Laslett contends that the extended family was not the dominant type of household, instead believing that the nuclear family was more typical.

   - Games and toys were played with by both adults and children.

   - Children performed an economic role, living in households with a wide range of adults and expected to tend to animals and help with sowing and harvesting.

   - Anderson found in his study of the 1851 census that extended families had not died out but were in fact quite common.

   - Some sociologists argue that other family structures, in particular extended families, would be more functional for industrial societies as discipline could be applied more easily by the family than by unrelated industrial bosses.

3. Using examples explain what is meant by:

   - A household
   - The nuclear family
   - The extended family

4. Explain why defining the family is so problematic.

5. According to Parsons what are the two 'irreducible functions' of the family?

6. Explain these two functions.

7. Give two criticisms of the functionalist view of the family.

Key terms

Expressive role: The role that Parsons suggests is performed by women within a family. Involves caring, nurturing and a supportive role that many functionalists believe women should naturally perform.

Extended family: A family group that consists of parents, children and other close relatives, often living in close proximity.

Geographical mobility: The extent to which labour is willing and able to relocate to different areas of the country.

Heterosexual: One whose sexual attraction is for people of the opposite sex.

Household: One person living alone, or a group of people (not necessarily related) living at the same address.

Industrialisation: A process of social and economic change whereby a human society is transformed from a pre-industrial agrarian economy to an industrial state. This process occurred during the eighteenth and nineteenth centuries in Great Britain.

Instrumental role: Parsonian phrase for the male wage earner in a household.

Nepotism: Favouritism towards one's relatives.

Pre-industrialisation: The period before the industrial revolution.

Patriarchy: The male domination of society.

Social policy: A governmental policy for dealing with social issues.

Section summary

- The family is a notoriously difficult institution to define.

- Without doubt the family is one of the most important social institutions; moreover, it is found universally in many forms across the globe.

- Functionalists take an optimistic view of the family. As with all structural theories they believe that the family plays an important role for the rest of society.

- Parsons believes that the family has merely two irreducible functions: the Socialization of children and the stabilisation of the adult personality.

- However, many, including Marxists, Marxist feminists and radical feminists, suggest that the family is far from functional for all, suggesting that women in particular seem to lose out with this family structure.

- Functionalist writers have developed a 'best fit' thesis to explain that the family has changed and developed to fit the requirements of industrialisation. They argue that the nuclear family structure has developed into the main family structure in industrialised capitalist countries.

- Writers such as Laslett, Anderson and Willmott and Young all believe that functionalists overstate this case, all suggesting that the extended family remained important even after industrialisation.

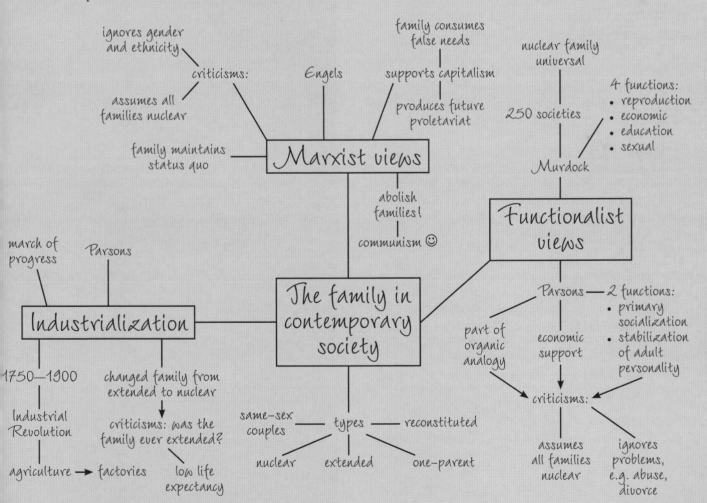

The extent of family diversity

Learning objectives

By the end of this section, you should be able to:

- Isolate contemporary trends of marriage and **cohabitation** in England and Wales
- Be able to explain what cohabitation is
- Understand why an increasing proportion of births are occurring outside of marriage
- Be able to comment on recent divorce rate changes in England and Wales
- Know and be able to explain reasons for changing divorce rates in England and Wales
- Be able to evaluate whether there exists only one ideal family type
- Describe with illustrations, as well as evaluate, the view that there now exists a range of family types which vary in a number of ways from the traditional nuclear family unit

Why the debate about marriage and marital breakdown?

With the ever increasing divorce rate in the UK it is hardly surprising that some writers equate these figures to a crisis in the family. Some writers, especially those from the right wing, stress that potentially there are dire consequences as a result of this trend.

Marriage in the UK

The latest statistics on marriage make bleak reading. Following an increase in marriage in the years 2002 to 2004, the 2005 marriage rate was the lowest on record. Apart from occasional years, marriage rates had previously been falling since 1973. The 2005 figures appear to be a return to the longer term trend. There were 244 710 marriages in England and Wales in 2005, down from 273 070 in 2004. This is the lowest annual number of marriages since 1896 when there were 242 764. Only 35 per cent of all marriages involved a religious ceremony in 2005, although surprisingly this figure is slightly higher than that for the previous year. However, this needs to be put in perspective by noting that 51 per cent of marriages involved a religious ceremony in 1991.

Longer-term trends are no less worrying: the proportion of the adult population (age 16 and over) who are married is projected to fall from 53 per cent in 2003 to 42 per cent in 2031 for males, and from 50 per cent to 40 per cent for females. The actual number projected to be married drops by a much smaller margin due to the expected increase in the adult population over the period in question. In 2003 only 44 per cent of women aged 25–34 were married, whereas in 1991 it was 63 per cent.

However, views of marriage do differ; traditional views are more likely to be held by religious and married people.

Differences in educational background are also indicators of differences in attitudes: those without qualifications hold more traditional views than those with them; those with higher educational qualifications are more traditional in their outlook than those with lower qualifications (Barlow et al., 2001).

Race is another source of difference, with Richard Berthoud of the Institute of Social and Economic Research, University of Essex, noting that three-quarters of Pakistani and Bangladeshi women are married by the age of 25, while other groups such as black British people being the group least likely to marry (2000).

The above has provoked a fierce debate amongst New Labour and New Right thinkers. New Right writers such as Patricia Morgan (2006) have compared the UK with other countries, in particular Sweden. New Right theorists see the nuclear family type as essential for the health and stability of family life. They argue that, ideally, government policies should encourage the 'traditional' nuclear family, rather than eroding it.

Focus on research

Family Policy, Family Changes, 2006

Patricia Morgan

In this study Morgan compared the state of the family in secular Sweden, Catholic Italy and Britain. One of the most striking points of comparison is the extent to which the state interferes in family life, especially the rearing of children, in each of the countries. On the face of it these countries have very differing systems.

Sweden is famous for its comprehensive, top-down, social engineering, which makes it difficult for people to live in any other way than that prescribed by the state.

Italy is the complete opposite People neither want nor expect the state to do anything to support families, and this is compounded by the Catholic church's traditional view that the family should be outside the state's sphere of influence.

Britain is more like Sweden as it treats people as units of production rather than unique individuals. Theoretically the state supports the family by supporting individuals in whatever choices they make, without discriminating in favour of any one family type. In fact, as Patricia Morgan shows, the system is so heavily skewed in favour of lone-parent and two-earner families that life is made difficult for single-earner, two-parent families, as in Sweden. 'The lone parent is the family form preferred by the tax/benefit system.'

Morgan found that, in Britain, marriage has not been supported by the tax system. She suggested that the promotion of policies to undermine the traditional family, like the scrapping of the marriage allowance and the transfer of rights and obligations which used to pertain to marriage to all relationships, was part of New Labour's programme of increased state control of our private lives: 'This is why totalitarian regimes in the twentieth century found themselves on a collision course with families and often preferred promiscuity and lone parenthood, since there are no boundaries and barriers here to state intervention'.

As with all statistics, those on marriage need to be contextualised. Most people will marry at some stage in their life. The reality is that men and women are now choosing to get married later in life, rather than not at all. For example, in 2005 the average age of first marriage for men was 32 and for women 29. This represents a marked change from previous patterns; 45 years ago the average was age 24 for men and age 22 for women. Women now tend to delay marriage so they can have a career and become financially independent. Other factors such as the high cost of housing and a movement to have children later in life all impact on the age at which we first get married.

The New Right view of the family	
The state of marriage	See the family in decline, as witnessed by increasing rates of cohabitation and births outside of marriage.
Their 'ideal' family type	Consisting of mother, father and children; financially viable and independent from the state. This type of family may involve a specialised division of labour or may rely on joint conjugal roles. The New Right prefer this family type with its specialised functions.
Evidence of the 'traditional' family being in decline	<ul><li>Fewer marriages.</li><li>Proliferation of single parent families.</li><li>Perceived declining 'morals', for example, homosexuality, abortion, female liberation.</li></ul>
How state policy undermines the family	The New Right argue that welfare policies encourage policies that favour those who don't want to be married, with generous welfare being offered to single mothers and children 'born outside of wedlock'.

The most recent *British Social Attitude Survey* (2006) indicates that couples still want to marry and see it as an essential part of life. Old-fashioned attitudes on having children still persist, which results in a general belief that it is better to have children inside marriage than outside it.

Moreover, when people get divorced an overwhelming majority want to remarry. Remarriages rose by a third between 1971 and 1972 following the introduction in England and Wales of the Divorce Reform Act 1969 and then levelled off. In 2003, 109 090 marriages were remarriages for one or both partners, accounting for just over two-fifths of all marriages. Provisional figures for 2005 show there were more than

113 000 remarriages, accounting for two-fifths of all marriages. These figures hardly indicate that marriage is not seen as desirable. Additionally, there is a trend towards relationships where there is a significant age difference. In England and Wales, the majority of women who get married marry men older than themselves. However, an increasing proportion of women are marrying younger men. The proportion of couples where the husband was younger than the wife increased from 15 per cent for those who married in 1963 to 26 per cent for those who married in 2004. Over the same period, the proportion of couples where the man was at most five years older than the woman fell from nearly two-thirds in 1963 to nearly one-half in 2004.

Many feminists believe that female attitudes towards marriage have radically altered over the last 30 years. A number of authors, including Sue Sharpe (1993) and Helen Wilkinson (1994), have discovered in their research that females often see marriage as a hindrance to their career. Instead of previously prioritising marriage, spouse and family, the newer generation have put these on the back-burner and opted for a career instead. This general trend has gone hand in hand with increased educational attainment of women both at GCSE and A level. With better qualifications women have thus opted to go to university or go on to training courses rather than into marriage. Whilst other feminists remain adamant that marriage is not a institute of love but a patriarchal institution, with feminists such as Victoria Dutchman Smith (2007) commenting that 'the very act of getting married has its roots in harmful, outdated notions of ownership and immutable gender roles'. Moreover, there is evidence to suggest that men in particular benefit from the institution of marriage rather than women.

Cohabitation in contemporary Great Britain

Cohabitation, or 'living together', has become increasingly common in England and Wales. The proportion of people cohabiting has increased greatly since the mid-1980s. The rise in cohabitation may in part be related to people marrying later in life. The proportion of non-married men and women aged under 60 who were cohabiting in Great Britain more than doubled for men between 1986 (the earliest year for which data are available on a consistent basis) and 2005, from 11 per cent to 24 per cent; and almost doubled for women aged under 60, from 13 per cent in 1986 to 24 per cent in 2005 (Social Trends, 37). Additionally, cohabitation is also becoming popular with older couples who have previously been married. **Berrington** and **Diamond** (2000) found that cohabitation was common amongst those who had been married before. In general the available research shows that couples view cohabitation as a prelude to marriage not necessarily as an alternative, as the vast majority (60 per cent) end up marrying after a five year period.

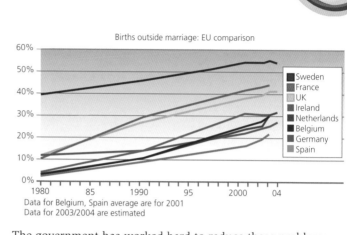

Births outside marriage: EU comparison

■	Sweden
■	France
■	UK
■	Ireland
■	Netherlands
■	Belgium
■	Germany
■	Spain

60%
50%
40%
30%
20%
10%
0%
1980   85   1990   95   2000   04
Data for Belgium, Spain average are for 2001
Data for 2003/2004 are estimated

In *Cohabitation and Breakdown* (2000) Carole Smart and Pippa Stevens found that cohabitation can mean very different things to different couples, ranging from those who started living together as a result of an unplanned pregnancy, to those who had ideological objections to marriage. Few couples, however, had reliable knowledge of their legal position on separation. The findings suggest that policy initiatives should not treat 'cohabitation' as a blanket term for one type of partnership. It is important that the children of cohabitees are not neglected by policy initiatives which tend to focus on married parents who are divorcing rather than on unmarried parents who separate.

Births outside marriage in contemporary Great Britain

Some commentators, particularly from the right wing, remain concerned about the number of births that occur outside marriage. Recent statistics (ONS, 2004) show the proportion of children born outside marriage in the UK has leapt from 12 per cent in 1980 to 42 per cent in 2004.

Interestingly, our own figures are in contrast to other countries in the EU who on average only show 33 per cent of births outside marriage. This trend towards births outside marriage is a reflection of the rising trend in cohabiting parents. The UK, in comparison with Europe, has a very high rate of teenage pregnancy. Recent figures (Family Planning Association, 2005) reveal that in 2005 the under-18 conception rate for England and Wales was 41.4 conceptions per thousand women aged 15-17, compared with 41.7 per thousand in 2004, a fall of nearly 1 per cent. Despite this the UK still has the highest teenage pregnancy rate in Europe (UNICEF, 2001).

Teenage birth rates in England and Wales are six times those in the Netherlands, nearly three times those in France and more than twice those in Germany. Not surprisingly this has led to a moral panic, focusing in particular on the high rate of pregnancy amongst the young, welfare benefits and likely social affects of such births. However, given teenage pregnancy rates are twice as high in the USA (2002–3) the UK is by no means the worst country in the world in this respect.

The government has worked hard to reduce these problems and set up the ten-year rolling National Teenage Pregnancy Strategy in 1999. Recent figures show conception rates for under-18s are at their lowest for twenty years and some authorities have reduced their rates by more than 35 per cent since the strategy began. However, in 2005 the under-16 conception rate for England and Wales was 7.8 conceptions per thousand girls aged 13–15 compared with 7.5 in 2004, an increase of four per cent. Nevertheless, overall the rate in this age group has been steadily declining since 1998 when the figure was nine per thousand girls aged 13–15. It seems, however, that certain groups, such as those from poor socio-economic backgrounds, and those children in care, are more likely to get pregnant. However, the reality is that teenage pregnancy is a rarity, with only three per cent of unmarried teenagers becoming mothers and four out of five births outside of marriage are registered to both parents with three-quarters of these living at the same address. It is perhaps also salient to note that, no matter the age, even those married and in a stable relationship suffer increased divorce rates as a result of the birth of their first child. This indicates that there are no guarantees of stability either in one-parent families or amongst those who are married.

More recently, there has been a concern about the fall in the UK birth rate with approximately one-third of women choosing not to have any children at all. More recently, however, in 2005, the birth rate has risen, with the average woman bearing an average of 1.79 children during their life course (Social Trends, 2007).

Divorce in contemporary Great Britain

Divorce is without doubt becoming more common in England and Wales, but until relatively recently in history, divorce did not occur. According to statistics the first divorce in Britain took place in 1551, with the church until then seeing marriage as sacred. However, it was only after the 1857 Matrimonial Causes Act that allowed divorce through the law courts, instead of the slow and expensive business of a private Act of Parliament. Under the terms of the act, the husband had only to prove his wife's adultery, but the wife had to prove her husband had committed not just adultery, but also incest, bigamy, cruelty or desertion.

More recently, Britain's divorce rate has remained high compared with many other countries in the EU. Recent figures show the UK has a divorce rate of 2.7 per 1000 of the population, the second highest rate in Europe, with only Denmark having a higher rate at 2.8 (Social Trends, 2002). Relationship research group, One Plus One (2006), comment that the UK divorce rate 'stuck out' compared to other countries figures.

Nonetheless, recent trends show some improvement, with provisional figures for 2005 showing an eight per cent fall in the divorce rate to 13.0 divorces per 1000 married population in 2005. In statistical terms there were 155 052 divorces in 2005, a decrease of seven per cent from the previous year's 167 138. This is the lowest number of divorces since 2000, and the first annual decrease since 1999–2000. This is 14 per cent lower than the highest number of divorces which peaked in 1993 (180 018).

One in two marriages end in divorce, which is still too high for many commentators, particularly when it is taken into account that half of all the divorces involved children under the age of 16. New Right sociologists argue that these figures reveal a crisis of marriage in the UK and they believe that a succession of policies that have made divorce easier have exacerbated this problem. It was perhaps with this in mind that the Labour government, who had been in office since 1997, decided not to replace the present system of five grounds for divorce with a no-fault clause that required no grounds have to be shown as to why the marriage has irretrievably broken down. It should also be noted that figures on separation are not collated and although separation orders are sometimes obtained and give some indication of separations, couples often separate without going to court, with the consequence that there are no available statistics. Additionally, there

---

> **Monogamy:** Can be defined as a person marrying another person (including same-sex marriages) and staying faithfully married to that person.
>
> **Serial monogamy:** The same as monogamy, but a person marries, divorces, and remarries again in a succession of monogamous relationships.

---

are couples who live in so called 'empty-shell marriages' (those marriages where couples continue to live together despite being unhappy). So although they live together as a couple they often have high levels of dissatisfaction with their marriage but refuse to divorce. It can consequently be concluded that definitive figures on divorce rates in the UK are almost impossible to surmise: all we can do is give some indication of general contemporary trends.

Explanations for marital breakdown

As is often the case, sociological explanations vary with the perspective that each sociologist writes from. We will start with the functionalist view of why marital breakdown has become more common.

The value of marriage

Functionalists including Talcott Parsons and Ronald Fletcher believe that the rise in marital breakdowns does not signify the fact that people do not want to be married. Instead they argue that people are increasingly expecting more and more from marriage; notions of love, fidelity and equal roles, both in relation to domestic chores and childcare have become more important. They argue that higher divorce rates suggest that these 'higher standards of marriage in society' (Fletcher, 1966) are not being met.

However, there is contradictory evidence that both supports and rejects this view from *The British Social Attitudes Survey* (2001). Although many respondents made comments about the importance of marriage and high expectations they had of the institution, they also believed that cohabitation was an acceptable alternative or a precursor to marriage. Thus, there seems little evidence to suggest that people attach a higher value to marriage than before.

Conflict between spouses

Structural changes to the family and the move away from extended families with close kin and a social support network has resulted in the modern-day family being isolated to meet the needs of capitalism. Functionalists such as William Goode state that had led to a 'heavier emotional burden' for the spouses with greater fragility and thus higher rates of marital breakdown. Additionally, with the economic role being stripped from the family there is less to unite the couple emotionally.

Allan and Crowe found in their 2001 study, *Family Diversity and Change in Britain and Western Europe*, that 'marriage is less embedded within the economic system'. The family no longer acts as a unit of production so there are fewer bonds between the spouses. Even more important is the fact that both spouses are economically independent of each other. They have greater choice about whether or not to endure an unsatisfactory marriage. Whereas previously the spouses might have been willing to forego problems and stresses in their relationship, nowadays they are much more willing to think of divorce as the first option, rather than the last.

The above issues particularly impact on the wife, as previously she often would not have an income and therefore the financial muscle to trigger a divorce. Now, however, women are often financially independent and are unwilling to stay in emotionally unfulfilling relationships. This is indicated by the figures relating to the petitioning of divorce. In 2005, 69 per cent of divorces were granted to women. This is in comparison with post-war rates where it was much more likely that the man would petition than the woman.

Attitudes to divorce

Writers such as **Beck** and **Beck Gernsheim** (1995) take a postmodern approach to divorce. With increasing consumer-related choice and freedom, couples are starting to see marriage in a similar light. With constant media messages about 'perfect love' and marriage, women are starting to compare their relationships with the idealised ones shown on TV. Whereas in the past strong societal pressures from family prevented divorce, individuals now feel they have the right to a happy and fulfilling marriage. If this is not the case, women in particular are obtaining divorce petitions, with seven out of ten being taken out by unhappily married women. This, along with the increasing opportunity for extramarital relationships in the workplace and use of Internet sites to meet partners, has led to an increased likelihood that women will exercise greater choice in their relationships.

Changes in divorce legislation

In the past it was both difficult and expensive to obtain a divorce; however, changes in legislation have been liberalised over the last 50 years, making the process far cheaper and socially acceptable. For example, before 1857 a private Act of Parliament was required for a divorce. Very few took this expensive and difficult route to get a divorce. Since 1857 divorce law has revolved around the idea of 'matrimonial offence', particularly adultery or the idea that one partner has 'wronged' the other. This idea was central to the much later 1950 Divorce Act which allowed other grounds for divorce including cruelty and desertion. This would then often necessitate long drawn out battles with an adversarial emphasis.

The most significant piece of legislation, however, was the introduction of the Divorce Reform Act passed in 1969 which came into effect in 1970. This act dispensed with the idea of 'matrimonial offence' and instead allowed the term 'irretrievable breakdown' of marriage. Although adultery could still be cited, it also introduced the idea of separation as grounds for divorce. Further acts in 1984 and 1996 were added which altered the time period before a divorce could be petitioned from three years to one, and the addition of a non-fault clause to prove that the marriage had simply broken down. For this, all the couple have to do is enter a one-year period of 'reflection' to consider any possible reunion, with the exception of those with children under the age of 16, or where one partner asks for more time, when the period of reflection is extended to 18 months. The latest proposed legislation has used mediation to allow cheaper divorces in relation to money and child access rights.

However, divorce is not that easy. It still remains an expensive procedure, with the average cost of divorce in the UK now costing £13 000. More than a third of couples are forced to sell their marital home when they split up (BBC, October 2006).

Family household structures

Although Anderson noted that a variety of family structures existed in pre-industrial and industrial times, it is generally accepted that with industrialisation the nuclear family has become the dominant family structure. More recent research has questioned this assumption. For example, in 2004 only 37 per cent of households consisted of mum, dad and two children (*General Household Survey*, ONS, 2005). As ever, we should be open-minded about statistics as they only give one snapshot in time.

Families tend always to be evolving, so married couples become nuclear families and with divorce may then also evolve to one-parent families. We should not assume that the nuclear family is becoming redundant. In 2004 two-parent families made up 78 per cent of all families (ONS, 2004). Despite this statistic it is undoubtedly true that other family structures are becoming more typical; one-parents families, cohabiting couples, and reconstituted families, which are also known as 'blended families'. This can be seen from ESRC research that shows that in Scotland one-person households will 'soon account for one-third of all households – the highest rate in the UK' (2006).

One-parent families

Families in the UK are increasingly likely to live in one-parent units. The ONS has found that children in the UK were three times more likely to live in one-parent households than they were in 1972. There are 1.9 million one-parent families in Britain, one-quarter of all families, caring for 3 million children (Labour Market Review, 2006).

Amongst one parent families about nine out of ten are headed by women. The previous marital status of lone-parent families is as follows: five per cent of lone parents have never been married, 30 per cent are divorced, 21 per cent separated from marriage and four per cent are widowed. Interestingly, only 12 per cent of lone mothers are under the age of 25, which goes against much of the moral panic that has been created about teenage mothers supposedly getting pregnant to receive benefits (*Labour Force Survey*, 2004). The average age for a lone parent is 35 and at any one time only three per cent of lone mothers are teenagers.

Some research has indicated that one-parent families do not provide a very stable environment, particularly for children. In a speech entitled *Changing Aspects of Family Life: Children and Divorce* (2003), **Carole Smart** believes that one-parent families encourage 'bad relationships', especially with the absent parent. Often unfairness can creep in with children being used to score points against their ex-partner. The New Right sees the family as in deterioration. They point to the following evidence to support their claims:

* Lone-parent families
* Fatherless families
* Divorce rates

Dennis and Erdos, in their book, *Families Without Fatherhood*, talk about fatherless families, claiming that it places disadvantages on the children. They state that on average, they have poorer health and lower educational attainment. Apparently, this lack of a father potentially leads to irresponsible, immature and anti-social behaviour amongst young men. Criticisms of the New Right views on the family include the argument that they tend to blame the victims of disadvantaged families and hold an idealized view of the past.

Reconstituted families

Stepfamilies consist of married or cohabiting couples who, between them, have at least one child from a previous relationship who either visits or lives with them. As the divorce rates rise, the formation of this type of family structure has increased. Childline (2002) estimates that in Britain there are currently over 2.5 million children in stepfamily life. One million live within their stepfamily; another million visit their stepfamily. To put it another way, stepfamilies represent six–eight per cent of all families with children. And around 85 per cent of stepfamilies are formed after a relationship breakdown. However, this family structure offers many difficulties for those involved. A potential obstacle to the successful

formation of a stepfamily is how the parties have handled the end of the previous relationships. An acrimonious divorce or separation can force a child to have divided loyalties between both birth parents, particularly when one or both find new partners. Children can often find themselves listening to one parent criticising the other. It is unsurprising, then, that in 2001 Childline received over 15 000 calls from children to talk about family relationships; many about problems in step families. For some children, coping with stepparents, stepbrothers and stepsisters can be a difficult and lonely experience. For other children problems can arise in relation to how well they do at school and their general health and wellbeing. This can result in depression or children feeling stressed and unhappy. These problems can particularly surface during Christmas.

Parentline (2005) also believes that stepfamilies assist by children gaining a wider family with more support, both financially and emotionally, whilst the stepfamily structure encourages children to become more adaptive and able to learn from their parents' past mistakes.

Same-sex families

This is the term used for families in which two people of the same sex live together as a family. If you were to believe the tabloid press one might assume that there had been a big increase in such families. The reality is that same-sex couples are a rarity throughout most of Britain. Across most of the country, less than a third of one per cent, below 0.3 per cent, of couples define themselves as same-sex and, in many areas, there are almost no same-sex couples. Nonetheless, same-sex families do exist and are common in certain parts of the country, with Brighton and Hove being the most inhabited locality by same sex-couples (whereas as many as 2.67 per cent of all couples define themselves as same-sex). The choice remains to live outside of traditional structures, even if on the face of it such groupings remain rare. As part of this greater choice, the Civil Partnership Act 2004 came into operation on 5 December 2005 and enables a same-sex couple to register as civil partners of each other. Civil partnership is able to be registered in England and Wales in a register office or in approved premise in a similar way to heterosexual marriage.

Section summary

- Marriage rates are falling in the UK.

- Marriage rates differ in relation to ethnicity and class in the UK.

- The likelihood is that most of us will marry at some stage in our life cycle.

- Cohabitation has become increasingly common in England and Wales.

- Having children outside of marriage has become increasingly common in England and Wales.

- The UK has the highest teenage pregnancy rate in Europe; however, it is still far lower than in the USA.

- There has been a long-term trend for increasing divorce rates in England and Wales, although this trend seems to be less certain than before, with recent figures displaying a falling divorce rate.

- Reasons suggested for this trend include the high value placed on marriage, conflict between spouses in the privatised nuclear family, attitudes and legislation.

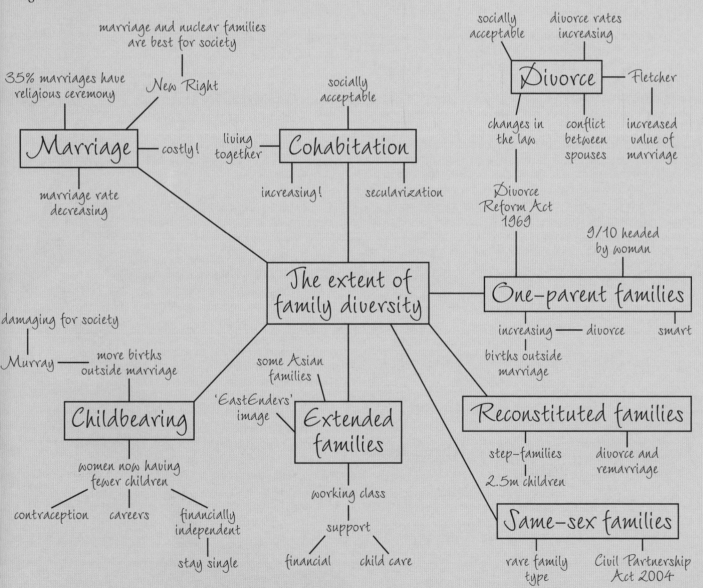

marriage and nuclear families are best for society

socially acceptable

divorce rates increasing

35% marriages have religious ceremony

New Right

socially acceptable

Divorce — Fletcher

Marriage — costly!

living together

Cohabitation

changes in the law

conflict between spouses

increased value of marriage

marriage rate decreasing

increasing!

secularization

Divorce Reform Act 1969

9/10 headed by woman

The extent of family diversity

One-parent families

damaging for society

Murray — more births outside marriage

some Asian families

'EastEnders' image

increasing — divorce — smart

births outside marriage

Childbearing

Extended families

Reconstituted families

women now having fewer children

working class

step-families

2.5m children

divorce and remarriage

contraception   careers   financially independent

support

stay single

financial   child care

Same-sex families

rare family type

Civil Partnership Act 2004

Domestic labour and gender roles in the family

Introduction

A useful starting point for this section is the work of the two British sociologists, Willmott and Young, who in 1975 declared in their book, *The Symmetrical Family*, which was based on a study of London couples, that the traditional segregation of tasks in the household with women doing domestic chores and men bringing in the weekly wage was breaking down. They went on to claim that the family was becoming what they called 'symmetrical'. In this symmetrical family Willmott and Young believed that a greater degree of equality was being shown where both did equal amounts of both paid and unpaid labour. This idea was picked up by social commentators who suggested that the 'new man' would be the saviour of the modern-day family, cooking, cleaning and multitasking in the home as efficiently as a woman. However, symmetry does not necessarily mean that roles are not gender segregated. So, men might do the garden or DIY tasks around the home, whereas women might do cleaning, washing and ironing; tasks which should ideally be done in relative equality in terms of time and commitment. This section area looks at arguments about whether this symmetrical family is a myth or a reality today. Of course, the idea of equality or **egalitarian** roles in the household is an ideal one, but it needs to be matched in a whole arena of areas. For example, men may spend an equal amount of time doing these tasks, but if women are left doing roles such as financial and emotional roles, the equality may not be as real as the statistics suggest.

Conjugal roles: The roles played by man and wife within a marriage. This term especially applies to who does what when it comes to domestic labour.

Studies on domestic labour

Feminists in particular oppose the idea that the family has become more symmetrical. Almost as soon as Willmott and Young's study had appeared, the feminist, Ann Oakley, claimed to have found a very different situation in her book, *The Sociology of Housework* (1974). Oakley, a radical feminist, used qualitative interviews amongst housewives in South East England and discovered that the majority of household tasks were performed by women rather than men. In her relatively small sample, 40 married women – 20 of whom were working class and 20 of whom were middle class and who had one or more children under the age of five – were questioned. A number of interesting aspects were revealed by her work. In terms of class, it appeared that the middle classes were more symmetrical than working-class families. However, in both classes there were very few men who delivered the majority of childcare and housework. She found that far from there being a 50:50 split it was more akin to an 85:15 ratio. Many women in her interviews commented on the unfairness and boredom that they felt about housework. Some felt their gender identity was being sacrificed along with their husbands, with some of the sample believing that men shouldn't do the housework, and that 'it was not mannish to stay at home. I like a man to be a man'.

Clearly there is a big difference of opinion here between feminists such as Oakley and functionalists such as Willmott and Young. To take this further we therefore need to look at more contemporary evidence on housework and childcare. **Helen Couprie** (2006) of Toulouse University in her research based on data from *The British Household Panel Survey* looked at working women; single or living with a partner, both with and without

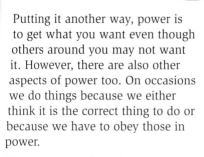

children. By examining information on more than 2000 people she concluded that, on average, an employed woman does 15 hours a week of housework when she lives with her employed partner, up from ten hours when single. Other research such as that of Xavier Ramos (2003) notes how housework increases with age and amount of children in the household. More recent surveys, such as the *Time Use Survey* (2005), paint a more hopeful picture with, on average, people spending less time doing housework. However, it also concluded that women in all economic categories spent longer on domestic work than men. Women who worked full time spent 151 minutes on domestic work compared with 113 minutes spent by men who worked full time. From this we can conclude that there is contradictory evidence. However, in general there seems to be some evidence that women appear to do a 'double shift': going to work for increasing amounts of time, yet at home doing the majority of the housework. It is hardly surprising that this leads to conflict, with writers such as Howard Dryden (1999) suggesting that this burden places relationships under a considerable amount of strain, and potentially leads to marital breakdown.

However, it is not merely housework that women are responsible for. There is a growing body of both sociological and psychological research that points to the responsibility placed upon women to care for the emotional welfare of both her partner and her children (Erickson, 1993; Duncombe and Marsden, 1993; Reay et al., 1998; Wharton and Erickson, 1995; Zajdow, 1995). This research shows that within families, women engage in emotional labour far more than most men, taking responsibility for maintaining the emotional aspects of family relationships, responding to others' emotional states and also acting to alleviate distress. This, it is argued, leads women to neglect their own emotional health with the result that although both men and women benefit from marriage, some investigators found that men gain more (Wilson and Oswald, 2005).

Decision making and power in households

Power is an important concept in sociology, so it is important to explain what we mean by power. Max Weber (1947) defines it as:

"Power is the probability that one actor within a social relationship will be in a position to carry out his will despite resistance, regardless of the basis on which this probability rests."

Putting it another way, power is to get what you want even though others around you may not want it. However, there are also other aspects of power too. On occasions we do things because we either think it is the correct thing to do or because we have to obey those in power.

There are a number of ways in which decision making and power are exercised in the family. We will first look at decision making. Early research in this area looked at how financial power was exercised particularly in middle class families. Stephen Edgell of Salford University (1980) found that when it came to major purchases, such as decisions about where to live, which car to buy or where to go on holiday, it was the man of the household, the major wage earner, who made these decisions. Women in comparison only made decisions on minor items such as food purchases and children's clothes.

Edgell believed that as he was looking at middle-class couples this would filter down to working-class couples. Although this study is rather dated it was corroborated by the work of Jan Pahl (1993) who examined who controlled the money within the household. The couples interviewed were split into two groups: those who had joint named bank accounts and those who had separate accounts. A further split was then made between those where the husband made the important financial decisions and those where the wife performed this function. Pahl found the following findings from the 102 couples who were interviewed:

- **Husband controlled pooling** was the most likely relationship, with 39 out of the 102 couples using this method to control their money. Here, although there was a joint bank account, the husband controlled the most important financial decisions.

- **Wife controlled pooling** was the second most common arrangement (27 couples), with the couple having a joint account but the wife having control of major expenditure. From the sample, this tended to be the case in middle-class couples, particularly where the woman had a higher income than the man.

- **Husband control** was found in 22 of the couples, where the husband had his own account and took control of the major financial issues in the family. Although this arrangement was found when the male had a high income, it was also the case in lower-income families where the wife didn't need an account as most of her income was spent in cash.

Other writers, such as Christine Delphy (1992), additionally note that when men do buy products for themselves they spend more than their wives do. Deplhy calls this 'differential consumption'.

- **Wife control** was the least likely arrangement, with only 14 of the couples using this system. This was commonly found in low-income couples where neither had a bank account and where the woman controlled the earnings to pay the bills.

This study reveals the complexities of financial arrangements within families. And although major decisions appear to be taken mostly by men, women do have some control, particularly in managing accounts on a daily rather than monthly basis. Pahl's findings showed that the most equal type of control is wife controlled pooling. In such families, because of the similar income of each partner, decisions tended to be made jointly and equally. However, Pahl found that this arrangement was only in operation in a quarter of all the families, suggesting that, in domestic financial arrangements, just like many other areas of life, women do not have equality even in the family.

Further evidence of a lack of equality is provided by the Fawcett Society's report, *Home Truths* (Geethika et al., 2002), which found some women resorted to stockpiling their own savings without the knowledge of their husbands to provide a nest egg for their own financial security, with some women being afraid that their husbands might spend their money if they found out about it. The report commented that despite a perception that many more couples were now sharing financial decision making, men still called the shots, particularly in low-income families. The report authors commented that "It is clear from this research that for many, the egalitarian family is a myth."

Men also appear to exercise control when it comes to the importance of their job. In *A tale of two nations? Juggling work and home in the new economy*' (2003), Irene Hardill wrote that women would often end up following their husband to a new part of the country, leaving behind their jobs and friends to further his career. Additionally, in the past men also often expected their wives to further enhance their careers by offering additional support and attending functions to make their husbands appear more powerful.

Domestic violence

Another area of power and control is through physical abuse. The Home Office defines domestic violence as "any incident of threatening behaviour, violence or abuse between adults who are or have been in a relationship together, or between family members, regardless of gender or sexuality". However, others believe that this definition is not complete enough. The Women's Aid Federation define domestic violence as

"… physical, psychological, sexual or financial violence that takes place within an intimate or family-type relationship and forms a pattern of coercive and controlling behaviour."

Given the complexity of this crime, The HM Inspectorate of Constabulary has more recently used the following definition: "any violence by current or former partners in an intimate relationship, wherever and whenever the violence occurs. The violence may include physical, sexual, emotional, or financial abuse."

Although this crime is thought to be under-reported, with **Ken Pease and Gary Farrell** (2007) estimating that domestic violence statistics are 140 per cent higher than those stated in the British Crime Survey, which only records a maximum of five crimes per person, *Crime in England and Wales 2004/2005* (Nicholas et al.) estimate that it accounts for:

- Sixteen per cent of all violent crime

- Has more repeat victims than any other crime (on average there will have been 35 assaults before a victim calls the police)

- Costs in excess of £23 billion a year. **Sylvia Walby** estimated in her study *The Cost of Domestic Violence* (2004) that when you take account of the cost of all factors, including that of the criminal justice system, health, social services, housing and cost to the economy, this amounts to a staggering £5.1 billion

- Claims the lives of two women each week and 30 men per year

- The largest cause of morbidity worldwide in women aged 19–44; greater than war, cancer or motor vehicle accidents

- Will affect one in four women and one in six men in their lifetime

Abused women are five times more likely to attempt suicide than the non-abused people, and one-third of all female suicide attempts can be attributed to current or past experience of domestic violence (Barron, 2005; Humphreys, 2003; Meltzer et al., 2002). Women's Aid (2006) comments "the causes of domestic violence are rooted in the issues of power and control and the perpetrators sense of entitlement within the relationships".

Child abuse

Sadly, this area is another negative aspect of power relationships within families, with a strong correlation between child physical abuse and domestic violence, with estimates ranging between 30 per cent to 66 per cent, depending upon the study (Hester et al., 2000; Edleson, 1999; Humphreys & Thiara, 2002). Statistics compiled by the NSPCC show that:

- Each week one child will be killed by their parent or carer in England and Wales (*Crime in England and Wales 2002–3*, Home Office, 2004).

- Six per cent of children experience frequent and severe emotional maltreatment during childhood.

- Eighteen per cent of children experience some absence of care during childhood.

- More than a quarter of all rapes recorded by the police are committed against children under 16 years of age (Harris and Grace, 1999).

Theoretical explanations of inequalities of control in the family

Sociologists see this inequality of power in the family differently depending upon which theoretical position they are writing from. Feminists, for example, take a diverse view on power in families.

Functionalists

Functionalists take a very traditional approach to the family, seeing a natural **division of labour** between spouses and suggesting that these differences are biological and 'natural'. Therefore, specialisation of labour allows each spouse to concentrate on roles to which they are best suited. So, for example, Parsons believes that women are better at the caring or expressive role with women, therefore taking on most of the childcare and providing the emotional support for the family. By contrast functionalists believe that men mainly perform the instrumental role, that of breadwinner, providing the financial support for the family.

Liberal feminists

Liberal feminists believe that the position of women has improved over time. They believe that the reason for this has primarily been due to changes in legislation that stop sexism. The Sex Discrimination Act and the Equal Pay Act have impacted on the way that people in general perceive women. With these acts, gradual and ongoing changes in the attitude and behaviour towards women have changed. They believe with continued legislation and progress, further improvements will be secured in the future. A tip to remember this is to equate liberal feminism with the 'L' word: 'Legislation' (the making of laws to improve the position of women in society).

Radical psychiatry

Radical psychiatry offers a critique of the idealistic notions of the family presented by functionalists. Writers such as **Edmund Leach** (1968) and **R. D. Laing** (1964) see the modern nuclear family as being too dislocated from other family members, leading to emotional overload similar to an electric circuit tripping with a fault. This emotional overload, he believes, is a consequence of too much expectation between family members. Moreover, the structural isolation of the nuclear family leads to it seeming like a private unit in which the family is fearful and distrustful of wider society in a way that doesn't sit with reality. So by contrast to functionalism, Edmund Leach suggests that we need to move away from the nuclear family and reintegrate with the rest of society. R. D. Laing uses this idea of isolation to explain how the nuclear family draws a defensive barrier around itself leading to maladjusted opinions of other groups of society and authoritarian figures being created within the family itself.

Marxist feminists

Marxist feminists believe that the inequalities we have outlined serve capitalism. This is done by reproducing the workforce and allowing workers to dissipate their anger against capitalist oppression when they go home to their families. Any abuse that occurs then is often a reflection of this anger and alienation. A tip to remember this is to equate Marxist feminism with the 'C' word: 'Capitalism' (the root cause of oppression according to these theorists).

Radical feminists

Radical feminists believe that men are the main cause of oppression for women. They believe that the family, and in particular the female role, is created by men for the benefit of men, allowing them to go to work without being burdened by childcare and with domestic work being completed by their spouses. A tip to remember this is to equate radical feminism with the 'P' word: 'Patriarchy' (the male domination of society).

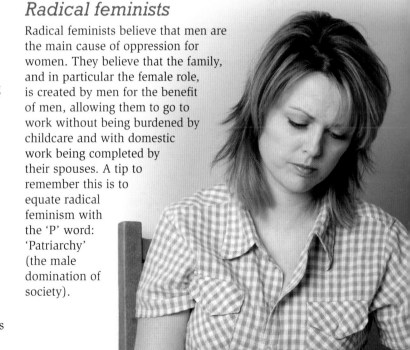

What do you know now?

1. Using examples explain what is meant by:
   - Domestic division of labour
   - Symmetrical family
   - Egalitarian

2. Explain, with examples, how males can exercise power in the family.

3. Explain the different forms that domestic violence can take.

Key terms	
Conjugal:	This refers to the relationship of a husband and wife.
Dual role of women:	The two main roles undertaken by a large number of women. These roles are those of wage earner and domestic housewife.
Egalitarian:	Belief in the equality of all people.
Division of labour:	Tasks that are allocated on the basis of traditional roles. For example, the mother specialising in childcare and domestic arrangements and the male of the household being expected to provide financially for the family.
Symmetrical:	Equal in terms of time and effort expended.

Section summary

- Functionalists such as Willmott and Young have argued that with the development of the nuclear family roles have become symmetrical.

- Most contemporary research refutes this idea. Women still perform a dual role: that of going out to work and that of housewife, where, in reality, men still do relatively little housework compared to women.

- Another area of power is that of decision making. It appears that men tend to make the major financial decisions in the household with women making peripheral decisions, often related to children.

- This power can also spill over into domestic violence which affects one in four women in their lifetime.

- Children are also not immune to abuse from the male in the household. Each week one child will be killed by their parent or carer in England and Wales.

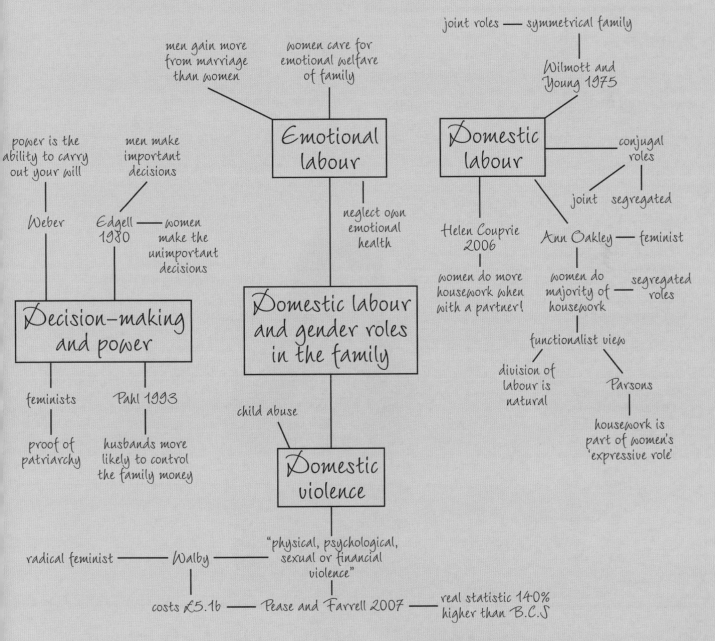

What is a child?

Children appear to be living for longer and longer in the parental home, although they appear to 'grow up' at an ever younger age. How do we picture 'a child'? Childhood is a **social construction** given the fact that the age of **childhood** appears to differ between different countries and changing time periods. It is not even straightforward to define childhood. Sociologists usually start by using two concepts:

- **Biological:** This is the rate at which we physically and mentally develop. In our own society, children are physically more mature than ever before.

- **Cultural definitions:** These are the meanings or words that people associate with childhood. Complexities arrive when we think about who we perceive as children. Firstly, it is virtually impossible to say when childhood ends. So anomalies occur, such as that a couple can get married (with parental consent) and have sex at the age of 16, but cannot go and see an 18 rated film. Further problems arise in the classifications that society uses for children at different ages. During the life course we move from being infants, to toddlers, to children and finally to teenagers.

Sociologists, despite these difficulties, usually start from a historical point of view in assessing the nature of childhood.

The child in pre-industrial times

The usual starting point used is the work of **Phillipe Ariès'** *Centuries of Childhood* (1962). This social historian studied the changing nature of childhood and the family in France and England from pre-industrial society up to modern times. He found that our present idea of childhood is a relatively recent social construction. He found that prior to pre-industrial society, childhood (as experienced by children today) didn't exist. He argued than in pre-industrial society children were not called 'children', nor were they treated as such. Ariès does not claim there were no young people. Rather, while there was an abundance of people between the ages of seven and 15, they were seen as 'small adults' who were expected to take place in the same work and activities as older members of the community. Although this seems a rather callous way to see children, we need to put this into context. Due to very high mortality rates children were seen more as an economic resource rather than an emotional resource. As little time was spent with them, nurturing and socialising them, it made sense to treat them like everyone else.

Art historians such as Berger (1972) give support to Ariès in artwork of the time when there are no children. There were babies but, what we call children now did not exist. Little adults are there; the nature of dress, expressions and mannerisms are all adult. Childhood is a later historical creation. However, Ariès has been criticised by **Harry Hendrick** in the 'Journal of Economic Social History' (1992) for using data that was unrepresentative or unreliable.

Childhood and industrialisation

In the early stages of industrialisation (perhaps similar to developing societies today) child labour was common, as children performed the role of cheap labour for employers and as economic asset for parents. This resulted in children often working 14 hours a day, six days a week. Gradually, a more enlightened view of childhood began to develop, firstly within more prosperous families and gradually into the working classes, with attitudes particularly starting to change from the middle part of nineteenth

century. This led to what Ariès calls the progressive removal of children out of adult society with a succession of acts that banned children from the mines and factories, where many had to work in appalling conditions, with death being a constant daily danger. By the mid-eighteenth century things started to change, particularly amongst the middle classes where children came to occupy a central place in the family. In Britain the development of education started with The Forster Act 1870, where children started to be separated from the world of the adult. However, that is not to say that children were still not treated badly, particularly those children who came from poor backgrounds; many children worked as servants in the homes of richer families. In the 1850s one in nine of all female children over the age of ten years worked in domestic service.

Childhood in the twentieth and twenty-first centuries

The start of twentieth century saw the development of the child-centred family with the 1908 Children's Charter classifying childhood to the age of 14, with children under this age being classified as minors. This led Hood Williams (1990) to believe that childhood had changed children from being productive contributors into consumers. Additionally, as the welfare state has developed, children have been seen as worthy of moral and social welfare. Feminist Diana Gittens (1998) believes that a decline in infant mortality and a decline in the birth rate after the Second World War meant that families were more able, and willing, to value and invest in their children. Children became objects of fun and pleasure for adults, objects of consumption (not production), whilst laws were created to protect children from exploitation and neglect by adults.

After the Second World War we saw the emergence of the 'teenager', with this category being differentiated from childhood. Youth cultures grew amongst people in their middle to late teens, working in their first jobs, with less responsibility and more disposable income to spend on fashion and music. However, with the development of youth sub-cultures teenagers started to become the subject of **moral panics**, a heightened level of concern about a particular group without warrant. Such moral panics included teddy boys in the 1950s and mods and rockers in the 1960s and the development of what Hendrick (1990) calls the focus on the 'delinquent child'.

On a more contemporary note, it was believed in the 1980s that with reduced working hours would come greater leisure time with children. This has not been the case, with parents (particularly men) having to spend long hours at work. With male workers being so worried about the loss of their jobs that they often go to work when ill (presenteeism), and feel obliged to arrive early and leave late. The work-life balance that should have been tipped towards greater family quality time has instead led to increased working hours. The 2001 census revealed that on average men work 42.2 hours per week. By 2003 this had increased to 43.2 hours per week (*Labour Force Survey*, 2003).

The state and children

With the development of the child-centred approach the state has become far more involved in the protection of children. The state has always played a role in defining childhood with acts such as the 1833 Royal Commission deciding that children could only work if they were 'of the ordinary strength and appearance of a child of his/her stated age'. This act also sets

14 as the minimum age at which children may be employed, and gives the following restrictions:

- No child shall do any work other than light work

- A 14 year old may not work for more than five hours on a Saturday or any other day

- On a school day, a 14 year old may not work: during school hours; before 7.00am or after 7.00pm; for more than two hours a day; or for more than 12 hours in any school week

- During the school holidays a 14 year old may not work for more than 25 hours in any week, or for more than four hours in any day without a rest break of one hour.

The state also socialised children by attendance at school so children can only leave school at the age of 16, with the 1997 Labour government "definitely looking into raising it further" to the age of 18, with this being reported that the change would take place by 2013: youngsters who entered secondary school during 2008 to be the first to be affected by the new regime. This also helps support children by offering parents child benefit and child tax credit and Educational Maintenance Allowance (EMA). Additional supplements are offered for those with disabled and severely disabled children.

Towards the end of the twentieth century a move towards children's rights, both nationally and internationally occurred. Nationally the Child Support Act 1991 supports children when their parents divorce with maintenance being paid until the child reaches the age of 17. This act was followed by subsequent legislation including a further Child Support Act in 1995, and the Child Support Pensions and Social Security Act 2000. This most recent act made radical changes to the system in an attempt to simplify the process, both for parents and for those working within the Child Support Agency, and to improve the accuracy and enforcement of child support assessments. However, by 2007 the government announced the Child Support Agency would be replaced by the new Child Maintenance and Enforcement Commission (CMEC). The CMEC agency would be given new powers to dock wages and

withdraw passports from those who fail to keep up with their child maintenance payments. The agency could also impose curfews and confiscate driving licences from non-payees.

Internationally, the United Nations General Assembly adopted the Convention on the Rights of the Child (UNCRC). The convention sets out the specific rights of children and their need for special care and assistance including:

- Children have the right to be kept safe and not neglected, exploited or hurt. Children with disabilities have the right to special care and training.

- Children have the right to education and to play.

- Governments should ensure that children are properly cared for, and protect them from violence, abuse and neglect.

Theoretical approaches to the family

The present debate amongst sociologists revolves around the ideas of two groups: functionalists and the New Right, whose approach is often referred to as the 'conventional' approach versus the alternative approach advocated by interactionists.

The conventional approach sees the state and the family as important institutions in the successful upbringing of children. They argue that children are under constant threat from adults and the liberal ideas of adult society. These liberal ideas, they argue, have led to children suffering more often in families where there is only one parent, or where children do not have access to parents of either sex. Traditional theorists are sceptical that gay couples are capable of bringing up children to be well-rounded and balanced citizens. In general there is a concern that modern-day youngsters are being brought up in a moral vacuum, in which ideas of right and wrong are not being taught from an early age nor being shown to their children in their parents' day to day existence.

Conventional-approach theorists argue that childhood has been destabilized by two trends: firstly, the belief that neo-liberal ideas has produced children who have no respect for their parents. They argue that this lack of respect is in response to children's rights undermining the hierarchical respect of their parents; for example, children 20 years ago were routinely physically punished by their parents. With the removal of acceptance of these penalties parents have allowed their children even more leeway. Secondly, conventional theorists argue peer groups and commerce are shaping children through teenage magazines and television to become adults before their time. So much so that in 2006, David Cameron, the Conservative Party leader, was moved to comment on a large department store's 'Little Miss Naughty' underwear range as being "harmful and creepy". Others are concerned about children's use of cosmetics to make them appear older than they actually are.

As a consequence, the age of 'childhood' is becoming ever shorter, as teenagers take on the views of the adults around them, encouraging them to have sex at an ever earlier age. The average age of first sex in 16.3 years old (Durex survey amongst 16–20 year olds, 2005), with attendant high teenage-pregnancy rates in the UK, but also additional problems, such as an increasing suicide rate amongst teenaged boys in particular. Some suggest that this influential group have impacted on social policy. Teenagers are seen to be too immature to make judgements and need to be protected by laws and the state.

> ### Children and decision making (2005)
> *Ian Butler, Margaret Robinson and Lesley Scanlan*
> Based on group discussions with 69 children and in-depth interviews with a further 48 children, all aged between eight and 11, the authors found that:
> - The ways in which families made decisions involved a subtle, complex and dynamic set of processes in which children could exert a decisive influence.
> - Most families operated democratically but children accepted the ultimate authority of their parents, provided that they felt their parents acted 'fairly'.
> - For children, 'fairness' had more to do with being treated equitably than simply having the decision made in their favour. Children could use claims to fairness as a moral lever in negotiations with parents.
> - Children regarded fathers as less actively involved in making domestic decisions, except where these affected the whole family or when decision-making concerned 'public' rather than simply 'domestic' matters. For most children it was mothers, rather than fathers, who were the most frequently consulted source of domestic authority.

These ideas have been taken up by American professor at the Steinhardt School for Education, **Neil Postman** (1985), who has attacked the mass media and claimed that childhood is ending. He believes that television is instrumental in this blurring between adulthood and childhood. "There's no such thing as children's programming", he claims. "Everything is for everybody"; television is "the total disclosure medium … Television and the Internet give children complete access to all information". He argues that potentially this is an extremely worrying trend as children's ability to trust, and believe in and rely upon the adult world diminishes with the result that adult authority is lost. Postman argues that this leads to children becoming more like adults in relation to their dress, criminality and sexuality, while in contrast adults seem to be regressing into childhood, wanting to look forever young and 'hip'.

Criticisms of the conventional approach to childhood

A number of criticisms have been levied on this group. Interactionists are critical of functionalist and the New Right.

Structural theories such as these tend to underplay the role of the individual and assume that citizens are merely the product of society, that we are simply blank canvasses told what to do and what to accept. They assert that the reality is far more sophisticated. Interactionists believe that we are a product of our contact with those around us and this is not a single process but a bilateral one. So, although we may be influenced by our parents and guardians, we too influence them. Children's influence in the family can often be profound, particularly in decision making. Ian Butler et al., in their study based on group discussions with 69 children and in-depth interviews with a further 48 children, found that the ways in which families made decisions involved a subtle, complex and dynamic set of processes in which children could exert a decisive influence, with children accepting the ultimate authority of their parents, provided that they felt their parents acted fairly.

This approach tends to generalise about children and childhood. As we have already seen, childhood is not universal but is influenced by the time period, by class, gender, ethnicity, culture and **locality**. To exemplify this:

- Childhood is very different in the Third World, with some 11 million children dying due to poverty every year. The *Growing up in Asia* report (2005) states that 600 million Asian children under the age of 18 lack access to food, safe drinking water, health care or shelter. Every day, almost 16 000 children die from hunger-related causes, that is, one child every five seconds (The Lancet, 2003).

- Experiences may also be very different between male and female. **Gender roles** may be different, stressing careers for boys and family roles for women. There is some evidence to suggest that more resources are spent on men than women in educational provision.

- The experience of childhood may differ according to social class, with children's social backgrounds being even more important than low birth weight in determining how well they achieve in school and later life, according to researchers. The study, published by The British Medical Journal (2002), firmly points at social deprivation and poverty as some of the most significant reasons why some children do less well than others. These differences may be exemplified by upper-class children being expected to attend boarding schools such as Eton and Harrow, staying away from the family for weeks on end, whilst the middle classes offer considerable financial and cultural support for their children, such as moving into areas where the best educational chances are offered. By contrast the working classes may be offered little encouragement and go to any local school regardless of its performance in league tables or its local reputation.

- There may also be differing experiences between ethnic and religious groups, with evidence to suggest that those from Muslim, Sikh and Hindu families, feeling a stronger sense of obligation to their parents than other groups.

What do you know now?

What do you know now?

1. Using examples explain what is meant by:
   - Childhood
   - Social construction
   - Biological

2. Explain how children were seen in pre-industrial times by writers such as Ariès.

3. Account for reasons for this perception.

4. How did industrialisation affect the role of children?

5. Explain the term 'child centred'.

6. Explain the role of the state for children in contemporary society.

7. Isolate at least two sociological theories on childhood and briefly explain their beliefs.

8. How does the conventional approach to childhood view children?

Key terms

Childhood: This is a broad term applied to the phase of development until a person is an adult.

Child centred: This means focusing on the needs and wants of the child.

Gender roles: A set of supposed behavioural norms associated particularly with gender.

Locality: A place or geographical position.

Moral panic: A heightened level of concern about a particular group without warrant.

Social construction: This is where something is constructed by social processes rather than just being natural or biological.

Section summary

- The concept of childhood is problematic.

- Children were seen as 'miniature adults' in pre-industrial society by writers such as Philippe Ariès.

- This view of children was a result of high mortality rates and the need for the child to be an economic asset.

- Industrialisation led to the 'progressive removal' of children from the economic role.

- The start of twentieth century saw the development of the child-centred family.

- With the development of the child-centred approach the state has become far more involved in the protection of children.

- Towards the end of the twentieth century a move occurred towards children's rights, both nationally and internationally, with acts such as the Child Support Act (1991).

- The present debate revolves around the views of those adhering to the conventional approach who believe that children are vulnerable and need to be protected. Writers such as Neil Postman believe that childhood is becoming ever shorter due to pressures from the media and Internet, and interactionists who believe that we are a product of our contact with those around us and this is not a one-way process but a bilateral one. So although children may be influenced by their parents and guardians, they too influence them.

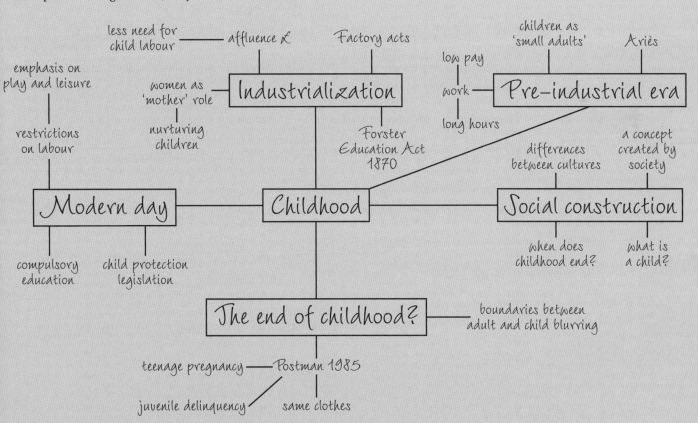

Demographic trends since 1900

Learning objectives

By the end of this section, you should be able to:

- Understand that there are different types of family and that the family has changed significantly over time
- Have an appreciation of the factors that have led to the demise of the family
- Understand where power resides in the family
- Understand how the family help society socialise new members and stabilise adults
- Appreciate the links between the family and the economy
- Understand that the notion of 'childhood' is actually a social construct

Population: 1901 to present day

- The population of the UK has grown throughout the period 1901 to the present day, but at a declining rate.

- The highest growth rate was observed between 1901 and 1911 when the growth rate was one per cent per annum. However, by 1981–91 this rate had fallen to 0.26 per annum.

- The average age of the population was 38.8 years, an increase on 1971 when it was 34.1 years.

- In mid-2005, approximately one in five people in the UK were aged under 16 and one in six people were aged 65 or over.

- The UK has a growing population. It grew by 375 100 people in the year up to mid-2005 (0.6 per cent). The UK population increased by 7.7 per cent since 1971, from 55.9 million.

- Population is expected to continue to grow, with latest projections suggesting that in 2031 the population will reach 67 013 million.

Year	Population
1901	38 323
1911	42 138
1921	44 072
1931	46 074
1941	48 216
1951	50 290
1961	52 807
1971	55 928
1981	56 352
1991	57 808
2001	58 790
2005	60 210

Source: 1901–71 British Historical Statistics (Mitchell, 1988); 1981–2001 ONS, Population Trends (1998)

UK population 1901–2005

Reasons for these changes

The main reasons for the overall change in population are due to a falling birth rate and a falling mortality rate, which led to an ageing population, particularly as we move into the twenty-first century. Another significant factor in the increase in the overall population rate is migration. Although the century began with a trend for net emigration (emigrants leaving their native country) particularly to commonwealth countries, more recently, since 2001, there has been significant net migration (leaving a native country permanently). It is virtually impossible to be sure of this figure as the number of people coming for at least one year, in relation to the number of people who were leaving, has been going up since 1987. In 1999–2000 100 000 more people came for a year than left, before reaching a high of 171 000 in 2001. That figure has dropped back since then. Another key measure is the figure for people giving 'grants of settlement': a right to stay permanently in the UK. This figure has been tracking the general trend and came to about 144 000 in 2004. It should be noted, however, that this figure excluded immigration of EU nationals who have an automatic right to stay within the UK.

Birth rates

- Throughout this period there has been substantial fluctuation in birth rates in the UK.

- Sharp increases occurred after both world wars as soldiers returned from the battlefield.

- The largest annual amount of births occurred in 1920 when there were 1 126 800 births.

- The largest sustained increase in population occurred during the 1960s in the so-called 'baby boom'. The highest amount of births during this period being recorded in 1963 with 1 014 700 babies being born.

- This was followed by a rapid decline in the numbers of births, reaching a low of 657 000 in 1977.

- With the increasing amount of women due to the baby boom, a 'mini baby boom' occurred in the late 1980s and early 1990s, which was further encouraged by affluence.

- Since then birth rates, although falling in the first part of the twenty-first century, have seen a rise due to increasing fertility. Live births in England and Wales increased for the fifth successive year in 2006. There were 669 531 births in 2006, compared with 645 835 in 2005; an increase of 3.7 per cent.

- Fertility rates for 2006 give an average number of 1.87 children per woman in England and Wales. This is an increase of nearly four per cent since 2005 (1.80) and is the fifth consecutive annual increase from a low point in 2001.

- Since 1995 the proportion of births occurring to mothers born outside the UK has been rising. This rise became steeper between 1999 and 2004. In 2004 19.5 per cent of all births were to women born outside of the UK.

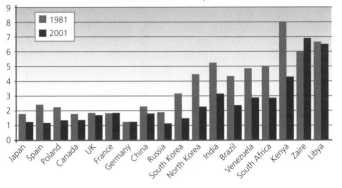

Fertility rates:
Number of children per woman

Source: Population et societes, INED

Reasons for these changes

- One of the major reasons for a falling birth rate has been the movement of women into the job market, with higher female wage rates depressing the birth rate.

- The high cost of having a child is another factor limiting increases in birth rate. Latest figures (Liverpool Victoria, 2006) puts the cost of having a child at a staggering £180 137.

- There has been a general trend for more women to choose to have no children at all. Dr Catherine Hakim has carried out some extensive research in this area and found that couples are increasingly deciding on the benefits of a childfree lifestyle. More recently the total fertility rate has increased to 1.79 children per woman; a rise from 1.77 in 2004 and the fourth consecutive annual increase since the record low of 1.63 in 2001. It is too early to predict whether this is the start of a sustained rise.

- The greater availability and efficiency of contraception has also impacted on the birth rate. After the introduction of the contraceptive pill in 1961 there was a marked fall in the birth rate.

- Increasing immigration has led to an increased birth rate for immigrants within England and Wales. This has helped to increase the overall birth rate over the last ten-year period.

Death rates

- In 2006 there were 502 599 deaths registered in England and Wales; comprising 240 889 male deaths and 261 710 female deaths.

- Over the course of the twentieth century, there have been steady falls in death rates.

- The rate for males fell from 25 829 in 1901 to 8477 in 2000.

- The rate for females fell from 21 705 to 5679 over the same period.

- Despite these trends there are dramatic variances, with death rates substantially increasing during flu epidemics and during cold and hot weather. Large annual increases,

for example, occurred in 1918 with over 200 000 people dying from the influenza epidemic in England and Wales.

- Around 80 per cent of deaths occurred at ages over 65 in 2000 compared with around 20 per cent in 1901.

- Male mortality, although declining, has not kept pace with female mortality reductions; although this gap has been substantially decreasing and it reached its narrowest point in 2006.

- Infant mortality has fallen dramatically during this period, down from 25 per cent of deaths in 1901 to less than one per cent in 2006.

- Overall life expectancy in 2006 is 76.9 for men and 81.2 for females in England and Wales. This compares with a life expectancy in 1901 of 48 for a male and 52 for females.

- Premature deaths fell by a sixth between 1994 and 2004 (the Poverty Site, 2007).

- In 2005, the main causes of childhood death were injury and poisoning.

- In 1901, 36.2 per cent of all deaths and 51.5 per cent of childhood deaths were from infectious diseases. By contrast in 2000, 11.6 per cent of all deaths and only 7.4 per cent of childhood deaths were from infectious diseases.

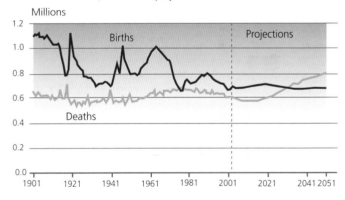

Births, deaths and projections from 1901 to 2051

- By contrast, in 2004, the two single biggest causes of death among people aged 55 to 64 were heart disease and lung cancer.

- Deaths are expected to start a sustained increase again to a projection of 800 000 deaths per year by 2051. The increase in the number of deaths will be added to in the 2040s and 2050s by the baby boom generation of the 1960s reaching old age.

- However, disparities still exist as Britain has the second highest child-death rate among the 24 richest countries in the world, with infants in the UK twice as likely to die before the age of five as children in Sweden (Collison, 2007). The researchers from Dundee University link child mortality with income inequality. They found that in the UK the gap between the haves and the have-nots was the third biggest among the 24 countries.

Reasons for these trends

Improvements in primary medical services, such as immunisation, have contributed substantially to decreasing death rates. The decline and virtual elimination of tuberculosis in England and Wales represents one of the most important and valuable health gains during the twentieth century. In 1901 tuberculosis represented about 11 per cent of all deaths versus the year 2000, when tuberculosis only represented about 0.07 per cent of all deaths in England and Wales (*Twentieth Century Mortality: 100 Years of Mortality Data in England and Wales*).

In the UK today, the population is probably better fed than at any time in history. Deficiency diseases have all but disappeared, we are taller and live longer than ever before, and infant mortality has declined. However, as diseases associated with malnutrition have disappeared, other diet-related illnesses have emerged; the result, not of food shortage, but of a diet inappropriate to our lifestyle and metabolism. Many of these improvements have stemmed from improved agricultural production and food handling processes.

Improvements in public health

With rapid industrialisation the UK has seen a huge improvement in hygiene and therefore lower mortality. Progress was made in this area from the mid to late 1860s with the development of a sewerage system in London and the introduction of filtered water supplies (from 1875 onwards). However, some researchers, such as McKeown (1979), believe that mortality rates were reduced due to less air pollutants.

Improvements in environmental conditions

As wealth has increased in the UK, better conditions have followed for workers, with consequential falls in death rates. Other improvements, such as the quality of air with the controlling of pollution by government organisations such as the Department for Environment, Food and Rural Affairs (DEFRA), have further reduced mortality.

However, the Joseph Rowntree Foundation (1997) finds that death rates have been falling in some areas more quickly than in others. The highest death rates were generally recorded in northern and urban areas. Glasgow residents were 66 per cent more likely to die prematurely in recent years than people living in rural Dorset, and 31 per cent more likely than people living in Bristol. The three areas with the highest death rates in the 1990s – Oldham, Salford and Greenock – had mortality ratios nearly a third higher than the national average, compared with only a fifth higher in the 1950s.

Family size

Households: by size (%) Great Britain					
	1971	1981	1991	2001	2006
One person	18	22	27	29	29
Two people	32	32	34	35	36
Three people	19	17	16	16	16
Four people	17	18	16	14	13
Five people	8	7	5	5	4
Six or more people	6	4	2	2	2
All households (= 100%) (millions)	18.6	20.2	22.4	23.8	24.2
Average household size (number of people)	2.9	2.7	2.5	2.4	2.4
Source: Census, Labour Force Survey, ONS					

Average UK household size

- The average household size halved in the last century: before 1900 the average size was 4.6 people, but it is now 2.4.

- There were 24.2 million households in Great Britain in spring 2006.

- The trend towards smaller household sizes has contributed to the number of households increasing faster than the population and hence an increased demand for housing.

- The number of households in Great Britain increased by 30 per cent between 1971 and 2006.

- The average household size declined over this period from 2.9 to 2.4 people.

- The proportion of households in Great Britain comprising a couple with dependent children fell from more than one-third in 1971 to less than one-quarter in 2006.

- Ethnic groups differ in terms of household size. Asian households tend to be larger than those of other ethnic groups and may comprise three generations.

- There was an increase in the proportion of women remaining childless. This increased from nine per cent of women born in 1945 to around 20 per cent for women soon to complete childbearing.

Households: by type of household and family (%) Great Britain					
	1971	**1981**	**1991**	**2001**	**2006**
One person					
Under state pension age	6	8	11	14	14
Over state pension age	12	14	16	15	14
One family households					
Couple					
No children	27	26	28	29	28
1–2 dependent children	26	25	20	19	18
3 or more dependent children	9	6	5	4	4
Non-dependent children only	8	8	8	6	7
Lone parent					
Dependent children	3	5	6	7	7
Non-dependent children only	4	4	4	3	3
Two or more unrelated adults	4	5	3	3	3
Multi-family households	1	1	1	1	1
All households (= 100%) (millions)	18.6	20.2	22.4	23.8	24.2
Source: Census, Labour Force Survey, ONS					

Households by type and family

Reasons for these trends

- The main reason for the trend towards smaller households includes more lone-parent families, smaller family sizes and an increase in one-person households, although the rise in one-person households has levelled off since 1991. Most of the increase in the proportion of one-person households since 1991 is a result of the rise in the number of people below state pension age living alone.

- This increase in one family household has been fuelled by the rapid rise in the divorce rate in Great Britain. Sixty per cent of households involve a divorced or separated partner.

- With increasing life expectancy the potential for the number of years a marriage can last increases. With life expectancy reaching 80 for females and late 70s for males, marriages have the potential to last for over 50 years. With

this increase may come the potential for increasing marital breakdown and mortality, particularly of the male of the household.

- With increasing wealth and career it appears that highly educated men and women, in particular, choose to have no children at all. Indicating that this particular group considers their single lifestyle to be paramount rather than having children. The development of The Contraceptive Pill in the early 1960s was fundamental to this change.

People in households: by type of household and family Great Britain					
	1971	**1981**	**1991**	**2001**	**2006**
One person	6	8	11	12	12
One family households					
Couple					
No children	19	20	25	25	25
Dependent children	52	47	53	39	37
Non-dependent children only	10	10	12	9	8
Lone parent	4	6	9	12	12
Other households	9	9	4	4	5
All people in private households (= 100%) (millions)	53.4	53.9	54.1	56.4	57.1
Source: Census, Labour Force Survey, ONS					

People in households by type of household

What do you know now?

1. Isolate where the following trends are related to 1901 or 2007:
   - High population growth
   - An ageing population
   - High levels of immigration from countries within the EU and outside it
   - Falling birth rate
   - Large households
   - Declining fertility rates
   - Poor nutrition and sanitation
   - Dramatic variances in the death rate with death rates substantially increasing during flu epidemics and during cold and hot weather
   - The high cost of bringing up a child
   - An increasing proportion of one-parent families
   - An increasing proportion of women choosing to have no children at all
   - Children staying at home until they are well into their twenties
   - The movement of women into the workforce rather than staying at home
   - Life expectancy of 48 for males and 52 for females

2. Using examples explain what is meant by:
   - Birth rate
   - Death rate
   - Fertility rate

3. Give one reason for the change in birth rate in the UK

4. Give one reason for the change in death rate in the UK

5. Explain what has been happening to family household size in the UK

6. Give one reason for the declining household size in the UK

Key terms

Birth rate: The number of live births per 1000 of the population over a period of time, usually a year.

Death rate: The number of deaths in a year per 1000 of the population.

Emigration: The act of leaving a home country to settle in another.

Immigration: The movement of people from one nation to another.

Total fertility rate: The number of children an average women would have assuming that she lives her full reproductive lifetime.

Section summary

- The population of the UK has grown throughout the period 1901 to the present day, but at a declining rate.

- The main reasons for the overall change in population are due to a falling birth rate and a falling mortality rate, which had led to an ageing population particularly as we move into the twentieth century.

- Throughout this period there have been substantial fluctuations in the birth rate in the UK.

- Reasons for a fall in the birth rate include women wanting careers, the high cost of having a child, a movement towards more childless couples and more effective contraception after the introduction of the contraceptive pill in 1961 in the UK.

- Over the course of the twentieth century there has been a continual fall in death rates.

- Reasons for this fall include: improvements in primary health care, better nutrition, public sanitation and advancing environmental health.

- Family size has halved since 1901: before 1900 the average size was 4.6 people but it is now 2.4.

- Reasons for smaller family households include: the increase in one-parent families, higher divorce rates and increased life expectancy.

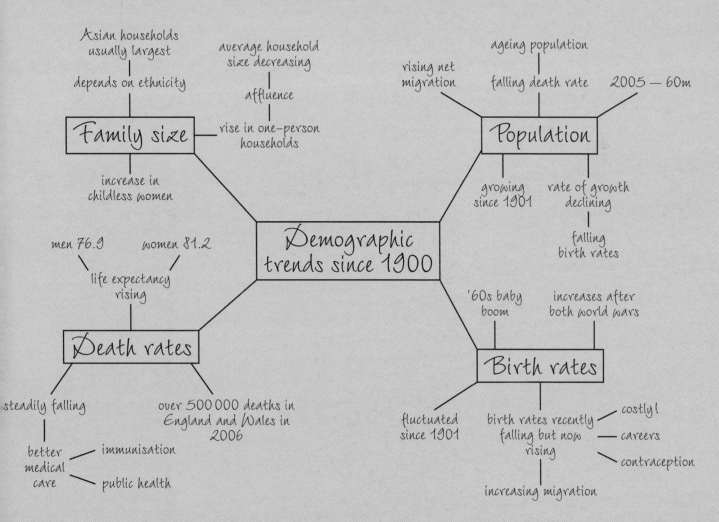

How to maximise your grade with AQA

How to maximise your grade with AQA

Family and Households is worth 40 per cent of the AS total mark and 20 per cent of A level. You will be expected to answer five questions on the family with graduated questions from two marks, four marks, six marks and then the large 24 mark questions. As with the previous specification the exam format is a stimulus response style question.

The Assessment objectives are as follows:

Assessment objectives		Weighting
AO1	Knowledge and understanding of the theories, methods, concepts and various forms of evidence linked to the specification.	45–55%
	Communication of knowledge and understanding in a clear and effective manner.	
AO2	Demonstration of the skills of application, analysis, interpretation and evaluation.	45–55%

AO1: You will need to know the following areas to obtain a high mark in knowledge and understanding:

- **The nature of sociological thought:** The AQA ask you to have a good knowledge of a range of theories, including Marxism, functionalism, feminism and interactionism. Other theories will also need to be covered such as the New Right and Weber's social action theory. Additionally, you will need to know how each of the theories sees social policy.

- **Methods of social enquiry:** As there is no coursework component the AQA have added a methods section to each unit. You will be required to know about the different methods sociologists use for research and how theory and methods are interlinked. So for instance, you would understand that quantitative methods tend to be linked with macro theories such as Marxism and functionalism.

- **Themes:** You are expected to cover two themes:

  1. Socialization, culture and identity: This theme is central to an understanding of the role of the family in contemporary society. For instance, the family plays an important role in the Socialization of children.

  2. Social differentiation, power and stratification.

AO2: This assessment objective asks you to be able to acquire and produce evidence and apply it to the question set. You will also be expected to be able to look at the strengths and weaknesses of each argument and come up with a reasoned conclusion. Evidence should be both from primary and secondary resources, and you will be expected to use both quantitative and qualitative data.

There are three sections you will need to tackle for AO2:

1. Collection and recording of evidence: Specifically you will need to evaluate the design of sociological research as it applies to the family and households. Secondly you must analyse and evaluate the methods used to collect data.

2. Interpretation and evaluation of evidence: It is essential that you do the following here: show objectivity, apply a range of theories to the questions set and use

appropriate concepts. So for instance, within the family you would be expected to understand what domestic labour is and which theorists would want to look at this debate within the family, to be able to interpret quantitative and qualitative data, interpret and evaluate trends within the family, such as divorce rates or birth rates, and most importantly be able to evaluate theories, knowing for example criticisms of functionalist notions of the family.

6. Presentation of evidence and argument: A level examiners expect you to be able to organise your written answers so there is coherence. This means that you are expected to start with an introduction, have a number of interlinked paragraphs and a conclusion. Within this answer you must use theory that would inform the question and include any evidence that would further answer the question. Within this you must draw conclusions and back these up with appropriate arguments.

Exam practice for AQA

Item A

The number of divorces granted in the UK has reached its highest level since 1996, new statistics reveal. In 2004, the number rose to 167 116 from 166 737 in 2003, the Office for National Statistics (ONS) figures show. In 1996 there were 171 700 divorces. Men and women aged 25–29 continued to have the highest divorce rates. Charity Relate said the rise was partly due to pressure being put on family life by an increasingly "individualistic way of living".

Item B

Children appear to be staying longer and longer at home, although they appear to 'grow up' at an ever increasing rate. The sociology of childhood is no longer straightforward to define. Even theorists disagree as to what is happening with childhood. So whilst some argue that childhood is being extended ever further, with children not being able to leave school until 16 years of age, others such as American Neil Postman argue that childhood is ending, with children having access to 'adult' information from an almost impossibly early age.

a. Explain what is meant by achieved status. *(2 Marks)*

b. Suggest two reasons why the number of first marriages has fallen. *(4 Marks)*

c. Suggest three reasons why lone-parent families are usually headed by women. *(6 Marks)*

d. Identify and briefly explain two reasons for the increase in the divorce rate apart from changes in divorce law. *(8 Marks)*

e. Examine the reasons for changes in the position of children in the family and society. *(24 Marks)*

f. Using material from Item 1B and elsewhere, assess sociological explanations of the increase in the number of divorces since the 1960s. *(24 Marks)*

g. increase in the number of divorces since the 1960s. *(24 Marks)*

Topic 4 · Education

Learning objectives

What the AQA spec says	Section in this book	Page
The role and purpose of education, including vocational education and training, in contemporary society.	Section One: Sociological views on education, training and the economy	152
The reaction of pupils to the education system.	Section Two: Educational achievement and different social groups (Part I)	162
Ethnicity and educational attainment.	Section Two: Educational achievement and different social groups (Part II)	168
Sociological methods used in educational research.	Section Two: Educational achievement and different social groups (Part III)	172
How schools are organised and how this structure helps the workplace. How the hidden curriculum impacts on educational success within schools. How different groups are affected by the processes that occur within schools.	Section Three: Relationships and processes within schools	182
Social policy and the education system.	Section Four: Educational policies	188
The differences between quantitative and qualitative research. Which methods are used. Whether sociology can be 'scientific'. The advantages and disadvantages of differing methods used in educational research.	Section Five: The application of research methods to education	198

Exam skill focus

Skills required	
AO1 Knowledge and understanding of theories.	Students need to know writers and theories associated with the UK education system.
AO2 Demonstration of the skills of application, analysis, interpretation and evaluation.	Students must be able to apply this knowledge of the education system and evaluate theories.

What it means to be studying education with AQA

According to sociologist Michael Rutter we spend 15 000 hours in the education system. Consequently the schooling process has a large role in forming our personalities. It also provides an excellent indicator of how political ideology affects social policy, with the changing of governments impacting on educational policy. This chapter provides an overview of how sociologists see the educational system. In **Section One** we look at the different theories that explain variations in educational attainment. Is the system fair? Why do some groups do well, whilst others fail? We examine whether the educational system is like a 'sausage-making machine', looking, for example, at the role of the hidden curriculum in shaping our personalities. **Section Two** examines individual groups and assesses the reasons for success or failure of the different classes, different ethnic groups and women. **Section Three** examines the social processes in schools. How important are teachers and the pupils themselves for success? Do labels impact on educational attainment? And how deterministic are such labels? In addition we examine which groups are most likely to suffer from stereotyping within schools. **Section Four** tracks the changes that have occurred within educational policy. Although students do not need to know all this detail, knowledge of the major acts is required. Finally in **Section Five**, we examine some of the methods used by sociologists to examine the 'black box' of schools, examining which are most appropriate, whilst also looking at the advantages and disadvantages of each of these methods.

Topic 4 Education

Sociologists studied in this topic

Louis Althusser (1965)	Argued that the bourgeoisie have at their disposal the ideological and the repressive state apparatus.
Louise Archer (2005)	Found that for Chinese and Asian girls, success and passive resistance can be seen as a problem as it can be a consequence of restrictive home cultures.
Stephen Ball (2003)	Looked at how market forces have affected parental choices about secondary school. He interviewed 150 parents.
Howard Becker (1963)	Claimed that social groups, teachers, doctors, the police, and so on create deviance.
Basil Bernstein (1961)	Claimed there are two speech codes. The restricted is associated with the working class and ethnic minorities. The elaborated code is the one used by the middle classes and in education.
Blackledge and Hunt (1985)	Evaluated the work of Willis and questioned his methodology.
Maud Blair (2001)	Concentrated on the over-representation of black boys in exclusions from school.
Raymond Boudon (1974)	Analysed the reasons that underpin inequality of educational opportunity and why it is that certain groups underachieve.
Pierre Bourdieu (1971)	Proposed the idea of 'cultural capital' and how the middle classes enable their children to achieve, generation on generation.
Bernard Coard (1971)	Thought that black children may develop an inferiority complex, low self image and low expectations of life as a result of being labelled educationally subnormal.
Isabelli Crespi (2003)	Examined gender socialization within the family and the way that this impacts upon girls experiences in education.
Davis and Moore (1945)	Looked at the way the social stratification system with differential rewards motivates people to work hard and apply themselves to the education system.
Sara Delamont (1990)	Found that girls reject 'failing working-class lads' because they cannot offer them the lifestyle that they seek.
Clifford Drew (1997)	Commented about some of the problems with using quantitative data in educational research.
Émile Durkheim (1961)	Looked at the role of education in society: how it unifies society and produces a homogenous mass.
Jannette Elwood (2005)	Used a weights analysis and found that coursework had less affect on girls' attainment than it did on boys'.
Leon Feinstein (2003)	Used secondary data to establish the variables that affect participation rates in education.
Alasdair Forsyth and Andy Furlong (2000)	Argued in their research that children from low-income families tend to opt for less prestigious colleges and courses.
Margaret Fuller (1984)	Examined how black students in London interacted with the stereotypes associated with being female and being black. Developed the idea of labeling and self-fulfilling prophecy.

David Gillborn and Deborah Youdell (2000)	Believed that policies within school to improve attainment have concentrated upon A–C students.
Michael Haralambos (1980)	Wrote *The Blue Bible* that many students have used to guide them through A level Sociology.
David Hargreaves (1967)	Examined the ways that teachers categorises pupils in terms of ability.
David Jesson and David Crossley (2006)	Believed that specialist school status has had a positive impact on GCSE results.
Nell Keddie (1971)	Concluded that the differentiation of pupils by teachers in comprehensive schools was as effective as official streaming in impeding the progress of working class children in grammar schools.
Colin Lacey (1970)	Noted that anti-school cultures are created, even amongst relatively high flying students because they saw themselves as being failures compared to their friends.
Mairtin Mac an Ghaill (1992)	Analysed the extent to which racism is evident in the education system.
Angela McRobbie (1975)	Implied that women actively negotiate their female identities in response to how the school sees them.
Heidi Safia Mirza (1992)	Discovered that there were wide variations of education success or failure amongst different ethnic groups.
Talcott Parsons (1950s)	Argued that the school was the main focal socialising agency in that it transmitted society's norms and values and ensured that pattern maintenance was being met. Made the distinction between ascribed and achieved status. Proposed that modern western democracies were 'meritocratic.'
Diane Reay (2000)	Found that there appears to be very little difference between the classes when it comes to aspirations for their children.
Tony Sewell (2002)	Suggested that the biggest problem for black pupils is peer group pressure.
Farzana Shain (2003)	Interviewed 44 girls as part of her thesis. Used a typology similar to Merton to show how Asian girls coped with racism in schools.
Sue Sharpe (1976)	Looked at how the aspirations of girls changed over time from being family orientated to being career orientated.
Anne West et al. (2003)	Established that the middle classes were in an advantageous position when it came to admission into secondary school.
Paul Willis (1977)	Argued that the education system does not offer equality of opportunity, but merely replicates the class system generation on generation.
Helen Wilkinson (1994)	Argued that what she calls the 'genderquake' has led to women wanting to be financially independent.

My mock examination for this topic is in ....

I will be examined on this topic in ....

Sociological views on education, training and the economy

Education as an agent of socialization

Education performs an incredibly important role in society and shapes us from the age of four until we are often in our early twenties. During that time education gives us the knowledge to pass examinations, but we also learn attitudes and expectations that are not taught as part of the formal curriculum. This knowledge is learnt by the process called the hidden curriculum. This phrase was coined by Philip Jackson (1968), with Michael Haralamboss' definition providing the best definition:

> *The hidden curriculum consists of those things pupils learn through the experience of attending school rather than the stated educational objectives of such institutions* (2004).

Whilst many children see little value in these attitudes and expectations, they play an important role in shaping us for our future role as an employee.

What important principles have shaped the education system?

People imagine that the education system has been around for a long time, given Britain's heritage as a major industrial producer during the eighteenth century, but the reality is rather different. Great Britain was economically successful during this era, despite the fact that there was no formal educational system. One of the reasons for this success was the often barbaric way children were used as a productive resource. By the middle part of the eighteenth century a succession of factory acts (1833, 1844, 1847 and 1850) started to limit the hours and employment of children. This inevitably led politicians to consider the educational needs of children. The beginnings of the system occurred relatively late, with the introduction of the Elementary Education Act 1870, more commonly known as the Forster Education Act in recognition of the role of William Edward Forster, Vice President of the Committee of Council on Education.

The act itself first introduced the idea of compulsory education for all those under the age of 13. There were a number of reasons why education was made compulsory. These included:

- **To create a highly trained and efficient workforce:** The importance of schooling for the economy has long been recognised by sociologists. Many sociologists are aware that good education leads to a more productive workforce, and thus high levels of literacy, numeracy and vocational skills are considered essential. It was argued by reformers that these skills would improve the quality of recruits in the forces, reduce crime and discourage revolutionary urges. One has to remember that around Europe revolution had occurred in countries close to England.

- **To sift and differentiate between pupils:** Another essential part of the system is the process of picking out the most talented individuals in a way that is entirely meritocratic: based on merit rather than class or ethnicity. It was felt that this would encourage academic talent from all parts of society, rather than merely concentrating upon the gentry.

- **Socialization:** Education is also an effective way to instil similar norms and values amongst all members of society.

Many of these remain important tenets of the educational system today, with the development of Specialised Diplomas being introduced in 2008, showing how important the government sees the introduction of vocational qualifications. Government plans to increase the school leaving age indicate that they see education as an important way of instilling

Émile Durkheim

norms and values that help within the workplace. What kind of socialization schools convey and who most benefits from the educational system forms the basis of the ideological debates within the sociology of education. What exactly is the role of the education system? Is the education fair and meritocratic? And why do some groups do so much better than others? These are questions that we need to answer to understand how different ideologies see the education system. We will now look in turn at each of the major theories that seek to explain these questions.

Functionalism

Functionalists argue that education performs a number of functions, laying particular emphasis on three areas in relation to stability:

- Education promotes social solidarity (**Émile Durkheim**) through learning the social rules of behaviour of a society from one generation to the next.

- Education promotes cooperation through the learning of social rules of behaviour. These are backed up by sanctions. People are socialised effectively to help them become more effective workers. Therefore functionalists have little problem with the idea of the hidden curriculum.

- Education develops all those special skills needed in society. These include the essential skills of literacy, numeracy and cooperation. People are able to locate their most appropriate role in society as a result of their experiences in school (**Davis and Moore**, 1967).

We will now briefly look at the most influential functionalist writers and how each sees the role of the educational system.

Émile Durkheim

Émile Durkheim (1858–1917) has been highly influential in the sociology of education, especially in the work of **Basil Bernstein**. He believed a vital task of the educational system was 'the welding of a mass of individuals into a united whole' (Bernstein, 1961). In other words, people from all backgrounds need to form a united society. This can best be done, according to Durkheim, by teaching subjects such as history (so they see themselves as part of something bigger than just themselves), English (to learn a common language) and having a national curriculum that instils shared norms and values to all races and creeds. Durkheim believed that the function of social institutions was to promote and maintain social cohesion and unity. One way of explaining social solidarity is to use the 'blu-tack' analogy. The role of society, according to Durkheim, is to bond people from lots of different cultures, and you can separate your 'blu-tack' to show this, consequently blending it again into a united whole.

Talcott Parsons

Since Durkheim's death, modern functionalists such as Talcott Parsons have built on his ideas; using his conservative and middle-American values to guide them. Parsons agreed that the educational system is important in providing a basis for Socialization. He also stressed the functions it performs in allocating individuals to their social roles.

Value consensus

If this system is to survive it must have a degree of compatibility. Many functionalists believe that this integration is based upon agreement about values. If this agreement is expressed in the institutions, those parts will be integrated in society. According to Parsons the two key values possessed by all societies are **equality of opportunity** and the **value of achievement**. What Parsons means by this is that there is a shared culture and agreement on what is important.

Universalistic judgement

Functionalists are very keen to stress that the education system is a **meritocracy**. This is the idea that everyone has equal opportunity for achievements, or that position and reward is based on effort or ability.

Therefore one primary role that Parsons envisages for education is allocating individuals to their social roles. He sees this as being achieved through an examination system, which awards qualifications according to merit. Individuals are filtered so that they can then be allocated to the most appropriate job for them. The educational system also provides the skills, values and attitudes that individuals will need to do their jobs properly and contribute as much as possible to society. The idea of judging pupils across all their age groups and sifting and sorting them according to ability is called **universalistic judgement**. Within schools such judgements are made at **branching points**. These are time periods when pupils move from one key stage to another, or transfer to a different school. Within the UK system branching points occur at ages 7, 11, 14, 16 and 18. At all these ages

pupils are expected to take exams that grade and sort them according to ability.

Functional prerequisites (AGIL)

From this perspective, society has certain needs that have to be met if society is to survive. Parsons believes that society has four basic functions to perform. To allow people:

- To adapt to their environment (**A**daptation)
- To mobilise their resources in order to achieve its goals (**G**oal attainment)
- To maintain the internal coordination of its parts and keep itself together (**I**ntegration)
- To maintain itself in a state of equilibrium (**L**atent pattern maintenance)

Role allocation: Davis and Moore

This perspective argues that inequality is a natural feature of society, since people are born with different talents. The functions of education are to allocate and recruit people to the wide range of positions in society. Moreover, for society to function there has to be a method of ensuring all the necessary occupational roles are filled. Many more factory workers are needed than doctors are for example. Davis and Moore thus believe that the functionally most important jobs need to be given to the most qualified or intelligent people.

Summary of functionalist view of the role of education

Functionalism lays emphasis on three areas in relation to stability:

- Education promotes social solidarity through learning the social rules of behaviour of a society from one generation to the next (Durkheim).
- Education promotes cooperation through the learning of social rules of behaviour. These are backed up by sanctions. People are socialised effectively.
- Education develops all the skills needed in society. People are able to locate their most appropriate role in society as a result of their experiences in school (Davis and Moore).

However, functionalism, although popular in the 1960s and 1970s, has come under fierce criticism more recently.

Criticisms of functionalism

- It is doubtful that all pupils **internalise** the same norms and values. This is because the educational diet of students varies according to class, gender and ethnicity.
- The ability of the educational system to equip students with practical and technical skills has to be queried. Most training in schools is too academic and there has never been a vocational sector that has the same status as 'educational knowledge'.
- The norms and values transmitted by schools are not necessarily those of society as a whole, but those from the middle classes. It is thus a class-centric approach.
- Functionalism fails to adequately deal with the role of interaction within the classroom. Sometimes failure is due to social processes not structural reasons.

Functionalism	Marxism
Writers: Parsons, Davis and Moore, Durkheim.	Writers: Bowles and Gintis, Paul Willis, Louis Althusser.
Based upon social consensus and the notion that all benefit.	Based upon conflict between the proletariat and the bourgeoisie, Marxists believe that the elite benefit from the educational system.
View education's role is to socialise and encourage the development of a common culture.	By means of 'symbolic violence', the ruling elite can define what is considered knowledge and deny access to those who are not from a middle-class or upper-class backgrounds.
Education allocates individuals to the most appropriate jobs. It does this by sorting them according to their ability.	Allocation is not based on meritocracy, but instead to the class in which a person belongs.

Marxism

So far we have assumed that education benefits all; However, Marxists reject this notion. The conflicting view is that groups have fundamentally different interests; thus some will benefit more than others.

Functionalists and Marxists share the belief that schools and training schemes transmit norms and values that create social stability in society. However, whereas functionalists believe that this stability is based upon the internalisation of socially agreed norms and values, Marxists believe that it is based upon the internalisation of the dominant ideologies that benefit a ruling elite. This, they argue, is done subtly, encouraging the majority to believe that the continuing domination of the ruling elite within the educational system is the result of higher intelligence or the failure of the working classes. They believe this working class failure is internalised without being challenged, leading to the continued compliance of the working classes.

TRINITY HALL

COLLEGE
CLOSED
NO ENTRY
FOR
VISITORS

How is this achieved?

The way in which the educational system serves to help capitalists is that it ensures that the pupils' personality, attitudes and values are shaped in such a way as to make the pupils useful for capitalism and to make money.

Schools act as an important agency of social control, which encourage children to learn and conform to the values and norms expected of society. This is mainly carried out through the hidden curriculum: so called because there are no obvious, organised courses in 'obedience and conformity' as there are in English and Maths. Nevertheless, this hidden curriculum is present throughout schooling, and those who conform are likely to be rewarded, whilst those who do not are branded as non-conformists by the school and may find themselves getting into trouble. The hidden curriculum is transmitted in a number of ways: students are conditioned to be pliable and subservient by the seating plans in classrooms, the layout of the classroom, the way they talk to and address teachers and the way that they are spoken to by teachers. Students are systematically disempowered and marginalised.

Marxists quote a number of key studies to show how the educational system shapes pupils to be useful to capitalism. We will now look at each of these in turn.

Bowles and Gintis

Bowles and Gintis argue that the major function of education is to reproduce labour power. In particular they maintain there is close **correspondence** between social relations that govern personal interaction in the workplace and the social relationships in education. The following quote gives an indication of how strong this relationship is:

Work casts a long shadow over the educational system; education is subservient to the needs of those who control the workforce, the owners of the factors of production. (Bowles and Gintis, 1976)

The ways in which the hidden curriculum shapes pupils

Bowles and Gintis argue that pupils are shaped in the following ways:

The educational system helps to produce a subservient workforce

In their study of a senior school in New York they found that 237 members of the school were rewarded more in relation to personality than academic abilities. Low grades had a tendency to be related to creativity, aggressiveness and independence; traits most likely to be attributed to the working classes. By contrast, higher grades were given related to persistence, steadiness and dependability and punctuality: character traits usually exhibited by the middle classes. Thus Bowles and Gintis found that the system seems to be producing passive, unimaginative and unquestioning workers.

The educational system encourages the acceptance of hierarchy

Bowles and Gintis believed teachers give orders, pupils obey. Students have little control over the educational process, preparing them for their lives at work. In the workplace similar patterns will be observed.

Motivation by external reward

Just as in the workplace people tend to be motivated by money, so similarly the boredom and monotony of school is helped by the future reward of high income, rather than any intrinsic enjoyment of the work itself. Thus, the idea of good qualifications that promise high incomes provide the incentive to study hard. Similarly, the workplace and jobs themselves

tend to be boring and workers are likewise motivated by **external reward**, such as monetary.

Fragmentation of knowledge

Lessons at school tend to be in single subjects. Often little effort is made to connect one subject to another even though there might be strong links. This aspect of education corresponds to what happens in the workplace, where individuals are given specialised tasks. This stops the possibility of workers gaining enough knowledge of the production process to set up in competition to the capitalist. It also divides workers into different areas with different pay. This helps to divide and rule workers, discouraging them from uniting to tackle the owners of the factors of production.

The benefits of the educational system to capitalism

The system thus produces passive and obedient workers who:

- Do not question capitalism
- Accept authority, and conform to what their bosses tell them to do
- Are motivated by external rewards
- Are suitably fragmented

The formal parts of the curriculum meet the needs of capitalists:

- What happens in the schooling system corresponds to the workplace, thus making it easier for workers to be easily assimilated into the rigours of Capitalism.
- Because the population is well educated as a whole this allows capitalists to have a wide choice of workers. This ensures a high level of people who are unemployed. It also provides a deterrent against non-conformity in the workplace. In reality a lot of jobs do not need high qualifications.
- It legitimates inequality. Those who fail are told the system is fair and that failure is down to their own shortcomings. This masks the true nature of their failure, which for Marxists is down to their class background.

How Marxists see role allocation

Marxists argue that the educational and occupational status is based upon social class rather than meritocracy. The process of cultural reproduction works against the meritocratic principles surrounding schools. In essence it is dictated that working-class children grow up to get working-class jobs, and the best, most enticing jobs, with the highest job satisfaction are reserved for the middle classes. As a result Marxists believe that there is very little social mobility with schools ensuring that the working classes believe their failure to be a result of their lack of intellectual prowess rather than anything to do with the system.

A Marxist analysis of the educational system

- Marxists such as Bowles and Gintis reject functionalist claims of meritocracy

- For them class is the most important factor in possible success

- Marxists claim that the ruling elite have much greater opportunities and thus tend to obtain better jobs, irrespective of their abilities

The Work of Paul Willis (*Learning to Labour*, 1977)

Willis provides the classic critique to the work of Bowles and Gintis. Willis' work is influenced in its structural part by the theories of the French sociologist, **Louis Althusser** (1972), who argued that the education system is primarily an **ideological state apparatus** concerned with the cultural reproduction of capitalism. Althusser's argument is that the main function of education is to ensure that privileges of one generation are passed down to the next by the process of ideological conditioning to be found in schooling. Willis draws on the idea of cultural reproduction, but wishes to examine the processes in schools which contribute to the transfer of privilege and disadvantage across the generations.

Paul Willis

Willis' methodology

The main question Willis attempts to answer is 'Why do working class kids fail?' To understand this phenomenon he adopted an **ethnographic approach** (using observation as a research method), which included observation and interviews. His approach can be considered innovative as he combined structurally-based, outside-school explanations with action-based, interactionist, inside-school explanations. Willis' combination of micro and macro perspectives is a classic example of what A. Giddens calls **structuration theory** (structure and action perspectives combined into one set of ideas). Classically this uses both quantitative and qualitative methods together. For example, Willis uses participant observation and personal diaries to achieve this when studying a group of 12 working class boys (the lads) during their last year-and-a-half at school and their first few months at work.

He watched the lads in a number of different situations. He then connected this small-scale interaction to the wider social structure. Willis' study was a sophisticated attempt at studying a small group in a number of different ways. The school he studied was in a small industrial town, chosen to be representative of all working-class schools.

Willis' findings

Unlike Bowles and Gintis, Willis found no clear **correspondence** between school and work. Nor did he find that the lads were shaped by the educational system. Instead the lads rejected school, and created their own counter school culture. Ironically, this very rejection of school prepared them for the low-skilled, low-status jobs they were to take. Features of the counter-culture included:

- The lads felt superior to the teachers and to the conformist pupils.

- They attached little or no value to school work.

- They had no desire to gain qualifications.

- They avoided going to lessons or, when attendance was unavoidable, did as little work as possible. For instance, Willis gives an example of the lads deciding to attend a lesson because the deputy head was the teacher.

- They resented the school taking control of their time.

- While not working, they kept themselves amused by "having a laugh". 'During films in the hall they would tie the projector leads into impossible knots, make animal figures or obscene shapes on the screen with their fingers, and gratuitously dig and jab into the backs of the "ear oles" in front of them'. In class they would annoy the teacher by as many means possible.

- Willis gives a description of a school outing to a museum: 'The back seats of the coach are covered with graffiti and names in indelible ink, and in the museum every possible "don't touch" sign is blatantly ignored … The lads are a plague of locusts … blackening out pomp and dignity'.

- For them, the real excitement was to be found in the outside world. It was their night-time activities in clubs and pubs that kindled their interest. They were even prepared to work to get money to indulge in the smoking and drinking that made them identify with the outside world.

- Their counter-culture was strongly sexist. They saw girls in a poor light, and saw the 'ear oles' as sissies, lacking masculinity.

- They were very racist, seeing people from other cultures as inferior.

- They wanted to leave school at the earliest possible opportunity and looked forward to going to work. They were prepared to take any work, so long as it was a masculine manual job. For them, white-collar jobs were all boringly similar and manual jobs were seen to be 'real' jobs.

- For the lads the extra effort needed to do well at school was not worth it.

From all of this, Willis notes that the education system does not seem to be producing the ideal worker. They are evidently neither obedient nor passive. Yet Willis suggests that they may have prepared themselves for the work they do. It was their very rejection of school that made them suitable for unskilled or semi-skilled jobs. Willis followed the lads into the workplace, where he observed that many of the behaviours that occurred in school were carried through into the workplace. Willis claims that their behaviour both at school and at work was a way of coping with the tedium and oppression of work and study.

Similarities between the counter-school culture and shop-floor culture

Willis found a number of similarities between the attitudes and behaviour developed by the lads in school and those of the shop floor at work. Having 'a laugh' was important in both situations as a means of dealing with monotony and authority. At work, as at school, the bunch of mates liked to mess around. So, like Bowles and Gintis, Willis argues that there is a strong correspondence between school and work. But the school does not produce

this: the lads are not the docile, obedient pupils of Bowles and Gintis' study. They created the correspondence by their rejection of the school and, in so doing, they prepared themselves for their place in the workforce. However, the lads' culture is not entirely adapted to the requirements of the capitalistic workforce. It contains an important, albeit largely hidden, criticism of the dominant ideology of individualism and equality of opportunity. There is an understood recognition that individual effort does not necessarily bring success, that a meritocratic society does not exist, and that collective action is needed to improve the situation of the working classes. However, this is a long way from recognising the true nature of capitalistic oppression and exploitation.

Criticisms of Paul Willis' *Learning to Labour*

Willis' study has come in for some harsh criticism:

- Willis' sample is considered too small. He chose only 12 working-class lads, all male, and not necessarily typical of the schools he studied or schoolchildren as a whole.

- Perhaps central to Willis' study is that it was conducted in the final years when most young men could be sure of getting fairly well-paid manual jobs. Almost immediately after his study the economy went into rapid decline.

- Willis is thought to have focused too much on counter-school culture and ignored the sociological significance of conformist sub-cultures.

- **Blackledge and Hunt** suggest that Willis misinterpreted some evidence. They argue that in his work there is little basis on which to claim that the lads develop the same attitudes as previous generations of workers.

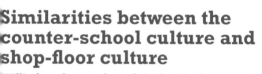

What do you know now?

1. Explain why it was considered important to make education compulsory in the UK.

2. Isolate the similarities between functionalist and Marxist views on education.

3. What functions does the education system perform for functionalists?

4. What functions does the education system perform for Marxists?

5. Explain why Bowles and Gintis suggest that personality attributes are more important than intelligence.

6. How does the work of Paul Willis offer a critique to Bowles and Gintis' research?

7. Give three criticisms of both functionalist and Marxist explanations of the functions of the educational system.

Key terms

Branching points: Clear points at which examinations are used to decide the future of pupils in the educational system.

Correspondence principle: Phrase coined by Bowles and Gintis to suggest that what occurs in school reflects what happens in the workplace.

Ethnographic approach: This would focus on the role of observation to uncover meanings and realities. Derives from the work of Weber and his central concept of 'Verstehen' meaning 'empathy.'

Equality of opportunity: Circumstances in which every person has an equal chance, particularly in areas such as education, employment and political participation.

External reward: Returns that are based upon financial remuneration, rather than any other reason, such as enjoyment.

Hidden curriculum: All those things that are learnt by pupils without them being formally taught as part of the official curriculum.

Ideological state apparatus: The term used by the French Marxist philosopher Althusser to refer to the agencies who are at the disposal of the bourgeoisie who use these tools to convey 'hegemony' to convey obedience and conformity: to get us all to sit down shut up and do what we are told when we are told.

Internalise: To take in and make an integral part of one's attitudes or beliefs.

Meritocracy: The idea that everyone has equal opportunity to achieve, or that position and reward is based on effort or ability.

Structuration theory: Advocated by Giddens. Tries to unite the macro and micro elements of sociology. People have choice and make conscious rationale decisions, but they do so within a limited and narrow spectrum of choice. For example, people have the choice to buy whatever clothes they wish, but the clothes that they have to opt for are the ones in the shops, thus reducing true choice. This applies to all areas of sociology.

Universalistic judgement: The way schoolchildren are judged against our peer group. From this they are sifted and sorted and allocated to sets in terms of ability.

Value of achievement: In modern complex societies we have a specialised division of labour. We have some jobs that require a great deal of skill and intelligence. Such societies have moved to the position where they promote 'value of achievement' in order to ensure that the most able apply themselves to the task at hand and rise up the social hierarchy.

Section summary

Education performs an important role in society and shapes us from an early age until we are often in our early twenties.

The education system was introduced to create a well-trained and efficient workforce, to sort pupils in order of ability and to socialise pupils into the prevailing culture.

Functionalists argue that education performs a number of functions: to promote social solidarity, to encourage cooperation and to develop the essential skills of literacy and numeracy.

Parsons believes that the educational system is important in providing a basis for Socialization.

Davis and Moore see the functions of education system as being to allocate and recruit people to the range of positions in society.

Functionalism has been criticised by writers who believe it is doubtful that all pupils internalise the same norms and values.

Marxists are critical of functionalists and suggest that it is the ideas of the ruling classes that are internalised rather than those of society in general.

Bowles and Gintis argue that the major role of education is to reproduce labour power. In particular they maintain there is close correspondence between social relations, which govern personal interaction in the workplace and the social relationships in education.

Willis' work criticises Bowles and Gintis in that he believes that the education system does not produce subservient workers. Instead he found in his study that there was no clear correspondence between school and work.

In general functionalists and Marxists have been criticised for ignoring the subjective feelings of the social actors within the education system.

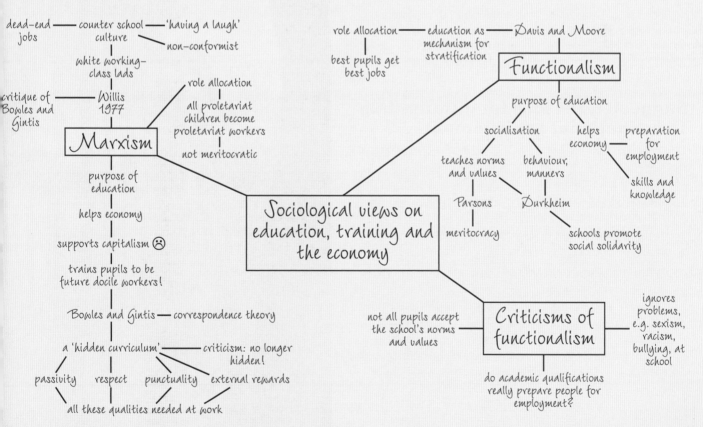

Educational achievement and different social groups (Part I)

Introduction

Sociologists have long looked at extensive patterns when it comes to educational results. This quantitative or macro approach has exposed a persistent trend, indicating that those from the working classes tend to do less well in examinations, have less motivation, and are more inclined to seek instant gratification rather than staying on to further their educational qualifications. A recent unpublished report by the Department for Education and Skills (DfES) (Webber, 2006) matched almost one million pupils with their individual postcode and exam scores at ages 11 and 15. The report showed that a child's social background is the vital factor in academic performance, and that a school's success is based largely on the class background of its pupils. Researchers have also found that other factors such as gender and ethnicity are also pivotal to educational success.

Suggested reasons for differentials in educational achievement

Home background has been a particular focus of sociology to explain underachievement in education. Four distinct explanations have emerged:

1. **Material deprivation theory:** Income inequality and the problems associated with it.

2. **Cultural deprivation theory:** Differing attitudes to education between the classes.

3. **Cultural difference theory:** Bernstein, Bourdieu. Derives from 'Social Darwinism'. The belief that certain groups are culturally inferior or superior to others: a value judgement.

4. **Interactionist theory:** Micro sociology, rejection of macro sociology, rejection of positivism. Looks at ways in which meanings and labels are created, applied and enforced; for example, deviance in the education system.

Material deprivation

Working-class parents tend to earn lower incomes than middle-class parents (although it should be noted that some do rather well, with plumbers and electricians often earning more than teachers, for example). As a result their children usually experience **material deprivation** such as a less than healthy diet and unsatisfactory housing conditions. This lack of income is said to hinder their chances at school as judged by examination and SATs results. For example, Douglas' 1964 **longitudinal study,** *Home and School,* offered partial support to this materialist approach. In the study he found that poor housing conditions in particular depressed school performance. Admittedly, this study was some time ago, but many would claim it is still relevant today.

Governments have long tried to tackle this issue by **positive discrimination** or **compensatory education** that targets

poor areas and then seeks to spend money on encouraging improved attitudes toward education. This compensatory education was first used in America during the Kennedy Presidency in the early 1960s as part of the War on Poverty and during the Johnson presidency with Operation Head Start. With these programmes additional capital was put into pre-school amenities for the poor. However, the results of this effort were considered disappointing for **cultural deprivation** theorists, with researchers finding that merely throwing money at the problem did not bring dividends.

In Britain, the ideas of Operation Head Start came later, ten years after the start of the American programme and resulted from calls by leading academics such as A.H. Halsey who asked for positive discrimination for schools in deprived areas. Geographical areas were designated educational priority areas (EPAs) in the 1960s – and later Educational Action Zones (EAZs) in the late 1990s – and teachers were paid more to work in EPA schools. More recent policies include the Sure

Start programme which was launched in 1998, with the aim to drive down child poverty and exclusion. To do this the programme sought to increase the availability of childcare for all children; improve children's health, education and emotional development; support parents in their role, and develop employment aspirations.

EAZs were created by the Schools Standards and Framework Act 1998 and were given a maximum lifespan of five years on their inception. EAZs were developed around a group of schools determined to raise educational standards in challenging area'. There were usually 15–25 schools in each zone. The aims of EAZs were to:

- Create new partnerships involving business, parents, local authorities, schools and their communities
- Raise standards
- Generate innovation from which the whole educational system can learn

To help them meet these targets each EAZ was allocated £1 million. However, the government decided that the scheme was not working as well as it liked and pulled the funding for this programme in 2003. The government also introduced the Excellence in Cities (EiC) programme which was launched in 1999. Its aims were to:

- Drive up standards higher and faster in schools in cities, towns and rural areas in order to match the standards of excellence found in the best schools.

- Improve leadership, behaviour, and teaching and learning.

- Increase the diversity of school provision so that the needs of all pupils could be met.

- Network schools together so they work with each other to overcome inequality and poor provision.

- Enhance the quality in all schools rather than reinforce existing inequalities. Make excellence the norm.

Although the programme was initially focused on secondary schools, it developed to include primary schools and worked closely with the Primary National Strategy (a way that the government via LEAs ensures that the schools are focusing on the correct areas [for example, Literacy, Science, IT]. Advice and support is given to schools in a desire to drive up standards.) As a result, over 1300 secondary and 3600 primary schools have been involved in the programme since it began.

The following five policy strands were central to the programme:

1. **Improve provision for gifted children:** This happened with the introduction of a national strategy which included summer schools held across the UK at universities such as Cambridge and Oxford.

2. **Learning mentors:** There are approximately 8000 learning mentors across the UK, with one of the main focuses being to reduce the number of exclusions amongst disadvantaged groups.

3. **Learning Support Units (LSUs):** LSUs are school-based centres for pupils who are disaffected with conventional schooling, at risk of exclusion or vulnerable because of family or social issues.

4. **Beacon schools:** These were established in 1998, prior to the introduction of the EiC programme. The Beacon schools programme as a central government-funded programme was phased out by August 2005 and as a result there will be no further designations or renewals of contracts in the future. The Beacon schools programme identified high-performing schools across England that represented examples of successful practice, and asked them to share good practice with other schools in the surrounding area.

5. **Specialist schools:** The programme was initially designed to encourage maintained secondary schools to specialise in technology (along with science and mathematics). It

was extended in 1994 to include modern foreign languages and in 1996 to cover sports and arts. There were, therefore, four types of specialist schools at the time when EiC was launched.

The government has also been trying to tackle the historically low staying-on rates of post-16-year-old students. One of its chief weapons to achieve this has been the introduction of **Educational Maintenance Allowance** (EMA). Its aims are to:

- Reduce the number of 16-year-olds leaving education

- Reduce the amount of time spent in part-time employment

- Contribute to transport costs, thereby allowing students to travel to school or colleges of their choice

- Provide the student with more money to spend on course-related costs

There is a concern that recent changes have encouraged fewer working-class pupils to attend university. **Alasdair Forsyth** and **Andy Furlong** (2003) of the University of Glasgow found that a number of factors put off the working classes from attending university. A primary concern is the cost of higher education, particularly the prospect of gaining large debts through student loans. This affected both students and their parents. The report comments that this often led working-class students to apply for shorter, less academic courses. And if working-class students do go to university, it often means that they have to work around their studies.

More recent figures, however, show that although there was a blip when top-up fees – which are paid after graduation – were introduced in 2005, by 2006 applications through UCAS had increased by 6.4 per cent. However, at present there has not been enough research to explore the impact these changes have had on lower socio-economic groups. Any decrease would be extremely serious given the overall increase in applications.

Cultural deprivation theory

This theory asserts that there are different attitudes towards education dependent on which social class a person belongs to. It is thought that working-class attitudes and values fail to adequately prepare children for education, wheras middle-class systems do.

This notion is based upon the assumption that most working-class parents have a value system that encourages children to drop out of education early and to underplay its importance. However, this attributes these values to the working classes as a whole; when in reality they may only exist in parts of it. It also ignores the long tradition of self-help in areas of the working classes. In terms of cultural deprivation theory, the solution to working-class underachievement lay in three areas:

1. Working-class culture would have to change; to become similar to middle-class culture.

2. Working-class children would have to be compensated for their home background by the provision of extra

educational resources that would give them an equal opportunity to compete with their culturally advantaged middle-class peers.

3. Extra education resources would have to involve pre-school educational compensation. According to educational psychology, the 'damage' done to children by exposure to the working-class culture by primary Socialization was too far advanced by the time a child reached school age for compensatory education to be of any real benefit.

A number of studies, such as Douglas' (1964) and the *Plowden Report* (1967), have found that working-class parents tend to offer less encouragement towards their children's education than middle-class parents, and that this goes some way to explain the differences between the classes. However, others note that the apparent lack of interest by working-class parents may mask a lack of confidence or knowledge of dealing with schools, rather than indifference to their children's fate.

A far more recent study was conducted by the University of Sunderland, looking into the differences in parental satisfaction, expectation and attribution in St. Petersburg, Sunderland and Kentucky (Elliott et al., 2002). The paper concludes that the important role of parents in supporting children's educational progress is undermined by the current emphasis in the UK on schools being fundamentally responsible for ensuring high levels of achievement.

In addition **Leon Feinstein**, Director of the Centre for Research on the Wider Benefits of Learning at the Institute of Education and London University (2007), proved that by the age of three children from underprivileged families lag up to a year behind wealthier social groups in social and educational development because of the more proactive attitudes of the middle classes.

Cultural difference theory

The cultural difference theory focuses on the mismatch between working-class and middle-class cultures in schools. It is most often associated with the work of writers such as **Basil Bernstein** and **Pierre Bourdieu**. The French sociologist Pierre Bourdieu starts with the idea that there is a dominant culture. The higher people's position in the class structure, the greater the amount of dominant culture they possess. This culture is generally regarded as superior because those at the top have the power to define it as such. Because it is highly valued and sought after, it forms the basis of the educational system. For example, the bourgeoisie's control over the economic system means their children pick up the **cultural capital** (knowledge, appropriate behaviour, language, taste and lifestyle) to give them material benefits (capital). Bourdieu introduced the concept of 'habitus': a set of acquired patterns of thought, behaviour and taste – passed on by each generation – which shape behaviour towards the educational system. Because the working classes do not possess similar acquired patterns, they are less likely to be educationally successful.

Pierre Bourdieu

Why the middle classes have an inbuilt advantage

Children who are born into middle and upper classes are exposed to a culture that is closer to the culture of school to those who are born into the lower classes. They are therefore more likely to be educationally successful. For example, their speech and writing tends to be closer to that of teachers, so they better understand what is being taught and are rewarded for their work. Marxists call this process **symbolic violence**; the dominant classes inflict definitions of which subjects are considered worthy of consideration. The middle classes thus impose and define their interpretation of what counts as intelligence and what a knowledgeable activity is, based on what they consider important.

The social function of elimination

As the pupil moves up the educational ladder, those from the working classes are progressively eliminated or sidelined into lower-status forms of education, particularly vocational qualifications. Although you can claim that the system acts 'neutrally' or fairly in the sense that it evaluates all children (universally), not all students start from the same educational point. The process of examination failure achieves this elimination.

Success at exams will therefore be limited for those from working-class backgrounds due to their lack of dominant culture. Self-elimination is achieved because working-class children know what is in store for them, with attitudes shaped by the system. From the outset they are taught not to value their particular skills as they are not in line with the dominant culture. The important thing here is that the working-class students accept their failure as being fair and normal, and don't question it.

Other ways cultural capital may be beneficial to the middle classes

Although the work of many of the writers discussed above has been criticised for lacking empirical sincerity, this has been remedied more recently in a study by **Diane Reay** (2000). Reay found that there appears to be very little difference between the classes when it comes to aspirations for their children, with almost all classes seeing education as a way to social mobility. Reay utilised the concept of 'emotional labour' to explain the crucial role that mothers play in passing on cultural capital and argued that this is achieved in a number of ways. Firstly, the middle classes are able to compensate for their children's poor performance; either by helping them with their schoolwork or by employing others to do this job. Secondly, because middle-class women tend to work part-time, this allows them to deal with teachers when they believe that their children are not being pushed hard enough or are suffering from substandard teaching.

West et al. (2003) found that the middle classes were in an advantageous position when it came to interviews for admission into secondary school. They believe that policymakers should promote socially diverse schools, thereby allowing the chance of educational success for the working classes as well as those in privileged positions.

Interactionist theory

The interactionist approach explains the differential educational attainment by seeing education as directed by meanings and definitions that are negotiated in school. From this perspective class differences in education are socially constructed in the classroom.

Labelling and the self-fulfilling prophecy suggest ways in which teachers' reaction to individual pupils can affect their educational career. It is also possible, however, that whole groups, not just individuals, can be treated in different ways. Despite the fact that under the comprehensive system all state-educated children attend the same type of school, this may not mean that they all receive the same type of education. In many comprehensives pupils are placed, for at least some of the time, in different classes according to their supposed abilities.

Diane Rea

According to **Becker** (1963) and other interactionist sociologists, the power of the label, backed by the authority of the teacher, is such that it is difficult for the pupil to escape it (similar to career-work in crime and deviance). The individual pupil will come to accept the label, their self-definition will be strongly influenced by it and their actions will reflect the behaviour usually associated with that label.

So a pupil, who is labelled by a teacher as 'disruptive', even though they may have only misbehaved in a relatively minor fashion, may well suppose that they are a disruptive student and act accordingly. One of the effects of being labelled in this way is the lowering of a pupil's self-esteem. Becker also showed that teachers frequently made their evaluations of pupils and students in relation to how close they corresponded to the concept of an 'ideal pupil'. Students were judged in relation to how they completed work, how tidy it was, and whether they were punctual and conscientious in their studies.

Interactionists then go on to assert that the process of banding and **streaming** creates pro- and anti-school cultures. Writers such as Hargreaves (1967) and Stephen Ball (1981) found that lower streams created an anti-school, anti-academic culture because the school had labelled them as failures. These pupils placed a high value on behaviour that teachers would regard as disorderly as they realised that this was the only way that they could gain status. This process is called **status frustration**. Other writers, such as Lacey (1970), found anti-school cultures being created even amongst relatively high-flying students because they saw themselves as being failures compared to their friends.

Further research by **Nell Keddie** (1971) examined the humanities department of a large, socially mixed, comprehensive school. Keddie was interested in the processes involved in the production of academic failures. The classes she studied were not streamed as tended to be the case with the new 'comprehensive system', yet careful scrutiny of teachers both inside and outside of the classroom revealed that:

- Although vigorously denied, teachers categorised pupils according to social class.

- Teachers determined this social background, not by personal knowledge of the pupils, but by superficial characteristics and stereotypes.

- Despite the absence of streaming, pupils were still thought of as A streamers or C streamers and treated according to these labels.

- Teachers differed in the materials made available to them, thereby denying equality of opportunity to all pupils.

- Teachers treated questions from pupils with a lower social background with suspicion, and they were rarely seen as genuine, but as attention seeking or plain disruptive. This differed from A streamers whose questions were seen as evidence of their enthusiasm for learning.

- Keddie concludes that the differentiation of pupils by teachers was as effective as official streaming in impeding the progress of working-class children.

You will notice that Keddie's findings are similar to those of Bowles and Gintis.

More recently **Stephen Ball** (2003) has reasserted his criticism of banding and streaming in his lecture given to The London University's Institute of Education. In his address he indicated that banding and streaming creates 'social barbarism' in that it allows middle-class parents to separate their children from what they view as 'inferior' pupils. This is a particular concern of Ball as more recent educational policy has moved towards the use of banding and streaming despite years worth of sociological research that consistently shows that it is educationally damaging to working-class pupils by further increasing educational inequalities. Moreover, Ball found that pupils suffered because bottom sets were taught by the youngest and least experienced teachers, with the highest rates of staff turnover.

Educational achievement and different social groups (Part II)

Learning objectives

By the end of this section, you should be able to:

- Describe which ethnic groups do best and worst within the educational system
- Understand the limitations of using quantitative data when measuring racism
- Explain how outside school factors impinge on the educational attainment of ethnic groups
- Outline how inside school factors may limit success

Ethnic minorities and life chances

Education is seen as a major factor affecting the future of black children. Because of the link between schooling and occupation, many of the arguments for working-class underachievement also apply to ethnic groups. However, proving a link between low attainment and ethnicity is not that easy as there are other factors that also affect how well they do. Moreover, we need to be aware that within broad groupings, such as 'Asian', there are often huge differences in attainment. However, looking at recent figures from 2007 a number of facts can be noted:

- Chinese pupils attain the highest grades at GCSE grades A*–C, with 83.3 per cent achieving this standard (using figures that exclude English and Maths).

- Indian pupils also do extremely well, with 74.4 per cent achieving GCSE grades A*–C.

- Any other Asian background, with 64.1 per cent achieving GCSE grades A*–C.

- White British, with 59.5 per cent achieving GCSE grades A*–C.

However, by contrast other ethnic groups do not do so well.

- Black students, with 49.1 per cent achieving GCSE grades A*–C. However, this group's results have been improving and are little worse than for white children of a similar social background (the figure for 2006 was 44.4 per cent).

- Pakistani, with 53 per cent achieving GCSE grades A*–C.

However, within these statistics it should be made clear that educational attainment is affected by class whether it is for English, Welsh and Scottish (EWS) students or Bangladeshi, Pakistani or black students (DfES, 2006).

Interpreting the evidence

The statistics presented only look at two variables: ethnicity and educational attainment. It cannot be assumed that ethnicity is the cause of the variation in educational attainment. Part of all this variation may be due to other factors such as social class. For example, **Drew** (1997) comments about some of the problems with using quantitative data in this area:

- Small sample sizes from local LEAs result in difficulties making generalisations from the data

- The lack of studies that **operationalise** (measure) class and ethnicity

- The lack of longitudinal data to assess patterns over time when it comes to class and ethnic educational performance

Barring

From such tables it is often not possible to ascertain whether certain ethnic groups have been barred from taking certain examinations because of their colour. For example, in a study of a northern comprehensive, it was found that Asian pupils of similar ability to white pupils were less likely to be entered for GCSEs (CFRE, 1992).

One snapshot in time

Statistics on school leavers are only a snapshot of a given point of time; they can thus be ambiguous. For example, pupils may improve and add to their qualifications after leaving school. There is evidence that ethnic minorities are more likely to do this. According to the *Youth Cohort Study* (2005), 92 per cent of Indians were in full-time education, thereby indicating that, in the long-term, ethnic minorities may improve their qualifications.

Outside school factors for ethnic underachievement in school

Social class

Part of the explanation for the high average examination success of Indian children is that this is a relatively middle-class group. The same is true of African-Asians, many of whom were business people excluded from various countries across the world. One line of argument concerning outside school factors is that the differential educational performance of ethnic groups reflects the social-class background of those groups, as well as their ethnicity. It is suggested that minorities such as Indians and African-Asians do well educationally because they have the economic advantages of being middle class, whilst groups such as Bangladeshis and black people tend to underperform in the education system because they have the material disadvantages of coming from working-class backgrounds.

However, this debate concerning the effects of social class versus ethnicity is not a simple one. Drew comments "There is a danger, though, that these general findings will generate myths because, although they are valid in an overall sense, the generalisations do not tell the whole story." Nevertheless, qualification differentials are larger for ethnicity than they are for gender, so clearly this is a fruitful line of enquiry. For example, Drew found that anomalies such as Bangladeshis being the highest performers in Tower Hamlets (an inner-London borough that is blighted with educational underperformance), whilst being the lowest performers nationally indicate the problems of making generalisations in this sphere. A much more recent study by Lucinda Platt (2007) established that although ethnic minorities used education for social mobility, others suffered an 'ethnic penalty' in being unable to obtain the highest occupational jobs or achieving high grades throughout their schooling career. She found this to be particularly the case for both Pakistani and Bangladeshi pupils.

Material factors

Such explanations take a number of different positions. Firstly, economic disadvantages in housing, employment and wages must be taken into account. For example, Platt (2007) found vast differences in poverty between ethnic groups, with likelihood of poverty being highest in Bangladeshi, Pakistani and black communities. Additionally, the *Labour Force Survey* (2002) reveals that only 29 per cent of white families and 22 per cent of black families live as couples, with New Right writers suggesting that the absence of a father figure may result in a lack of motivation for male pupils during their educational career.

Whilst the employment rate for ethnic minority groups is currently 58 per cent – compared to 75 per cent for the population overall (2007) – this gap of sixteen percentage points has remained continuous for over a decade. Again, this indicates that low income is always more likely to affect those from ethnic minority backgrounds than for the majority of the population. This has an attendant effect on income, with Platt finding that many groups have no savings and are much more likely to be users of means-tested benefits. Census material (2003) shows that even when in employment Pakistani and Bangladeshi households are more likely to experience poverty. Platt also disturbingly found that, despite black people achieving high levels of attainment at GCSE and A level, they did not reach the employment positions that might have been expected if they had come from an EWS background. This indicates a wider problem of racism within the workplace.

Language

Another area of research looks at the impact of language on educational attainment. It has been argued that some Asian students, such as Bangladeshis, experience communication problems because for many of them English is their second language, finding it hard to understand and be understood by their teachers. Moreover, they can experience difficulties reading textbooks and examination papers. It is suggested by **Mac an Ghaill** (1988) that black students encounter educational problems because the 'Creole or patois they speak' does not fit the standard English taught in schools. Typical problems they experience include misunderstanding the meaning of everyday expressions and being misunderstood by teachers.

Gender

Research shows gender and ethnicity is another cause for educational failure. Whilst black boys in particular tend to fail throughout their educational careers – only 44 per cent obtain five GCSE grades A*–C – this is not the case for black girls. Ethnographic work shows a very different response to schooling by black girls compared with their peer groups. Interactionist **Fuller** (1980) studied a small group of people with West Indian parentage that formed a discernable sub-culture, by virtue of the girls' positive acceptance of being black and female. These girls, unlike their black male peers, directed their frustration and anger towards achievement in school through the acquisition of educational qualifications. Their response to racism was to work hard and prove their worth. They were not, however, conforming, 'good pupils'. They were pro-education, but had clever and subtle ways of showing their defiance. Teachers' expectations were unimportant to them.

Inside school factors

As we have seen in previous studies of interactionism, inside school explanations focus on the concept of the hidden curriculum. Many sociologists believe that the hidden curriculum operating in schools is a racist one that discriminates against ethnic minority pupils. However, some debate exists about whether this racism is intentional or unintentional. Either way, the evidence suggests that the racist hidden curriculum serves to create a resistance to schooling on the part of certain ethnic groups and leads to their eventual underachievement.

The ethnocentric curriculum

There has long been a concern that the curriculum in UK schools reflects the cultural norms of the country concerned. As a consequence many believe that by definition other cultures and different ways of life tend to be underplayed. Moreover, when they are depicted in literature they are often shown in stereotypes that fail to demystify marginalised groups and tend towards imperialism.

History and Geography textbooks have been singled out by writers such as Cole (1992) and Wright (1986) as putting forward unacceptable views of black people. Descriptions of black people in these texts was often negative, with them being portrayed as 'uncivilised savages', whilst white people were described in positive language, such as 'fine and fair'. And although multi-culturalism, with its emphasis on a varied culture, improved matters in the 1980s, this was reversed by the introduction of the national curriculum.

Institutional racism

Since the 1970s there has been a view that schools are institutionally racist. In other words, not only are individuals, such as teachers and pupils, racist, but also the school itself as an institution. Institutional racism is inherent within the policies and practices of schools and has the effect of disadvantaging ethnic groups.

Bernard Coard (1971) believed that black children may develop an inferiority complex, a low self-image and low expectations of life. Teachers expect black children to fail and this produces a self-fulfilling prophecy in which they live up to their label.

Setting

A number of researchers have found that this racism also occurs in what should be the meritocratic allocation of pupils into sets. Most recently the work of **David Gilborn** (2005) established that black pupils are over represented in lower sets, with many students being misallocated by the internal judgements made by the school. Moreover, this process is further compounded by the likelihood of lower sets being taught by junior or poorer teachers.

Anti-school culture

Some writers, such as *Voice* columnist and black academic in education at Leeds University, Tony Sewell, believe that the culture of the streets is anti-educational and can affect attainment at school. He comments that:

> "I say that, because in Peckham today if you go to the library with a book in your hand, you're considered 'weird' by your peers and it's that culture that I think we need to deal with at the moment." (2000).

Black culture, he argues, puts style and instant gratification ahead of the values of school and college. For Sewell, black males see educational success as a feminine thing. The way for them to get admiration is through credibility of the street.

In Sewell's terminology, the young man wants to be a "street hood". Success in the schoolroom marks the black boy out from his peers or classmates and is likely to make him the target of derision or bullying. Educational failure becomes a badge to wear with pride.

Role models

The most up-to-date statistics (January 2004) indicate a lack of black role models within the education system. The last published data on the percentage of black teachers in England reveal that only 1.5 per cent of the teaching profession are from a black background, although this percentage rises to seven per cent in London. It therefore appears that black teachers are under-represented. Given that in England and Wales 1.1 per cent of people are black Caribbean, 0.9 per cent are black African and a further 0.2 per cent are from other black groups, one would expect similar figures within the teaching profession. Carrington et al. (2001), McCreith et al. (2001) and Ross (2002) note that initial teacher training figures indicate that this state of affairs is unlikely to change in the short to medium term. Other research (McCreith et al., 2001) indicates that even when black teachers are appointed in schools, they are much less likely to be found in positions of power, with only four per cent of head teachers and deputy head teachers coming from a black background. Moreover, black male role models are even rarer in the primary sector; in 2004 only 15.7 per cent of teaching staff were men, whilst even in the secondary sector men only made up 45 per cent of the secondary teaching staff (DfES, 2005). Educational policy needs to encourage more black male teachers to act as role models for black students.

Teacher interactions

A report commissioned by the London Mayor, Ken Livingstone (2004), was of the opinion that black students had been 'betrayed by the education system'. Specifically, black boys complained of racism and stereotyping from teachers. They said chances of success were also limited by the old-fashioned curriculum:

"The consensus was that low teacher expectations played a major part in the underachievement of African-Caribbean pupils. In addition, inadequate levels of positive teacher attention, unfair behaviour management practices, disproportionately high levels of exclusions and an inappropriate curriculum took their toll."

This is especially gloomy given a 2003 DfES report:

"Black teachers play a critical role in supporting, encouraging and educating black pupils. They also provide a positive role model and validate black pupils' culture and identity. More black teachers are needed in the UK schooling system and there needs to be a clear strategic focus on recruiting, retaining, training and supporting black teachers."

Dianne Abbott, writing in *The Observer* (2002), notes that teacher interaction between female teachers in particular, shows that these teachers are physically intimidated by black pupils, even in primary schools. However, it should be noted that racism is very hard to operationalise. It is practically and ethically problematic to investigate, and whilst racist sentiments may be shown in the classroom, writers such as Hammersley, Professor of Education and Social Research at the Open University, remain unconvinced that it necessarily permeates into the classroom.

Exclusion

Exclusion is one of the methods of social control that schools can use to deal with students they regard as troublesome. Once again, it appears that black students are much more likely to be excluded. In a 2004 DfES study it was suggested that black pupils remain three times more likely to be excluded from school than white children. Even after special educational needs and free school meal) students were taken out of the equation, black students were still 2.6 times more likely to be excluded. In statistical terms every year, 1000 black pupils are permanently excluded from school and 30 000 more are suspended. Moreover, the study showed that excluded black pupils were much less likely to mimic the backgrounds of equivalent white pupils. So whilst white pupils were statistically likely to have special educational needs, poor attendance records, or being children in care, this was not the case for black children. This evidence seems to support the work of writers such as Gilborn and Maud Blair who have long believed that black children are treated differently to white pupils, whilst Wright, Weekes and McGlaughlin (2000) of Nottingham University believe that black pupils and their parents have been failed over the issue of exclusion and that "individual and institutional racism clearly exists within schools".

Labeling theory

Labeling theory explores the way that teacher stereotypes can affect their pupils. Writers such as Gilborn have consistently found that many teachers felt that black pupils in particular opposed their authority. Teachers interpreted their dress and aspects of behaviour as a deliberate challenge. One of the consequences of this was that black students were disciplined, for example by detention, far more than other groups. The reasons given by teachers for this discipline demonstrated that they were really interpreting behaviour as requiring discipline rather than the pupil actually having broken clearly defined school rules. For example, attitudes interpreted as 'arrogance' could easily lead to a detention for a black pupil. In a study commissioned by the government, Steve Strand (2007) argued that labelling leads pupils to become "demotivated and to try less". It goes on further to comment that if teachers continually label black pupils in this way it can have the consequence of distorting judgements on their academic ability.

Stereotyping

Some writers, such as Cecile Wright (1986), believe that stereotyping amongst white teachers is a common practice, with teachers excluding pupils on the basis of their race. Peter Figueroa (1991) believes that such stereotypes have the following results:

- The misassessment of black students due to the use of culturally-based tests that discriminate against black groups.

- Black students being misplaced into lower sets based, not on meritocracy or results achieved in tests, but on stereotypes. This is known as 'misplacement'.

- Teachers encouraging black students to voluntarily opt out of academic work to take up what they consider more appropriate channels, such as sport. This is known as **channelling**.

This general belief by teachers about black students again leads to the self-fulfilling prophesy, where black students end up failing themselves because of the racist stereotypes the teachers hold of them.

However, Peter Foster (1990) found in the school he was studying that black students received little racism from their teachers. Even this study, though, showed Foster underestimated the effect of negative comments on ethnic minority students.

Summary

Claire Hunte (2004) neatly summarises the causes of black students' underachievement:

- The poor quality of schooling
- Discriminatory school practices
- An ethnocentric curriculum
- The inability of parents, due to low-paid jobs involving long hours, to support their children with schoolwork
- A lack of role models, particularly male, within schools
- Wider misperceptions about the black community by the rest of British society
- Poor self-esteem and peer pressure

Educational achievement and different social groups (Part III)

Learning objectives

By the end of this section, you should be able to:

- Describe the basic trends in achievement between the genders over the last ten years
- Outline outside school explanations for differences in achievement by gender
- Explain why in more recent times girls are outperforming boys at both A level and GCSE
- Describe why boys tend to underachieve
- Assess whether such trends mean the end of the 'glass ceiling' in the workplace for women

Introduction

Concern about gender and educational attainment focuses mainly on the degree to which females and males perform differently in different subjects and their predisposition to study different subjects given the choice. However, it is not true that males generally obtain more qualifications or higher grades than females at school; in fact the reverse is the case. Until the late 1980s, however, the major apprehension was about the underachievement of girls. This was because girls did better at primary school, but from GCSE level onwards they tended to fall behind.

Educational performance and gender

Below are some recent statistics that indicate the level of difference in educational attainment between the genders:

- Girls outperformed boys in every Key Stage in 2007, barring Maths Key Stage 2
- Gender differences in Science are relatively small
- Taking into account prior achievement and other factors, there is only a small variation between boys' and girls' progress at primary school, but a larger difference at secondary school (equivalent to two grades' progress).
- At Key Stage 4 (GCSEs) 62.1 per cent of girls obtain five or more grades A*–C compared to 52.2 per cent of boys
- At Key Stage 5 girls continue to outperform boys in every major subject, except for modern foreign languages and further maths, though the gender gap again narrows very slightly (DFCFS, 2007).

Outside school factors

Wilkinson (1994) argues that what she calls the 'Genderquake' has led to:

- Women wanting their own money and a fulfilling career.
- Women's increasing willingness to take on part-time and

tertiary sector jobs. This is an area that traditionally suits women, who demonstrate better interpersonal skills and analytical awareness than their male counterparts. Some sociologists comment that these skills are related to those used within the private sphere of the family, making women much more adept at looking after and understanding the needs of customers in the service sector.

Other writers, such as Sue Sharpe note that while in the 1970s women's expectations of life revolved around gaining a husband and having children, by the 1990s women no longer saw this part of their lives with the same importance. Instead, she found that women see men as a liability to their career. This may explain the increasing age of women in the UK having their first child.

Socialization

From the moment we are born we are shaped into what society expects of us to be by the process of socialization. We learn how to direct our behaviour. In the past gender identities tended to be fixed, with masculine and feminine identities being reinforced from childhood. Girls, for example, were encouraged to play with gender-specific toys (Norman, 1988). However, more recently, these perceptions of femininity and masculinity have begun to change. Riddell (1992) found, for example, that schoolgirls had a dual notion of their futures, linking their subject choices at school to the local labour market (especially working-class girls), whilst also accepting that motherhood and domesticity were important parts of their identity as women. But the girls in Riddell's study were not submissive in this process of socialization. Rather they absorbed both accepting and undermining messages about traditional female roles.

In addition, working-class and middle-class girls expressed different gender codes, with middle-class girls opting for academic education and thus gaining the approval of the middle-class female teachers who they most closely resembled.

Work by Italian sociologist **Isabelli Crespi** (2003) suggests that a wider range of identities is now possible to women, allowing them to explore careers that in the past would have been gender-specific, perhaps revolving around part-time employment that met the needs of their children.

Reasons for improved examination attainment in girls

Social policy aiding females

This analysis suggests a number of policy changes that have been effective in encouraging female students to achieve in those areas where they have traditionally performed poorly. The first initiative was Girls into Science and Technology (**GIST**), which was intended to encourage females to choose science and technology. This included policies such as arranging visits from female students to act as positive role models, developing curriculum materials that reflected female interests, non-sexist career advice and raising teachers' consciousness of gender role stereotyping. More recent policies include Women in Science and Engineering (WISE). However, critics suggest that it is difficult to pin down a general increase in female standards to this particular initiative as GIST was fairly narrow in its scope and affected only a few selected schools, nor were these policies necessarily always followed through because they were expensive to implement. More recently, Machin and McNally (2005) found that the National Numeracy Project, or numeracy hour, had the affect of reducing the gender gap between boys and girls in Maths at Key Stage 1.

The introduction of the GCSE examination

The introduction of this exam, which replaced O levels and CSEs, is argued to have favoured females. The principles behind GCSE are that students should be allowed to show what they know, understand and can do. In order to achieve this coursework was been introduced as a prominent feature of GCSE courses. This component is said to favour the consistent and conscientious work characterised by female students. Similarly, the increased emphasis on oral assessment is supposed to favour female skills. Researchers who disagree about the educational merits and social justice of new forms of assessment, Stobbart et al. (1992), suggest that coursework and new curriculum content in the national curriculum and in examinations have had a positive effect on girls' performance. However, the notion that it's all down to coursework is not supported by the way in which girls' enhanced performance has not been entirely in sync with changes in assessment approaches: English moved from being 100 per cent coursework, and over the period of introduction of coursework and its reduction, the gender gap continued to increase. Moreover, research by Elwood (2005) utilised a weights analysis and found that coursework had less affect on girls' attainment than it did on boys', and, although she agrees that coursework may be a factor, it is not the only cause.

Revision at home

A large number of students said they did not realise that revision would be so important. As girls tend to revise more than boys, girls are more aware of what is needed to obtain good qualifications. Whereas boys are more likely to be involved in sport or gang activities, girls are more likely to spend their leisure time talking (McRobbie, 1976). Girls are consequently more likely to work harder and do more revision as they feel that they have something to aim for. Jean Rudduck's work on GCSE preparation suggests that boys tend to leave it to the last minute and rely on 'natural talent'; in subjects where you need to build skills and knowledge over time (for example, languages, English, and so on).

Homework

There is a considerable amount of sociological evidence available that suggests that there is a connection between homework and educational attainment. Research in Britain and the USA indicates that working-class boys who do at least one hour's homework a night perform as well as middle-class boys in examinations (Estelle and Morris). Other writers such as Mitsos and Browne (1998) maintain girls work harder, are more meticulous, spend more time on homework, are better organised, and are more likely to meet deadlines than boys. In a recent study, Lyon et al. (2006)surveyed 7000 pupils and parents, and found that parents reported their daughters did all or almost all of their homework. By comparison boys finished 61 per cent of theirs. Interestingly, the survey showed that both boys and girls received the same proportion of time when they asked their parents to help, indicating that lack of parental involvement in doing boys homework was not a factor.

Relationship with teachers

The type of relationship that the student has with their teachers has a considerable bearing on exam results. Teachers have different ideas about the type of behaviour that is consistent with the pupil's role. Similarly, pupils have conflicting views about what makes an ideal teacher. Some pupils are unable to live up to the model of the ideal pupil held by their teacher. As a result it may lead to new patterns of behaviour, which influence their levels of attainment. A considerable amount of research has been carried out into how teachers make sense of, and respond to, the behaviour of their pupils. In his book, *Outsiders* (1963), Howard Becker puts forward his labeling theory of behaviour. His theory suggests that the classifying of behaviour by teachers leads to labels being attached to pupils. This classification will then affect what will eventually happen to the pupil and thus will lead to the self-fulfilling prophecy. Ball, for instance, in 1986 found that teachers' labels had affected performance. Howe (1997) found that boys make more contribution to classroom discussion, therefore receiving more teacher time. Moreover, during these interactions teachers will praise and chastise boys in a way that does not occur with girls. Arnot (2004) notes in comparison that girls use a private learning strategy in that they ask teachers questions after the lesson, thereby making up any shortfall in time they have received from their teachers.

Relationships between girls and their teachers are generally better than those of boys and their teachers (Abraham, 1995). One reason for this is that a higher percentage of girls than boys share the values of the teacher.

Single-sex classes

Another initiative that has been claimed to be successful is the introduction of single-sex classes. This builds on the arguments in favour of single-sex schools. Female-only classes provide positive role models as, for example, the science teacher too has to be female. In science lessons, having no boys in the class removes the domination of laboratory equipment by boys (Kelly), and also allows female students to answer questions and follow their interests. The positive outcomes of female-only classes are said to increase female confidence and lead to a more positive attitude to science. More recent research by the DfES found that the proportion of A grades achieved at A level in all-girl independent schools was, on average, ten per cent higher than that of girls in co-educational independent schools across a broad range of subjects. Critics of this belief argue that female-only classes do not guarantee that teachers' attitudes are changed or that sexist material is not used. As with GIST, this approach has only been adopted by a very few schools as it is relatively expensive to implement. Furthermore, some, including Janette Elwood, claims that while pilot single-sex classes held in some schools have indicated that segregation boosts performance, not enough research has been done on the subject. She points out that even if single-sex teaching did improve results, it

would raise the girls' achievement as well as that of boys and the gap between the sexes would still remain: "When are we going to be happy? When boys and girls achieve the same, and there is no gap?"

> **Focus on research**
>
> **Effects of single-sex versus co-educational classes and schools on gender differences**
>
> *Van de Gaer, E., Pustjens, H., Van Damme, J. and De Munter, A. (2004)*
>
> The authors examined the effects on single-sex as opposed to coeducational classes. The study itself examined pupils at the end of year eight. The results indicate that for boys the gender composition of the classes has more impact than the gender composition of the schools, whereas for girls the gender breakdown of the schools is more important. Boys make more progress for language (but not for mathematics) in co-educational classes, even after the selective nature of the classes has been taken into account. Girls, on the other hand, make more progress for mathematics (but not for language) in single-sex than in co-educational schools.

Others, such as Alan Smithers (2006), conclude in research that single sex schools for boys and girls 'have not shown any dramatic or consistent advantages'.

Why boys are underachieving

Behaviour of pupils in class

Ongoing reports by government inspectors suggest that bad behaviour in the classroom is responsible for children underachieving at GCSE (Ofsted, 1996). This appears to be supported by research. Licht and Dwect, for instance, noted that boys seem to be more easily distracted in the classroom. Boys are also more likely to cause discipline problems. For example, nationally, 80 per cent of pupils excluded from secondary schools are boys (Ofsted, 1996). In an interview, a number of pupils suggested that image was an important factor. Pupils did not want to be seen as doing as much work because it did not look good for their image. Peter Woods (1979) argues that boys are more concerned with the approval of their **peer group** than the approval of teachers. This is reiterated by Jackson (1999), who has pointed out how many of the failing working-class boys are tied deeply into a traditional macho culture where academic work is **feminised**. There is a strong relationship between their failure and their perceived limited work opportunities. They therefore turn to compensatory sources of status. Madeleine Arnott (1997) argued that the most significant issue in explaining difference is the way in which boys and girls regard school. Amongst boys, it's 'cool' to be seen not to work or comply. Alongside this, boys tend to blame poor performance on externalised factors (bad teaching, wrong test questions, and so on), while girls tend to blame themselves and their competence, and work harder as a consequence to improve and to overcome problems.

Sets and performance

Research shows that some boys underachieve because they were placed in the wrong set. There was very little difference between the sexes on this issue. Some students thought that they had been unfairly placed into the wrong sets. As David Hargreaves has pointed out, the set that someone is in will influence teacher expectations. This in turn will influence performance. Students believed that there were more behavioural problems in the lower sets. This was more of a problem for boys as their peer group more easily influenced them (Bly, 1996).

Peer group status

As far back as the 1970s Willis showed that male peer groups are a powerful force within the education system. So, whilst boys tend to be hyper competitive and hierarchical in their composition, leading to an over-emphasis on 'doing things', this leads to an increased likelihood of males leaving schools for the workplace and proving their 'masculinity'.

Is the future really female?

During the 1995 BBC programme *Panorama* it was claimed in the title that the 'future is female'. However, feminists remain sceptical that women's dual roles will change at all. Sharpe (1994) indicates that many of the females in her 1990s study, like those in the 1970s, anticipate life as a 'dual worker', combining waged employment with family and domestic responsibilities. She additionally acknowledges that the desire to gain educational qualifications may partly reflect female's recognition of the fragility in the labour market in a period of recession (six months of zero growth in production in the economy).

It should also be pointed out that the increased employment opportunities are less impressive than at first sight. It may be that the **glass ceiling** has been lifted slightly, so that women are found in significant numbers in middle-management positions, but females are still under-represented in the top echelons of management and over-represented in the part-time work they have traditionally dominated. This lack of gender equality is recognised by Sharpe, and she sees it as potentially denting the expectations of females in the twenty-first century.

Other writers such as Weiner (1997) claim that female rather than male underachievement is still characteristic of the education system, particularly in higher education. She notes that the backlash concerning male underachievement is exaggerated, whilst Mitsos and Browne point out that girls are still under-represented in science and engineering subjects at university. They do not question the problems that boys have but suggest that girls too have similar problems in certain areas, particularly in Maths and Science.

The Equal Opportunities Commission's report, *Sex and Power: Who Runs Britain* (2005) found the following facts, which indicate that despite women attaining better qualifications than men, women have a long way to go:

- Women make up over half of the workforce and the proportion is ever increasing, yet the main decisions are still made by men in society.

- They found in the report that 20 per cent of women face being sacked or financial penalties as a consequence of becoming pregnant.

- One-third of women, because of their caring role, had turned down employment opportunities.

- The report also revealed that we lag far behind our European colleagues in terms of the proportion of male to female MPs. After the 2005 election only 126 female MPs were elected to the House of Commons, with just 20 per cent of MPs in the House of Commons currently being female, despite commitments from various parties to increase the number of women in office. By comparison in 2004, 45 per cent of MPs in Sweden were female.

What do you know now? (Part I)

1. Look at the following sentences. Are they strengths or weaknesses of interactionism?

   - This theory is more sophisticated as it looks at the role of teachers rather than just looking at structural explanations.

   - The theory ignores structural influences. Class and how society operates are the real reasons for educational failure.

   - The explanations have highlighted important implications for the way that teachers should be trained.

   - Taken collectively, this research supports the idea that school processes associated with teaching, learning and assessment are biased in favour of the 'good pupil'.

   - As Willis found, this theory may explain why deviant anti-school cultures occur.

   - Qualitative theory is low in reliability.

   - Labeling theory may explain why some children do very well and why some do badly.

   - The self-fulfilling prophecy recognises that teachers attitudes can unconsciously influence pupils' self-image and hence their achievements.

   - The schooling system appears to deal with the genders differently.

   - Research indicates that teachers label students within hours of first acquaintance.

   - Working-class failure further indicates labelling is happening in schools.

2. Why not consider doing some observation in class?

   - Do teachers label their pupils?

   - What impact does this have on them?

   - Compare bottom and top sets in English or Maths. Interview students as to how they view themselves and their teachers.

   - Consider the problems of observation: will the teacher change their behaviour? Should you perhaps use covert participant observation?

3. Give three government policies that have sought to alleviate material deprivation.

4. Explain, giving one example, how material deprivation can affect educational attainment.

5. What is cultural capital? Give an example to explain the concept.

6. Explain the likely methodology used by interactionist sociologists.

Key terms (Part I)

Compensatory education: Education that has the intention of conquering the perceived educational deficiencies suffered by the working classes.

Cultural capital: The accumulation of both subjective and objective cultural competencies that allow economic success.

Cultural deprivation theory: The idea that academic underachievement is a consequence of a culturally poor home environment.

Education Maintenance Allowance (EMA): A weekly payment to 16–18-year-olds attending a course of further education.

Longitudinal study: A study of the same group of people at different points in time.

Material deprivation theory: Underachievement in education that results from the circumstances of poverty.

Positive discrimination: Actions intended to improve the prospects of disadvantaged groups.

Self-fulfilling prophesy: When a person lives up to the label given to him or her.

Streaming: A form of organisation in schools where pupils are grouped according to their overall ability.

Symbolic violence: Phrase coined by Pierre Bourdieu to explain coercion that is imposed without physical force.

Section summary (Part I)

- Those from the working classes tend to do less well in examinations, have less motivation and are more inclined to seek instant gratification rather than staying on to further their educational qualifications.

- Four distinct reasons for these differences between the classes have emerged:

  - Material deprivation theory: Lack of income hinders academic performance. Governments have tacked this by using compensatory programmes which target poor areas and then seeks to spend money on encouraging improved attitudes toward education. Such policies have included EAZs, Sure Start and EMA.

  - Cultural deprivation theory: Varying attitudes towards education are shown by the classes. It is claimed that working-class attitudes and values to education are in some way inferior than those of the middle-class.

  - Cultural difference theory: This theory focuses on the disparity between working-class and middle-class cultures in schools. It is most often associated with the work of Marxist writers such as Basil Bernstein and Pierre Bourdieu.

  - The interactionist approach Education is directed by meanings and definitions that are negotiated in school. From this perspective class differences in education are socially constructed in the classroom. It is argued by interactionists that labelling, particularly of working-class children, can lead to self-fulfilling prophesy and failure.

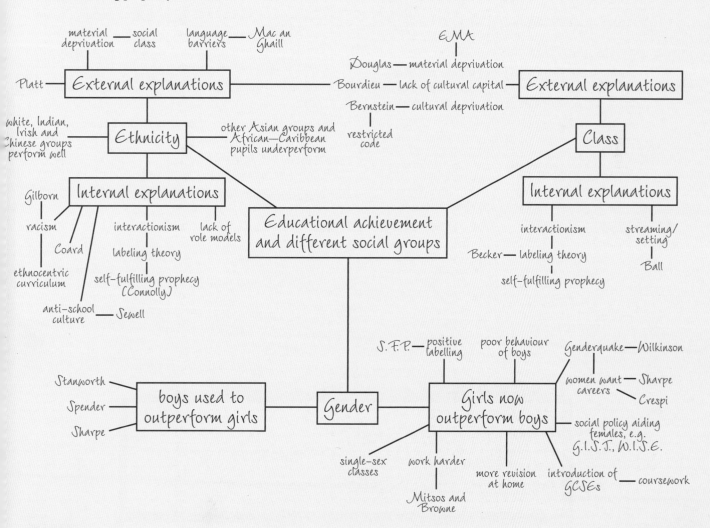

1. Looking at the following, are they strengths or weaknesses of the inside school explanation for black students' underachievement?

   - The approach attempts to see things from the social actors' point of view and therefore allows insight.

   - Some research evidence (Foster, 1990) demonstrates that not all teachers are racist.

   - Studies such as Fuller's indicate that the power of the hidden curriculum may not be as pervasive as these writers suggest.

   - Liberation theorists may scoff at the idea that black people are passive in educational success. Possible resistance may in the end lead to liberation, not merely educational failure.

   - Much of the inside school explanations of ethnic minority underachievement ignores structural influences such as class and poverty.

   - A lot has been done through multicultural education to reduce racism and to foster a spirit of understanding and empathy for all members of society.

   - More recently ethnic minority groups have seen improved educational performance and now almost match that of ESW pupils.

   - The inside school explanations of ethnic minority underachievement have helped us to understand the nature of social inequality and injustice.

   - Many of the black writers, such as Coard, Wright and Mac an Ghaill, it could be argued, are suffering from ideological bias.

   - The research ignores other factors, such as defective socialization and arguments that black people are merely genetically less intelligent than other groups.

   - The success of other ethnic minority groups, such as Indians and African-Asians, suggests that the schooling system is far from racist.

   - Feminists would argue that the research detailed ignores patriarchal influences, especially concerning the failure of black females in the schooling system.

   - Much of the research is ethnographic in orientation and thus small-scale and lacking in validity.

   - Some sociologists argue that racism in schools cannot be a complete explanation of educational underperformance because Indian and African-Asian students experience such racism but perform well educationally.

   - It could be argued that the explanations overstate the case. A number of schools have adopted multicultural and anti-racist approaches to education that reduce the level of racism that inside school explanations claim exists in schools.

   - Most of the findings are based on qualitative research and therefore are high in validity.

   - Evidence, such as the high exclusion rates of black people, confirms many of the findings of this type of research.

2. Give one reason why differential achievement occurs between ethnic groups.

3. Name one ethnic group that does extremely well within the UK educational system.

4. Name one group that does extremely poorly within the UK educational system.

5. Explain how cultural differences may impact on educational attainment.

6. Explain the phrase 'self-fulfilling prophesy'. Explain how this may operate in the arena of ethnicity.

7. Describe the importance of teacher expectations for educational success of black pupils.

8. Outline why the lack of male role models hinders black boys' attainment.

9. What does 'ethnocentric' mean? Why might such a curriculum disadvantage ethnic minorities?

Key terms (Part II)

Channelling: To direct or guide along some desired course.

Ethnocentric: To look at the world mainly from the viewpoint of one's own culture.

Operationalise: The process of converting concepts into specific observable behaviours that a researcher can measure.

Section summary (Part II)

- There are huge differences in attainment by ethnicity, with those from Chinese backgrounds doing particularly well, whilst in contrast black and Bangladeshi pupils underperform. It should be noted, however, that all groups have improved their attainment at GCSE in recent years.

- It cannot be assumed that ethnicity is necessarily the cause of these differences. Drew argues that qualitative data may mislead as studies are often small-scale and offer statistics only in one snapshot in time.

- Explanations for differences are split into two areas: outside and inside school explanations.

- Outside school explanations believe that class, material factors and language may all disadvantage those from different ethnic groups.

- Inside school explanations suggest that the implementation of an ethnocentric curriculum (white bias), racism within the classroom (the ways in which teachers anglicise students' names, for example), institutional racism (the fact that the school holidays fit in with Christian celebrations), a *street culture* that sees education as being 'uncool' and the lack of positive role models hinders academic progress.

- Other issues that impact on performance include the overuse of exclusion on those from ethnic backgrounds and the labelling of students.

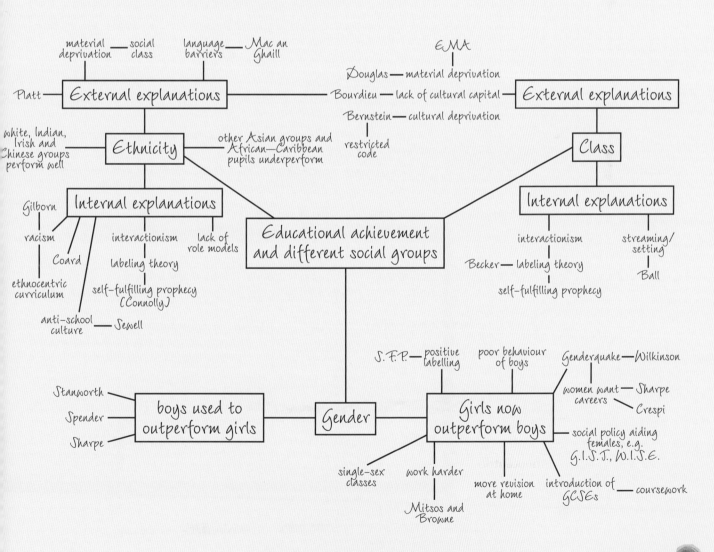

What do you know now? (Part III)

1. Identify the strengths and weaknesses of this argument:
   - Although girls may be doing better at examinations at school, this is not to say that females will make strides in achieving top managerial positions.
   - Evidence from the workplace and elsewhere support the assertion that female attitudes to success have changed. Women are having children later in life, and see careers as vital.
   - A lot of the work lacks empirical data to support it. It is often small-scale, and thus generalisations are difficult to make.
   - These studies give an up-to-date account of classroom attainment in the 1990s.
   - The work fails to take into account class differences. In reality it is not boys in general who fail, but working-class boys.
   - This debate is sterile. In reality it is a smokescreen to divert attention away from the real gains women have made, and to divert attention back again on the male of the species.
   - Many of the so-called initiatives were only narrow in their scope and can thus not be said to be responsible for added female achievement.
   - Much empirical quantitative data show that this trend is consistent and widening, and thus cannot be dismissed easily.

2. Explain general trends in educational attainment between the genders over the last ten years.

3. Outline why changes in the job market have encouraged women to achieve educational success.

4. List three educational policies that have improved female educational achievement.

5. Outline four ways male attitudes to school damage their chances of educational success.

6. Describe how the workplace remains a sexist environment despite ever improving female examination results.

Key terms (Part III)

Feminised: To cause to assume female characteristics.

GIST: Programme introduced before the Education Reform Bill 1988 to encourage girls to study science and technology.

Glass ceiling: The discrimination that stops women getting into top positions in the workplace. Women can see the position of power but they are unable to break through the barriers to get these jobs.

Peer group: A friendship group with similar status.

Tertiary sector: Also known as the service sector. For example, the retail and banking industries are part of this category.

WISE: Women into Science Engineering and Construction, another programme to encourage females into these traditionally male areas of expertise.

Section summary (Part III)

- Concern about gender and educational attainment focuses mainly on the degree to which females and males perform differently in different subjects and their predisposition to study different subjects given the choice.

- However, it is not true that males generally obtain more qualifications or higher grades than females at school; in fact the reverse is the case both in at primary school (SATs) and secondary school (GCSE and A level).

- Explanations for this again look at outside and inside school explanations.

- Outside school explanations for gender differences focus on the changing attitudes of women, particularly to work.

- Other reasons why girls outperform boys include their greater willingness to revise, their painstaking attitude to homework, and better relationships with teachers than boys.

- However, the jury is out on the role that single-sex classes play in better female attainment. Whilst some believe this segregation to be a reason for girls' good results, others are less convinced.

- By contrast, boys underachieve because of their behaviour in class which can often result in an anti-school culture being formed.

- Nonetheless, feminists note that despite women outperforming men, the fact is that the most important positions and roles in society are still taken by men. For instance, only 20 per cent of MPs are women, whilst women remain a rarity in the boardrooms of top companies.

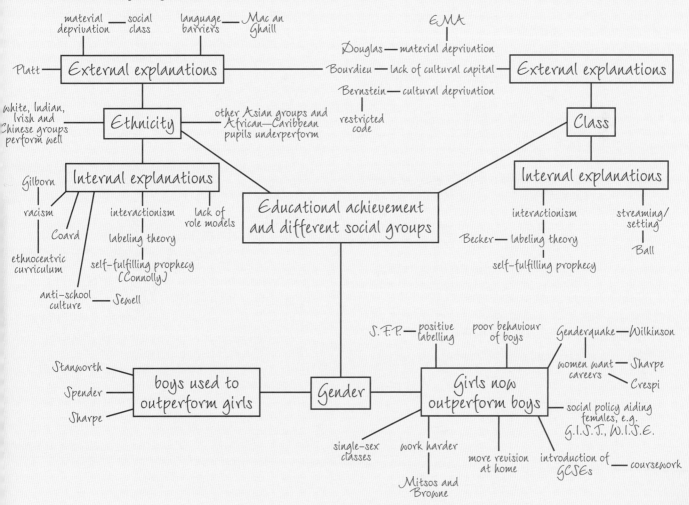

Relationships and processes in school

Introduction

Although structures are important in schools, the reality is that to discover what is really happening in education we need to look at the interaction between pupils and teachers. Why, for example, do some pupils end up failing themselves and creating anti-school cultures? How far does teacher influence stretch?

The organisation of schools

Central to an understanding of pupil reaction is an understanding of how the processes in schools lead to different outcomes for pupils. Essentially the social organisation of schools has changed very little over the last one hundred years. Schools are seen as:

- Mimicking hierarchical structures outside of the education system:

  A few members of staff, such as the senior management, have considerable power whereas others, who are less experienced and less well qualified, have very little autonomy in school. It is also interesting to note that often these hierarchical relationships within schools are similar to those in wider society. So, for example, although women make up the majority of staff in primary schools, it is men who are much more likely to become head teachers.

- Operating like mini businesses:

  Sociologists often use the analogy of a sausage making machine to explain how they process pupils. Children enter at five years of age and are processed to:

  - All wear the same uniform with little concern about individualism or targeted programmes
  - See success as being linked to examination success alone

  - Understand that success is based upon universalistic judgements being made about them
  - Understand that knowledge is never linked together; it is always fragmented
  - Believe that the school's time is far more important than pupils
  - Believe that rules are to be obeyed regardless of what they are

- Having a rigid curriculum:

  Many argue that the main problem with the education system remains the inflexible curriculum; a curriculum that has changed little over the last 150 years and one which only meets the needs of the most academic pupils (the top 20 per cent) but ignores the majority. There remains a deep unease that the educational diet we are offering our children is not meeting their needs, or the needs of society. The curriculum is more a throwback to the 1950s, an age where we knew what knowledge was and how to apply it. However, in the twenty-first century these 'truths' are no longer applicable. So whilst the present curriculum seems committed to the ideas of marketisation and efficiency, our employers still complain that those who go into the workforce are unable to act pragmatically, make decisions and solve problems. It is with this in mind that some schools are introducing an 'open minds' curriculum which stresses the importance of the following 'competencies':

  - **Learning:** Learning how to learn, being systematic, think and reflect, but also enjoying the learning process.
  - **Citizenship:** Learning how to relate to people from diverse backgrounds.
  - **Relating to people:** Learning how to relate to people in different contexts and roles, thereby understanding and being able to manage personal and emotional relationships.
  - **Managing situations:** Coping with the use of time, new situations, whilst celebrating success and learning from failure. Students are also expected to develop the capacity to be entrepreneurial and to take risks.
  - **Managing information:** Learn how to access information, evaluate it and then apply it critically.

  In some schools in the UK this has resulted in year seven, eight and nine students being taught these 'competencies' by one teacher, rather than having separate teachers for each curriculum subject. However, main national curriculum subjects, such as Maths and English, continue to be taught by specialist staff.

The hidden curriculum

Work into the **hidden curriculum** and misbehaviour, particularly of working-class boys, encouraged sociologists to explore why some pupils were able to internalise and follow the hidden curriculum whilst others developed anti-school cultures that opposed the school with vigour. As we have seen in Section One, Paul Willis in particular wanted to understand the motivations for working-class pupils creating an anti-school culture. He discovered that much of their behaviour was a direct response to the reality that they were expected to fail. Thus as a result of their low status within school, the only way that they could find status was through the creation of an anti-school culture. Poor behaviour, mucking about and taking control from the teacher were not considered by the group to be inappropriate, but a legitimate way of responding to their lack of status or **status frustration**.

Male sub-cultures

Whilst in the past males could almost ignore the idea of gaining good educational qualifications, this is no longer the case. The Sixties and early Seventies was a period of incredible economic growth and this ensured that any boys that wanted a job could get one. Often these jobs were well paid and had good progression. This resulted in many males feeling that education was not that important and work was more important than gaining what they considered useless qualifications. This response led particularly to working class males almost failing themselves on purpose and certainly creating an anti-school culture. Much of the male sub-culture that was created was reactive to the treatment they received from the teachers. However, the treatment was often as a consequence of how they saw education. Willis realised this and noted that the boys understood that the system was going to fail them, and responded or reacted accordingly. However, writers such as Hargreaves (1967) and Peter Woods (1983) believe that the reaction of working-class male pupils is far more complex that merely the creation of anti- and pro-school cultures. Woods, for example, used Merton's Strain Theory (1968) to suggest that pupils respond in a variety of ways, from ingratiation and compliance to outright rebellion.

It now seems that male working-class boys have not moved away from this perception that jobs will always be there for them, despite a seismic shift in the economy away from the manufacturing sector which favours males to the tertiary sector that does not. Given that they imagine that jobs will not be a problem, it is hardly surprising that boys on *The New Deal* commented in a study by Anne Gray (2000) that they resented the "poor quality training, inappropriate attitudes of supervisors, low remuneration on options and fear of pressure to accept a low-paid job."

More recently studies have started to look at other areas of sub-culture away from reactive explanations. Mac an Ghaill (1994) provided an even more sophisticated typology to explain male subcultures. He noted a range of sub-cultures such as:

- Academic achievers: boys from working-class backgrounds who want to do well in education but who have to cope with jibes from the other boys in school.
- New enterprisers: pupils who embraced vocational qualifications such as GNVQ and GCSE Business Studies, realising that these subjects offered a successful career pathway.

Female sub-cultures

The majority of girls, as witnessed by female educational attainment, tend to embrace a pro-school culture. Girls therefore tend to value education and see it as an excellent route to career success. Therefore, although girls often do not necessarily see education as enjoyable, they seem to understand that it offers benefits beyond the instrumental. For example, they use school as an arena within which to socialise with their friends. Their collaborative and communicative stance allows them to support each other, particularly when it comes to examinations.

However, some qualitative studies indicate that similar to their working-class male contemporaries, they form anti-school oppositional cultures. Conversely, these studies indicate that female identities are constructed differently to that of the boys. Studies such as McRobbie and Garber (1975) and Griffin (1985) imply that women actively negotiate their female identities in response to how the school sees them and how it responds to female pupils. On occasions this leads girls to see their schooling within traditional notions of female identity such as homemakers and wives.

Contemporary research has examined fragmented identities and sought to widen the debate within a post modern context. For example, examining how consumer consumption affects female and male identities, Delamont (1990) found that girls reject 'failing working-class lads' because they cannot offer them the lifestyle that they seek.

Ethnic sub-cultures

Sociology textbook writers like O'Donnell (1992) point out that prejudice and discrimination is faced by all ethnic minorities in Britain. However, O'Donnell argues that it is the reaction to this discrimination by different ethnic groups that helps us understand differential educational performance. He observes that black males often respond with anger and oppose white institutions, including schools.

In contrast, Indian people, although they are resentful of racism and show anger, do not always rebuff the powerful white institutions. It therefore follows that black people, particularly males, are more likely to underperform as they show strong resistance to schooling, whilst Indian people perform well because they use the educational system to their advantage.

More radical theorists have utilised the work of Willis to develop a resistance theory. Willis argues that subordinate groups in schools do not just passively accept their disadvantage but develop coping strategies for resisting practices that lead to their underachievement. Giroux argues that these strategies may be adaptive as well as resisting, but that the strategies of resistance, such as those adopted by ethnic minorities, have the potential to liberate the oppressed from their exploitation. It is by treating individuals as able to mediate their 'lived existence' that ethnic educational disadvantage may be overcome.

Tony Sewell writing in *The Independent* (2002) suggests that the biggest problem for black pupils is peer group pressure which makes it 'uncool' for students to aspire to educational success. A questionnaire of 150 black 15-year-olds in five secondary schools, conducted by Dr Sewell, revealed 80 per cent cited peer-group pressure as the biggest barrier to their learning. One girl told the researchers: "I don't blame the teachers. Everyone knows it ain't just the teachers. It's mainly black kids, with some whites, all wanting to act as if they're the rudest."

However, studies by Fuller and Mirza show a very different response to schooling by black girls compared with their peer groups. **Mirza** (1992) found that although girls were often put down and offered inappropriate advice, black girls nonetheless did better in exams than their peers and that black girls yearned to gain qualifications similar to their middle class counterparts. She found that in her study 74 per cent of black females expected to find work in social classes one and two, compared with only 27 per cent of black boys and 35 per cent of white females. Mirza explains the differences by a comparison of second generation black and Irish pupils. The black girls in her sample discarded the economic dependency desired by young Irish women. They looked forward to relationships which have joint responsibility towards the household within the context of relative autonomy between the sexes which are a common feature of West Indian family life.

From the study, Mirza believes that positive attitudes to education and lack of restrictions of the female labour market participation within West Indian families account for their high aspirations in contrast to their male brothers.

Shain (2003) has looked at Asian girls' experience of education. She sees racism as fundamental to understanding Asian reaction to schooling. However, she makes the point that because we are dealing with humans this response is not homogenous. Shain believes that racist attitudes of seeing Asian girls as hardworking and passive stem from historical assumptions of Asian cultures. This perception was reinforced by the sharp differences of behaviour shown in particular by black pupils in contrast to Asian girls.

Connolly's comprehensive overview and assessment of the examination of Asian boys' behaviour in school showed that Asian boys tend to be treated more leniently than black boys, with poor behaviour being overlooked by the teacher (1998).

Louise Archer (2005) found that for Chinese and Asian girls, success and passive resistance, although admirable for the pursuit of high level academic qualifications, can be seen as a problem as it is as a consequence of restrictive home cultures.

From work on sub-cultures it is clear that although sub-culture is important to the success or failure of a variety of different groups, its impact is highly individual and complex. Whilst one group appears to respond in a negative manner, other groups often turn around their perception of racism and work even harder to prove that self-fulfilling prophesy wrong.

An evaluation of sub-cultural reponses to educational attainment

From the available literature a few comments can be made about the strengths and weaknesses of such research:

- One clear advantage is that they open up the 'black box' of what happens within the classroom and show us the differences of response from a variety of different ethnic cultures.

- The multitude of studies that show such consistent responses indicate that there must be some validity to their findings.

However:

- Most of the studies are small-scale and therefore low in validity. Can we be certain that the response of a few pupils in one school is typical?

- Consequently, it is problematic to make generalisations from their findings.

- Studies indicate vast variations in the response to education by different groups. What is needed here is for researchers to concentrate on small sub-cultural groups rather than claiming the same response by all ethnic minorities.

What do you know now?

1. Explain the term 'labeling'.
2. Outline why the response of working classes, although appropriate in the Seventies, is not suitable now.
3. Indicate how female sub-cultural response is different from that of males.
4. Outline two criticisms of sub-cultural responses to educational failure.
5. Explain two strengths of this work.

Key terms

Hidden curriculum: The hidden curriculum consists of those things pupils learn through the experience of attending school rather than the stated educational objectives of such institutions.

Status frustration: Where groups feel frustrated by their lack of success given the judgement of dominant groups. Such frustration often leads to these groups rebelling and creating an anti-school culture.

Section summary

- Central to an understanding of pupil reaction is an understanding of how the processes in schools lead to different outcomes for pupils.

- Whilst in the past males could almost ignore the idea of gaining good educational qualifications, this is no longer the case. The Sixties and early Seventies was a period of incredible economic growth and this ensured that any boys that wanted a job could get one. Often these jobs were well paid and had good progression.

- The majority of girls, as witnessed by female educational attainment, tend to embrace a pro-school culture. Girls tend to value education and see it as an excellent route to career success. Therefore, although girls often do not see education as necessarily enjoyable, they seem to understand that it offers benefits beyond the instrumental.

- Writers, like O'Donnell (1992), point out that prejudice and discrimination is faced by all ethnic minorities in Britain. However, O'Donnell argues that it is the reaction to this discrimination by different ethnic groups that helps us understand differential educational performance.

- In contrast, Indians, although they are resentful of racism, do not always rebuff the powerful white institutions. It therefore follows that black people, particularly males, are more likely to underperform as they show strong resistance to schooling, whilst Indians perform well because they use the educational system to their advantage.

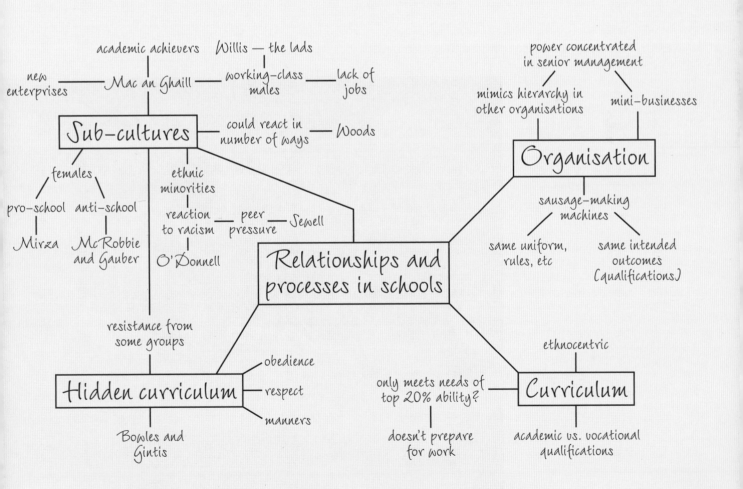

Educational policies

Introduction

In this section we explore the impact of educational policy on the schooling of pupils since 1945.

The education system up until the Butler Act of 1944 was disorganised, with all pupils being schooled until 14 years of age. However, pupils received vastly different experiences from the system. For the most privileged this meant attending public school; with excellent facilities, high expectations and the likelihood that students would progress onto university. However, most people's education provision was determined by the 'postcode lottery'. Some places in the UK were well catered for; for others the provision was sparse or poor. During the Second World War, however, it was recognised that the education system did not provide the basis for a strong army, navy or air force, whilst poor **vocational** skills hampered economic activity during the war years. Consequently central government set about ensuring that once the soldiers returned from the war, the education system would be 'fit for heroes' and particularly for their children.

The easiest way to understand educational policy is to look at it chronologically. The reason for this is that educational policies are produced as a result of the ideas of the party in power at each point of time. For much of the time period concerned there was a considerable amount of agreement about educational policy.

There were two central planks upon which consensus was achieved:

1. The education system should be meritocratic:

   A meritocracy is a system where individuals are rewarded on the basis of merit or ability and effort rather than social background. The concept of meritocracy is important because it provides the explanation for the social system as it currently operates. If everyone is rewarded for their skills and abilities rather than, for example, who their parents are, then people will see their position in society as a justifiable position. Reform since 1944 has tried to achieve this, with varying degrees of success. For many years there was consensus about this major goal, and as much as possible was done to encourage opportunity for all regardless of class, gender and ethnicity. Despite this there was some disagreement, with the left wing, such as Marxists, believing that the reforms did not lead to equality of opportunity, whilst others such as the New Right believed it did.

2. To generate a highly trained and efficient workforce by transferring vocational skills:

   Many sociologists accept that good education leads to a more productive workforce. However, many observe that the schooling system also appears to favour certain groups, such as middle-class pupils, often at the expense of their working-class counterparts.

1944–65: secondary education for all

The Education Act of 1944 made secondary education completely free and obligatory up to the age of 15 (although this was raised in 1972 to age 16). The act had two main aims, namely:

1. To improve economic efficiency by developing the skills of everyone and as a consequence create a more effective workforce.

2. To create a more equal society by giving everyone the opportunity to be educated, allowing them either to progress to university or obtain a secure occupation.

The tripartite system

The tripartite act itself established three types of school hence the name: tri (three) partite (parts) system. The three component schools were:

1. **Grammar schools:** Offered a traditional academic education. Only the top 15–20 per cent of students went to this type of institution upon passing the eleven-plus exam.

2. **Technical schools:** Provided a practical and vocational education, aimed at occupations related to skilled manual jobs. However, this part of the system was never properly funded. Consequently, most pupils either attended grammar schools or secondary modern schools.

3. **Secondary modern schools:** Offered a halfway house between grammar and technical schools, with some emphasis on academia but also providing pupils with vocational skills that would be useful for the workplace. Many students and their parents felt that going to a secondary modern school represented failure.

Allocation to each of these schools was meant to be completely fair. All children were required to sit the eleven-plus examination to correctly identify which one of the schools they would be most suited to. Only those who managed to pass the eleven-plus went to grammar school or to technical school, with the remaining going to secondary modern school. Thus, we can see the system took many of the strands associated with functionalism. It offered a system that was functional for pupils, which allocated them appropriately in relation to their ability, and was, on the face of it, meritocratic. However many, including middle-class parents, disliked the system, claiming that pupils were often misallocated and branded as failures.

Criticisms of the tripartite system

The system had a number of problems. Many pupils, particularly boys, develop academically after the age of 11, yet had already been allocated to a secondary modern school. This lead to one in ten pupils being misallocated. This criticism was true of all classes, with the middle classes particularly disapproving of an exam that they saw as being as an inequitable and imprecise way of allocating schools to pupils.

Despite the fact that all schools were meant to have a **parity of esteem** (schools that are equal in status), the reality was that secondary modern schools were seen as a 'school for failures', with often both teachers and pupils having low expectations of the system. For many this led to a **self-fulfilling prophesy** of failure as the pupils lived up to the failure label that they had been given aged As a consequence there was concern that the aptitudes of the working classes were being wasted in secondary modern schools.

Technical schools were not expanded in the way that the act suggested. The high cost of equipping the schools resulted in them not being available to the majority. They only accounted for about five per cent of the educational provision. Again it was a matter of 'postcode lottery'. The vast majority of students attended secondary modern schools.

There were big differences in the number of grammar school places available throughout the country. Children in Wales had the highest chance of a grammar school place, with one out of three children passing the eleven-plus. Children in the south of England had the lowest chance of passing the exam, with only one in eight getting a place in grammar school. As well as this, Local Education Authorities often provided better facilities for their grammar schools than for the secondary modern schools in their area.

Some believed that the examination-based system disadvantaged those who were nervous doing formal written assessments and, as a result, would favour those from middle-class backgrounds who could, for example, afford private tutoring to help with exam practice.

Because of the need to achieve a gender balance, some girls, despite gaining high scores in the eleven-plus did not get into grammar school. This led to accusations that entry was biased towards boys.

Other commentators point to the cultural specificity of the eleven-plus. The exam's middle-class language ensured that the majority of successes were likely to come from the dominant classes. As such, it was seen as an unfair examination.

As a consequence by the mid 1950s there was general agreement that the tripartite system needed to be replaced with a system that provided genuine opportunity for everyone. The system chosen was the comprehensive system.

1965–79: comprehensive schools (comprehensivisation)

A comprehensive school is a secondary school that accepts pupils of all abilities. By 1964 Wilson's Labour government had instructed Local Education Authorities to introduce comprehensive schools, thereby leading to the end of the unpopular eleven-plus examination and the three-tier tripartite system, although it actually took until 1976 until all councils were told to prepare plans for comprehensive schools.

Children would, for the first time, be educated in the same school regardless of their social class, gender and ethnicity, and it was believed that this 'cultural rub-off' would lead to greater equality and acceptance of diversity. Although traditionalists were not happy with the abolition of grammar schools, which were seen as centres of excellence, many other educationalists favoured the change. It was also felt that comprehensives, because of their large size, offered scope for considerable economies of scale. As a result large

investment in comprehensives occurred, with better facilities being offered to students and higher levels of teacher training, ensuring that the quality of teaching matched its new and improved surroundings. However, there were a number of criticisms of the system:

- Some argued that because comprehensive schools were so large they became impersonal 'factories' and as a result pupils often felt alienated by the impersonal nature of the education. It was argued that this could lead to discipline problems, as well as some middle-ability children not being noticed nor their abilities being developed.

- It was argued that where pupils were taught in mixed-ability groups, the brightest were hindered by the slower learners and their attainments affected.

- Many comprehensive schools put their pupils into streams according to their ability. Essentially, such school are little different from grammar schools, resulting in similar feelings of lack of self-worth for those in lower bands and streams.

- As with the previous system, there was not a homogeneous provision. So, although some comprehensives did have excellent facilities, others were not as fortunate. This resulted in better-equipped schools being over-subscribed, whilst other 'sink schools' (schools that are failing with a poor reputation, poor behaviour and poor standards of teaching) had falling roles, with parents keen to avoid the sink schools doing what they could to get places for their children in other schools. Consequently, the sink schools had few applicants.

- Finally, there was no guarantee that the most able students would necessarily do any better in a comprehensive rather than in a grammar school.

By the end of the 1970s the tide had turned against the comprehensive school, with the media in particular making much of the fact that comprehensives, with their policy on mixed-ability teaching and progressive teaching, were 'out of control', with teachers failing to provide an excellent standard of education. And, whilst the ideas of child-centred learning sounded a panacea, to disaffected students forced to sit in classes the reality was far different. As a result, parents started to question the educational policies of the Labour Party (1974–9). With this would come a huge shift in policy; the days of progressive education and teacher control were soon to become a thing of the past.

Despite this, we do still have a grammar school system, which is operated on a selective entry basis, with the top 10 per cent in particular catchment areas being offered places. The system still operates in areas as geographically dispersed as Northern Ireland, Kent, Buckinghamshire, Essex, Trafford and Wiltshire.

Harold Wilson

1979–97: twenty years of Tory educational policy

Due to the fact that the Labour government introduced the comprehensive ideal after World War Two and then Callaghan instigated the 'Great Debate' at Ruskin College, Oxford, that led to the demise of the comprehensive system, it is ironic that the advocate of the reforms that followed during this period was James Callaghan, the then Labour Prime Minster (1974–79). In a speech at Ruskin College in 1976 he spoke of "legitimate public concern [about]trendy teaching methods". With this he initiated what has since been called 'The Great Debate'. This debate was a response to the fact that many felt that teachers had too much autonomy in the classroom and that more government control was needed to safeguard the quality of education being received by pupils. However, Callaghan's speech infuriated the teaching unions who resented interference from government. Nonetheless it had a huge influence on public debate about education and paved the way for the introduction of a number of major reforms. These included:

Basic skills

There was a feeling within industry in particular that schools were not producing efficient workers. Callaghan believed that employers in industry felt that school-leavers "sometimes do

James Callaghan

not have the basic tools to do the job that is required." As a result of this observation, in 1978 the Labour Party introduced the Youth Opportunities Programme (YOP) which offered every school-leaver a job, a training place or employment experience as an integral part of their benefit, with the Manpower Services Commission (MSC) being established to assist with the programme.

A core curriculum

Given Callaghan's observation that parents were "uneasy about the new informal methods of teaching", Labour set out "the strong case for the so-called core curriculum and basic knowledge". These two concepts proved vital to an understanding of educational policy instigated throughout the 1980s, in particular New Vocationalism and the 1988 Government Education Reform Bill (GERBIL), which was introduced by Thatcher's Conservative government (1979–91).

New Vocationalism

In a period of rising unemployment and the noticeable decline of Britain's economy, the concern was that education was failing to produce properly skilled and motivated young workers. That it should produce equality of opportunity was deemed less important than the needs of industry. This new set of initiatives was called New Vocationalism and with it came a commitment to train workers as opposed to just educating them.

The assisted places scheme

The **assisted places scheme** was introduced in 1980 and offered children who could not afford to go to fee-paying independent schools a free or subsidised place if they were able to score within the top 10–15 per cent of applicants in the school's entrance examination. This scheme, which assisted up to 32 000 pupils per annum, was abolished by the latest Labour government to help pay for reductions in class sizes in the primary sector.

Decentralisation and centralisation

The Conservative Party also instigated a less centralised system of educational control that allowed schools to be autonomous with their financial decision making. This change in policy reflected the view that Thatcher was unimpressed by overspending Labour local education authorities (LEAs) and considered that one way to control excessive local authority spending was to decentralise decision making away from the locality to the schools themselves. This led to the introduction of grant-maintained schools and local management of schools (LMS). Having said this, despite Thatcher's rhetoric to 'roll back the state', she in fact centralised education as never before. For instance, the national curriculum and grant-maintained status took control from the locality and replaced the power in those within government.

The Education Reform Act 1988

The Education Reform Act of 1988 is generally considered as the most important single piece of education legislation in England, Wales and Northern Ireland since the Butler Education Act 1944. The following measures were introduced:

- Testing and attainment targets were introduced for 7, 11, 14 and 16-year-olds:

    These targets were introduced in the hope that standards would rise as schools competed against other. **Standard Assessment Tasks (SATs)** also allowed national targets to be set in order to monitor if the system was working effectively, whilst also allowing parents to compare schools.

- National curriculum was introduced:

    Within the national curriculum each pupil was required to study Maths, English, Science, History, Geography, Technology, Music, Art, Physical Education (PE), and a foreign language. This was intended to ensure that pupils concentrated on what the government saw as essential subjects. It also, for the first time, allowed pupils to pick up their studies easily if they if they moved schools.

- The act emphasised parental choice in the educational market (marketisation):

    In theory parents had the right to decide to send their children to the school of their choice. This would help to encourage competition. A policy of open enrolment compelled every school to take on the maximum of pupils that could be accommodated in their buildings.

- The act allowed the setting up of City Technology Colleges (CTCs):

    CTCs were located in inner cities and concentrated on specialising in technology. They were sponsored by private industries so that the state would not have to pay the

full costs of building the colleges and so they would be independent of the LEAs. CTCs were designed to cater for the 11–18 year-old age group and to compete with existing schools.

- Existing schools were able to opt out of LEA control and be funded by central government:

The opting out category created the grant-maintained schools, so called because they received their finance from a central government grant. Their board of directors were, for the first time, allowed to manage their resources directly and unhindered by LEAs.

- The act gave greater autonomy to the schools in how they spent their money:

LMS gave the responsibility for managing school budgets to head teachers and governors, thus reducing the power of LEAs. Under the new system of formula funding the financing of schools was largely based upon the number of pupils (per capita). This was intended to reward successful schools with more money.

A number of important changes were not part of the GERBIL:

Technical and Vocational Education Initiative (TVEI):

TVEI started as a pilot scheme in 1983 in 14 LEAs. It was a scheme for 14–18 year-olds, which ran alongside the conventional curriculum and included work experience. TVEI became available to all secondary schools in 1986 and was later extended to include sixth form, further education and tertiary colleges.

- Certificate of Pre-Vocational Education (CPVE):

CPVE was similar to TVEI, in that it stressed preparation for the workplace. CPVE, first taught in 1985–6, was for those over 16 who were unsure about what they wanted to do. It offered work experience and was taught in schools and colleges. CPVE taught practical skills, but could be combined with taking exams in traditional subjects, although in practice students who were unsuccessful in traditional subjects tended to follow the CPVE route.

CPVE was not a great success and was later replaced by vocationally orientated exams such as GNVQs and NVQs and later, VGCSEs.

- The National Council for Vocational Qualifications (NCVQ) was set up in 1986:

The NCVQ was introduced to help standardise vocational qualifications related to particular occupations. In 1990 around 170 NVQs had been established. These were intended to reward practical achievement, with qualifications being obtained by demonstrating competencies. NVQs have four levels from level one (GCSE standard) to level four (postgraduate level). GNVQs were introduced nationally in 1994. These were intended to provide a vocationally-orientated alternative to traditional exams like A levels.

- General Certificate of Secondary Education (GCSE) replaced the O level system and the CSE system:

All students were entered for the same exam, the GCSE. GCSEs introduced a considerable amount of coursework, much against New Right thinking. This encouraged pupil-orientated approaches rather than 'chalk and talk'.

- The Introduction of Office for Standards in Education (Ofsted):

Introduced in 1992, the main aim of Ofsted was to improve standards of education and childcare. To achieve this it was given the task to inspect the 24 000 maintained schools in the UK.

Ofsted also inspects independent schools, colleges of further education, LEAs, initial teacher training, further education teacher training, nursery schools and childminders; releasing reports that specify how each institution is performing.

- Greater competition in post-16-year-old education:

To further encourage competition, colleges of further education were able to operate independently of LEAs from 1992 onwards. Additionally, polytechnics were allowed to become universities, thereby offering greater competition to the old universities that dominated the higher education sector.

An assessment of the Government Education Reform Bill 1988

Overall then this important bill had a number of pros and cons:

- Having a national curriculum means that, theoretically at least, all children have access to the same quality of education no matter where they live in the country.
- However, many felt it offered a paradoxical shift in power away from LEAs, who were accountable, to central government.

- Although the idea of comparing schools sounds straightforward, in reality schools are a reflection of their intake. **League tables** offer no indication of these difficulties, yet were published as a straight comparison between educational institutions.

- Some schools started trying to cheat the system by not entering low-ability children or introducing easier examinations that allowed greater points per pupils (GNVQs and VGCSEs).

- Some feel that schools spend too long preparing children to pass tests rather than just teaching them.

1997 onwards: New Labour

The Blair government came to power in 1997, with education at the top of its agenda. This was exemplified by Blair's proclamation in his keynote address to the 1996 Labour Party Conference when he commented "Ask me for my three main priorities for government and I tell you: education, education and education".

Yet in reality policy changes were small, with Labour continuing Thatcher's marketisation policies, although a greater degree of state intervention was introduced. This 'no change' policy was perhaps most exemplified by Blair's refusal to replace the Chief Inspector of Schools, Chris Woodhead. Without doubt Labour has invested strongly in education, with the government spending nearly £1.2 billion on education per week. Some central policies introduced in this wave of investment include:

Primary

- The creation of the Standards and Effectiveness Unit which set ambitious targets for literacy and numeracy. To assist reaching these targets numeracy and literacy hours (sections of the timetable that were set aside so that teachers were directed to focus on these initiatives) were made compulsory in primary schools across the UK.

- Establishing reduced class sizes in the first three years of primary school. For the first time class sizes above 30 were prohibited.

- Nursery Education: All three-year-olds now have access to a free nursery place, amounting to five sessions of two-and-a-half hours of free nursery education a week. Each LEA, in association with their Early Years Development and Childcare Partnership (EYDCP), keeps a list of nursery education providers approved to offer free places.

Secondary

Curriculum 2000 reformed A levels, with the new A levels consisting of six units: three units taken in year one called AS levels, and three in the second year, called A2 levels. Assessment was also altered so that A levels became modular, offering all pupils the chance to be able to retake modules to gain higher marks. Additionally, a new qualification called

Tony Blair

Key Skills was introduced, designed to improve the vocational skills of post-16-year-old students. However, as many pupils were exempt from taking this qualification if they had obtained A*–C grades at GCSE, this left many classes empty. Generally apathy towards these courses from Universities and Colleges Admissions Service (UCAS) and the majority of universities resulted in Key Skills being dropped by many LEAs from 2003 onwards.

School diversity

Within the secondary sector, a range of schools have been developed during Blair's time as prime minister. These include:

- **Specialist schools:**

  Specialist schools are state secondary schools that aim to be local 'centres of excellence' in their chosen specialism, and which benefit from public funding under the Specialist Schools Programme (a government initiative to ensure that all schools pursue a specialism; be it drama, business, the International Baccalaureate, science, and so on) and from private sector sponsorship. Bids for specialist status are acknowledged by the Department for Education and Skills (DfES) in March and October each year. There are ten specialisms approved by the DfES: Arts, Business and Enterprise, Engineering, Humanities, Language, Mathematics and Computing, Music, Science, and Sports and Technology. A school may be specialist in respect of a maximum of two of these areas, and must apply separately for each designation.

The impact of the specialist schools programme on exam results

Jim Taylor (2007)

Jim Taylor found that the specialist schools programme is not the success story that the government claimed it to be. Whilst Business, Technology and Enterprise, and Science and Art schools showed an average of between one and three per cent GCSE grade A*–C points increase, the overall average of all specialist schools is just one per cent greater than would have been attained if the school had not gained specialist status.

These findings contrast greatly with the early study of Jesson and Crossley (2004–5) that indicated that specialist schools increased the percentage of pupils obtaining five A*–C grades by up to four to five per cent.

- **Beacon schools:**

    The Beacon schools initiative was designed to raise standards through the dissemination of good practice. Beacon schools are schools which were identified as amongst the best performing in the country and represent examples of successful practice. They were expected to spread this good practice across other local schools that were underperforming in comparison.

- **Foundation schools:**

    Foundation schools are schools that are maintained by the local authority. Other types of schools include community, voluntary-aided and voluntary-controlled schools. Foundation schools share a number of characteristics with voluntary-aided schools in that they own their land and buildings, employ their own staff and determine their own admission policies subject to any comments by the Schools Admissions Forum. In future they will also be allowed to set their own programme of study.

- **Academies:**

    The Academy programme has been one of Labour's most contentious educational reforms over the last decade. The programme offers the opportunity for businessmen or church groups to take over the running of an academy if they are willing to donate a maximum of £2 million. This then allows them to set the school's ethos and appoint governors. In return the government pays the institution's running costs and most of the £25 million construction bill, even though the school remains free of local authority control. There are plans to double the number of academies from 200 to 400 to transform the educational experience of pupils and parents in deprived inner city areas.

An over-concentration on GCSE grade A*–C students

Since the Education Reform Act (ERA) (Baker) in 1988, educationalists such as **Gillburn and Youdell** (2000) believe that policies within school to improve attainment have concentrated upon grade A*–C students. According to Gillburn and Youdell, this has further improved privileges for the middle classes, who are primarily picked out to be assisted in obtaining five A*–C grades. By contrast they suggest that other, underprivileged and discriminated groups, such as those from black backgrounds and travellers, have been left by the wayside as the drive for better exam results and a better standing within the league tables dominates.

Gillburn and Youdell

Higher education

David Watson (Centre for Higher Education Studies, 2007) believes that Labour's policies towards higher education have not been as generous as those towards the secondary school sector. The higher education community points to the following as evidence of this:

- Other than investment in Science, which has been funded by the Treasury rather than from the Department of Education, the higher education sector has seen declines investments.

- Labour has introduced, in effect, what is considered to be a 'maximum flat fee' of £3000, with little chance that this will be increased in the near future.

- Widening participation has stalled. After Blair promised a '50 per cent participation rate', now only vague aspirations are being offered by Brown.

Recent educational policy

The Tomlinson Enquiry (2004) proposes sweeping reforms to the 14 to 19 education system. It advocates that A levels, GCSEs and vocational examinations such as VGCSEs and BTECs should be phased out, to be replaced by a diploma offering students the opportunity to study up to four different levels of attainment. It is envisaged that such a change will at last help to remove the perception that vocational qualifications are inferior to academic ones.

1. Link the following to the tripartite system or the comprehensive system, or both:

   - 1944 Butler Act
   - The eleven-plus
   - Separating the social classes
   - Technical schools
   - Progressive teaching
   - Mixed ability
   - Grammar schools
   - The secondary modern school
   - Selecting from catchment areas
   - Mixing the social classes
   - Traditional talk and chalk.

2. How did the schooling system operate up until the 1944 Butler Act?.

3. Explain the reasons for the Butler Act being established.

4. Which school had the higher status in the tripartite system?

5. Describe the most important components of the Education Reform Bill 1988.

6. Identify criticism of the Education Reform Bill 1988.

7. Evaluate how Labour policy has differed from Conservative educational policy.

8. What is 'diversity'? Give examples of how Labour has encouraged diversity with their educational policies.

Key terms

Academies: State-maintained independent schools set up with the help of external sponsors. Tony Blair established academies in 2000 to drive up standards by closing down failing schools in struggling education authorities.

Assisted places scheme: A scheme established in 1980 in which the government assisted parents with the cost of fees at independent schools on a means-tested basis. The scheme was phased out in 1997.

City technology colleges: Schools usually based in deprived inner-city areas which are funded by the private and public sector. City technology colleges offer a curriculum with a particular focus on science and technology.

Curriculum 2000: Overhaul of the A level system which allowed post-16-year-old pupils to take more subjects in their first year (AS) which is assessed in modules.

Eleven-plus: Examination taken by 11-year-olds based upon cognitive IQ tests that allocated pupils either to grammar schools if they passed the exam or to a secondary modern school if they failed.

Foundation schools: With these schools the governing body employ the school staff and have primary responsibility for admission arrangements. They are owned by the governing body or by a charitable foundation (hence the moniker 'foundation schools').

Hidden curriculum: All those things that are learnt by pupils without them being formally taught as part of the official curriculum.

League tables: Tables published annually which provide a guide to how well a school is doing. Four tables are published which list national curriculum test results for each school in England and Wales.

Marketisation: The process of introducing market forces within the educational system; for example, parents should have free choice where to send their children.

New Vocationalism: A set of educational reforms designed to bridge the gap between education and training, thereby ensuring that schooling meets the specific needs of employers.

Parity of esteem: Equal status often relates to different examination regimes.

Standard Attainment Tests (SATs): National tests that assess pupils at the ages of 7, 11 and 14 at the end of Key Stages 1, 2 and 3.

Vocational: Relating to an occupation or career.

Section summary

The Education Act of 1944 made secondary education completely free and obligatory up until the age of 15 (although this was raised in 1972 to 16 years of age).

The 'Butler Act' itself introduced the tripartite system. The three schools that were introduced were: the grammar school (intended for the top 20 per cent of students), the technical school (intended as a vocational route) and the secondary modern school (considered to be a halfway house between the academic and the vocational specialisms of the other two schools.

This system was criticised for its reliance upon using the blunt instrument of the eleven-plus.

Comprehensivisation occurred from the early Sixties onwards. A comprehensive school is a secondary school that accepts pupils of all abilities. By 1964 Wilson's Labour government instructed LEAs to introduce comprehensive schools, resulting to the end of the unpopular eleven-plus examination and the three tier tripartite system.

In 1979 the great debate on education was initiated by James Callaghan. This debate itself was a response to the fact that many felt that teachers had too much autonomy in the classroom and that more government control was needed to safeguard the quality of the education being given in schools.

- The Education Reform Act 1988 introduced: SATS, league tables, opting out of local authority control (grant maintained status), the introduction of vocational programmes such as TVEI and CPVE, and the replacement of GCE O levels with GCSEs and school inspections by Ofsted.

- The bill itself was criticised as it decreased the accountability of the education system by shifting power from the local area to government.

- Since Blair's election in 1997 policy changes were small, with Labour continuing Thatcher's marketisation policies, although a greater degree of state intervention was introduced.

- Blair's government focused on primary schools, introducing the 'literacy hour' and 'numeracy hour' to help meet ambitious targets for these.

- Within the secondary sector, Curriculum 2000 was implemented, reforming A levels into the modular exams of AS and A2.

- Not everyone has been happy with these changes. Some feel that these polices have encouraged schools to concentrate upon grade A*–C candidates at GCSE, whilst those in higher education believe that resources have not been lavished on their sector in the same way.

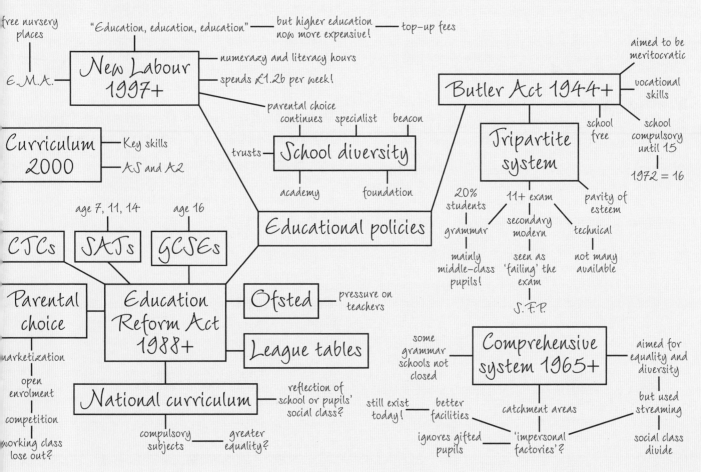

The application of research methods to education

Introduction

Educational research uses methods which are similarly used in other branches of the natural sciences and the social sciences. As a new component of the new A level syllabus pupils need to be able to apply these methods to the study of education. Whilst in the past students were able to achieve this by producing a piece of coursework, now you will be expected to use your knowledge of research and your own research to exemplify studies you have examined within this topic. During this module you will perhaps have noted that most of the research has been performed in schools and looked in particular at the way teachers and pupils respond to each other. Additionally, it is noticeable that while pupil and teacher interaction was considered important in the 1960s and 1970s, the focus of research has moved towards other areas of research, particularly the examination of how small groups respond rather than larger sub-cultures.

Methodology

There are two main approaches used when it comes to researching the educational system. The method chosen will of course result in particular from the ideological standpoint of the researcher undertaking the work. Methodology can be defined as an analysis of different methods. Two general approaches can be taken by researchers:

1. **The use of quantitative data:** This refers to data that is usually in numerical form, as a percentage, a number or a rate (often per head of the population). The **quantitative** approach is used when the researcher wants to obtain entire trends or statistical truth in the research. Examination data therefore that indicates that girls do substantially better at GCSE grades A*–C is an example of quantitative data. This method is used mainly by macro approaches which seek to explain responses in relation to a whole ideology. Marxism and functionalism are the best known of these. They believe that by looking at wide (macro) trends a more meaningful and valid set of results can be obtained. Typical examples of quantitative research methods include the use of questionnaires, surveys, experiments and using secondary data.

2. **The use of qualitative data:** By contrast **qualitative** data is usually in words, not in numerical data. Because words are used researchers are able to look at how pupils experience differences in the classroom and they can examine why pupils respond in different ways to the same people. This data, it is argued, is far richer in detail than data obtained by quantitative means. Examples of qualitative research include participant observation and unstructured interviews.

It should be noted that although I suggest that methods are polarised into quantitative and qualitative methods, the reality is that most modern day research tends to use the two in tandem. This is known as 'triangulation'.

Methods of data collection

Researchers can use the following ways to obtain data:

- **Primary data:** This is data collected directly by the researcher. This involves the researcher finding out things at first hand. Primary data has the advantage of allowing the sociologist to obtain data that may not be in the public domain. They can additionally ask questions that specifically allow any **hypothesis** to be answered. Examples of sources of primary data include questionnaires, interviews and participant and non-participant observation.

- **Secondary data:** This data is not collected directly by the researcher but is used nonetheless to explore and answer hypotheses. Examples of secondary data include the use of official statistics, the press, books and magazines.

What influences the methods used by researchers? Positivism versus interpretivism

Researchers are influenced by three factors:

1. The method must be appropriate to the topic to be investigated

2. It should be a method that is practical given the circumstances of the research

3. The researcher's ideological stance

Positivism

Positivism sees the world governed by social rules. Because people's behaviour is the result of socialization and social rules, this approach believes that behaviour is consistent and from this patterns can be isolated. Methods utilised include experiments and questionnaires. This approach is based on the attempt to imitate the methods of the natural sciences:

- Identification and observation of a problem.

- Collection of data.

Explanatory hypothesis.

Analysis of results.

Retesting if necessary. Positivists believe that further ongoing testing allows us to ascertain how close to the truth certain phenomena are.

Interpretation of results and issuing of a report.

The implications of this approach are as follows:

It is best to use the deductive approach. This is when a start is made from things that are assumed to be true, and conclusions are drawn that must be accurate if the assumptions are true.

There is an objective world which is capable of being understood in objective, scientific terms.

The whole of society is subject to investigation to see how behaviour is influenced by the structure and function of institutions.

Scientific analysis using structured interviews, surveys and statistical data shows the extent to which people are shaped and controlled by agencies of socialization.

Behaviour is predictable, since the 'actors' are trained to keep to their 'scripts'. Order is thereby maintained and conflicts managed.

Any research needs to be large-scale, thereby allowing generalisations to be made.

The advantages of questionnaires in educational research

Questionnaires are a common method used by sociologists. This questioning can take many forms:

Questionnaires administered within the school itself: This has the advantage of the researcher giving out the questionnaire and personally collecting it. This allows

the sociologist to explain what they want and clarify any difficulties that may arise. It also has the added advantage that sampling procedures can be used in allocating questionnaires within a school setting.

- **Postal questionnaires:** This method allows researchers to widen the geographical scope of their enquiry.

The advantages of personally distributed questionnaires

- Although slightly more expensive than postal questionnaires, this method is still relatively inexpensive
- This method allows the researcher to clarify any question that is not fully understood
- Results from personally distributed questionnaires can be analysed by computer with trends being isolated and graphs being produced
- Personal questionnaires reduce interviewer bias as standardised questions are more reliable
- Personal questionnaires are less intrusive than telephone questionnaires and are more personal

The disadvantages of personally distributed questionnaires

- Due to their standardised nature questionnaires do not allow further probing by the researcher
- The respondent may feel inhibited by the presence of the researcher
- Time pressure may lead to respondents giving answers that may not reflect their true opinions

The advantages of postal questionnaires

- It is a cheap and inexpensive method that eliminates interviewer bias
- Results can be analysed and interpreted with spreadsheet packages
- Allows pupils within the school to give honest, heartfelt responses
- Because similar questions are used again and again, this method achieves greater validity than more personal methods
- Particularly within a school setting, it allows the pupils to ponder on their responses rather than being harried by the researcher
- Offers the possibility of a wide geographical spread, thereby ensuring a more valid sample, and the chance to make more sweeping generalisations

The disadvantages of postal questionnaires

- Because the researcher is not close at hand, pupils and staff are unable to ask for clarification.

- Mailed questionnaires in particular tend to achieve low response rates, particularly when sent out to busy schools. Many teachers receive so much mail that much merely gets placed straight into the bin.

- With mailed questionnaires the researcher cannot be certain that the responses have been completed by the intended research target.

- Qualitative researchers remain dismissive of this method because it limits the answers of the respondent. Far from finding out about what happens in school, it offers only a sanitised peek into the world of education.

- On occasions, particularly with postal questionnaires, respondents are asked to complete the questionnaire outside of the setting that it is being asked. This may limit validity.

Interpretivism

Interpretivists see the world very differently from positivists. Instead of believing social facts, this group of researchers suggest that behaviour is far more fluid that positivists assert. We need, so they argue, to understand the meanings and values held by 'actors'. Therefore we can summarise this approach by:

- They believe that it is impossible to make laws of human nature. Therefore there is no point being 'scientific'.

- They use methods that uncover the values and meanings of those being studied.

The implications of this approach are as follows:

- That human behaviour is unique and cannot be predetermined. Humans have free will.

- The aim of social research is to investigate the meanings and interpretations of social actors in specific situations.

- Research is therefore likely only to be small-scale, as cost and time prohibit large-scale questioning.

The use of interpretive methodology

Participant observation

Participant observation refers to a form of sociological methodology in which the researcher takes on a part in the social situation under observation. The social researcher immerses themselves in the social setting under study, getting to know key actors in that location in a role which is either covert or overt. Overt participant observation involves telling the subjects being observed of your presence, whilst with covert participant observation the subjects are kept in the dark about the existence of a social researcher in their midst.

The aim is to understand events in the manner in which the subjects under study also experience them. Sociologists who employ participant observation as a research tool aim to discover the nature of social reality by understanding the actor's perception, understanding and interpretation of that social world. Whilst observing and experiencing as a participant, the sociologist must retain a level of **objectivity** in order to understand, analyse and explain the social world under study.

This method has been used extensively within educational research by writers as diverse as Paul Willis (1977) Mac an Ghaill (1994) and Hargreaves (1967). It offers the following advantages within a school setting:

- It allows for material straight from the horse's mouth

- The researcher actually experiences what the subjects go through

- Because the researcher becomes part of the group the subjects tend to change their behaviour less, particularly over time

However, as with all methods, it has its problems. These include:

- The researcher may become too close to the group and lose their objective stance as a result, which limits the validity of any findings

- Because of the small-scale nature of participant observation generalisations may be difficult to make

- Participant observation relies upon the skills and talents of the researcher, making replication almost impossible

- Whilst access may not be difficult within a school setting, the reality is that any older researcher is going to be seen with suspicion

Interviews

Interviews are a typical method used within schools. They can be of two types: either structured or unstructured. With the structured interview the researcher uses an interview frame to aid the task of reading out questions to the respondent. This method is favoured by quantitative theorists who believe that this consistent approach offers greater validity and reliability than open-ended questions. The other method utilising interviews is the unstructured interview. This allows the respondent to give answers that digress from the original question. Questioning is therefore more of a channel from which the respondent can further their responses. This is a highly appropriate method within a school setting, allowing pupils the space to explain and explore how they see the construct of the educational system. The middle approach is to use a selection of structured and semi-structured questions. The method was originally pioneered by Robert K Merton. It is ideal as a method of exploring pupil responses within a school.

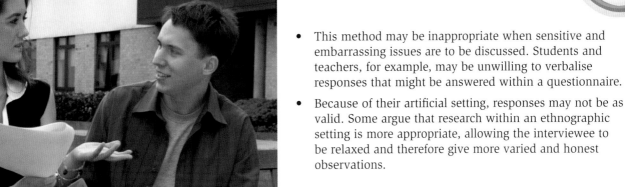

- This method may be inappropriate when sensitive and embarrassing issues are to be discussed. Students and teachers, for example, may be unwilling to verbalise responses that might be answered within a questionnaire.

- Because of their artificial setting, responses may not be as valid. Some argue that research within an ethnographic setting is more appropriate, allowing the interviewee to be relaxed and therefore give more varied and honest observations.

Ethical issues

It is important that research is conducted in an ethical way. Being ethical means that we should be aware of the rights and wrongs about how we should conduct sociological research … and how not to! Practically, this means we need to assess:

- **Whether consent has been gained:** As far as possible participation in sociological research should be based on the freely given informed consent of those studied. This means you need to tell those who you are observing.

- **Whether the research affects the rights and well being of the participants:** The British Sociological Association (2002) informs researchers that members have a responsibility both to safeguard the proper interests of those involved in or affected by their work and to report their findings accurately and truthfully. Practically, within research in an educational setting we should avoid distressing participants when conducting sociological research.

- **The possible consequences of participation:** Researchers need to be honest about any possible consequences, tell the participants of these, and allow participants to complain if needs be.

- **Whether the researcher is overstepping the boundaries of their professional competencies:** We must not research areas that we are not qualified to investigate. Researchers should satisfy themselves that the research they undertake is worthwhile and that the techniques proposed are appropriate. They should be clear about the limits of their detachment from and involvement in their areas of study. Ideally, when researching within schools it would be helpful if the researcher had some experience of teaching or some related discipline.

- **Whether any safety risks are involved:** Researchers face a range of potential risks to their safety. Safety issues need to be considered in the design and conduct of social research projects and procedures should be adopted to reduce the risk to researchers. Participants can refuse to take part whenever they like.

- **If you are breaking the law:** Laws, such as the Data Protection Act, limit the storage and retrieval of data, whilst the Human Rights Act stops researchers libelling or infringing copyright legislation.

The advantages of interviews

- Response rates are high as they are collected directly by the interviewer

- As the questions are asked directly, they tend to be shorter and more straightforward than with questions asked within questionnaires

- As the researcher is in situ, they can observe non-verbal signals from the respondent and use these to assist with the interview process

- They offer the chance for the interviewee to clarify their responses if the researcher feels that this is necessary

- Their main advantage is that they allow a far more rich and varied response, thereby increasing validity

The disadvantages of interviews

- It is a more costly method than questionnaires because time-consuming journeys and interviews need to be conducted.

- Interviewer bias can limit the validity of the responses, with pupils and teachers giving the responses that they think the researcher wants to hear.

What do you know now?

- Explain the difference between quantitative and qualitative research.
- Outline the types of methods used by these two theoretical approaches.
- Indicate the advantages of the scientific approach.
- Why are questionnaires an effective way to gain data from pupils and teachers?
- Explain the methods most likely to be appropriate to a classroom setting.
- Give an example of participant observation being used by a sociologist in an educational setting.
- Outline why interviews may be a flawed method.

Key terms

Hypothesis:	A statement than can be proved or disproved.
Objectivity:	Not allowing personal opinions to cloud judgement.
Qualitative research methods:	Methods that lead to main qualitative data. Examples of the methods employed include: participant observation, observation, unstructured interviews and ethnography.
Quantitative research methods:	Methods that lead mainly to quantitative data. Examples include questionnaires and structured interviews.

Section summary

- Educational research uses methods which are similarly used in other branches of the natural sciences and social sciences.

- There are two main approaches used when it comes to researching the educational system: The use of quantitative data refers to data that is usually in numerical form, either as a percentage, a number or a rate (often per head of the population). The quantitative approach is used when the researcher wants to obtain entire trends or statistical truth in the research. The use of qualitative data refers to date that is usually in words, not numerical data.

- Primary data is collected directly by the researcher. Any data collected involves the researcher finding out things at first hand. Primary data has the advantage of allowing the sociologist to obtain data that may not be in the public domain.

- Secondary data is not collected directly by the researcher, but is used nonetheless to explore and answer hypothesis. Examples of secondary data include the use of official statistics, the press, books and magazines.

- Positivism sees the world governed by social rules.

- The advantages of questionnaires are that they are cheap and allow generalisations to be made if a large sample is used. However, they do not allow follow up questions and mailed questionnaires have low response rates, whilst interpretivists believe that questionnaires limit the responses of pupils.

- Interpretivists see the world very differently from positivists. Instead of believing social facts, this group of researchers suggest that behaviour is far more fluid than that positivists assert.

- Qualititative methods, however, can be criticised in general for not being scientific. They are often small-scale and therefore generalisations are difficult to make.

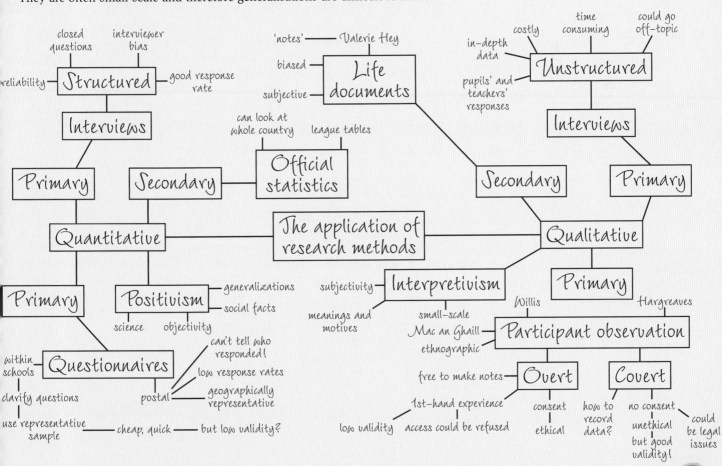

Topic summary

How to maximise your grade with AQA

Education is worth 60 per cent of the AS total mark and 30 per cent of A level. You will be expected to answer five questions on the family with graduated questions from two marks, four marks, six marks and then the large 24 mark questions. As with the previous specification the exam format is a stimulus response style question. As a result of the decision to dispense with coursework this module includes one question on sociological research methods in context and one question on research methods.

The assessment objectives for the A level are as follows:

Assessment objectives		Weighting
AO1	Knowledge and understanding of the theories, methods, concepts and various forms of evidence linked to the specification.	48%
	Communication of knowledge and understanding in a clear and effective manner.	
AO2	Demonstration of the skills of application, analysis, interpretation and evaluation	52%
Overall weighting		60%

AO1: You will need to know the following areas to obtain a high mark in knowledge and understanding:

- **The nature of sociological thought:** The AQA ask you to have a good knowledge of a range of theories that predominate in the sociology of education. Specifically, this means knowing the major writers and theories associated with functionalism, Marxism, interactionism, the impact of social class on attainment (cultural and deprivation theory), the sociology of ethnicity and gender, and underachievement in school. Additionally, students must know how government policy has evolved over the last century. It is particularly important that you are aware of recent policies such as the introduction of Specialist Diplomas and academy schools. Finally, for the first time in this module, students are expected to understand the methods used by sociologists to study education and be able to apply these methods appropriately. Under this heading you will be expected to know the difference between quantitative and qualitative research and understand how methods vary between these two sociological perspectives.

- **Methods of social enquiry:** As there is no coursework component, the AQA have added a methods section to each unit. Specifically, the AQA want you to apply your knowledge of methods appropriately. You will be expected to know how primary and secondary data is collected and understand which factors influence the design of research. Finally, you need to be aware of the practical, ethical and theoretical issues has can arise when studying pupils and teachers. Because much of the research involves minors, researchers need to be vigilant as to the ethics of their research.

- **Themes:** You are expected to cover two themes:

Socialization, culture and identity: Education is a vital way of socialising students: you will need to know how the education system achieves this and why this is important.

Social differentiation, power and stratification: This theme is central to education and is a way of explaining why the elite are able to extract so much more cultural capital from education than those from the working classes.

AO2: This assessment objective asks you to be able to acquire and produce evidence and apply it to the question set. You will also be expected to be able to look at the strengths and weaknesses of each argument and come up with a reasoned conclusion. Evidence should be both from primary and secondary resources, and you will be expected to use both quantitative and qualitative data. There are a number of ways could can do this. When talking about the education system you can be critical of areas such as the methodology used, whether the study is dated, whether the researcher is suffering from ideological bias, and so on. It is important that you learn at least two criticisms for each major theory. However, remember that evaluation also includes strengths of theories.

There are three sections you will need to tackle for AO2:

- **Collection and recording of evidence:** Specifically you will need to evaluate the design of sociological research as it applies to the education system. You must analyse and evaluate the methods used to collect data.

- **Interpretation and evaluation of evidence:** It is essential that you do the following here: show objectivity, apply a range of theories to the questions set and use appropriate concepts. So for instance, within the education system you would be expected to understand what the role of education is and which theorists would want to look at this debate within the education system, to be able to interpret quantitative and qualitative data, and interpret and evaluate trends within the education system. Such trends might include examination results by gender, ethnicity and social class.

- **Presentation of evidence and argument:** A level examiners expect you to be able to organise your written answers so there is coherence. This means that you are expected to start with an introduction, have a number of interlinked paragraphs and a conclusion. Within this answer you must use theory that would inform the question and include any evidence that would further answer the question. Within this you must draw conclusions and back these up with appropriate arguments. Examiners suggest that the best way to do this is to carefully plan your essay. Make sure that you make one substantive point per paragraph and then evaluate and provide a link sentence for the next point you want to make.

Exam practice for AQA

Section A: Education with research methods

You are advised to spend approximately 50 minutes on Question 1

You are advised to spend approximately 25 minutes on Question 2

You are advised to spend approximately 40 minutes on Question 3

Topic 4

Topic summary

Item A

It is said that boys continue to lay behind female attainment in GCSE examinations. Although the gender gap has narrowed in recent times (2006–7), boys are still said to be years behind the performance of their female brethren. A number of reasons have been suggested for this. Outside explanations have examined the impact of government policies such as the introduction of GCSE coursework on boys. Plus there appears to be evidence to suggest that boys see the world of work and the ideas of instant gratification being more important than staying on at school. Inside school explanations see the poor results of males are to do with factors such as boys' inability to organise themselves and do their homework. By contrast girls appear to have better social networks that encourage them to talk and help each other to pass examinations.

Explain what is meant by the term 'instant gratification'. (*2 Marks*)

Suggest three ways in which it could be argued that the curriculum is said to be ethnocentric within schools.

Outline some of the reasons apart from those mentioned in Item A why girls do so well at both GCSE and A level. (*12 Marks*)

Examine the role of processes in schools in producing different educational attainment amongst pupils from different social groups. (*20 Marks*)

Section B: Education with research methods

This question requires you to apply your knowledge and understanding of sociological research methods to the study of this particular issue in education. Read Item B below and answer the question that follows.

Item B

The issue of ethnic minority underachievement has been a constant source of sociological investigation since the 1980s. An increasing amount of research has focused on pupil interactions and staff. A major study commission by Ken Livingstone (2004) was of the opinion that black students had been 'betrayed by the education system'. Specifically, black boys complained of racism and stereotyping from teachers. They said chances of success were also limited by the old fashioned curriculum. Using a variety of methods such as interviews the commission found evidence of direct discrimination within the classroom.

Using material from Item B and elsewhere, assess the strengths and limitations of one of the following methods for the study of ethnicity and educational attainment:

- Questionnaires
- Participant Observation

This question permits you to draw examples from any areas of sociology with which you are familiar.

Explain the term 'representative'. (*2 Marks*)

Suggest two ways of operationalising 'ethnic minority underachievement' line 1. (*4 Marks*)

Suggest two reasons why sociologists like to use questionnaires. (*4 Marks*).

Examine the problems sociologists might encounter with the use of interviews when examining the educational underachievement of ethnic minority groups. (*20 Marks*)

Topic 5

Health and illness

Learning objectives

What the AQA spec says	Sections in this book	Page
Health, illness, disability and the body as social and biological constructs.	Section One: Health, illness and the body	212
The unequal social distribution of health and illness in the UK by social class, age, gender, ethnicity and religion, and internationally.	Section Two: The social distribution of health and illness by social groups	220
Inequalities in the provision of, and access to, health care in contemporary society.	Section Three: Health inequalities	228
The sociological study of the nature and social distribution of mental illness.	Section Four: Mental illness	236
The role of medicine and the health professionals.	Section Five: Medicine and health professionals	244
The application of sociological research methods to the study of health.	Section Six: The application of research methods to health	252

Exam skill focus

Skills required	
AO1 Knowledge and understanding of theories.	You should know both theoretical explanations of health and illness and be able to quote studies that inform this process. You are be encouraged to use examples drawn from your own experience of small-scale research.
AO2 Demonstration of the skills of application, analysis, interpretation and evaluation.	You should be able to apply your knowledge of health and illness to any question set, whilst analysing and evaluating the theories.

What it means to be studying health and illness with the AQA

At first sight it might appear that health is a rather strange topic to be studying in A level Sociology. Taken from a doctor's perspective, illness, you might argue, is straightforward: it consists of specific biological symptoms that need to be treated. Yet the reality is that health is a far from simple subject. For instance, in **Section One** we explore the way that key concepts such as health and illness are socially constructed in that illness is perceived differently across different societies, during different eras and amongst different societies.

In **Section Two** we look at further variance. Why, for example, is illness so unevenly distributed between British society? Why do the citizens of Teesside in the North East of England only have an average life expectancy of around 55 years of age? Why do some ethnic groups, such as Pakistanis and Bangladeshis, similarly suffer from poor health? It is clear that poor health appears to be the result of a range of geographical and social factors. But how do sociologists explain these differences?

In **Section Three** we examine the role of the health service in these inequalities. Given that we all pay for our health by way of taxation, one might expect that resources should be targeted to those most in need. Yet the evidence suggests that just the reverse occurs. Why does this occur and what policy implications are there for such a state of affairs?

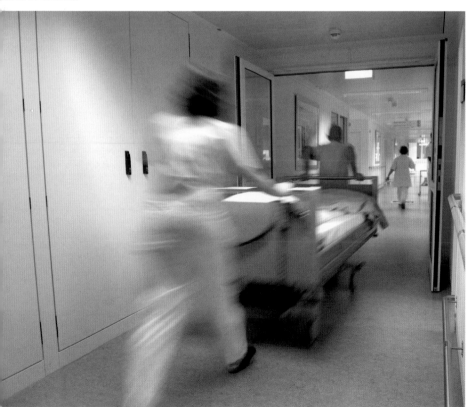

In **Section Four** we look at the subject of mental illness, and in **Section Five** we examine medicine and the role of health professionals. Finally, in **Section Six** we look at the application of research methods to health.

Topic 5

Health and illness

Sociologists studied in this topic

Robert Alford (1975)	Noted the existence of structural interests within the health service, each possessing differing amounts of power.
Helen Allen (2006)	Examined how working as a nurse in a fertility unit affected the nurses. Allan's study looked at the day-to-day emotions suffered by nurses as part of their everyday activities.
Mildred Blaxter (2004)	Gave a lay definition of health.
Richard Bundy (2001)	Believed that financial pressures are often given as a dominant reason for poor mental health.
Phyllis Chesler (1997)	Suggested that males dominate and run society and that women are more likely to be labelled as having mental illness due to the patriarchal nature of the medical profession.
Barbara Dobson (1994)	Her research shows that mothers sometimes skip meals so their children don't go without a decent meal.
Vic Finkelstein (1993)	Argued that it may be appropriate to use different definitions of disability depending on the context and purpose the definition is intended to serve.
Michel Foucault (1961)	Gave a critical evaluation on the role of the institutions found in the health system. His ideas are often associated with postmodernism.
Eliot Freidson (1970)	Looked at the way that the medical profession dealt with strain and conflict within the profession.
Anthony Giddens (1997)	A leading social commentator, and Tony Blair's 'guru', looked at the notion of 'authority' and how this has become a fluid phenomena in a postmodern world.
David Gordon and **Peter Townsend** (2003)	Provided the most convincing definition of absolute poverty.
Erving Goffman (1961)	Explained how the disabled were excluded on the basis of stigma.
Hiliary Graham (1984)	Examined how socio-economic factors shape women's lives and their health.
Emily Grundy (2005)	Utilised life histories to examine how childhood experiences influence health and mortality in later life.
Albert Harris (1971)	One of the first sociologists to define disability.
Cecil Helman (1990)	Has researched how health and social and cultural factors can impact on health care and health education.
Lisa Iezzoni (2002)	Looked at the way in which the medical profession treats autism.
David Johnstone (2001)	Examined how discourse within the medical profession is used to create and shape reality.
Jackie Landman and **John Kennedy Cruickshank** (2001)	Observed the link between diet and health and ethnicity.

Jean Francois Lyotard (1970)	A founding father of postmodernism. Argued that the meta-narrative was dead.
Michael Marmot (1994)	Investigated mortality rates over 10 years among male British Civil Servants aged 20–64 and found that men in the lowest civil servant grades had a three-fold higher mortality rate than men in the highest grade (administrators).
Walter Miller (1958)	This theorist notes that the working classes have their own culture, which differs from the mainstream culture.
Craig Morgan (2006)	Psychiatrist at London University who has examined whether schizophrenia is merely a brain disease or is related to adverse social factors within the lives of those suffering from it.
Mike Oliver (1990)	Set out the 'social model of disability', the idea that it is society which disables disabled people.
Ossi Rahkonen (1997)	Investigated health-related social mobility amongst employed men and women in Britain and Finland.
David Rosenhan (1973)	Showed how mental institutions are not able to differentiate between sane and insane.
Lauren Slater (2004)	Outlined a number of well known psychology experiments, told via the medium of story.
Karen Spilsbury (2004)	Used both quantitative and qualitative research methods to investigate the complex and changing role of the modern health care assistant.
Robert Spitzer (1975)	Believed that, as with all medical science, psychiatry must rely upon the reported symptoms of the patient.
William Thomas (1929)	Leading member of the Chicago school who famously noted that "if men define situations as real, they are real in their consequences", that is, people are affected by their subjective reading of a social situation.
Richard Wilkinson (2006)	Looked at the correlation between income and health.
Philip Wood (1981)	Developed a definition of disability which was adopted by the World Health Organization.

My mock examination for this topic is in ....

I will be examined on this topic in ....

Health, illness and the body

Introduction

Although we tend to take our health and our bodies for granted, the understanding of health, illness and health care is heavily influenced by social constructs. This is apparent from the varying ways in which definitions of health and illness have been viewed over time and in the response of doctors and other healers to their patients. And although we often say we feel ill, what does this mean? How does illness vary between people? And what makes someone 'healthy' as opposed to being 'abnormal'? This chapter looks at how sociologists seek to understand the terminology of illness and how these labels affect those who receive them.

Health is a relative term; it means different things to different people. There is no universally agreed definition of being healthy. So whilst for the elderly being healthy might mean not being on medication or being able to actively take part in life, for other groups it may mean different things. Moreover, the ideas of health have changed with time.

Lay definitions of health and illness

One source of definition comes from those who suffer from illness in the first place: the general public. And whilst these surveys have the problem of variance between one patient and another, they at least give some indication of what health and illness are. **Mildred Blaxter** (2004), Professor of Medical Sociology at UEA, defines lay beliefs as "commonsense understandings and personal experience, imbued with professional rationalizations." A number of studies have being conducted over the last twenty years, ranging from surveys conducted in Scotland (Rory Williams, 1983, 1990; Blaxter and Patterson, 1982), in Wales (Pill and Stott, 1982,1987), and finally more surveys conducted in London (Cornwall, 1984) and throughout the UK (Blaxter, 1990).

Blaxter, in the survey *Health and Lifestyles* (1990), sampled 10 000 respondents on how they viewed health. She found that a number of clear definitions resulted. And whilst general ideas of being well were articulated, along with having no pain and being able to get on with everyday activities, she found that there is no simple way that 'health' can be defined. As such, she believes that if we do try to define health we are in danger of including all human life and happiness under the label of 'health'. Health then, it is argued, is a subjective state that varies between one person to another. Interpretivists

see health as socially constructed, that decisions on health are based upon a range of social processes and decisions, particularly by medical professionals and the reactions of other social actors.

Factors that influence lay definitions of health

If we accept that lay definitions of health vary, we need to understand what factors affect these notions of health. As with most areas of sociology, these factors vary between cultures. In particular sociologists believe that culture, age, gender and social class are variables that influence our perceptions of health.

Age

As we age we tend to reassess our perceptions of health. Blaxter for example, in her 1990 study found that as people aged they viewed their health as the ability to cope with everyday activities. This contrasts to younger people's definition of health as being physically fit and children who view energy and vitality as signs of health. Middle-aged males tended to emphasise the quality of their mental health instead of being physically fit. Females view health in terms of their satisfaction with life, particularly in reference to their social relationships. So whilst younger people may consider the elderly as being ill, the group themselves felt that as long as they were able to lead a satisfactory everyday existence and were able to carry out day-to-day activities the elderly considered themselves to be healthy.

Gender

There is a saying used by doctors that neatly summarises the difference and experiences of illness by gender: "Women get sicker, but men die quicker." Although this area of research is relatively new, perhaps showing the patriarchal malestream research that dominated, studies show that women do indeed visit their GP more frequently and have more illness than men in general. There are a number of reasons for this. Firstly, medical professionals note that this increased incidence of attendance is merely physiological, indicating that women are more likely to suffer from difficulties because of their more complex reproductive systems. Secondly, male socialization results in men seeing themselves as less likely to be ill. So whereas women are much more likely to visit their GP if they experience any symptoms, men by contrast will often ignore similar ailments. This is one reason why, despite their rarer visits to their doctor, and higher female rates of suicide and mental illness, that **mortality rates** are significantly higher for men than for women. And whilst the life expectancy rates between males and females are starting to shrink, they are still significant. These differences are a consequence of men being more likely to have risky jobs, having higher levels of smoking and drinking, being more likely to have an unhealthy diet and being less likely to use health services for prevention of diseases. It also may be that men suffer on average greater levels of social stress linked to their working life and their social status, although feminists would point to the far greater perceived social stress that women suffer.

Social class

There has always been an association between health and social class and, despite the welfare state and the improvement in health in all sections of societies over the years, this discrepancy remains. This variance led to the publication of the *Black Report* (1980), which looked at the health of the nation and concluded that there were major differences in health according to social class. The differences between social classes apply to all aspects of health including expectation of life, infant and maternal mortality and general

level of health. For example, the *General Household Survey* continually shows that lower social classes are much more likely to have 'limiting and long standing illnesses'. Moreover, the *Black Report* notes that such class differences were more marked in Britain than in many other countries.

In Blaxter's survey (1990) those from the working classes mirrored studies into sub-cultures by **Walter Miller** (1958). She concludes that the working classes are more fatalistic about their health – this means that the working classes accept poor health as 'just one of those things'. The corollary of this is that that those from the working classes are less likely to visit their GP and will only do so when they are often seriously unwell. This offers another reason for the high mortality rates in particular of working-class males who often fail to present themselves to their GP until they are often terminally ill. Unfortunately these social class differences remain persistent. Nevertheless, the working classes are also more adept at relying upon community help and assistance; for instance, within extended families to help those who become ill; practically and emotionally.

Cultural differences

Helman (2000), Littlewood and Lipsedge (1997) and Kleinman (1980), amongst others, have written extensively of the need to have some understanding of cultural symbols in making sense of a patient's communication of distress. So whilst those

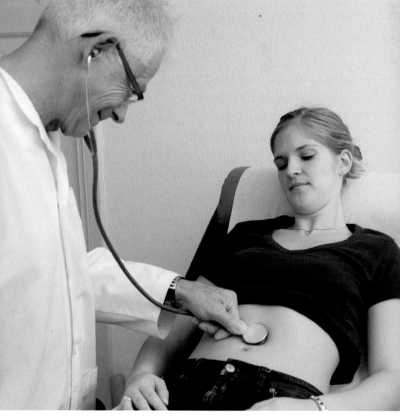

from English cultures present with specific symptoms, patients from other cultures use symbols, dress, gestures and other behaviours for communicating their problems. Some cultures explain mental disorder as the working of evil forces that are external, spirit possessions and bad luck.

In many cultures patients are encouraged to use their bodies to express their distress. Studies like that of Kleinman, Krause (1989) and Ots (1990) each describe different cultures using parts of the body, like the heart, liver and limbs to name a few, as the medium in which their psychological problems are relayed. For example, in the case of Krause, Sikh patients in her research used the metaphor of the 'sinking heart' to talk about their troubles. It becomes necessary to understand what these signs or metaphors represent if one is going to accurately make sense of their problems. These cultural differences remain unlike anything presented by those from a British background.

Medical definitions of health and illness

As can be seen from the above, the concept of health is far from clear-cut with different meanings of 'health'. There are two basic models that seek to explain the causes of ill health and the solutions needed to cure this problem.

The medical or biomedical model of health

This has been the model that has dominated health since the mid-nineteenth century and it has informed the expansion of western medicine. The model sees ill health in relation to objective, scientific measurement. The **biomedical model** suggests that the role of the doctor is to diagnose and treat the physical symptoms of illness.

The biomedical model can be summarised by the following key features:

- Its main emphasis focuses on the physical processes that cause disease, along with how to treat it with drugs and the composition of the disease.

- The body is likened to a car. When it needs a service, or is running 'rough', it is taken for treatment; diagnostic tools are used to find out what is wrong for; example, by using chemical processes such as analysing the exhaust. From this the doctors or mechanics are able to treat that part of the machine that needs to be mended. As a consequence the patient or car will be treated and cured of its ailment.

- Central to treatment is the use of scientific methods, such as the use of drugs or surgery.

- Illness itself is seen as being the result of poor maintenance by the body owner; for example, eating too much, taking illegal substances or smoking too much.

- As a result of the above beliefs, this model suggests that large amounts of money need to be spent on the provision of specialised facilities that employ highly-trained medical personnel in hospitals.

Limitations of the biomedical model

In more recent years a distinction has been made between illness and disease by critics of social medicine. According to Kleinman (1988), illness "refers to the innate human experience of symptoms of suffering." Whilst in contrast Kleinman believes that disease "is what the practitioner creates in the recasting of illness." From Kleinman's quotes we see that he believes that illness is the symptoms that patients feel, whereas diseases are the observable presentable condition shown to the doctor. Kleinman claims that with the biomedical model there is an overemphasis on disease rather than illness.

Arthur Kleinman

Non-western definitions of health

Although the biomedical model has become dominant in western society, in other societies a more holistic approach is taken to treat illness. For example, in Chinese medicine, health is the result of the balance between two basic powers. Disease is perceived as the consequence of disequilibrium and health is achieved by harmony. In African culture they believe that ill health is the result of spiritual factors. These examples suggest that other cultures see ill health not merely as the result of physiological factors, but related to both body and mind, with ill health occurring via psychosomatic symptoms; the mind influencing the body to create or exacerbate illness. However, publicly funded medical care has been dominated by the biomedical model that dismisses these ideas in favour of the high-tech knowledge epitomized by western medical treatment.

The growth of complementary medicine

Increasingly in western society patients have become fascinated by alternative treatments that offer a very different approach to the biomedical model. **Complementary medicine** includes treatments such as acupuncture, chiropractic, homeopathy, hypnotherapy, herbal medicine and osteopathy. The increase in popularity of complementary medicine in the UK is reflected in the increase in registered therapists. From 1981 to 1997, the number of non-medically qualified registered practitioners trebled from around 13 500 to 50 000. There are also thousands of conventional healthcare professionals who practice some form of complementary medicine as an addition to their 'conventional' use of drugs therapy.

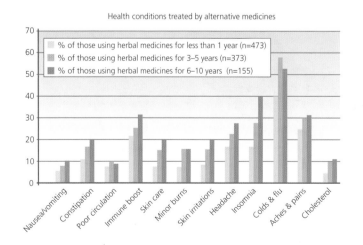

Health conditions treated by alternative medicines

% of those using herbal medicines for less than 1 year (n=473)
% of those using herbal medicines for 3–5 years (n=373)
% of those using herbal medicines for 6–10 years (n=155)

Nausea/vomiting · Constipation · Poor circulation · Immune boost · Skin care · Minor burns · Skin irritations · Headache · Insomnia · Colds & flu · Aches & pains · Cholesterol

The move towards integrating conventional and complementary medicine is explained by **Anthony Giddens** in terms of 'consumerism' and 'pluralism'. Giddens argues that in a postmodern world patients now can choose their treatments and mix and match to their wants. Postmodernists claim this new reluctance of patients merely to accept the prevailing biomedical model is the result of the decline of **meta-narratives**. So whilst 20 years ago patients accepted the authority of the medical profession without question, now in modernity, they look at the choices available to them, perhaps accept some degree of conventional medical intervention, but also favour seeking alternative therapies that offer something completely different from the medical model.

Consumerism, pluralism and the growth in plastic surgery

The above ideas have contributed to the large-scale growth in cosmetic surgery with 32 453 surgical procedures carried out in 2006 by members of the British Association of Aesthetic Plastic Surgeons. Women were most likely to go under the knife; there were 29 572 procedures in 2007, up from 26 469 the previous year. Males have also become more likely to want to surgically enhance themselves, with male surgery increasing by 17.5 per cent with 2881 surgical procedures carried out (compared to 2452 procedures in 2006). The most popular operation continues to be breast augmentation with

over 6497 operations being performed in 2007. Rhinoplasty is the most common male operation, with 716 operations being performed in 2007, equating to a 36 per cent increase from the 2006 figures for this operation. These increases have left some sociologists wondering whether the next generation will be the last to be 'pure' humans (Deitch, 1992).

New reproductive technologies

Ever since the birth of the first test-tube baby, Louise Brown, in 1978, reproductive technology has become another growth industry that has matched the wants of couples across the world. Since 1978 over three million babies have been born as a result of this technology worldwide. One in seven British couples experience problems conceiving and more than 20 000 women seek treatment each year. Assisted Reproductive Technology (ART) is so popular that it is reckoned that that every primary school now has at least one test-tube baby. This trend reflects the requirements of health consumers that now want to delay having a child until their late thirties or early forties.

Definitions of disability

Recent estimates report that there are 11 million people aged 16 or over in Great Britain classified as disabled (Department for Work and Pensions [DWP], 2002). Given this huge number, definitions of **disability** remain important: if humans

Anthony Giddens

eek to define disability they tend to tend to orientate their ehaviour towards those who are disabled in terms of how efinitions see them. As W. I. Thomas (1929) observed, If men define situations as real, they are real in their onsequences." The main theory that has dominated this ehaviour has been the idea that being disabled is a **personal ragedy**, a term coined by **Oliver** (1990), with the assumption hat being disabled is an impediment that stops people from perating normally within society.

t has been the disabled themselves who have sought to hallenge this definition of disability and develop new trategies for defining disability. This initially started with the vork of **Harris** (1971) and then of **Wood** (1981), who were ommissioned by the World Health Organization (WHO) to levise a classification system for disabilities. However, these lefinitions have not been universally accepted, especially >y those who are disabled and the bodies that seek to epresent them.

As a broad definition, **Iezzoni** (2002) suggests a general understanding of disability can be defined as "difficulty onducting daily activities because of health, sensory, ognitive and emotional conditions interacting with the social nd physical environments." This broad definition takes into onsideration the individual and social aspects of disability.

inkelstein (1993) argues it may be appropriate to use lifferent definitions depending on the context and purpose they are intended to serve. For example, in transport issues, benefits provision or medical assessments. However, the use of varying definitions may lead to inconsistencies and confusion. In response to this a number of definitions have been formulated to cater for these differing contexts. Examples include the Disability Discrimination Act (DDA, 1995): "A physical or mental impairment, which has a substantial and long-term adverse effect on his ability to carry out normal day-to-day activities." This broad definition includes the idea that the disabled person is labelled as 'non-functioning' by others and that this label may become

internalised and lead to the self-fulfilling prophecy, whilst also considering attitudinal discrimination, particularly for those with disfigurement.

Perhaps one of the most universally accepted definitions that take an individual approach is that of the WHO International Classification of Impairments, Disabilities and Handicaps (ICIDH):

- **Impairment:** Any loss or abnormality of psychological, physiological or anatomical structure or function.

- **Disability:** Any restriction or lack (resulting from an impairment) of ability to perform an activity in the manner or within the range considered normal for a human being.

- **Handicap:** A disadvantage for a given individual, resulting from an impairment or a disability, that limits or prevents the fulfilment of a role that is normal, depending on the age, sex, social and cultural factors, for that individual Wood (1980). (It should be noted that the term 'handicap' to mean 'disability', can be seen as having negative connotations.)

A number of pressure groups fight for the rights of the disabled. For instance, the United Kingdom's Disabled People's Council is run entirely by disabled people.

Criticisms of definitions

Nonetheless, even the definitions discussed above have come in for criticism, with writers such as Oliver and **Johnstone** (2001) believing that definitions tend to be too close to the individual model of disability that see disability as a factor that negatively affects the individual. It is argued that most models do not think about the wider social aspects, such as societal barriers, discrimination and rights. Johnstone states: "Nearly all acts of parliament concerning disabled people have tended to reinforce the domination of the medical [individual] model and the perception of disability as an illness."

Disability and stigma

The work of **Erving Goffman** (1963) is useful to gaining an understanding of how the rest of society sees disabled people being excluded. Goffman identifies two types of **stigma**:

- **The discredited:** People who are visibly different from the 'norm', with symbols such as being in a wheelchair.

- **The discreditable:** People who do not visibly differ from the 'norm', but are living with illnesses such as Hepatitis C and AIDS.

Goffman asserts that once an individual is labelled with a stigma; for example, as someone who is disabled, all other statuses previously gained by that person will cease to be relevant.

What do you know now?

1. To assess the health of the UK population have a go at the following quiz:

   a. What is the percentage of people who smoke in the UK? (*General Household Survey*, 2005)

      - 5%
      - 15%
      - 24%
      - 35%

   b. What is the percentage chance of children in the UK born into the lowest socio-economic group dying in the first 10 years of life compared with children born into the highest group? (*General Household Survey*, 2007)

      - 10%
      - 20%
      - 30%
      - 40%

   c. How much higher do you think infant mortality is amongst the 'routine and manual' social class? (2003 figures)

      - 0.9%
      - 9%
      - 15%
      - 19%

   d. Estimate the proportion of respondents by sex in the *General Household Survey* reporting their health to be 'good'. (2001)

      - 42% (m) 40% (f)
      - 56% (m) 54% (f)
      - 62% (m) 58% (f)
      - 66% (m) 64% (f)

   e. According to *Minitel* what was the value of the complementary medicine market in 2004?

      - £50m
      - £100m
      - £130m
      - £147m

2. Explain the following terms:

   - Illness
   - Disability
   - Health

3. Outline factors that affect the definitions above.

4. Explain what the medical or biomedical model suggests that we should treat patients in the western world.

5. Outline how disability is different from stigma.

6. Explain which groups are likely to be stigmatised and why this might be the case.

Key terms

Biomedical model: This model is reliant upon the scientific framework of knowledge and relies upon focusing on the physical causes and treatment of any illness. Tends to liken the human body to a car.

Complementary medicine: Practices often used to enhance or complement standard treatments. Common forms of complementary medicine include: acupuncture, aromatherapy, homeopathy, hypnosis, osteopathy and yoga.

Disability: A physical or mental incapacity, either inherited or resulting from an injury or illness.

Health: The state of well-being when a person believes that they are free of disease.

Illness: The condition of feeling less well than is normal.

Lay definitions of health: Are common sense definitions used by the general public who whilst not medical professionals use such ideas to define health and illness.

Meta-narrative: Term used by **Jean Francois Lyotard** … 'grand, large-scale theories and philosophies of the world, such as the progress of history, the knowability of everything by science'.

Personal tragedy: Term used by Oliver who explains disablement as an individualised problem and a personal misfortune rather than a public issue.

Stigma: A negative stereotype of a group of people.

Answers: (a) 24% (b) 40% (c) 19% (d) 62%/58% (e) £130m

Section summary

- The understanding of health, illness and health care is heavily influenced by social constructs.

- One source of definition comes from those who suffer from illness in the first place: the general public. Blaxter defines lay beliefs as "commonsense understandings and personal experience, imbued with professional rationalizations."

- Definitions of health vary with age, gender and social class.

- Helman, Littlewood and Lipsedge, and Kleinman, among others, note that different cultures display illness in varying ways.

- There is a basic model that seeks to explain the causes of ill health and the solutions needed to cure them. This is called the biomedical model.

- The Biomedical model has been dominant since the mid-nineteenth century and has informed the expansion of western medicine. The model sees ill health in relation to objective, scientific measurement.

- Although the biomedical model has become dominant in western society, in other societies a more holistic approach is taken to treat illness.

- The move towards integrating conventional and complementary medicine is explained by Giddens in terms of 'consumerism' and 'pluralism'.

- These ideas have contributed to the large-scale growth in cosmetic surgery, with women most likely to go under the knife. Men have also become more likely to want to surgically enhance themselves.

- Reproductive technology has become another growth industry that has matched the requirements of couples across the world.

- Disabled people have sought to challenge definitions of disability and develop new ones.

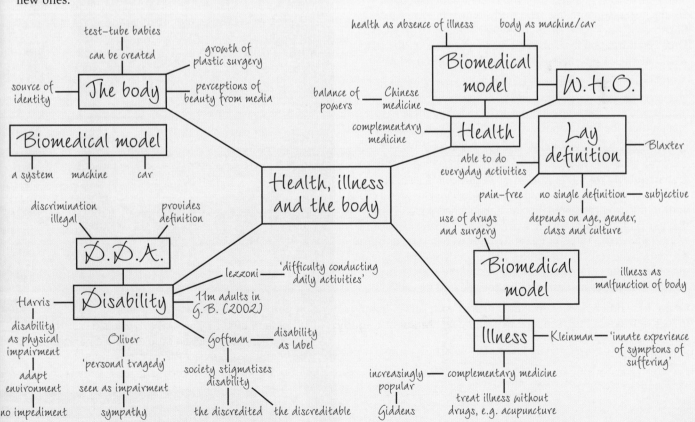

The social distribution of health and illness by social groups

Learning objectives

By the end of this section, you should be able to:

- Quote examples of the 'health divide' found in the UK
- Clarify how different approaches explain social class differences in health
- Isolate how different approaches explain differences in health by gender
- Explain how different approaches explain differences in health by ethnicity

Introduction

Although official statistics show that in general the UK population is becoming a healthier nation, nonetheless, there is still strong evidence to suggest that health is correlated to a number of differing social factors such as social class, age, gender and so on. Despite the ongoing expenditure on the National Health Service (NHS) there are discrepancies between groups on a range of factors such as life expectancy, infant mortality, and general well-being.

A study published in the *British Medical Journal* (2001) reveals the health gap, or differences in health, between the richest members of society and those who come from the poorest groups, increases with age. The study, which followed 10 000 British civil servants aged 35 to 55 over a period of 20 years, found that those on low incomes aged eight years earlier than would be the case if they had been on higher income levels.

And despite government pledges to reduce inequality as measured by infant mortality and life expectancy, recent figures (ONS, 2007) show that far from reducing these inequalities, they are actually widening. Although some progress has been made in tackling mortality rates for diseases such as cancer and heart disease, there is still a long way to go.

Embarrassingly for a Department of Health-commissioned report (Marmot, 2005), the gap in life expectancy between the bottom fifth and the population as a whole had widened by two per cent for males and five per cent for females between 1997–9 and 2001–3. Infant mortality rates were a staggering 19 per cent higher during the period 2001–3 between the poorest members of the community and the rest of the population. This was an increase on similar figures released for 1997–9.

Given these differences we will now look at each social group in turn and assess the likelihood of each being healthy in the UK.

Social class

Social class is measured by the occupation of the father or sole breadwinner in a household. However, since 2001 this system has been replaced by a more complex socio-economic classification – the National Statistics Socio-Economic Classification (NS-SEC) – which is now used in most statistical publications. Although mortality rates have fallen in all social class groups since 1930, they have fallen more in the better-off groups. Mortality rates are similar today in unskilled groups to those for professional groups in 1930. By contrast, mortality rates in professional groups have fallen substantially, and are now almost three times lower than for unskilled groups. It is important to note that health inequalities are not just indicated by mortality. People in manual occupational groups also fare worse on almost every indicator of ill health, be it hospital admissions, GP consultations or self reported illness. These issues lead to males in the professional classes living on average to the age of 78.5 in comparison to males from an unskilled manual background living to 71.1 years.

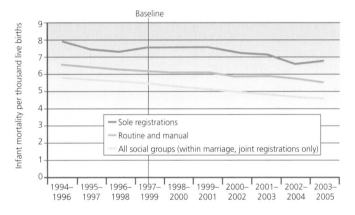

Infant mortality rates

What are the explanations for the differences in health between social class and health?

The artefact approach

The artefact approach suggests that social class inequalities do not exist. They appear on the face of it to be the result of statistical methodology employed by researchers. But are they fact? If you want to find a correlation you will; for example, by using extremes such as the differences between the lowest social classes and the highest social group, researchers are looking at small groups that remain at opposite sides of the social scale. However, when the available evidence is looked at, there is overwhelming support for the view that there are substantial differences between the classes. These differences have remained ongoing; for example, showing that the lower the social class of a person, the younger they are likely to die and the increased likelihood that they are to suffer from persistent chronic health problems.

The social selection approach

This explanation implies that while the healthy are more likely to move up the social class system, or indeed stay in the highest social classes, in comparison those from the working classes will find it difficult to obtain a well-paid job because of risk of illness. There is some evidence to support this model; for example, the 1946 British Birth Cohort found that children with serious illnesses were more likely than those without to be downwardly mobile (Wadsworth, 1987). The general consensus though, according to Blane et al (1993), is that **social selection** plays a tiny, but significant, role.

However, by contrast, in a recent analysis of the *General Household Survey*, almost no evidence of downward mobility was found for those with poor self-rated health or limiting longstanding illness (Rahkonen et al., 1997). Moreover, other commentators believe that although good health might be important for social mobility, it is no guarantee of higher social status given the ever increasing demands of better qualifications and high level of experience to obtain a high-status job. Additionally, it can be said that this explanation offers a deterministic view of those with illnesses. There is no certainty that illness in childhood necessarily leads to social demotion. Indeed, some will be able to adapt to their illness and its circumstances and ensure that social demotion does not occur as a consequence.

The cultural approach

The **cultural approach** seeks to pin the chances of ill health on the cultural behaviours made by different social groups within the population. Blaxter (1990) notes that judgements are usually made on the basis of smoking, drinking, diet and exercise. We will examine each of these in turn:

Smoking: A recent study in the *Lancet* (Peto, 2006) concluded that smoking is to blame for half of the difference in death rates between men in the top and bottom social classes. A *General Household Survey* (2005) revealed that only 18 per cent of men and 16 per cent of women from the professional classes smoke; by comparison 33 per cent of men and 30 per cent per cent of women smoke from the routine and manual classes.

Drinking: In terms of social class and employment, alcohol dependence is significantly higher amongst the unemployed and from those in social class five. However, figures from *General Household Survey* indicate that alcohol consumption is far too high for all social groupings and, in fact, those admitting to 'drinking more than eight units in one day' were only slightly higher for the routine and manual classes than for the professional ones.

Diet: The semi-routine and routine occupations are two-and-a-half times more likely to consume none of the five-a-day portions of fruit and vegetables, whilst also having a higher consumption of biscuits and cakes, salty snacks and chips (Joint Health Surveys Unit, 1998).

Physical activity: Socio-economic differences in physical activity are complex; however, there are marked social class differences in activity patterns, with participation in sport tending to increase with social class, particularly by men. According to Sport England (2004), participation in sport and exercise and walking was strongly related to social status, with men and women in social classes one and two being more likely to take part in these activities. With for example, 48 per cent of men and 47 per cent of women in social class one participated in sport and exercise, compared to 38 per cent of men and 28 per cent of women in social class five.

Social class classifications	
I	Professional occupations and so on
II	Managerial and technical occupations
III	N Skilled non-manual occupations
III	M Skilled manual occupations
IV	Partly-skilled occupations
V	Unskilled occupations

Criticisms of the cultural explanation

Can we really believe that the working classes are at fault for their own early deaths? It would appear that such a blame culture is not new and this new focus is the result of 'the New Right viewpoint that citizens should take responsibility for their own consumption patterns. In reality, the greater cultural capital of the middle classes gives them the knowledge for greater longevity. However, we have to ask why the working classes smoke and drink more than the middle classes. And why, when the New Right lectures the working classes on what to eat, how many times per week they should exercise, and so on, they are unwilling to redistribute income by means of higher taxation, for example, to promote healthier lifestyles and diet within the education system.

Material and structural explanations

This explanation believes that although it is true that the working classes do make more poor choices about their lifestyles than the middle classes, the real reason for their poor health relates to the different living and working environments to those from the middle classes. This has long been recognised, even by government, with a succession of reports such as the *Black Report* (1990), with more recent government policy leading to the commissioning of the *Independent Inquiry into Inequalities in Health* (1997).

Employment and health

There is evidence from the Health and Safety Executive (HSE) that there are differences between death rates between occupations. And although death rates are declining – for example, in 2005–6, the finalised figure was 217 – this was the lowest annual figure on record. Finalised figures reflect changes to the coded details of records should more accurate information subsequently become available. Nonetheless, even though a long-term downward trend is still apparent, the rate of decrease has slowed over the last 15 years and there has been very little change in the overall rate over the last five years, with those working in routine and manual occupations appearing to be particularly at risk. Fatalities are highest in agriculture work, however this can be seen to be a relatively dangerous industry. Twenty-four per cent of these deaths were categorised as deaths due to agricultural vehicles overturning (HSE, 2005–6) and construction work (due to falls and trips), with these two sectors together leading to 46 per cent of fatalities for 2006–7. These occupations provide risks such as exposure to dangerous substances, dangerous situations and long hours, that are not associated with higher status occupations. There is also evidence that non-manual workers who have boring and repetitive low-status jobs also suffer from stress-related health issues and, as a secondary factor, problems due to the measures used to combat stress and alienation; namely, drinking, smoking and recreational drugs (Marmot, 1991).

Unemployment

A variety of studies by Moser et al. (1984), Iversen et al. (1987), Martikainen (1990), Morris et al. (1994) and Ruhm (2000) have shown that mortality rates among the unemployed are higher than among the employed, with the belief that unemployment leads to stress and increased alcohol and cigarette consumption, with unemployment leading to a lowering of living standards and available financial resources. Additionally, Morris et al. reveal that unemployment experience, as well as the length of unemployment, increases the risk of early mortality after taking into account factors such as age, race, marriage, income and occupational class.

Positions at work

Employees with low degrees of autonomy and control continually show higher levels of mortality than those who have more control over their work environment. A study by Marmot et al. (1994) that examined mortality rates over ten years among male British civil servants aged 20–64, found that men in the lowest civil servant grades had a three-fold higher mortality rate than men in the highest grade (administrators). Studies also reveal that grade is also associated with particular illnesses likely to be suffered, with lowest grade workers being twice as likely to suffer from cardiovascular heart disease.

Poverty

The link between poverty and poor health was recognised in the *Black Report* (1980). The report showed that the unemployed suffer worse mental and physical health than the employed. Unemployment can lead to poverty, ill health and premature death.

Gender

Women on average live to a greater age than men and death rates for both sexes have consistently fallen. Yet despite this women are more likely to visit their GP. And according to the Mental Health Foundation, 20 per cent of women suffer from mental health problems as opposed to 14 per cent of men. The Twenty-07 study by the Medical Research Council (MRC) reports that the picture of greater female ill health for most health outcomes is an oversimplification.

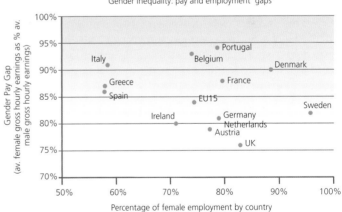

Gender inequality: pay and employment 'gaps'

Inequality in society

There has been a recent increase in interest in the relationship between income inequality and health within and between nations. Richard Wilkinson of Nottingham University (2006) believes that in societies where inequality is reduced people are more trusting of each other, there are lower levels of violence, and health is better. Indeed, Wilkinson notes that life expectancy is higher by several years, prison populations are lower, teenage pregnancy rates are reduced, and educational attainment in school is increased.

Explanations of health differences between the genders

Genetic and biological explanations

Although women have a greater chance of living longer than men, they subsequently have increased risks of suffering from degenerative illnesses as they reach the later stages of their life. Women also suffer from different illnesses because of their sex. Nonetheless, even 'female' illnesses, such as those that result from reproduction, can still be the result of a complex mix of both biological and genetic factors, as well as cultural and social ones. For example, in some western cultures women often start taking the contraceptive pill at an early age. The age at which this occurs is influenced by the social factors inherent within that culture. Genetic and biological factors have been criticised for their narrow focus, as they tend to look at certain medical illnesses which ignore, for example, female psychological health. Additionally, for structural theorists, such as Marxists, it underplays the role of structural factors, such as the differences between men's and women's pay.

Importance of gender equity in health

Men have different health needs to women or children, are affected differently by various diseases and illnesses, and access services in different patterns and for different reasons.

Over the last 30 years, women have argued that they have been poorly served by a male-dominated health service. They argue that health policies and practices must change to reflect the specific needs of women. Yet it is now becoming increasingly clear that, perhaps surprisingly, men have not benefited from a male-dominated health service either. Men need a new approach to health care; one that takes into account the needs of their gender.

Gender matters in health care

Understanding gender is crucial to understanding male health issues. It helps to explain, for instance, why so many men take risks with their health. Even today, traditional attitudes towards gender remain surprisingly strong and prevalent. Boys and young men continue to be socialised to be tough and strong, to appear in control and to take risks. This creates dangerous behaviours such as fast driving and cigarette smoking.

Gender roles also make it harder for young males to ask for help. Indeed, men often believe that they should 'tough out' illness for as long as they can, rather than admit to what feels like a weakness. The emphasis placed on being rational also makes many men feel disconnected from their bodies and their physical needs. Men often speak about their bodies as if they were machines and think about illness in terms of the failure of a particular body part. The *British Medical Journal*

(2001) has suggested that the "development and maintenance of a heterosexual male identity often requires the taking of risks that are seriously hazardous to health." Not only are men at high risk of dying prematurely from occupational accidents or disease but also at special risk through homicide, traffic accidents and dangerous sports. The need to be seen as 'hard' also has implications for men's mental health, preventing them from taking their health seriously and inhibiting them from seeing a doctor when problems do arise.

It is important to understand that gender is not biological, but neither is it an identity that can be easily put on or taken off. Gender roles are primarily socially and culturally determined and, because they have existed for a long time, are very difficult to change. This means that health policymakers and professionals must improve their understanding of male gender roles and seek to develop and deliver services that are aimed at men as they are, and not as some might wish them to be. For example, as men are not socialised to reveal weaknesses publicly, providing them with ways of accessing health information anonymously and confidentially, for example, by the Internet or telephone helplines, may be more useful than clinics. Health promotion materials that use metaphors which are relevant to men, such as those comparing bodies to machines, may also prove more successful.

Cultural and behavioural explanations

There is contradictory evidence when it comes to the above. Whilst women are less prone to taking risks than men; for example, being less likely to be involved in road traffic accidents, to smoke less and consume fewer alcoholic beverages, their private role within the family may place a considerable burden on their health. Statistics show that women have an increased chance of being single parents on low incomes. Some believe this may lead to women being less likely to exercise regularly; and research shows that mothers even skip meals so their children don't go without a decent meal (Dobson, et al., 1994). Other indications show that women not only take better care of themselves; for example, going to the doctor at the first sign of unusual symptoms (Graham, 1984), but additionally make appointments for their husbands and boyfriends to see the doctor (MORI, 2004). This may be a cultural difference between the sexes with men being less willing to accept they are ill, whilst women find socially acceptable to admit their ailments.

However, other research found that women were no more likely to visit their GP when experiencing five of the most common conditions: musculoskeletal, respiratory, and digestive, heart and mental health problems (Hunt and Ford, 1999). Moreover, women are subject both to **structural** and **material** poverty, with some five million women (20 per cent) belonging to households in poverty. Many of these are single-parent households, where 73 per cent of single-parent mothers live in inadequately-heated accommodation (Gingerbread,

2006). Fuel poverty is becoming a major problem with gas bills on average rising by over £500 since 2004 (Ofgem, 2008). The burden of worries about money leads to women experiencing high levels of stress, anxiety and guilt. These factors impact on women's mental health, particularly because women seem to be less resigned to poverty than men (Syeandle et al., 2003).

Ethnicity and health

The links between health and ethnicity are invariably difficult to pin down given the huge diversity between ethnic groups within the UK. This makes generalisations difficult and academic. Nevertheless, studies do show some significant differences between ethnic groups. Large-scale surveys like the *Health Survey for England* (2007) show that black and minority ethnic groups as a whole are more likely to report ill-health, with ill-health starting at a younger age than in white people. There is more variation in the rates of some diseases by ethnicity than by other socio-economic factors. However, patterns of ethnic variation in health are extremely diverse, and interlink with many overlapping factors. Nonetheless, it is true that certain groups, particularly those in poverty such as Pakistani, Bangladeshi and black-Caribbean people report the poorest health, whereas East African-Asian, black-African and Indian groups report similar health to the majority of the population.

Mortality rates indicate that primarily due to higher poverty rates black and minority ethnic groups live shorter lives than other groups. Significant variations show that South Asian men are 50 per cent more likely to have a heart attack than the rest of the population. By contrast men born in the Caribbean are 50 per cent more likely to die from a stroke than the rest of the population, but are much less likely to die from a heart attack. All black and minority ethnic groups of both gender are interestingly less likely to suffer from cancer.

Reasons for differences in health by ethnicity

The following are considered to be influential for explaining different levels of health between ethic groups:

Inequality

Poverty remains the predominant reason for inequalities in health in the UK. For example, Platt (2006) reveals that ethnic groups have the highest rates of poverty, both adult and child, income insecurity and low rates of economic activity. All these factors increase the chances of increased mortality amongst the poorest members of the ethnic minority groups.

Racism and poverty

We would expect racism to be less of an issue than ever before, given the black rights movement and legislation that should have outlawed racism in the UK. Research by BBC Five Live (2004) found that white candidates were far more likely to be given interviews than black and Asian candidates with similar qualifications. Yet it is clear, from the example that black and minority ethnic groups suffer from racism that is often institutional, with the result that black and minority ethnic groups are significantly more likely to live in poverty and that this racism is likely to increase stress levels.

Cultural and material factors

Landman and Cruickshank (2001), in their study of ethnicity, health and nutrition-related diseases, comment that it is very difficult to make definitive judgements on diet and health. Yet they found that Asian men suffered higher levels of obesity and larger waist measurements than other ethnic groups, leading to those from African-Caribbean or Asian cultures being up to four or five times more likely to develop diabetes than Caucasian members of the population. This is further exacerbated by less reported physical activity among minority ethnic groups than in the majority population (Acheson, 1998). The *Manchester Inner City Survey* (1994) found the highest participation in life-enhancing activities among men of African-Caribbean origin (59 per cent) and the lowest among men of Bangladeshi origin (45 per cent), with men of Indian origin (54 per cent) and Pakistani origin (49 per cent) in between. All these factors may decrease health amongst the black and minority ethnic groups.

Evidence also suggests that black and minority ethnic groups' households are affected disproportionately by homelessness and housing problems. The Department of Communities and Local Government (DCLG, 2007) found that black and minority ethnic groups are significantly more likely to live in overcrowded conditions, especially in London. For white people the national rate of overcrowding is 1.8 per cent, but for black and minority ethnic groups it is 11 per cent. In London the rate for whites rises to four per cent, and for black and minority ethnic groups to 13 per cent. These issues all lead to black and minority ethnic groups suffering from stress and poor health because of the material conditions in which they live. This is exemplified by the fact that black and minority ethnic groups suffer from a range of mental health problems with the disease burden associated with mental disorder appearing to fall disproportionately on minority ethnic populations. For instance, Craig Morgan (2006), a senior lecturer at the Institute of Psychiatry, King's College, found that African-Caribbean people are nine times more likely than white people to be diagnosed as schizophrenic, and six times more common in people from black-African origin than in the white-British population.

What do you know now?

1. Link the following to their correct definition to explain social class differences:

   a. The artefact approach

   b. The social selection approach

   c. The cultural approach

   d. The material approach

   - This explanation concentrates upon hazards which are innate in society and to which some people have no option but to be exposed.

   - This explanation suggests that social-class differences in health are a result of the behaviours which people chose to engage in.

   - This explanation suggests that observed social class differences in mortality may be an error in the process by which they are measured. In summary, this explanation suggests that since it is difficult to measure both social class and health: how can we show any link between the two?

   - This explanation suggests that the healthy are more likely to move up the social classes and the unhealthy move down.

2. Explain one reason for geographical differences in health across the UK.

3. Describe two examples of how social class affects health in the UK.

4. Using your own words explain what is meant by the cultural approach.

5. Isolate three examples of how structural factors can influence health.

6. Give two reasons why women live longer than men.

7. Isolate three reasons for differences in health between ethnic minority groups.

Key terms

Artefact approach: Believes that statistics on social class and health tend to overplay the real situation and are often the product of the methodology used by the social researcher concerned.

Cultural explanations: Explanations that particular look at lifestyle and the behaviours of any one cultural group.

Degenerative illnesses: An illness that slowly causes the body to deteriorate.

Mortality rates: the proportion of deaths in a population or to a specific number of the population.

Structural explanations: A macro explanation that seeks to look at the structure of society to explain inequality.

Section summary

Although official statistics show that in general the UK population is becoming a healthier nation nonetheless, there is still strong evidence to suggest that health is correlated to a number of differing social factors such as social class, age, gender etc.

Social class remains an important factor in explaining poor health.

The artefact approach suggests that social class inequalities do not exist. They appear on the face of it to be the result of the statistical methodology employed by researchers.

The social selection model implies that the sick will slide down the social scale while the healthy will have a greater chance of social advancement.

The cultural approach seeks to pin the chances of ill health on the cultural behaviours made by different social groups within the population.

Material and structural explanations believe that although it is true that the working classes do make some poor choices about their lifestyles, the real reason for their poor health relates to the different living and working environments of those from the middle classes, as opposed to those from poorer sections of society.

- Cultural and behavioural explanations describe how whilst women are less prone to take risks than men, for example, being less likely to be involved in road traffic accidents, to smoke less and consume fewer alcoholic beverages.

- Variations within the health of ethnic groups make generalisations difficult to make. However, it is true that certain groups, particularly those in poverty such as Pakistani, Bangladeshi and black-Caribbean people report the poorest health.

- Inequality, racism and cultural and material factors are all given as reasons for this.

- Platt reveals that ethnic groups have the highest rates of poverty, both adult and child, income insecurity and low rates of economic activity.

- Institutional racism, along with higher poverty rates, increase stress for those from black and minority ethnic groups.

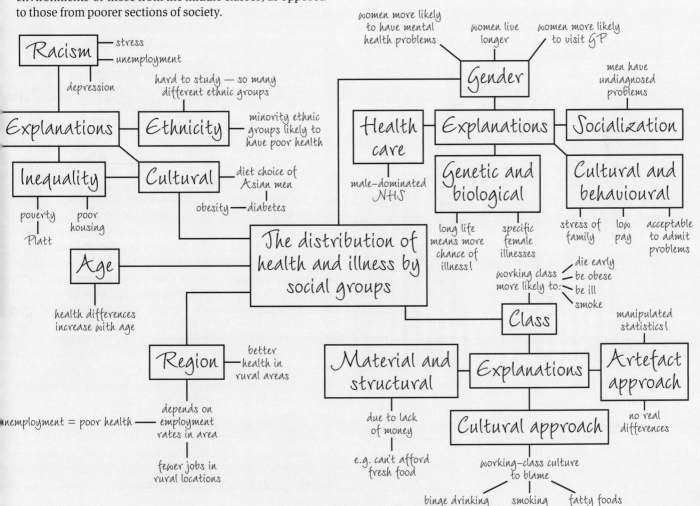

Health inequalities

Introduction

The NHS is the publicly funded system of health care within the UK and is free at point of use with no payment being made when treatment is needed in hospital, despite the huge costs to the country of providing this service. These costs are paid for by National Insurance (NI) contributions. In 2007 £90 billion was spent on the NHS and the government estimates that in the following three years £110 billion will have to be spent to allow new investment to reduce waiting times, increase access to GPs and to provide cleaner hospitals: all this within a context of an ageing population and rising birth rate fuelled by immigration.

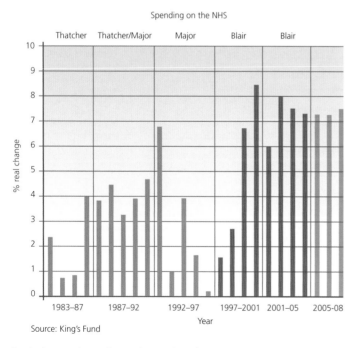

Spending on the NHS

Graph shows real spending on the NHS in cash terms. However, we need to remember that not all of this money is necessarily spent on medical services. For instance, the costs of drugs, wages and pensions all need to be paid for.

Yet despite this huge spending there is evidence that some groups are able to extract more use out of the service than others. Funding is obtained by means of the taxation system, health care should be routinely available for all patients, and the level of service should remain the same, whether that is in Scotland, Wales or England.

We are led to believe that the NHS is based on equity and need. This implies by definition that more money 'needs' to be spent on those groups who have the poorest levels of health. Yet this does not appear to be the case. There are a number of reasons for this:

- The poorest groups do not appear to have the most spent on them
- Certain groups are more likely to use the NHS than others

It is therefore vital that the government considers how it best provides for the patients who use the service. Financial provision is affected by a number of factors. These include:

Geographical provision

There is a widely-held view that rural populations are healthier than their urban counterparts. Using national key health measurement indicators, rural health can indeed be shown to be better. For instance, average life expectancy tends to be higher in rural areas. It would therefore make perfect sense to ensure that these areas with less healthy members of the population gain greater funding than those areas that are currently more favoured. And indeed, this is what the financial NHS system is meant to achieve by its government formula funding that is meant to isolate these differences.

However, this has never been the case. It is claimed by the government that one reason for this is the greater input costs in the South East, such as labour, land and buildings. The Healthcare Commission found that the 2002 formula for assessing health needs was not being introduced quickly enough because the government feared the response from voters in the more affluent areas, as services were lost and transferred to those areas with greater need. The Healthcare Commission notes that funding is so paradoxical that trusts such as Westminster Primary Care Trust receive 31 per cent more than they should, whilst other areas with far greater social inequality and poorer health, such as Easington Primary Care Trust in County Durham, receiving a shortfall of £26.5 million. These figures result in areas which receive favoured funding having on average one more GP per 10 000 residents. Areas such as Richmond, Cambridge and Oxford all gain from this system. By contrast, **Primary Care Trusts** (PCTs) such as Tendring, Liverpool, Birmingham and Basildon are net losers.

Professor Ian Kennedy, the chairman of the Healthcare Commission, was moved to comment: "The NHS must serve the whole nation, not just those who live in certain areas or those best able to demand health care of good quality." (2004)

The influence of doctors

High-ranking doctors and pressure groups like the British Medical Association (**BMA**) can influence how funding is allocated within the NHS. As with all jobs, some areas are more lucrative than others, and surgeons and doctors realise that London in particular offers rich pickings for them, both in terms of guaranteed patient numbers from their NHS work, but also the prospect of earning extra income from private consultations. This is the main reason why **specialist hospitals** for ailments such as cancer tend to be located in specialist teaching hospitals, either in London or one of the major conurbations in the UK. So powerful are they that doctors have also urged the main political parties to reconsider the way the NHS is funded. Doctors would like to see an end to the entirely public funded NHS. This pressure is the result of the government desperately trying to reduce spending within the service. Deficits remain a real problem; these are the direct result of new contracts for surgeons that imagined doctors and surgeons would reduce their working hours to help the quality of their life. However, this has not been the case and top surgeons saw an increase in their wages of 30 per cent as a consequence of the government's new contracts. As wages constitute a high proportion of the total cost of the NHS this has had a dramatic affect, hence the medical profession seeking to influence future funding.

Variable quality of PCTs

The quality of medical care is essential for positive health outcomes. Yet an international comparison joint study by a team from the University College Hospital, London (UCL) and Mount Sinai Hospital, New York (2003) focusing on the surgery outcomes of 1000 patients who had undergone the same sort of major surgery revealed significantly higher mortality rates in the UK hospital (10 per cent), compared to Mount Sinai (2.5 per cent). This indicates that the quality of care remains poor in the NHS compared to other countries, especially in contrast to the USA. Moreover, national data on mortality rates, published in *The Times Hospital Consultants' Guide* (2003) which compares mortality rates for coronary heart bypass surgery, found that United Bristol Healthcare PCT has the lowest standardised mortality rate in the UK, some three times lower than the worst-performing hospital, the Walsgrave Hospital in Coventry. Similar differences occur across a range of serious operative conditions.

Private health care

One clear inequality between patients is the existence of a private market for health care for those who can afford it. It is estimated that the independent health market provides £15 billion in health services (*Guardian Unlimited*, 2007). There are approximately 230 **private health care** hospitals run by three main providers: General Healthcare Group, BUPA and Nuffield Hospitals. Increasingly, the private sector has started to play an important role in non-urgent operations.

For example, one-third of all hip operations are done by the private sector and nearly one-half of all abortions. And whilst much of the rhetoric about the NHS talks about public funding, in reality there is a mix of private and public funding, with the government seeing the private sector as a way to reduce waiting lists. It is argued that private health care increases inequalities by:

- Allowing those with money to skip waiting lists, whilst those who are unable to pay have to wait for operations. At present no patient should have to wait any longer than six months; however, in some instances such a wait may be the difference between life and death: the ultimate inequality.

- Taking NHS-trained doctors away from their core NHS responsibilities. Often this leads to surgeons being unable to attend to NHS patients as they prefer to do more lucrative private sector work.

- By utilising doctors, who each cost the taxpayer £250 000 to train on the NHS, the private sector are acting as 'freeloaders', gaining the services of well-trained doctors and nurses without ever paying for them.

Demand factors: social-class differences

The Department of Health publication, *Tackling Social Class Inequalities: Status Report on the Programme for Action*, reveals that although health is improving overall, "the difference in overall mortality between the highest and lowest social classes increased moderately from 1986–92 to 1997–9, continuing the trend for increasing inequality shown in earlier periods. Although mortality fell substantially in all social classes, there was a greater fall in social classes one and two than in social classes four and five. For women aged 35 to 64, the gap in all-cause mortality between social classes one and two and four and five narrowed between 1986–92 and 1997–9."

There are a number of reasons for increased mortality rates for social classes four and five. These, according to Dixon and Le Grand (2003) include:

- Socially deprived groups use the NHS less than their needs would suggest. For example, not seeing their GP as regularly as those from higher socio-economic classes. This is true across a number of different health conditions including: heart and surgical care, hip replacements and in-patient oral surgery. For example, they discovered that in Yorkshire, even though lower social classes have a 30 per cent greater need for hip replacements, the actual operation rate was 20 per cent lower than higher socio-economic groups.

- Lower socio-economic groups typically experience longer travel times to visit specialists or their GPs.

- Less car ownership causing difficulties in travelling to see health professionals.

- People in different groups have to make decisions on whether to attend health care at all; for example, finding it difficult to take off time from low-paid jobs and long shifts to see medical professionals.

Julian Tudor Hart (1971), a GP in Wales, was moved to coin the term 'The Inverse Care Law' to describe a perverse relationship between the need for health care and its actual workings. In other words, those who most need medical care are least likely to receive it; conversely, those with least need of health care tend to use health services more (and more effectively) and have longer consultations with their GP.

Gender

The health of females

While women can expect to live longer than men, they are also more likely to have more years in poor health. On average, males in England spend 59.1 years in good health and 15.9 years in poor health; for women the corresponding figures are 61.4 years and 18.6 years. As sociologists we need to be aware of whether some of these facts are related to the provision that is offered to women. Such is the concern on this issue that the government have introduced the Gender Equality Act (2006), which is designed to reduce the amount of gender discrimination that occurs by heath-service providers. As part of the act heath-service providers will have to ensure that they can isolate groups such as women who underuse or who are less satisfied with the service on offer. There remains the feeling, particularly by feminists, that the health service remains a patriarchy. So, whilst huge sums are spent on diseases that men are more likely to contract, by contrast midwifery services, for example, remain outmoded in comparison. And although gender positive policies such as the breast screening programme and the cervical cancer screening programme (1988), sociologists still note the disparities of usage between social class and ethnic groupings. Feminists would suggest that these initiatives, although laudable, do not make it easy enough for all women to access, and this issue is something that the Gender Equality Act will have to address.

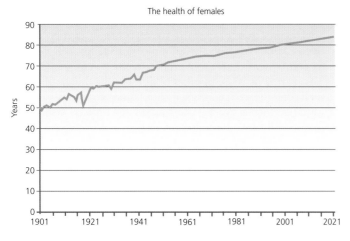

The health of females

(graph: y-axis "Years" from 0 to 90; x-axis years 1901, 1921, 1941, 1961, 1981, 2001, 2021)

The health of males

We should also be aware that one of the main concerns of this act is to improve provision for men. Organisations such as The Men's Health Forum believe that in contrast to women men's health issues are often overlooked. Men take more risks with their health with a range of behaviours, such as:

- **High levels of alcohol consumption:** In 2006 the male death rate (18.3 deaths per 100 000) was more than twice the rate for females (8.8 deaths per 100 000) and males accounted for two-thirds of the total number of deaths.

- **Drug abuse:** An *Observer* poll (2002) uncovered that among the UK population of those aged 16 or over, 28 per cent (about 13 million adults) have taken illegal drugs at some point, with men more than twice as likely to have done so as women (38 and 18 per cent respectively).

- **Sexual habits:** Similarly men appear more willing to take risks with their sexual health. The *National Survey of Sexual Attitudes and Lifestyles* (2001) showed that since the previous survey in 1989–90 the median for lifetime sexual partners had increased for women from two partners to four partners. In comparison men reported an increase from four to six lifetime partners.

Suicidal tendencies: Despite male suicides declining to their lowest rates for 30 years (due to a range of factors including the fitting of catalyst converters to cars and thus reducing carbon monoxide deaths, increased use of anti-depressants and lower levels of unemployment) males still accounted for 75 per cent of all suicides in 2006.

Some argue that perhaps the focus should now be more on men than women. However, this is to oversimplify biological and cultural arguments as to why these differences exist.

Ethnicity

Black and ethnic minoritygroups tend to use the NHS less than others. There are a number of reasons for this:

- **The ethnocentric nature of the NHS:** Although real progress has been made with the introduction of initiatives such as the use of interpreters for 999 calls and the use of 'language line' for front-line ambulance crews, the NHS can still be accused of being too ethnocentric by tending to look at medical issues from their own cultural norms.

- **Poverty:** The factors that limit the lower socio-economic classes have a similar effect on ethnic groups. Lack of suitable transport and difficulty gaining time off work all limit access to health services.

- **Cultural differences:** The prevalence of male doctors, particularly in the higher echelons of the NHS, may limit NHS use. This is particularly true of Asian users who prefer female doctors to examine them rather than male doctors.

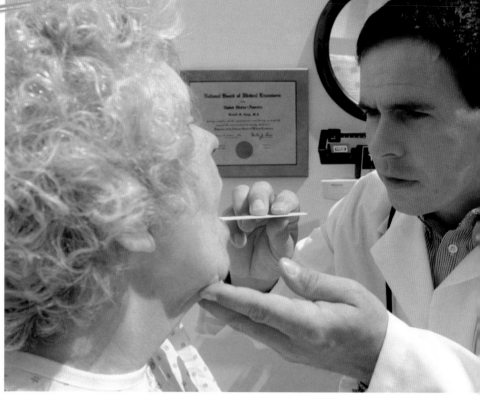

However, the picture is not all negative. The Parliamentary Office of Science and Technology (2007) found similar uptake of services amongst the black and minority ethnic groups than the rest of the population based on need. Nevertheless, there is still some indication that certain groups do not access health care as much as they need it. For instance, South Asians have been found to have lower access to care for coronary heart disease. When looking at preventative health care, levels of smoking remain higher amongst black and minority ethnic groups than for white groups, indicating that access to these preventative services for black and minority ethnic groups is poor. Moreover, dissatisfaction about health care remains higher than for white people, with South Asians reporting high levels of dissatisfaction to the *Healthcare Commission Patient Survey* when being admitted into hospital.

Age

Despite being the group most expected to use the NHS, there is evidence that compared to need this group underutilises the service. Generational differences can also lead to the elderly being unwilling to 'pester' their GP when they are ill. The elderly are also often unwilling to take preventative measures to assist their health; for example, take-up of influenza vaccinations remains low, despite high-profile advertising campaigns. Yet despite these facts, it is true that the elderly are the largest users of hospital and community care within the NHS. Moreover, with our rapidly aging population and projections that five million people will be over the age of

80 in 2030, spending will have to continue to increase in response. The *Wanless Report* in 2002 estimated that NHS spending is going to have to increase from its 2002 level of £70 billion to more than £180 billion by 2022.

Because of the very specific needs of elderly patients, spending will have to be allocated, not only to primary (first care that is usually by a GP) and secondary care (treatment by specialists after referral), but also on long-term care. The *Joseph Rowntree Foundation Report* (2004) estimates that expenditure on long-term care will have to rise from £13 billion in 2004 to what it estimates to £54 billion by 2051. The report also suggests that the private sector is likely to benefit from the ageing population, with demand for nursing and residential care likely to triple to 1.1 million places.

Theoretical explanations of inequalities in health provision

Inequalities in health provision has become a key political issue in the UK and other countries. There are a number of competing explanations for these differences that include Marxism, pluralist and structuralist approaches.

Marxism

Marxism is a conflict theory and suggests two classes, the bourgeoisie and the proletariat, and the economic system (or infrastructure) shapes all aspects of life, be it health-care provision or education. Traditional, or crude, Marxists believe that the health service has been allowed to develop for three reasons:

1. It ensures that workers are healthy and therefore well enough to make surplus value for the bourgeoisie. When workers are ill they do not produce enough surplus value and therefore the health service treats them, returning them when they are fully productive again. However, some sociologists are sceptical about this and believe that the

middle classes have benefited far more than the working classes from a 'free' health service. And as the previous explanation shows, the working classes actually use the health service considerably less than the middle classes, despite having a far greater need (Le Grand, 1993).

2. It gives the proletariat the illusion that capitalism cares for them, even when they are not being 'wage slaves'. Workers are far more willing to accept the vagaries of capitalism in the knowledge that when they are most in need the capitalist system will help them.

3. Louis Althusser (1969), a neo-Marxist, argued that the bourgeoisie need to invoke hegemony amongst the proletariat. This is done via the ideological state apparatus, which consists of: the education system, the family, the media, the health care system, and so on. Essentially these structures are used to placate the proletariat and perpetuate 'false class consciousness.' Navarro (1979) argues that the medical profession are able to make illness seem an individual predicament rather than resulting from the inequalities that Marxists believe are instrumental.

However, Marxists have been criticised for their approach:

- Marxism ignores the real tangible benefits that capitalism offers those from the working classes. If the capitalist state really was as uncaring as Marxists suggest surely they wouldn't bother with benefits such as sickness benefits and unemployment payments.

- Interactionists see Marxist attempts to explain the medical system as missing out the role of the doctor. Do patients just accept that their illnesses are the result of biological or individual problems, or do they question why they are ill? Marxists have concluded that patients are 'brainwashed' by the medical system.

- There is also a lack of empirical data to support the view that a dominant ideology of health exists within the medical profession. It is easy to make statements about the system, but far less easy to prove them.

- Marxists, although being critical of health care in capitalist states, cannot show that under socialist states that equality necessarily occurs. Indeed, within the old Soviet Union there were huge differences in health between those at the top of the Soviet system and those at the bottom.

Pluralism

Pluralists believe that to understand decision making in relation to health provision we need to look at how power is used by groups. For this approach, although some groups do have greater power (elite pluralism), overall they believe that power is shared by everyone (hence pluralism), with no single group necessarily dominating. Any decisions that are made are the result of complex negotiating so decisions are made in a consensus (Held, 1996). Marxists, by contrast, would not accept that power is made by a consensus and that instead the

elite group – the bourgeoisie – are able to impose their will at the expense of the rest of the working classes. In relation to health care, pluralism contends that a complex power play between the competing groups occurs. So all the protagonists from the various health groups, health workers (for example, the health union, UNISON) , health administrators and competing pressure groups such as political parties, and the BMA fight with widespread and spirited competition. This will often lead to the power of one group often cancelling out the power of another.

An example of this was the proposed closure of Monklands Accident and Emergency in Airdrie (2007–8) by the then ruling Scottish Labour Party. Upon the announcement of the downgrading of this hospital from a full accident and emergency facility, local protests continued for over a year. Local support led to the signing of a 55 000-signature petition against the closure, and the then home secretary, John Reid, whose constituency was Airdrie, also lent his support to the cause, despite his affiliation to Labour. This example shows how organised local support, if allied to medical and political pressure, can be successful.

Structrualist approaches

Structural responses seek to fuse the structural approach of Marxism with pluralism. Using **Alford's** framework (1975), Alford asserts that structural interests within the health service will mould administrative devices to their advantage. Alford notes the existence of three such structural interests in the National Health Service:

1. **Dominant:** The medical professionals who compete for power within the NHS. This group serve the interests of the political, economic and social institutions. They do so by ensuring a healthy and productive workforce capable of producing large amounts of surplus value for the bourgeoisie.

2. **Challenging:** This group is headed by health service managers who seek to introduce changes that challenge the dominant group. For instance, health service managers may seek to cut back on medical services or reduce the amount of doctors within any single hospital.

3. **Repressed:** This group includes all those groups who receive universal coverage from the NHS, be they patients or other business groups. This group is the least powerful and has to accept the decisions made by both the dominant health professionals and health service managers who control the NHS on a day-to-day basis.

Essentially, Alford is offering an elite pluralist explanation of power within the NHS. His framework understands that not all groups have the same power and influence when it comes to decision making in the NHS. And his work introduces a Marxist slant to his analysis by pointing out that the dominant medical professionals are highly influenced by the political, economic and social institutions inequalities that occur throughout capitalist society.

What do you know now?

1. Isolate which approach the following statements are from, indicating whether they are strengths or weaknesses.

   - This approach offers a conflict approach to the medical profession which ignores the way that 'wage slaves' work effectively for the benefit of society.

   - Inequalities between the social classes indicate that this theory has much to commend it. Indeed, the differences in health between social classes one and five seem to be widening rather than improving.

   - This approach ignores the fact that the real power lies with those at the top of society: those who legislate, for example, those in the cabinet and medical professionals.

   - This approach realises that there is a need to join together Marxist and functionalist notions in the sphere of health.

   - There are many competing groups within the NHS: doctors, managers and patient groups. The reality is provision reflects these groups' needs with no one faction getting it all their own way.

2. Explain the term 'National Health Service' or NHS

3. What does 'equity and need' mean?

4. Isolate how private health care increases health inequalities in the UK.

5. Give three reasons why lower socio-economic classes use the NHS less than the middle classes.

6. Clarify why, despite living longer, women are not necessarily any healthier than men.

7. Describe the pluralist explanation of equalities in health care provision.

Key terms

BMA: Sectional pressure group that represents the interests of practising doctors and medical students.

Primary Care Trusts (PCTs): The organisations responsible for delivering health care and health improvements within a locality. They are the largest spenders of NHS money, providing a range of services ranging from provision of GPs, medical prescriptions and commissioning of mental health services.

Private health care: Health care that is paid for privately by individuals.

Specialist hospitals: High status hospitals that receive extra funding to train medical professionals.

Section summary

- The NHS is the publicly-funded system of health care within the UK and is free at point of use with no payment being made when treatment is needed in hospital, despite the huge costs to the country of providing this service. These costs are paid for by NI contributions.

- Despite huge investment into the NHS, there is evidence that some groups are able to extract more use out of the service than others.

- Geographically, rural populations are healthier than their urban counterparts. Using national key health measurement indicators, rural health can indeed be shown to be better.

- High-ranking doctors and pressure groups like the BMA can influence how funding is allocated within the NHS.

- One clear inequality between patients is the existence of a private market for health care for those who can afford it.

- The Department of Health publication, *Tackling Social Class Inequalities: Status Report on the Programme for Action*, reveals that, although health is improving overall, "the difference in overall mortality between the highest and lowest social classes increased moderately from 1986–92 to 1997–9, continuing the trend for increasing inequality shown in earlier periods."

- While women can expect to live longer than men, they are also more likely to have more years in poor health.

- We should also be aware that one of the main concerns is health provision for men. Organisations such as the Men's Health Forum believe that, in contrast to women, men's health issues are often overlooked.

- Black and minority ethnic (BME) groups tend to use the NHS less than others. There are a number of reasons for this. Firstly, the ethnocentric nature of the NHS; secondly, due to low income they often cannot attend hospital appointments because of travel costs and getting time off work; and lastly, cultural reasons.

- Despite the elderly being the group most expected to use the NHS, there is evidence that, compared to need, this group is underutilising the service.

- Pluralists believe that to understand decision making in relation to health provision we need to look at how power is used by groups.

- Structural responses seek to fuse the structural approach of Marxism with pluralism.

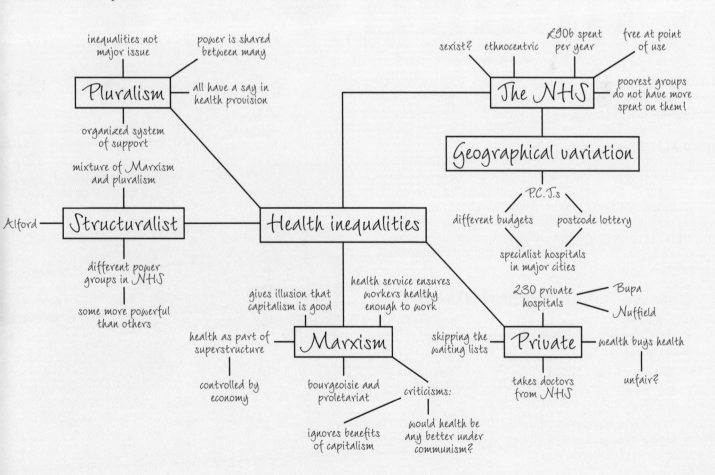

Mental illness

Learning objectives

By the end of this section, you should be able to:

- Clarify different definitions of 'mental illness' by using the concepts of social realism, social constructionism and interactionism
- Isolate differences in mental health in the UK by gender, social class and ethnicity
- Evaluate explanations of these differences

Introduction

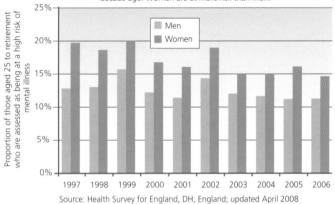

The proportion of adults aged 25 to retirement who are deemed to be at a high risk of develping a mental illness is somewhat lower than a decade ago. Women are at more risk than men.

Proportion of those aged 25 to retirement who are assessed as being at a high risk of mental illness

- Men
- Women

1997 1998 1999 2000 2001 2002 2003 2004 2005 2006

Source: Health Survey for England, DH; England; updated April 2008

Regardless of age, gender, race or religion, mental health is a major health concern that affects us all. In the course of any one particular year, one in four of us will experience some mental health problem, with 4000 committing suicide and 250 000 being admitted into mental health hospitals per year. Yet we only tend to hear about mental health when inadequacies of how the system deals with those who are mentally ill, such as the death of Jonathan Zito, who on 17 December 1992 was murdered by Christopher Clunis, who suffered from paranoid **schizophrenia**. As with many other areas in sociology, problems of definition and differences between gender, ethnicity, class engender considerable and heated debate.

How we define 'mental illness'

Unfortunately, there is no definitive definition of mental illness. However, the following terms are often used within this debate:

- **Neurosis:** Means literally to have 'weak nerves'. It is the more or less chronic state of being unsure of oneself, regularly running into states of fear.

- **Psychosis:** A symptom of mental illness characterised by a radical change in personality and a distorted or diminished sense of objective reality.

- **Obsessive-compulsive disorder (OCD):** An anxiety disorder characterised by recurrent thoughts (obsessions) or rituals (compulsions), which feel uncontrollable to the sufferer. Rituals such as hand-washing, counting, checking or cleaning are often performed with the hope of preventing obsessive thoughts or making them go away.

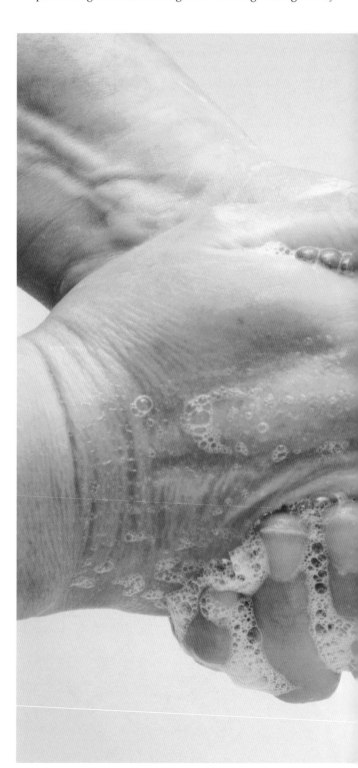

Trying to define mental illness is often split up into two approaches:

Social realism

The **social realism** approach believes that mental health disorders tend to have distinctive patterns of behaviour that are distressing to those who encounter it. Such exhibited behaviour is seen as mental illnesses. It suggests that there are observable symptoms that indicate mental illness; however, writers such Pilgrim and Rodgers do accept that there are variations. This differs in relation to time period and culture; nonetheless, this does not alter their main assertion that classification of mental illness is perfectly possible.

Social constructionism

The **social constructionist** perspective takes an interactionist perspective on mental illness, noting, similarly to Becker, that mental illness is socially constructed. Such adherents believe that we should take a critical stance toward our 'taken-for-granted' ways of understanding the world. They suggest that the ways in which we commonly understand the world, the categories and concepts we use, are historically and culturally specific. So, for example, heroin use was considered to be perfectly normal during Victorian times and used for medicinal purposes, but now its use is an indication that the user has dropped out of society.

This theory therefore sees mental illness being defined through the co-construction of knowledge through social interaction. So what is seen as mental illness in one specific time, culture is the construct of societal reaction within that culture. This suggests that mental illness in one culture does not necessarily mean that it will be labelled as such in others. Social constructionism argues that there are no essences inside things or people that make them what they are. And any 'truth' about what is or what isn't mental illness is problematic.

The interactionist perspective

From the above we can see that there are two schools of thought: One that sees mental illness as being easily defined, whilst social constructionist researchers deny such a notion. Researchers such as Becker (1963) and Heather (1976) believe that labels applied to mental illness are the result of the mindset of the psychiatrist treating the patient. Foucault (1976) uses the term 'gaze' to explain how the medical profession views mental illness, and how their dominant interpretation becomes accepted. Goffman (1968) realises the power that labels exert to stigmatise those suffering from mental illness.

To really understand mental illness interactionists believe that we need to understand how the label of mental illness is applied and how western notions contribute to this process. Even more importantly for interactionists are the effects that any labels have on the 'patient'. Bruce G Link has examined the effect of these labels. In a variety of linked studies ranging from 1987, 1989 and 1997, he and his colleagues concluded that being labelled can have negative consequences for the patient. In particular it can lead to the sufferer withdrawing from society in general. This withdrawal is increased by the patients being additionally punished by societal reaction to their illness. Some writers, such as Brand and Claiborn

(1976) found that those labelled as "ex-mental patients" found difficulty in renting housing and gaining employment. However, it should also be realised that the labels associated with mental illness can also lead to treatment, both with medication and cognitive therapy. Here lies the difference of labelling for those living with mental illness as opposed to criminality; for example, the master status label as applied to paedophiles, although allowing treatment, never leaves the patient. With mental illness the master status is not nearly as strong. And although for a time the label may stick and make applying for jobs problematic, ultimately, over time, the label will reduce in importance.

The effects of being labelled

In a famous study by **David Rosenhan** (1973), he wanted to discover whether mental health professionals are able to tell the difference between those who are mentally healthy and those who aren't. He wanted to know what the consequences were if the patients were misdiagnosed. He also wanted to know whether the characteristics that lead to physiological diagnoses reside in the patients themselves or in the situations and contexts in which the observers (those who do the diagnosing) find the patients.

In the experiment Rosenhan had eight pseudo patients pretend to be mentally ill and try to gain admittance into various psychiatric institutions. There were five men and three women from various backgrounds used in the study: three psychologists, one graduate student, one psychiatrist, one homemaker and one painter. At the start of the experiment participants were instructed to call 12 different hospitals on both the east and west coasts of the US and set up appointments. To help with consistency, all participants complained of the same thing: hearing voices saying "empty", "hollow" and "thud". All participants were then admitted into the institutions with all but one being diagnosed as having schizophrenia. Each pseudo-patient then took notes whilst they were patients in each hospital. Interestingly, once admitted, despite the participants being told to act completely normally, the doctors considered them as mentally ill. This, Rosenhan believes, shows the problems with the diagnosis of mental illness: on the face of it, one single symptom resulted in perfectly well patients being admitted into psychiatric hospital. Thus, how valid are psychological diagnosis across mental health settings? Perhaps diagnosis is more a matter of subjective opinion rather than the scientific fact as believed by social realists.

However, inevitably the study has drawn a number of criticisms, most notably from Robert Spitzer (1975) who believes that, as with all medical science, psychiatry must rely upon the reported symptoms of the patient since a number of researchers have repeated Rosenhan's study and which appear to support Rosenhan's view. The most recent of which was by Lauren Slater (2004), who presented herself to an accident and emergency with similar symptoms of hallucinations presented in Rosenhan's study. Although she was never admitted as an

inpatient, she says she received multiple prescriptions and was diagnosed with "depression with psychotic features" every time. Rosenhan also found in a repeat of his study that staff were unable to detect the presence of a 'stooge', with 41 patients being judged as an impostor when no stooges were ever sent to the ward. Thus we can conclude that even medical professionals find it difficult to diagnose mental illness. Indeed, failure to do this is seen as an indication of continued illness. Therefore the effect of their stigmatisation is the stripping of their personality, so much so that they accept the label given to them.

Goffman (1968) further claims that, once institutionalised in psychiatric hospitals, patients have to change their behaviour and self-identity by accepting medication and what Goffman calls 'the mortification of the self'. Goffman explains mortification as the process whereby the patient is denied both social support and their own identity. This is done by the routine humiliation of the patient, both by staff and fellow patients. This is known as stripping a person's identity; for instance, Goffman stresses the way that patients have to wear uniforms and are given a number. Institutionalisation also means that access to social networks such as family and friends is also often denied.

Criticisms of the interactionist approach to mental health

Walter L. Gove (1982) argues that society has no effect on mental illness and that the majority of people that are admitted to psychiatric hospitals have mental problems that need to be treated. Therefore the mental illness is the first stage of the process and this may or may not be compounded by the labelling process that occurs on entry to the hospital. Although as a theory it has lots of say about societal reaction, it gives us no indication of why people develop psychiatric illnesses.

Caribbean people and mental illness

Caribbean men are at no greater risk than white men of suffering from schizophrenia or psychosis, according to research, despite the fact that they are up to five times more likely to be hospitalised for these conditions. At the same time, other aspects of mental illness among Britain's ethnic minorities may be higher than previously suspected, and going untreated. For example, not one of the Caribbeans suffering from depression in the *Policy Studies Institute Survey* (1997) was receiving medication for it.

Ethnicity and Mental Health (Dr James Nazroo, 1997) is based on the first systematic study of depression and psychosis among a representative sample of ethnic minority groups in Britain. The exhaustive study included interviews with 5196 Caribbean people and Asian people, and 2867 white people, followed by detailed clinical examinations. The research clarifies several important questions about the level of mental ill-health in Britain's minority communities. Among the key findings:

- The rate of psychosis was no greater among Caribbean men than among white men (about one per cent). However, other research has shown that Caribbean people, particularly young Caribbean men, are far more likely than white people to be receiving hospital treatment for psychosis.

- Caribbean people were 60 per cent more likely to suffer depression than white people, and Caribbean men were twice as likely to be depressed as white men. However, single people and lone parents experienced lower rates of depression than those who were married or cohabiting.

- Overall, Caribbean people had the highest rates of mental illness, but Irish and other minority white people seemed to suffer similar rates. The author of the study suggests that "ethnic minority status might increase the risk of mental illness, regardless of skin colour." Chinese people suffered the lowest rates of mental illness.

- Contrary to research on deaths from suicide, South Asian women were no more likely to harbour suicidal thoughts than white women. Caribbean people, Irish and other minority white people were most likely to have thoughts of suicide. Indeed, as many as 7.2 per cent of young Caribbean people (aged 16–24) thought life not worth living, compared to 2.5 per cent of their white peers.

- Indian, Pakistani and Bangladeshi peole appeared less likely to suffer mental health problems than white people. However, this apparent shortfall occurred mainly in people who had recently arrived in Britain, who may not have been able to report their feelings of stress in terms which western diagnostic techniques recognised. These findings suggest that western psychiatric medicine may be failing to identify mental illness among South Asians.

- Marriage or cohabitation increased the risk of mental illness for Caribbean women, although it reduced the risk for white people and South Asian people. By contrast, class was inversely related to mental illness for all ethnic groups.

Foucault: mental illness and civilisation

The French sociologist, **Michel Foucault**, offers another view on mental illness. Foucault believes that modern notions of mental illness have resulted from the changes of the way that we think in modern society. As we moved to a modern society, we became more scientific and rational in our thought processes, and society in turn started to reject the old ideas of irrationality and superstition. Foucault suggests that we can only understand notions of mental health within the context of what is happening in wider society. Given this move to rationalism and science, Foucault believes that it is hardly surprising that notions about mental health have moved in a similar direction.

Foucault notes, as a result of rationalisation, health care for those suffering from mental illness is all about classification, institutionalisation and close monitoring. Foucault believes that the term 'mental illness' is a term that is designed to segregate and control those who are not rational.

To summarise the complex work of Foucault: he sees mental illness as a relatively recent phenomena, with those suffering from mental illness as seen to represent the irrationality of pre-enlightenment; an age based on superstition and lack of knowledge.

Realist explanations

Individual social groups and mental illness

Using the social realist definition of mental illness, we will now look at whether as this theory would suggest that there are clear differences that are scientifically observable between social groups.

Ethnicity and mental illness

This is a controversial area of the sociology of health as it is accepted that ethnicity in itself is a difficult term to define and statistics of the prevalence of mental health amongst this huge group vary considerably. However, it cannot be denied that past and present research shows that people from black and ethnic communities may face increasing difficulties, including higher rates of mental illness in some communities, and subsequent problems with access to the right care and treatment. This is particularly the case from the results of a national census of inpatients in mental health hospitals and facilities in England and Wales for black Caribbean, black

Michel Foucault

African and other black groups (Commission for Healthcare Audit and Inspection, 2005), which are over-represented in psychiatric hospitals. Some studies show schizophrenia rates as being as much as eight times greater for those from an African-Caribbean background compared to the indigenous white population (Harrison, 2002).

Research undertaken by King's College, London (2003), which focused on south London, indicated that members of ethnic minorities may be more likely to experience discrimination and institutionalised racism when in a small minority, leading to increased stress. Stress is thought to be a contributing factor in the development of schizophrenia. As well as this, the more isolated a member of an ethnic minority, the less protection they gain from social networks within ethnic minorities, which can protect against the effect of such stresses.

Broadly, there are a number of explanations for schizophrenia:

- **Genetic explanations:** This explanation believes that the disease is a 'genetic inheritance' and that those born to parents who suffer from schizophrenia are more likely themselves to develop the condition. However, twin studies by Harrison (1995) show that the risks of picking up the condition genetically are in fact no greater if one member of the family has schizophrenia.

- **Social constructionist explanations:** These theorists believe that mental illness is the consequence of labelling by doctors and mental health workers. They claim labels are applied on the basis of the experiences of the health worker. These judgements may be tainted by, for example, the privileged background of the psychiatrists making these judgements.

- **Family explanations:** Some writers believe that flawed family relationships can cause schizophrenia.

- **Social class explanations:** These suggest higher rates amongst the lower socio-economic groups due to the increased stresses of lower income living.

In response to these issues, the Labour government decided to embark on a five-year plan for reducing inequalities in black and minority ethnic patients' access to, experience of, and outcomes from mental health services (*Delivering Race Equality in Mental Health Care*, 2005). The report seeks to develop:

- More appropriate and responsive services for all

- Community engagement by talking to black and minority ethnic groups in the planning of services

- Better information through improved monitoring of mental health care and dissemination of good practice

Gender and mental illness

There are some startling differences between males and females in relation to mental health, with research by the Mental Health Foundation (2005) indicating that 20 per cent of women and 14 per cent of men in England have some form of mental illness. Likewise, 18 per cent of women have a 'neurotic disorder' (including anxiety, depression, phobias and panic attacks), compared with 11 per cent of men. However, not all the data is so conclusive; it should be noted that men are three times more likely than women to be dependent on alcohol, and two times more likely to be dependent upon drugs.

Structuralists point to a number of factors that lead to increased poor mental health. These include:

- Women tend to be the main carers for both their children and relatives. This role can impact on mental health.

- Women often have multiple roles: mothers, partners and employees (WHO, 2001).

- Because women are over-represented in low-paid employment, particularly part-time work, they are more likely to live in poverty. A consistent reverse relationship has been found between social class and mental health (Women's Health Council, 2003; Prior, 1999; WHO, 2003).

- Physical and sexual abuse can have a long-term impact on mental health.

However, radical feminists, such as **Phyllis Chesler** (1997), believe that males dominate and run society and that women are more likely to be to be labelled as having mental illness due to the patriarchal nature of the medial profession. She states that because women have different problems to men, women's problems are viewed as mental illness, whereas men's mental symptoms are considered to be 'normal'.

Social class and mental illness

Social class affects the likelihood of mental illness, with the poorest fifth members of society being around twice as likely to be at risk of developing a mental illness as those on average incomes. The differences by income are somewhat more pronounced for men than for women (*Health Survey for England*, 2005). Studies from a variety of countries (New Haven, USA; Hollingshead, USA; Redlich, USA; the UK, 1958) all indicated that there was a direct relationship between the experience of poverty and a high rate of emotional disturbance, as well as differential availability and use of treatment modes and facilities by different social classes (Meltzer et al, 1995).

A number of reasons have been postulated for these differences:

- The impact of deprivation and structural inequalities in health: A number of studies that look at the experiences of health-based professionals point to the link between economic disadvantage and mental health. Rogers and Pilgrim (2003) believe that mental health can be seen as a psychological response of demoralisation that comes with low income. The ongoing despair and discrimination felt by the lower classes impacts directly on their psychological health. Structural inequality can lead to people feeling distressed and hopeless. Bundy (2001), for example, believes that financial pressures are often given as a dominant reason for poor mental health.

- The incidence or the impact of negative life events and experiences for individuals; for example, abuse, relationship breakdown, long-term illness or disability. Patton et al. (2003) discovered that single or multiple life events increased the chances of mental illness five fold and eight fold respectively. Myers (1975) calls this the life course model.

- Social isolation and exclusion: Social support is an important protective factor for mental health and for physical health that can act as a buffer to protect against adverse life events. It has long been recognised that poverty and surviving on a low income have social consequences that can lead to exclusion from social activities and opportunities. Poorer mental health is associated with perceptions that the locality is in decline, whilst less neighbourliness and fewer leisure opportunities further increases the problem (Huxley and Rogers, 2001).

What do you know now?

1. Link the following phrases or words to either (a) interactionism, (b) Foucault, (c) gender, (d) ethnicity, (e) social class:

   - Labelling
   - Patriarchy
   - Chesler
   - Institutionalised racism
   - Link between economic disadvantage and poor mental health
   - Rationalism
   - Male doctors
   - Segregation and control applied by means of rationalism
   - Harrison
   - Rosenhan

2. Isolate two approaches that differ in their definition of mental illness.

3. Explain the differences between these two approaches.

4. Describe the importance of labels and explain how these labels are imposed.

5. What processes, according to Foucault, have resulted in the way the medical profession deals with those who are mentally ill?

6. Isolate two processes that result in ethnic minorities as being more likely to be defined as 'mentally ill'.

7. Describe why, according to feminists, women are more likely to be defined as mentally ill.

8. Isolate three reasons why those from lower socio-economic classes are more prone to mental illness.

Key terms

Social constructionism: Looks at how individuals' realities are social constructs and are influenced by the society in which the individual is located.

Social realism: This approach believes that there are observable symptoms which affect both the sufferer and those around them. Mental illness is thus a condition that does exist and is observable.

Schizophrenia: A group of mental disorders categorized by abnormal thoughts, moods, and actions; sufferers have a twisted sense of reality and thoughts that do not logically fit together.

Section summary

Regardless of age, gender, race or religion, mental health is a major health concern that affects us all. In the course of any one particular year, one in four of us will experience some mental health problem, with 4000 committing suicide and 250 000 being admitted into mental health hospitals per year.

Unfortunately, there is no definitive definition of mental illness.

This social realism approach believes that mental-health disorders tend to have distinctive patterns of behaviour that are distressing to those who encounter it. Such exhibited behaviour is seen as mental illnesses. It suggests that there are observable symptoms that indicate mental illness.

The social constructionist perspective takes an interactionist perspective on mental illness, noting that mental illness is socially constructed.

Researchers, such as Becker and Heather, believe that labels applied to mental illness are the result of the mindset of the psychiatrist treating the patient.

Foucault suggests that we can only understand notions of mental health within the context of what is happening in wider society. Given this move to rationalism and science, Foucault believes that it is unsurprising that notions about mental health have moved in a similar direction.

Past and present research shows that people from black and ethnic minority communities may face increasing difficulties, including higher rates of mental illness in some communities.

There are some startling differences between males and females in relation to mental health.

Social class affects the likelihood of mental illness, with the poorest members of society being around twice as likely to be at risk of developing a mental illness as those on average incomes.

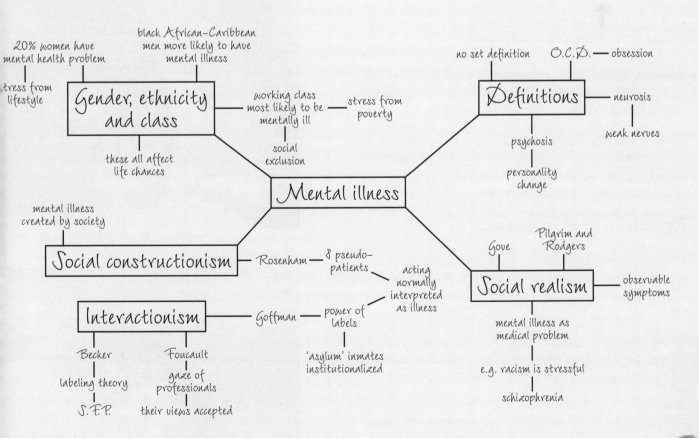

Medicine and health professionals

Learning objectives

By the end of this section, you should be able to:
- Explain different theoretical approaches that explain why medical professionals have so much power
- For each explanation be able to evaluate by explaining strengths and weaknesses of each

Introduction

Medical professionals, such as GPs and surgeons, tend to enjoy high status and high pay. A standard family doctor in the UK earns on average £110 000 a year (as of October 2007), an increase of 10 per cent from the previous year. But why do we hold doctors in such high esteem? Is this the result of the many years it takes to train to be a doctor? Or the high qualifications needed to go to medical college? Sociologists are always suspicious of any group that has great professional and economic power and this section looks at how differing theoretical approaches believe that this power has been achieved.

There are a number of different theoretical approaches that seek to explain the power of medical professionals:

- Functionalists believe that medicine performs positive functions for individuals and society.

- Weberians believe that function of the medical profession is to serve its own professional interests.

- Marxists see the medical profession as part of the superstructure and therefore suggest that it seeks to control the proletariat and hide the medical inequalities apparent within capitalism.

- Foucault believes that medicine serves its own interests through medicalising a range of conditions and behaviours. Consequently it is able to increase its power and influence.

- Feminists believe that women have been marginalised and controlled by the medical profession.

Functionalist approach

Functionalism is a macro, or wide, theory that seeks to explain all aspects of sociological life and its writers remain consistent throughout. The most well-known functionalist writer is Talcott Parsons, who argues that the medical profession has important functions that allow society to flourish.

Functionalists argue that doctors have a high status as they possess specific specialist skills that necessitate long and arduous periods of study. Moreover, doctors have to prove their knowledge of medicine on the basis of a meritocratic examination system, which only passes on the basis of ability, rather than social class, gender or ethnicity. This status then is the result of two factors. Firstly, the **deferred gratification**

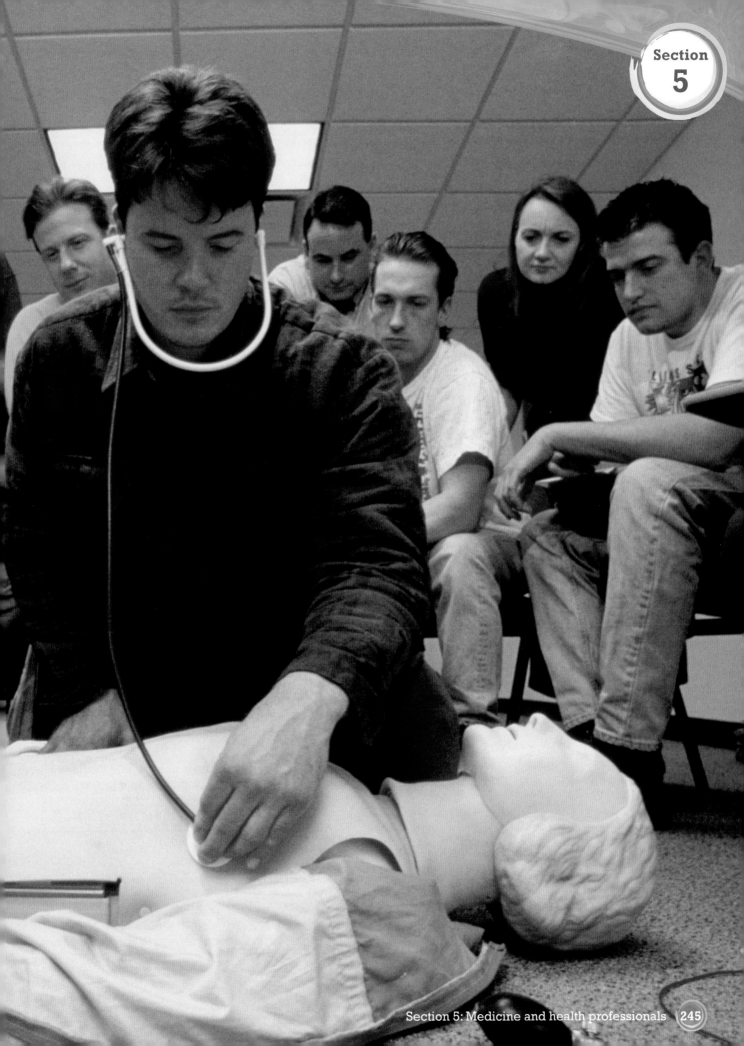

experienced by doctors before they qualify (this can take up to seven years, and involves both assessment by examination and work placement). And secondly, an appreciation of the vital role that doctor's play in society: dealing with vulnerable patients, and treating them equally, ethically and professionally.

Although there is a concern by functionalists that doctors may abuse the amount of power they have, they note that:

- Doctors maintain high standards of ethics, treating all patients equally
- Common criteria are used to judge all patients
- Under the rule of functional specificity, contact is limited only to improving health
- They are professionally regulated by the **General Medical Council** (GMC) who ensure proper standards of medical practice, being able to 'strike-off' doctors whose quality of care does not match these criteria

As a consequence functionalists believe that through the process of role allocation, it is only fair that such talented individuals should be rewarded for the sacrifices they endure during their training.

Criticisms of the functionalist view of the medical profession

- Marxists believe that functionalism ignores the power of the medical profession to manipulate what is seen or not seen as illness, and secondly to extract high levels of pay paid by taxation. Moreover, they believe the rewards given to doctors are not matched when looking at the differences between the costs of providing medical care and the benefits received by society.

- Marxists believe the model overplays the importance of doctors. Health studies show that patients use a range of medical professionals, not all of whom are highly qualified doctors.

- Functionalists tend to ignore the negative side of medicine. For example, some treatment is carried out without or against patients consent, such as those who have been sectioned as mentally ill. Modern medicine can also create illness and dependency, particularly prescription drugs such as methadone and antidepressants.

- This comfortable model has been badly shaken with the failures of professional standards and regulation, such as that we have seen with Harold Shipman (Shipman poisoned patients for financial gain) and the Bristol Children's Hospital (this hospital kept the hearts and other organs of more than 170 babies and children who died after operations, without the parents' consent).

The Weberian approach

The Weberian approach is typified by the work of **Eliot Freidson** (1970) who argues that doctors have created a system of **social closure** that has benefited the medical profession rather than the whole of society. Weber believed that the medical profession are similar to other groups in society, always ensuring that their power is considered to be more legitimate than other similar elite groups. Weber argued that doctors have created an aura of professionalism that has allowed them to achieve high status. The medical profession has achieved this by:

- **Restricting the social background of doctors:** The high examination qualifications needed for entry into the medical school invariably means that most doctors come from the middle or upper social classes. Furthermore, the length of medical courses, the high cost and social isolation allow those from the elite to continue without 'hindrance' from the working classes. Such closure even goes so far as to limit female entry into the profession and those from ethnic minority groups. This process can be said to be ongoing as the nursing profession operates a graduate-only entry scheme.

- **The mystification of medical knowledge:** Jamous and Peloille (1970) argue that the medical profession has managed to exclude the patient as to how decisions are made about drugs and surgery. As a consequence, patients rarely question the professionalism or high status of the medical profession.

- **Exclusion:** The formal medical profession has excluded alternate therapies such as homeopathy, thereby suggesting to patients that it is not a rational source of healing. This has resulted in many such treatments being only available outside of the formal NHS. Moreover, the prestige of these treatments is often questioned with formal medicine suggesting to patients that these alternatives to formal treatment are in some way inferior. This has been achieved despite considerable support for alternative therapies from the UK population and its promotion by high-profile people such as Prince Charles.

- **Occupational autonomy:** Doctors have fought to ensure that their presence is considered vital in many aspects of health care; for example, by stopping nurses being able to inject and prescribe pharmaceutical medicines.

Professions

Professions are occupations; for example, law and medicine which regulate themselves by setting exacting standards for their members to follow. This regulation allows professionals the power to dictate how many graduates enter the profession in any one year. Because of their knowledge base, professionals have a high status and authority over their clients.

You will notice that both functionalism and Weberian views of the medical profession are very similar, with functionalism stressing that role allocation is needed to attract the most intelligent students into the medical profession. By contrast, Weberian approaches view the medical profession as maintaining and extending their status position.

Marxist approaches

Marxists explain the power of the medical profession with reference to capitalism. As an elite group doctors are part of the bourgeoisie, which Marxists believe seek to protect the interests of capitalists at the expense of the proletariat. Professionals from all walks of life serve capitalism by justifying and legitimising inequality. Navarro (1978) argues that the medical process does this by creating **false consciousness** as to why there are huge inequalities in health. Medical professionals play an important role in creating this illusion. Rather than stressing that illness and mortality is linked fundamentally to a person's class position, doctors encourage patients to believe that their illnesses are due to other factors, such as genetics and cultural factors. By doing this, doctors are diverting attention away from some actual causes of mortality: dangerous working conditions, poor health and safety, inadequate housing and poverty. Doctors also assist capitalists by maintaining a healthy workforce that creates extra surplus value for capitalists thereby increasing productivity and profit.

Marxists additionally consider that doctors play an important role by socially controlling sickness. They do this by acting as 'gatekeepers', limiting access to sick notes and thereby encouraging appropriate work discipline, such as regular attendance and a realisation that sick leave limits productivity and profits for employers.

Criticisms of the Marxist approach

Marxism has been criticised for the following reasons:

- Are doctors and those who form part of the medical profession merely puppets of capitalism? Most medical professionals' first and sole interest is to the patients; not to serving capitalism.

- Marxists are often accused of being too economically deterministic. Do we really accept that the medical profession's main role is to serve capitalism? It reduces us to believe that we live in a conspiratorial world that has no morals and ethics. Much of the medical world is based upon helping others in the face of suffering; not merely serving capitalism.

Foucault's approach

For postmodernists such as Foucault (1976), power is essential to an understanding of the position of medical professionals. An important part of Foucault's theory is the belief that those who are in power have specialist knowledge. In cases such as these, "the production of knowledge and the exercise of administrative power intertwine, and each begins to enhance the other." For those who have this knowledge, Foucault believes that they are able to control their patients, thereby dismissing any opinions their patients may have about their treatment.

Foucault notes that control of this knowledge has been achieved by creating the illusion that all doctors are wise and omniscient (know everything), who use science and rationality to guard our health. Another upshot of this is that other alternative treatments are regarded by the medical profession as 'quacks' in comparison to the highly-trained scientific medical profession whose superior knowledge allows us to conquer disease. This has allowed the medical profession to be seen as essential as their rationalism provides the perfect antidote to the old ideas that presided before enlightenment. Consequently, doctors have been able to gain high positions in contemporary society and achieve high pay, particularly in comparison to other professional workers such as teachers and lawyers.

Criticisms of the Foucault approach

- Some suggest that Foucault's dislike of modern medicine is said to have been prompted by an early personal experience when he was taken by his father (who he was said to have loathed) to be treated for showing sexual interest in young men. He can consequently be accused of suffering from ideological bias against the medical profession.

Ivan Illich, *Medical Nemesis: Cultural Iatrogenesis* (1976)

Ivan Illich believed that the successes of modern medicine are unfounded. Indeed, Illich went so far as to comment that medical intervention is harmful to the patient. As far as Illich was concerned, long life was not a product of medical intervention, but the consequence of a healthy environment and strong social bonds. Illich's faith in this assertion was shown by his refusal of any conventional medical treatment when diagnosed with cancer. He found that seven per cent of all patients who were hospitalised came to harm.

Direct harm to the patient caused by medical intervention is called clinical **iatrogenesis**. Since 1974, iatrogenesis has increasingly been recognised by the medical profession. This harm occurs in the following ways:

- **Technical errors in surgery:** Liam Donaldson (Chief Medical Officer for the UK) admitted in 2005 that that the odds of dying as a result of clinical error in hospital are 33 000 times higher than those of dying in an air crash.

- **The side effects of drugs:** In 2006 there were reports of 964 patients in the UK who died as a result of an adverse reaction to the medication that they were prescribed by the medical 'professionals', compared with more than 1000 the previous year, and 861 in 2004.

- **Infections being caught within hospitals:** Organisations such as the Office for National Statistics report on deaths from infections. However, Graham Tanner, chairman of the National Concern for Healthcare Infections, has warned there is vast underreporting of Clostridium difficile and MRSA. The number of hospital-acquired infections in England alone is, according to his organisation, really 230 000 a year, with an average mortality rate of 15 per cent (2005).

Illich also recognised other types of iatrogenesis. For instance he asserted that social iatrogenesis results from the medicalisation of life. Good examples of this include the way depression and sexual problems have been medicalised and the fact that spending on the NHS has reached £13.5 billion in 2007. Finally, Illich argued that cultural iatrogenesis is the destruction of traditional ways of dealing with, and making sense of, death, pain and sickness. Do we need to take endless pills for our depression? Or perhaps it would be better to treat the causes of illness rather than the symptoms?

Criticisms of Ivan Illich and iatrogenesis

- It is argued that Illich ignored the need that society has for the medical profession. Longevity has increased rapidly over the last century. If the medical profession really did harm patients in the way that Illich argued then this would not have happened. In most cases, medical professional care assists human existence, it does not harm them.

Feminist approaches

Feminist sociologists believe that the medical profession is little different from most patriarchal organisations in British society. As such they argue it is run by men and for the benefit of men. One example of this is the way that the medical profession seeks to marginalise and control female health professionals whilst offering few opportunities to them in general. Additionally, it is interesting to note that the majority of cosmetic surgeons performing operations on women are men.

However, there is plenty of contradictory evidence suggesting that patriarchy in the medical profession is not as strong as it once was. For example, in 2002, 60.8 per cent of those accepted into UK medical and dental schools were women. The proportion of women compared with men has been rising steadily from 54 per cent in 1996, to 57 per cent in 2000, and 58 per cent in 2001. However, other data is more compelling, with women in 2001 accounting for only six per cent of the 4640 consultant surgical posts in the UK, although they comprise well over half of medical school intake. (British Medical Journal [BMJ], 2001). This contrasts markedly from what had gone on previously; for example in the eighteenth century women often took the role of herbal healers, pharmacists and abortionists.

Anne Witz (1992) contends that two methods have helped marginalise female medical professionals:

1. A gendered exclusionary strategy where women were prevented from entering the medical profession.

2. A gendered demarcation strategy where women were channelled into only limited areas of medical practice such as midwifery and nursing.

However, Witz believes that to counteract these patriarchal strategies, women have pursued the following two counteracting policies:

1. Witz argues that women have used a variety of methods of gaining as much entry into the profession as possible by, for example, using legislation and political action.

2. Dual closure: This process refers to closing off an area of medical practice by excluding doctors and thereby developing a new profession with specialist knowledge and procedures. This is exactly what is happening in the nursing profession in the UK, with the role of the nurse being extended to allow them to prescribe drugs; alleviating hard-pressed doctors who can be freed up to concentrate on more complex problems.

Other ways that female illness has been medicalised by men

- Feminists such as Oakley (1984) and Deborah Lupton (1994) claim that doctors use their power to control women in a wider sense. For example, natural processes such as pregnancy, childbirth, conception, beauty and the menopause have become medicalised conditions to be controlled largely by male experts. For example, Lupton suggests that women are so determined to use reproductive technologies, such as ultrasound, which, in the past, was only used in problematic pregnancies, as they are persuaded by the medical profession that such an intervention is necessary. Lupton sees this process as part of a number of situations where women's pregnancies are medicalised, thereby allowing males to control women, almost from the moment of conception to birth.

- Recent research in the BMJ (2003) by Ray Moynihan implies that the pharmaceutical industry has 'created' a disease out of female sexual problems, with large drug companies seeking to recreate similar demand for sexual dysfunction medication for women as for men, even when there is no evidence that women suffer sexual dysfunction.

Criticisms of the feminist approach

- Feminism ignores the fact that many male patients are also harmed by the patriarchal decisions made by doctors and consultants.

- Feminists can be accused of suffering from ideological bias. Other groups are also subject to poor medical provision and care. For example, some ethnic groups' medical needs are not provided for, despite obvious need.

The rise of complementary medicine to challenge the power of doctors

The male dominance of health care in the UK has been under threat from a range of influences. Firstly, there are far more women qualifying and training in the NHS that ever before, whilst additionally female ethnic representation is greater for medicine than would be expected, given the percentage of the population. Moreover, male patriarchy and dominance has been shaken by the continued growth of complementary medicine. Despite there being little research on how effective these treatments are, figures from a 1993 survey indicate 33 per cent of the population had used some form of complementary medicine and that over 10 per cent had consulted a complementary practitioner in the previous year. Surveys of patients with chronic and difficult-to-manage diseases such as cancer, HIV, multiple sclerosis, psoriasis, and rheumatologic conditions, give levels of use up to twice as high to use complementary medicines (partly due to the fact that these may be offered by some hospitals).

Postmodernists such as Giddens argue that this growth is due to a number of factors:

- The decline in metanarratives: Postmodernists such as Jean Francois Lyotard argue that whilst in the past grand theories were applied to life, such as scientific rationality, as we have moved towards modernity these explanations no longer have the same credence. As the medical profession is one branch of science, belief in traditional doctors and their power has also declined. Instead people look towards the narratives of individuals or local communities, such as complementary medicine. For postmodernists 'quality, not truth' becomes the focus.

- With modernity there is a far greater emphasis on choice. These choices can be made throughout medicine, choices on how to look, whether to have a sex change operation or to choose IVF, just in the same way patients are less inclined to merely accept old notions of treatment and are far more willing to explore other notions of medical assistance.

Criticisms of the postmodern view

- Onora O'Neill observed in her Reith Lectures (2002) that in practice people do not behave as if they have lost their trust in doctors. Patients continue to rely upon the NHS and demand for old fashioned medical intervention is not decreasing, but increasing.

- Coulter (2002) believes that patients, although wanting choice, still do not want a consumerist system in which they have total autonomy in health.

What do you know now?

1. How many workers were employed in the NHS in 2006?
   - 500 000
   - 1 million
   - 1.3 million
   - 1.7 million

2. What is the average wage of a GP?
   - £50 000
   - £60 000
   - £70 000
   - £110 000

3. By contrast what do you think is the average wage of a nurse in the UK?
   - £18 400
   - £28 400
   - £30 400
   - £35 400

4. How much do you think it costs to train a doctor in the UK?
   - £100 000
   - £150 000
   - £200 000
   - £250 000

5. How much, on top of their NHS wage, can top surgeons earn by working in the private sector?
   - £50 000
   - £100 000
   - £500 000
   - £1 million

6. Explain why functionalists believe that the medical profession has a high status in contemporary society.

7. Isolate the meaning of the phrase 'social closure' and explain its importance in explaining Weberian perceptions of health professionals.

8. Describe how Marxists claim that medical professionals serve the interests of the bourgeoisie.

9. According to Foucault, how has the medical profession gained power?

10. Give two examples of how the medical profession have 'medicalised' natural processes.

11. Isolate two ideas that postmodernism suggests has led to the growth of complementary medicine.

Key terms

Deferred gratification:	The ability to wait in order to obtain something that one wants.
Ethics:	A system that defines right from wrong.
False consciousness:	Marxist concept that that economic and institutional processes within capitalism deludes the proletariat into believing that exploitation is due to factors other than capitalism.
General Medical Council (GMC):	Regulates the medical profession by issuing licenses to practice and has the power to 'strike-off' doctors whose standards fall below those considered acceptable.
Iatrogenesis:	Means 'brought forth by the healer'. It can refer to the positive or negative effects of medical treatment. However, it has been most used to describe the damage western-style medical treatment can inflict on patients.
Social closure:	Phrase used by Max Weber to explain how powerful groups, such as medical professionals, exclude others from privileges and rewards.

Section summary

- Medical professionals, such as GPs and surgeons, enjoy high status and high pay.

- There are a number of different theoretical approaches that seek to explain medical professionals' power.

- Functionalism is a macro theory that seeks to explain all aspects of sociological life and its writers remain consistent throughout. Talcott Parsons argues that the medical profession has important functions that allow society to flourish.

- The Weberian approach argues that doctors have created a system of social closure that has benefited the medical profession rather than the whole of society. Weber believed that the medical profession are similar to other groups in society, always ensuring that their power is considered to be more legitimate than other similar elite groups.

- Marxists explain the power of the medical profession with reference to capitalism. As an elite group doctors are part of the bourgeoisie, which Marxists believe seek to protect the interests of capitalists at the expense of the proletariat.

- For Postmodernists such as Foucault, power is essential to an understanding of the position of medical professionals. Foucault believed that those who are in power have specialist knowledge.

- Ivan Illich believed that the successes of modern medicine are unfounded. Indeed, Illich went so far as to comment that medical intervention is harmful to the patient.

- Feminists sees the medical profession as little different from most patriarchal organisations in British society. As such they argue it is run by men, and for the benefit of men.

- The male dominance of health care in the UK has been under threat from a range of influences. Firstly, there are far more women qualifying and training in the NHS than ever before, whilst additionally female ethnic representation is greater for medicine than would be expected given the percentage of the population. Moreover, male patriarchy and dominance has been shaken by the continued growth of complementary medicine.

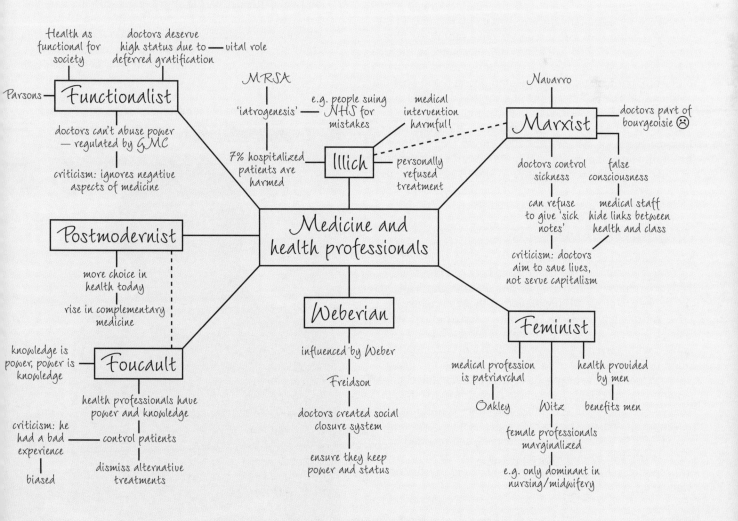

The application of research methods to health

Asking questions

A vast number of surveys are published by the Department of Health, often with the aim of showing whether government policy is being successful in the fight against illness. Examples include:

Surveys

The Health Survey for England (HSE): First performed in 1991, provides a series of annual surveys to monitor trends in the nation's health. HSE uses a representative **sample** of adults over the age of 16 who live in private households in the UK. It has been used in particular to monitor government targets on health, particularly cardiovascular illness, blood pressure and obesity. The HSE is an ongoing survey conducted every year throughout the year, with a new sample issued monthly. The survey runs to a five-year plan, with a particular focus in some years; for instance, the 2004 survey focused on the health of ethnic minorities, and the 2000 survey on the health of older people and social exclusion. Since 1995, it was also helped by *The Guardian's* survey of children age 2–15, with children aged 0–2 also being surveyed since 2002.

Structured interviews

The Health and Lifestyle Survey: First conducted in 1984–5, this survey examines the relationship between lifestyle, behaviour and circumstance in relation to the physical and mental health of the UK population. Although originally cross-sectional, it has since 1991 been a **longitudinal study** using the same sample. An in-depth interview-based system is used with nurse visit allowing respondents to complete the questionnaire. Because of its longitudinal slant the survey seeks to look at how health alters with differing life changes. Additionally, its brief is to examine how attitudes to health change over time, whilst refining and either confirming or rejecting data obtained from the original survey. Questions asked include basic socio-economic data; self-reported health, such as whether respondents smoke,and so on; along with a self-reported set of questions on personal and psychiatric well-being.

Unstructured interviews

When looking at health and illness, the interviewer will set the topic area. Although the interviewer may ask more open-ended questions to allow the interviewee to say what they want about their health and how they see illness. The recording of unstructured interviews always provides problems as it can hinder the conversation. Within a health setting very rough notes or video recordings can be utilised as a way of avoiding this problem. The advantages of using this method is that it allows the respondent to comment on these issues in their own words, therefore avoiding the issues of the interviewer misinterpreting what is being said. Nonetheless, this is a very costly and time-consuming method. It is up the researcher to decide whether these costs are justified.

Life histories

- Emily Grundy (2005) has used life histories to examine how childhood experiences influence health and mortality in later life. The research has predominantly focused on how particular partnership experiences and parental histories have an effect on mortality on both UK and US citizens. The research has revealed that those who remain childless, have teenage pregnancies or have short intervals between births are at higher risk of poor health or death later in life. The US part of the study showed that the shorter time men are married or those men with multiple partnerships have higher mortality rates.

Emily Grundy

Group discussions

- Norris (1996) used group discussion to explore women's perceptions of sexual aggression. She found that focus groups offered an ideal environment to understand and develop future hypotheses on this difficult subject area. By its very nature it allows far richer and more detailed information to be delivered to the researcher on the experiences of women. Within group discussions students were asked to discuss the link between the use of alcohol and sexual aggression.

Observation

Participant observation

Helen Allen (2006) has looked at how working as a nurse in fertility units affected nurses. Allan's study looked at the day-to-day emotions experienced by nurses as part of their everyday activities. Allan conducted 48 visits to the clinics to Assisted Conception Units of two–three hours per visit over a period of two years. **Participant observation** data comprised of field notes taken during and after sessions in the field. She found that staff used spaces within the hospital to distance themselves from patient's emotions. This gave the appearance of nurses being uncaring professionals. Although Allen believes that the hospitals organisations of 'private' and 'public spheres' assisted in stopping potentially damaging emotions being displayed by the nursing staff to those in their care. Allen believes that the use of participant observation uncovered this dynamic in way that other methodologies would have failed to reveal. The use of participant observation and interviews was especially vital in finding out how nursing staff coped with their emotions within a health setting.

Non-participant observation

Karen Spilsbury (2004) used this method to understand the duties of health care assistants in a hospital setting. She was interested both in varying backgrounds of health care assistants and how their role was changing in the NHS. Spilsbury looked what health care assistants say they do, compared to what they actually do. For ease of research one hospital was chosen, with findings indicating that duties are the result of active negotiations on the ward, often resulting in the misuse of health care assistants. Spilsbury believes that these findings are the result of changes in the role of nurses within the NHS and she believes that their change in role will result in the continuing extension of responsibilities for health care assistants. By observing this group, she was able at first hand to see the duties that assistants had to perform, offering an illuminating glimpse beyond the supposed duties as outlined on health care professionals' job descriptions.

Experiments

Controlled experiments

A controlled experiment generally tries to compare the results from an experimental sample to a controlled sample, with one variable being changed with the experimental sample. As a consequence any differences in results can be attributed to the change in the one variable. A good example would be a drug trial. The sample, or group, receiving the drug would be the experimental group; and the group receiving the placebo would be the control one; the idea being that the patient is receiving a form of treatment with the placebo, which, although not containing an active ingredient, can sometimes have an effect on the recipient. This is best used in tandem with the double-blind method in which neither the researcher nor the individual knows if they are in the control or the experimental group. This has the benefit of limiting possible cues from the researcher as to which group they belong it.

Uncontrolled experiments

These experiments do not have all the same conditions and therefore the control groups are different and the conditions that the experiment is conducted in are also different. Although uncontrolled experiments are easy enough to conduct under laboratory conditions, human beings in situ offer more complications, given that to observe humans changing environments should be used. As such, experimenting on human beings is fraught with difficulty.

Secondary data

There are two types of data that can be collected by social researchers:

- **Primary data:** This is where data is collected using methods such as interviews and questionnaires. The key point here is that the data collected is unique to you and your research and, until it is published, no one else has access to it.

- **Secondary data:** This is data that is neither collected directly by the user nor specifically for the user, often under conditions not known to the user. An example is government reports: secondary information has already been collected for some other purposes. It may be available from internal sources, or may have been collected and published by another organisation. Secondary data is cheaper and more quickly available than primary data, but likely to need interpretation before it is useful.

In this section we will look at the variety of health data available to the sociologist. The following statistics are published by the government:

- **Mortality statistics:** This data offers a review of the Registrar General on deaths by cause, sex and age, in England and Wales and is published annually. This annual report explains changes in death rates, the causes of

death by age, and sex. However, it should be remembered that mortality statistics only examine deaths; they do not look at illness, or at the stage or grade of an illness, and therefore non-fatal diseases are included in these figures.

- **The usage of medical facilities:** Examples include *Hospital Episode Statistics* (HES) which provides data on bed availability and occupancy, how many people attend outpatient clinics by sector and consultant, attendance at accident and emergency, the use and availability of NHS Day Care Provision, a summary of official complaints, and adult critical-care figures that look at the use of intensive care facilities in the NHS.

- **Absenteeism:** Sickness and absence data by sector in the economy (private or public), by region, occupation, in relation to dependent children, and by age and sex.

- **Waiting times:** These are published by operation and are linked to government targets in relation to operative care. Statistics on both inpatient and outpatient waiting times are collated.

- **Mental health:** Information on the prevalence of electroconvulsive therapy (ECT), and those formally detained under the Mental Health Act, 1983.

Patient choice: Shows how far patients have been able to exercise their choice at Primary Care Trust level.

Pharmacies and prescriptions: statistics on community pharmacies, GP prescriptions issued, and cost of prescriptions to the NHS.

Screening and immunisation: Statistics on breast and cervical screening in England, and the number of immunisations for diphtheria, tetanus, polio, pertussis (whooping cough), haemophilus, influenza, measles and tuberculin skin tests by age. All statistics are by region, NHS trust, and health authority.

Advantages of official statistics

- Statistics can be compared over time, allowing the sociologist to make generalisations from them. For example, Émile Durkheim used official statistics on suicide that allowed him to construct a new paradigm on why certain groups were more likely to commit suicide.

- It is a quick and easy method to use as the sociologist has no need to collect the statistics for themselves.

- Statistics allow sociologists to look at data before and after social policy has been introduced. Consequently, they act as a good yardstick as to how successful or unsuccessful government legislation is.

- Positivists claim that official statistics are more reliable and scientific than other methods of collection. If collection is similar year in year out, any differences between the statistics should reflect real tangible divergence.

Problems with statistics on health

- Marxists claim that any data produced by the government will always attempt to put a gloss on statistics. This can be done by omitting embarrassing statistics, publishing data on a 'quiet news day' or not publishing at all.

- Statistics are merely a 'snapshot of time'. As such, just like books, they are out of date from the moment they are published.

- The basis for the collection of statistics by the governments may change over time making comparisons almost impossible.

- It has been argued that official statistics simply show a person's judgement rather than objective facts. Phenomenologists, for example, tend to regard the way that statistics have been collected as far more interesting and telling that the statistics themselves.

- Statistics are good at giving us generalisations; they do not reflect a reality; they impose one.

- Interactionists believe that they fail to offer any meaning. What do they prove? It would perhaps be far more relevant to ask workers within the NHS about their perceptions on mortality rates, waiting times, and son on. Interactionists claim that this would be far more illuminating than the dry statistics produced by the ONS.

- Feminist and ethnic minority writers believe that official statistics tend to underplay issues such as gender (being too malestream) or ethnicity (tend to be ethnocentric).

Using triangulation in the study of health

Although much of the presented literature suggests a clear demarcation between positivists and anti-positivists, that is, those who use quantitative data as opposed to qualitative material, there is a third course that can be used: triangulation. This combines both the methodological advantages and disadvantages of both methods. A number of sociologists have used a combination of quantitative and qualitative methods, including Paul Willis's study, *Learning to Labour* (1984), and Eileen Barker's study of the Moonies, *Making of a Moonie* (1984).

Within the arena of health studies this method has also been utilised. Anne Rogers and Gerry Nicolaas's research shows how this can be done (1998). The study was conducted in three areas of the North West of England and was designed to look at how the use of health care impacted on health. Rogers and Nicolaas used a two-stage methodological approach. They asked patients to complete a survey and a study diary to find out how much they used the NHS and the quality of the respondents' health. There then followed a linked qualitative study asking in-depth interviews on a sample of respondents indicating that they had experienced problems with the quality of the primary care they have received. By using this wide range of methods, the researchers were able to have a broader understanding of how people used local hospitals. The research pointed to the fact that patients were much more likely to use self-care than necessarily attending their local PCT, with patients using their own perceptions and remedies to assist in their well-being.

What do you know now?

1. Explain the difference between a structured and unstructured interview.
2. Isolate an example of a survey used within the sphere of health.
3. Describe the term 'longitudinal study'. Why is it a particularly useful method?
4. Why are experiments a 'scientific method of inquiry'?
5. Explain the difference between non-participant and participant observation.
6. Give an example of data that the government publishes on health in the UK.
7. Explain one advantage and one disadvantage of official statistics.
8. Choose an appropriate method for each of the following examples:
   - Finding out how many prescriptions were issued in the NHS by PCT
   - Mortality rates by gender
   - How nurses are affected by their emotions
   - The experiences of women in relation to childbirth
   - How acute a patient's hearing is
   - The amount of patients 'sectioned' in the UK
   - The hours spent working in the NHS by doctors
   - Uncover the lifestyle choices of the UK population

Key terms

Longitudinal study: A study of the same group of people at more than one point in time.

Non-participant observation: A research method where the researcher merely observes the subjects in their study, rather than taking an active part in the process.

Participant observation: Involves entering the world and participating with the group concerned. Qualitative sociologists argue that through this process more detailed observations can be made.

Sample: A collection of individuals selected from the population to be studied.

Structured interviews: In its simplest form, a structured interview involves one person asking another person a list of predetermined questions about a carefully-selected topic.

Unstructured interviews: A spontaneous conversation, not a specific set of questions asked in a predetermined order.

Section summary

A vast number of surveys are published by the Department of Health, often with the aim of showing whether government policy is being successful in the fight against illness.

Emily Grundy has used life histories to examine how childhood experiences influence health and mortality in later life.

Norris used group discussion to explore women's perceptions of sexual aggression.

Helen Allen has looked at how working as a nurse in fertility unit affected the nurses.

Karen Spilsbury used the non-participant method to understand the duties of health care assistants in a hospital setting.

A controlled experiment generally tries to compare the results from an experimental sample to a controlled sample, with one variable being changed with the experimental sample.

- Primary data is where data is collected using methods such as interviews and questionnaires. The key point here is that the data you collect is unique to you and your research and, until you publish, no one else has access to it.

- Secondary data is data that is neither collected directly by the user nor specifically for the user, often under conditions not known to the user. Examples include government reports.

- Although much of the presented literature suggests a clear demarcation between positivists and anti-positivists, that is, those who use quantitative data as opposed to qualitative material, there is a third course that can be used: triangulation. This combines both the methodological advantages and disadvantages of both methods.

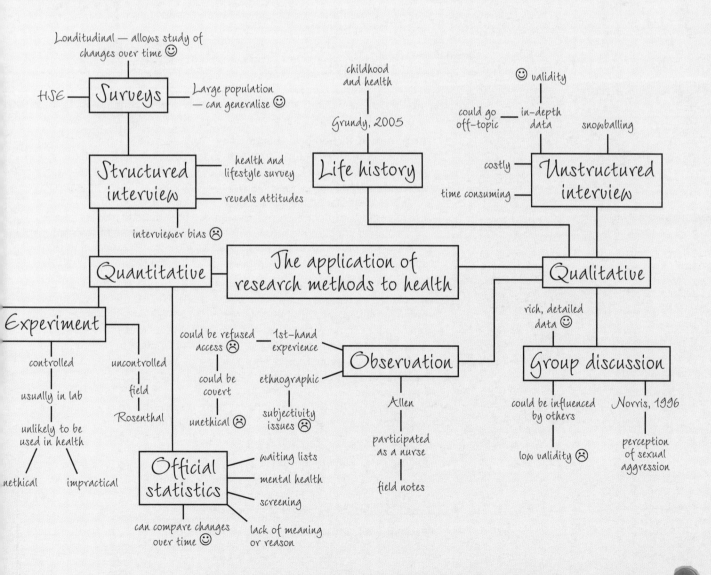

How to maximise your grade with AQA

Health and illness is worth 60 per cent of the AS total mark and 30 per cent of A level. You will be expected to answer five questions on the family, with graduated questions from two marks, four marks, six marks and then the large 24 mark questions. As with the previous specification the exam format is a stimulus response style question. As a result of the decision to dispense with coursework this module includes one question on sociological research methods in context and one question on research methods.

The assessment objectives for the A level are as follows:

Assessment objectives		Weighting
AO1	Knowledge and understanding of the theories, methods, concepts and various forms of evidence linked to the specification.	48%
	Communication of knowledge and understanding in a clear and effective manner.	
AO2	Demonstration of the skills of application, analysis, interpretation and evaluation.	52%
Overall weighting		60%

AO1: You will need to know the following areas to obtain a high mark in knowledge and understanding:

- **The nature of sociological thought:** The AQA ask you to have a good knowledge of a range of theories that predominate in the sociology of health and illness. Specifically, this means knowing the major writers and theories associated with pluralism, material and structural explanations and the different approaches to health. Additionally, students need to know about genetic approaches and differences in health and illness between gender, ethnicity and social class and be able to explain these. Students should also be aware of the inequalities of access and provision of medical care. There is also an expectation that candidates should be aware of issues such as mental health and disability.

- **Methods of Social Enquiry:** As there is no coursework component, the AQA have added a methods section to each unit. Specifically, the AQA want you to apply your knowledge of methods appropriately. You will need to apply this knowledge to show you understand how sociologists undertake research into health and illness and the advantages and disadvantages of these methods. Finally, students should know how theory and methods are interrelated and how this impacts on the study of health and illness. Overall then, a wide knowledge of primary and secondary methods is needed. It is expected that these skills will be used practically as there will be far more opportunity to undertake project work, with this new specification having few modules.

- **Themes:** You are expected to cover two themes:

- **Socialization, culture and identity:** Health and illness has long been considered as a source of identity, with many groups being labelled as being 'ill' via social construction. Health and illness offers an ideal way for students to explore how these identities are formed and self-perpetuated.

- **Social differentiation, power and stratification:** There are huge differences in how illness impacts on different groups within contemporary society.

Factors such as class, gender and ethnicity can be explored here to achieve an understanding of these disparities.

AO2: This assessment objective asks you to be able to acquire and produce evidence and apply it to the question set. You will also be expected to be able to look at the strengths and weaknesses of each argument and come up with a reasoned conclusion. Evidence should be both from primary and secondary resources, and you will be expected to use both quantitative and qualitative data. There are a number of ways you can do this. When talking about health and illness, you can be critical of areas such as the methodology used, whether the study is now dated, whether the researcher is suffering from ideological bias and so on. It is important that you learn at least two criticisms for each major theory. However, remember that evaluation also includes strengths of theories.

There are three sections you will need to tackle for AO2:

Collection and recording of evidence: Specifically you will need to evaluate the design of sociological research as it applies to health and illness. You must analyse and evaluate the methods used to collect data.

Interpretation and evaluation of evidence: It is essential that you do the following here: show objectivity, apply a range of theories to the questions set and use appropriate concepts. So for instance, within the health system you would be expected to understand what the role of doctors is and how this powerful group affects social policy. At all times, sociology students need to be aware of the highly subjective nature of sociology and apply a range of theories using their 'tool kit' of concepts to achieve this.

Presentation of evidence and argument: A level examiners expect you to be able to organise your written answers so there is coherence. This means that you are expected to start with an introduction, have a number of interlinked paragraphs and a conclusion. Within this answer you must use theory that would inform the question and include any evidence that would further answer the question. You must draw conclusions and back these up with appropriate arguments. Examiners are especially keen to see that sociology students have a wide knowledge of society. Make sure that when you write essays you are able to contextualise your knowledge. Do you know who the secretary of state for health is? Although students may think that such details are unnecessary, examiners like to see an overall knowledge of the topic areas studied.

Exam practice for AQA

Health with research methods

You are advised to spend approximately 50 minutes on Question 4

You are advised to spend approximately 25 minutes on Question 5

You are advised to spend approximately 40 minutes on Question 6

Item C

Although women live longer than men in England and Wales, that is not to say that they are actually healthier during their lifetime. There is a saying used by doctors that neatly summarises the difference and experiences of illness by gender: "Women get sicker, but men die quicker". The different genders do act differently when it comes to illness. Whilst women are often quicker to go to their doctor at the first sign of illness, men often wait until it is too late for effective treatment. There are also other notable differences. For instance, women are more likely to suffer mental

illness and depression than men. This leads to women being three times more likely to try to commit suicide. However, mortality rates for suicide are greater for men than for women.

(a) What is meant by 'mortality'? (*2 Marks*)

(b) Identify three reasons why higher social classes live longer than those from the working classes. (*6 Marks*)

(c) Outline some of the reasons why some ethnic minority groups suffer worse health than other groups. (*12 Marks*)

(d) Using material from *Item C* and elsewhere, examine the reasons why different social groups appear to have different rates of mental illness.

This question requires you to apply your knowledge and understanding of sociological research methods to the study of this particular issue in health.

Read *Item D* below and answer the question that follows.

Item D

Some sociologists like using participant observation to get an understanding of the role of health professionals. Karen Spilsbury (2004) wanted to understand the duties of health care assistants in a hospital setting. She was interested both in varying backgrounds of health care assistants and how their role was changing in the NHS. Spilsbury looked at what health care assistants say they do, compared to their actual reality.

Other sociologists such as Erving Goffman (1968) have examined the impact that medical institutions have on their patients. Goffman found in his study, *Asylums*, that once stigmatised patients changed their behaviour and self-identification.

Using material from *Item D* and elsewhere, assess the strengths and limitations of one of the following methods for the study of interaction between doctors and their patients:

- Interviews

- Participant observation

This question permits you to draw examples from any areas of sociology with which you are familiar.

Explain the term 'systematic random sampling'. (*2 Marks*)

Suggest two social factors that could be used for the creation of a quota sample apart from ethnicity. (*4 Marks*)

Suggest two reasons why social researchers might want to use social surveys. (*4 Marks*)

Examine the problems that may result from the use of participant observation in researching health and illness. (*20 Marks*)

Sociological methods

Learning objectives

What the AQA spec says	Section in this book	Page
Quantitative and qualitative methods of research, their strengths and limitations; research design.	Section One: Quantitative and qualitative methods and research design	264
Sources of data, including questionnaires, interviews, participant and non-participant observation, experiments, documents, and official statistics; the strengths and limitations of these sources.	Section Two: Sources of data; their strengths and limitations	272
The distinction between primary and secondary data, and between quantitative and qualitative data.	Section Three: Primary and secondary data	282
The relationship between positivism, interpretivism and sociological methods; the nature of 'social facts'.	Section Four: Positivism and interpretivism	290
The theoretical, practical and ethic considerations influencing the choice of topic, choice of method(s) and the conduct of research.	Section Five: Theoretical, practical and ethical considerations	300

Exam skill focus

Skills required	
AO1 Knowledge and understanding of theories.	You should know the different methods used by social researchers, whilst understanding the link between theory and methods.
AO2 Demonstration of the skills of application, analysis, interpretation and evaluation.	You must be able to apply your knowledge of methods to a variety of situations and be able to assess the strengths and weaknesses of each.

What it means to be studying sociological methods with AQA

Sociology is littered with debates about a whole range of topics, including health, education and the mass media. However, what separates sociologists from the views of the public is that these debates are not merely the opinion of the writer concerned; rather than being subjective, their claim is that their research is based upon fact. Within this topic we will examine the variety of methods that researchers use to formulate their views. This will enable the student to both understand the strengths and weaknesses of each method used, but also allow them to engage in their own research. Throughout this topic key terms are explained to help guide you through the maze of terminology that is a feature of the sociological methods part of the course.

In **Section One** we explore the difference between quantitative and qualitative research, looking at the advantages and disadvantages of each. We also look at the 'third way' to do research which is now used by most sociologists; triangulation. Lastly in this section, we concentrate upon factors that impact on the choice of method chosen by the social researcher.

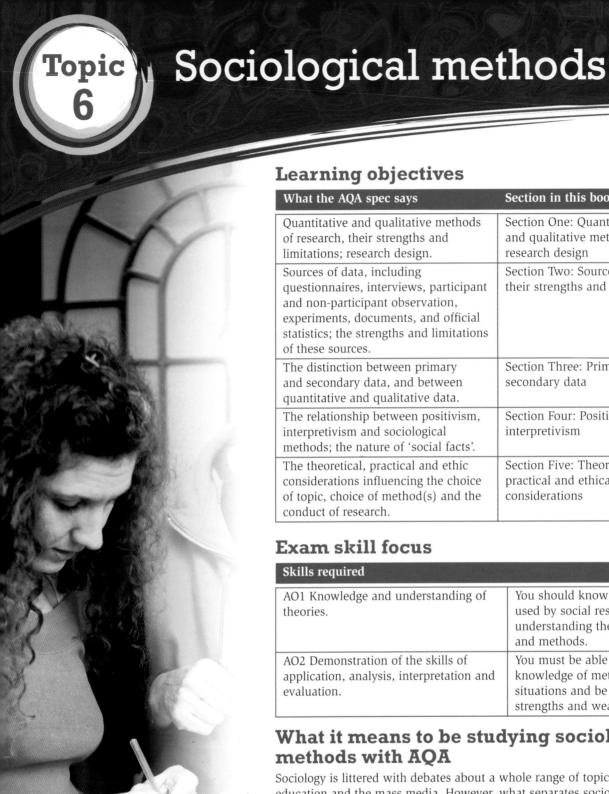

Section Two places the above into context. We consider which methods tend to be used by quantitative and qualitative researchers and the processes that are needed for successful social exploration. We examine each method, including social surveys, interviews, official statistics, experiments, longitudinal surveys, comparative method and different observation techniques.

Section Three delves into the differences between primary and secondary data, evaluating examples of each of these. Lastly, we look at the relationship between theory and methods in more depth.

Section Four offers more detail about the strengths and weaknesses of questionnaires, and practical tips about how to construct these. Interviews are also scrutinised. We study how observation is used as a research tool, looking at the ethical and practical constraints of this controversial research method. Lastly, we explore whether sociology can ever be value free.

Finally, Section Five analyses how social research can be fraught with practical and ethic considerations. It looks at the purpose of social research, how ethical issues can arise, and how theory and methods can impact on the method chosen.

Sociologists studied in this topic

Eileen Barker	Used triangulation to examine the Church of Unification (otherwise known pejoratively as the Moonies).
Rebecca Dobash and Russell Dobash (1980)	Husband and wife team who have looked at how domestic violence is a 'hidden' crime. By using interviews as their methodology they were able to develop a close rapport with their interviewees, thereby increasing validity.
Émile Durkheim (1897)	Important functionalist. Famous for his empirical study on suicide.
Simon Holdaway (1977)	As a sergeant kept a covert diary on the day to day working of the Metropolitan Police.
John Kitsuse and Aaron Cicourel (1963)	Found in their study, *The Educational Decision Makers*, that interviews provided the perfect foil for getting the most out of their respondents.
Ann Oakley (1981)	Feminist and founder of the Social Research Unit. Wrote *From Here to Maternity*, a study that examined women's perceptions of maternity.
James Patrick (1973)	The pseudonym used by social researcher who discovered that performing covert participation observation could result in the researcher being exposed to danger.
William Foote Whyte (1943)	Lived for four years in the Italian community of Boston researching gangs and gang culture.

My mock examination for this topic is in ....

I will be examined on this topic in ....

Quantitative and qualitative methods and research design

Primary and secondary data

Primary data

Data is said to be primary if is collected by the sociological researcher specifically for the research project in hand. Primary data includes questionnaires, statistics, observation records, and so on. Once collected, data then can be analysed by the social researcher using a variety of statistical techniques; for example, with the use of spreadsheets, and so on. As with all data collected, the sociologist needs to mindful of the personal nature of data gained and follow guidelines as outlined by the British Sociological Association (BSA).

Secondary data

Secondary data is information that has already been collected and published by others. Examples of secondary data include data published by the ONS, journals, press articles, magazines and so on.

Quantitative research methods

This method starts with the premise that sociologists should seek to replicate the methods used by the **natural sciences** such as physics, chemistry and biology. Thus adherents believe the following procedures should be used:

- Data should be collected objectively and scientifically. By collecting statistics, behaviour is being quantified. This then allows the data to be expressed either numerically, as a percentage or as a per capita figure (rate per 1000 of the population). From this data comparisons can be made over time, culture, and so on. This method was, of course, utilised by **Émile Durkheim** when collating data for his study on suicide.

- This data should be collected from as large a sample as possible, allowing generalisations to be made. Generalisations are propositions that result from a study of group of people who have similar features. Generalisations should only be attempted if the group being studied are typical of the sample being considered.

- Once the data is collected, it should be compared with other similar studies and correlations made. Correlation is the strength of the relationship between two or more variables. For example, height and weight are related: taller people tend to be heavier than shorter people. In this case the relationship is not perfect as people of the same height can vary in weight. Nonetheless, the average weight of people height 5 ft 5 in is less than the average weight of people 5 6 in', and their average weight is less than that of people 5 7 in', and so on.

- Once enough studies indicate similar findings, quantitative theorists believe they are moving towards a 'truth'.

The advantages of quantitative data

- **Reliability:** Often used in connection with the use of quantitative data. For research to be reliable it needs to be able to be easily replicable and when done so should produce similar results. As the collection of data is less personal and based upon fact rather than supposition, positivists who believe that we should use scientific principles, argue that, although it may miss contextual detail, it allows the researcher to remain objectively separated from the subject matter. Reliability can be further enhanced through the use of methods that use the same questions to many respondents. This 'standardised approach' ensures that any differences found between the respondents are tangible and real, rather than influenced by the way a question has been asked.

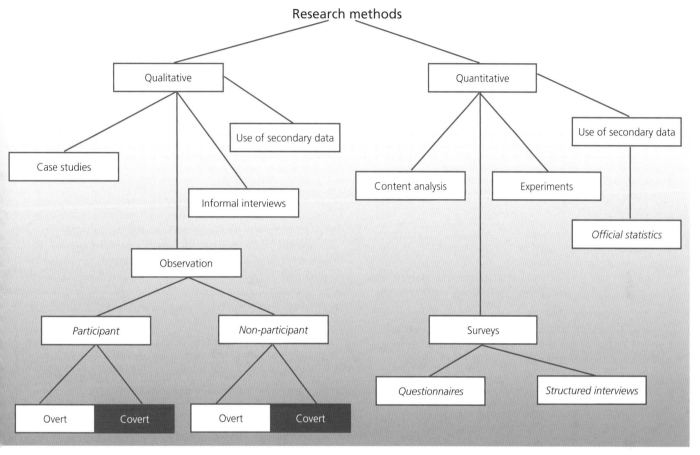

Research methods

- Qualitative
  - Case studies
  - Use of secondary data
  - Informal interviews
  - Observation
    - *Participant*
      - Overt
      - Covert
    - *Non-participant*
      - Overt
      - Covert
- Quantitative
  - Content analysis
  - Experiments
  - Use of secondary data
    - *Official statistics*
  - Surveys
    - *Questionnaires*
    - *Structured interviews*

- **Replication:** Another important idea for positivists is to repeat studies. Although writers such as Karl Popper note that you can never be certain of 'truth', the more times similar results are recorded, the closer to the truth it can said to be.

- **Statistical analysis:** Through the use of data, social phenomena can be classified without allowing personal opinion cloud judgement. The aim is to classify features, count them, and construct statistical models in an attempt to explain what is observed. Additionally, it allows for the researcher to easily track changes over time, especially if data has been collected similarly. For instance, comparisons on poverty can be made; moreover, correlation can be assessed to examine the relationship between two variables. **Kruger** (2003) believes that quantitative data "allows us to summarise vast sources of information and facilitate comparisons across categories and over time".

The disadvantages of quantitative data

- **Validity:** Although it can reveal statistical insights, it fails to offer any kind of insight as to the reasons for any statistics. So, for example, if we were to examine thefts within a school, data would be available to show the amount of thefts, the percentage increase and trends over time; however, this method fails to reveal the reasons for

school crime. So whilst statistics might be issued by the school, they show no context. For example, did the school pupils themselves consider each offence to be a crime? What is the definition of a theft? And so on.

- **Meanings:** This method therefore fails singularly to look at the complexities of human interaction, seeing all statistics as social facts, rather than looking at them in relation to a social dynamic. In the above example, pupils have their own ideas of what a theft is. Many of these will be similar to adults. However, not all. For example, students may borrow items and whilst this may be classified as a theft by the school, it certainly would not be seen as such by the pupils concerned.

Methods used by quantitative researchers

Examples of methods used by quantitative researchers include the following:

- Questionnaires
- Closed, formal and structured interviews
- Official statistics
- The comparative method
- Longitudinal surveys

Qualitative data

The advantages of qualitative data

- **Validity:** This kind of data is rich and holistic, revealing detail that would not be gleaned from quantitative methods. As it allows respondents to speak in their own words, we are far more likely to gain a whole and true understanding of the research project we are examining.

- **Reveals complexity of meanings:** Qualitative data allows researchers to understand why people do things, allowing them to speak in their own words and explain their emotions and feelings. So, in the example above, pupils would be able to explain what they consider to be a theft and how the theft had an impact on them. This method allows latent issues to be explored.

- **Sensitivity:** Rather than respondents being constrained by pre-coded responses, qualitative data allow sensitive areas, such as sexuality, to be explored because the researcher is able to use their interpersonal skills to gain trust.

- **Creates openness:** Because meanings are not imposed it allows for greater honesty and transparency between researcher and respondent. As a consequence, new hypotheses can be generated.

The disadvantages of qualitative data

- **Reliability:** Studies are very difficult to replicate so they raise the issue of lack of reliability. Indeed, similar studies of life in the Mexican village of Tepoztlan by Redfield (1926) and Lewis (1951) indicate the problems in replication. The different findings of each author resulted in each dismissing the other's methodologies and research findings.

- **Using the data:** With the huge amount of data that is collected by qualitative research there is a danger of the researcher imposing their own reality on what is collected.

- **Comparability:** Because of the methods used to collect qualitative data, it is very difficult to compare data because it is produced in a non-standard way. Questions may be asked in different order, or may indeed be completely different.

Triangulation

Using one of the data collection methods discussed above invariably brings problems. Much modern-day research gets around this problem by utilising both quantitative and qualitative design methods. A number of famous studies have done just this. The starting point of doing this stems from the view of Derran (1970) who sees **triangulation** as a way of assessing the validity and reliability of research and the data and information that it highlights.

Eileen Barker's study, *Making of a Moonie: Choice or Brainwashing* (1984) set out to examine the truth behind the Moonie sect. Do people choose to become Moonies or are they brainwashed? She examined the Unification Church by using a selection of quantitative and qualitative methods such as participant observation, questionnaires and interviews. By utilising these methods in tandem Barker believed that she would be able to look at how the church was organised, whilst also examining the day-to-day interactions of believers.

Eileen Barker: Making of a Moonie: Choice or Brainwashing?

"Of course it was known that I was not a Moonie. I never pretended that I was, or that I was likely to become one. I admit that I was sometimes evasive, and I certainly did not always say everything that was on my mind, but I cannot remember any occasion on which I consciously lied to a Moonie. Being known as a non-member had its disadvantages, but by talking to people who had left the movement I was able to check that I was not missing any of the internal information which was available to rank-and-file members. At the same time, being an outsider who was 'inside' had enormous advantages. I was allowed (even, on certain occasions, expected) to ask questions that no member would have presumed to ask either his leaders or his peers. Furthermore, several Moonies who felt that their problems were not understood by the leaders, and yet would not have dreamed of being disloyal to the movement by talking to their parents or other outsiders, could confide in me because of the very fact that I was both organisationally and emotionally uninvolved.

The advantages of using triangulation

The advantages of using such research design (be careful not to call it a method) are as follows:

- The weaknesses of both quantitative and qualitative methodologies are naturally overcome.

- The reliability of each method can be cross-checked. For example, McDonald and Tipton's oral history study, *Belfast in the 1930s*, used a cross-method triangulation ensuring that every bit of oral evidence was cross-referenced against a range of written sources.

- The researcher can check that their own interpretation of data is correct.

However, triangulation has its disadvantages …

The disadvantages of using triangulation

- It is a time-consuming method. As much research only uses one or two methods it is hardly surprising that using a variety of methodologies will lead to time constraints.

- Related to this problem is the issue of cost. Again, using multiple methods means using more time, more personnel and therefore increased cost.

- Lastly, theoretical problems can creep in. Some sociologists remain adamant that only one type of data is collected and find it hard to accept that multiple methods are valid.

Choice of method

Social researches do not live in a vacuum and are influenced by a number of factors. These include:

- **The interests of the researcher:** Just as students like to do their coursework on an area of sociology they find interesting, social researchers are exactly the same. If you browse the sociology lecturers' of any university you will find biopics that include the areas they like to spend their time researching. Often their choices reflect their ideological stances, with women, for example, often researching gender issues and so on.

- **Cost and funding:** The high cost of social research means that the costs of sundry items need to be paid for by grants obtained from the Economic and Social Research Council (ESRC). However, there is still competition for these pots of money, leaving some researchers with limited funds with which to conduct their studies. Large scale surveys can cost millions; for example, the 2001 census in the UK costs £255 million.

- **Opportunity:** Some organisations are far more difficult to study than others. For example, Marxists are critical of the fact that very few studies are performed on decision making bodies such as the cabinet. By contrast sociology seems instead to concentrate on the lower echelons of society. Invariably, this difficulty affects how sociologists come to choose their method.

- **The personality of the researcher:** Whilst some sociologists might enjoy the 'rough and tumble' of participant observation and difficulties gaining access to the group, writing notes and then leaving the group; other researchers prefer instead to conduct questionnaires, which are less taxing, time consuming and all-encompassing.

General issues with research

As with so much sociology, it is the jargon that sociologists, examiners and teachers use that make it seem far more difficult than it really is. Therefore in the next part of this section we will examine phrases and terms used by both quantitative and qualitative researchers.

Reliability

Reliability is used to assess how methods of data collection produce accurate data. For authority, social researchers should aim to be consistent in their research methods. Preferably data can be considered reliable if the same results can be gained by different researchers asking the same questions to the same people. Thus the beauty of standardised questions within a questionnaire is that any differences in response should relate solely to the question asked, thereby making it high in reliability. By contrast, a researcher conducting a participant observation study has to rely upon their own interpersonal and observational skills. As a consequence, two researchers observing the same group could come up with very different findings.

Validity

Validity refers to whether data gained from a research study is an accurate picture of what actually happened. For validity to occur, research must actually measure what it claims to be measuring. For there to be validity, sociological studies should offer an insight into what is being examined beyond what seems to be the case on a purely superficial level.

So, for example, if we were to use official statistics to examine the rate of unemployment, as sociologists we know that such data is collected on a monthly basis. However, can we be certain that these statistics give an accurate picture of the reality of unemployment? To be certain about this we would need to find out how many times the definition of 'unemployment' had changed over a period of time. Without a stable definition it will make comparisons over time difficult to make. We would also need to know whether those categorised as unemployed is accurate. Does it, for example, include all people who would like a job, but who cannot obtain one? Which groups does it exclude? And does this lead to inaccuracies in the statistics?

Representative

This is literally as the name suggests. Does the individual, group or situation being studied 'represent' the entire group under investigation? If so, then generalisations can be made on this basis. One way of looking at being representative is seeing the data as a scaled-down version of the whole of society. Whilst representativeness can be achieved fairly straightforwardly through the use of statistical techniques, such as sampling, for quantitative research it is far more problematic when, for example, conducting participant observation. Small-scale surveys can never hope to offer a cross-section of all the UK population.

Objectivity

Quantitative data is often claimed to be objective. This suggests that the sociologist collecting the data is following the methods advocated by natural scientists. In other words, that they act as a detached researcher who is seeking the truth To achieve this they need to be focused on the task in hand and not influenced by their own beliefs, money or prestige. However, even for those actually in the natural sciences, this is difficult to achieve. One readily thinks of examples where this has occurred; for example, Professor Hwang Woo-Suk made claims that he cloned the first human embryo in 2004 and followed this up a year later with a claim that he had derived individually tailored stem cells from a further 11 cloned embryos. Neither claim was true. Given such things can happen in the natural sciences, it is hardly surprising that with work on human beings, rather than inanimate embryos, sociologists are often accused of letting their personal opinions clouds their judgement.

Operationalisation

With sociological research researchers need to be able to define the phenomena that is being investigated so it can be measured in a objective and scientific manner that is systematic and consistent. For some sociological research this is easy. Very few researchers are going to argue about how to measure age, gender or date of birth. However, for other phenomena things start to become problematic. Consider a phrase often used within sociology: 'child'. How do we define this?

- A person under the age of 16 or 18?

- Do they need to be in full-time education?

- At what age does childhood become adulthood?

Research design

We are going to use social surveys to exemplify how sociologists design their research. First of all, why do sociologists use social surveys? Social surveys have the advantage of obtaining information using standardised questions that therefore allow generalisations to be made. This method is used because:

- Huge amounts of information can be generated quickly and cheaply.

- A large geographical spread can be obtained.

When designing a questionnaire the following factors need to be decided:

- Who to be asked to complete the survey.

- What questions will be asked.

- The best way to obtain these answers.

After these questions have been answered a number of processes need to be followed:

- Develop a hypothesis. Put simply, this is a statement that can be proved or disproved.

- Think about who is going to be asked to fill in the social survey.

- Draft a questionnaire, thinking carefully about what questions need to be asked, and what information need to be found from the questionnaire.

- Issue a pilot questionnaire. This will help to ensure that the questions are ideally worded and contain no ambiguities.

- Isolate the sample.

- Conduct the social survey.

- Analyse the results obtained.

- Write the research results.

Who to ask to complete the survey

Because of cost and practicality sociologists use sampling. This is where statistical techniques are used to ensure that the group being asked to complete the questionnaire closely mirror the attitudes of the British population. Sociologists use the following sampling methods to ensure that who they ask are representative:

Random sample

A simple random sample gives each member of the sampling frame an equal chance of being chosen. This should therefore ensure that those chosen by this method represent a selection of all of the UK population. Simple random sampling can be obtained in a number of ways. The researcher first has to obtain a sampling frame (a list of all those in the population to be studied). From this names can be taken from the list in a random manner (for example, by using a computer). The most commonly used sampling frame is the electoral roll, which is a list of all those over the age of 18 entitled to vote.

Different types of random sample

There are number of different types of random sample methods that can be used. These include:

- **Systematic random sampling:** Often called the 'Nth Name Selection Technique'. After the required sample size has been calculated, every nth record is selected from a list of population members. Whilst not a perfect random sample, as long the list does not contain any hidden order, it is an effective way to sample.

- **Stratified random sample:** With this type of sample, the sampling frame is first divided into a number of parts, or 'strata', according to some characteristic, chosen to be related to the major variables being studied. So, for example, in a political survey it would be important to replicate the composition of the UK population in regard to age, sex, and ethnicity and so on. Once the various compositions are obtained, respondents are chosen at random as above.

- **Cluster sampling:** With this type of sampling the units are separated into clusters which are usually group cluster or organisational clusters, subsequently a random sample of this cluster is chosen. This method is ideal when the population to be examined is geographically spread.

Non-random

- **Quota sampling:** This method is widely used by market research organisations such as Gallup and MORI. The quota is first identified by the social researcher by using population estimates for different social characteristics such as age, sex, ethnicity, social class, and so on to determine the numbers and proportions needed for the sample. Interviewers are then given quotas based on these numbers that they are asked to achieve (hence quota sampling). This method of sampling is considered preferable to other methods because results should be an accurate representation of the whole of the population under review.

- **Snowball sampling:** On occasions it can be difficult to obtain any sample at all, particularly if the group is ashamed or shy about volunteering for research projects. In such cases researchers will ask interviewees to volunteer a name of someone else they know who would be willing to be interviewed. From the initial interviewee, the sample becomes larger and larger, just like rolling a snowball down a hill. Snowball sampling has been used in studies of drug users (Avico et al, 1998; Griffiths et al, 1993; Kaplan et al, 1987), prostitution (McNamara, 1994), pickpockets (Inciardi, 1977), AIDS sufferers (Pollak and Schlitz, 1988) and the seriously ill (Sudman and Freeman, 1988).

What do you know now?

1. Match the statement to the correct concept below:

- A complete list of names of the population to be studied.

- Here the selection of the sample goes through various stages. Each stage involves the selection of a sample from the previously chosen sample, until the researcher arrives at a list of individuals.

- Interviews that are non-directive, giving the interviewee lots of opportunities to say what he or she wants to say.

- Everyone in the population has an equal chance of appearing in the sample.

- It is based on identifying a number of clusters in the population, such as schools or classes within schools, and then selecting individuals from the clusters.

- This refers to the question of whether the group of people or the situation that is being studied is typical of others.

- The sample is constructed by any of the methods outlined; it is then questioned a number of times over a lengthy period of time.

- A study that aims to gain data from large numbers of people, generally through using various types of questionnaires and interview methods.

- Allows only a limited number of responses.

- Instead of choosing randomly from strata within the population, the researcher sets a quota precisely outlining the number of individuals meeting certain criteria that are to be included in the sample.

- Where the sample is not representative of the population.

- Interviews are directive and give the interviewee much less leeway.

- Here the researcher selects people on the basis that they are likely to be relevant to the subject studied.

- Here people volunteer to be studied. For example, a questionnaire on a packet of breakfast cereal.

- A group to stand in, for the population they seek to study.

- Where the researcher starts with very few people and asks them for recommendations of further people to interview who fit from the criteria of the study. When interviewing the people the same procedure is used, so gradually a sample is built up.

- This method involves dividing the research population into a number of strata based on what are seen to be significant criteria.

- Here respondents are given space to construct their own answers.

- Here the researcher studies all individuals he or she meets over a given period.

- Scanning the population list and selecting every tenth member.

a. Random Sampling

b. Non-random Sampling

c. Representative

d. Open questions

e. Accidental sampling

f. Panel study

g. Quota sampling

h. Snowball sampling

i. Closed questions

j. Stratified random sampling

k. Volunteer sampling

l. Social survey

m. Multi-stage sampling

n. Systematic random sampling

o. Sample

p. Sampling frame

q. Structured interviews

r. Unstructured interviews

s. Purposeful sampling

t. Cluster sampling

Key terms

Natural sciences: The sciences including chemistry, physics and biology.

Triangulation: Type of research design that includes both quantitative and qualitative elements within it.

Qualitative data: Data that is rich in detail and description, usually given in non-numerical data rather than numbers. This thereby allows meanings and opinions to be explored.

Quantitative data: Data that is expressed statistically.

Section summary

- Primary data is collected by the sociological researcher specifically for the research project in hand. For example, primary data includes questionnaires, statistics, observation records, and so on.

- Secondary data is information that has already been collected and published by others.

- Quantitative research methods replicate the methods used by the natural sciences. Thus adherents believe the following procedure should be used: Data should be collected objectively and scientifically. This data should be collected from as large a sample as possible, allowing generalisations to be made. Once this data is collected, it should be compared with other similar studies and correlations made. Once enough studies indicate similar findings, quantitative theorists believe you move towards a 'truth'.

- The advantages of quantitative data are that it is reliable, allows easy replication, and statistical analysis can be utilised.

- The disadvantages of quantitative data are that although it can reveal statistical insights it fails to offer any kind of insight as to the reasons for any statistics.

- The advantages of qualitative data are that this kind of data is rich and holistic, revealing detail that would be never gleaned from quantitative methods. Qualitative data allows researchers to understand why people do things, allowing them to speak in their own words and explain their emotions and feelings.

- The disadvantages of qualitative data are that it can be unreliable. Studies are very difficult to replicate so they raise the issue of lack of reliability.

- Triangulation is when the researcher uses at least three methods across the quantitative and qualitative spectrum, therefore avoiding the singular weaknesses of each.

- Reliability is used to assess how methods of data collection produce accurate data.

- Validity refers to whether data gained from a research study is an accurate picture of what actually happened.

- Representativeness literally means as it suggests. Does the individual, group or situation being studied 'represent' the entire group under investigation?

- Objectivity is the idea that social researchers do not let their personal opinions and judgement cloud their social research.

- Social surveys have the advantage of obtaining information using standardised questions that therefore allow generalisations to be made.

- Because of cost and practicality, sociologists use sampling.

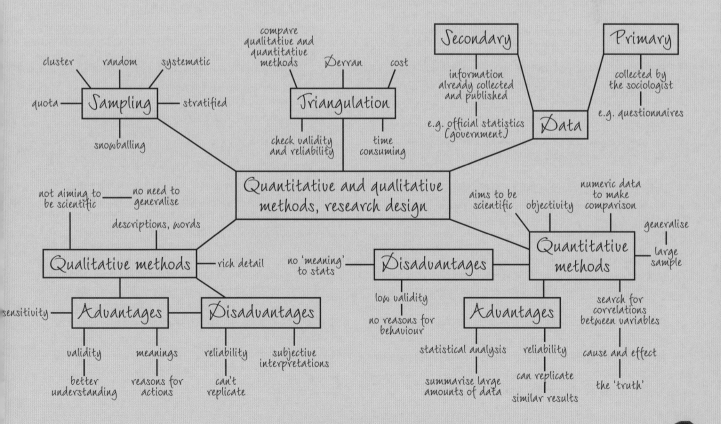

Sources of data; their strengths and limitations

Social surveys

Social surveys involve:

- Collecting large amounts of empirical data from a large cross-section of the population
- Data being obtained through the use of either questionnaires or structured interviews
- Analysing the results, often by computer, and data presented
- Comparing the results of the social survey to test hypotheses of research already in the public domain

What types of social survey are there?

- **Factual surveys:** Used to collect data that describes what is going on. Surveys on poverty are examples of factual surveys.
- **Attitude surveys:** Used to collect data on how people feel about the social world. Classic examples of attitude surveys are opinion polls carried out by organisations such as MORI or Gallup prior to a general election. These seek to uncover the feelings of the electorate about particular policies or personalities.
- **Explanatory surveys:** These seek to go beyond the descriptive and attempt to test theories or hypotheses, or indeed generate new hypotheses altogether.

Questionnaires

The advantages of using questionnaires

It is a simple and relatively cheap way to collect data on a large scale through the use of a standardised questionnaire. And whilst it takes time to construct such a tool, once created a large number of **respondents** are able to complete it. For example, the *British Crime Survey* that is carried out on behalf of the government by the British Market Research Bureau (BMRB) asks 50 000 people aged 16 and over that live in private households if they have been a victim of crime.

- The data that is produced is considered to be of high validity because it uses sampling procedures to allow **generalisations** to be made about the population being surveyed. Moreover, through the use of computers, **correlations** and new hypotheses can be generated. Additionally through the use of standardised questions any differences between the respondents should be real and tangible. And once collated results can be tested again by other social researchers replicating the methods used before.
- Unlike some qualitative methods, social surveys offer the chance to obtain valid data without becoming too involved with the group being studied. And whilst with qualitative observation it is very difficult to write up observations, by comparison surveys can be easily put into meaningful and accurate datasets.
- Social surveys allow a degree of **anonymity** for the respondent. This is particularly important for questionnaires that are carried out on delicate topics that respondents would not be willing to answer if they had to be identified. For example, the *National Survey of Sexual Attitudes and Lifestyles* is much more likely to be completed under such circumstances.

British Social Attitudes Survey (BSA)

The *British Social Attitudes Survey* is the leading social research survey in Britain. Each year around 3300 randomly selected adults are asked to give their views on an extensive range of topics. The questions asked are developed and funded in collaboration with grant-giving bodies and government departments. Topics include housing, work, transport, government spending and voting habits; as well as religion, racism and illegal drugs. New areas of questioning are added each year to reflect policy changes and current affairs, but all questions are designed with a view to repeating them periodically to chart changes over time. The *British Social Attitudes Survey* is independent of political pressure, which is an important reason for its success and longevity.

The disadvantages of using questionnaires

Theoretically interactionists deny the possibility that questionnaires provide the forum from which to explore human behaviour.

Despite claims that questionnaires are scientific and valid, many suggest that processes such as the 'interviewer effect', where respondents give the answer they think the social researcher desires, limit validity.

Response rates can be very low, particularly for postal surveys, which may lead to expensive construction of an appropriate survey being made worthless by an inadequate sample.

Questionnaires limit the answers available to the respondent. Almost by definition this means that the social researcher has imposed their reality what answers they consider to be important.

Open-ended questions are very difficult to code and any attempt to achieve this may lose the meaning given by the respondent.

Research design of questionnaires

Surveys are about asking questions. So it's vital for the success of a survey that the right questions are asked and that they are well presented. Poorly conceived questions and questionnaires will reduce response rates and provide inaccurate data. Questionnaires should achieve the following:

- Think carefully about the words being using. For example, avoid jargon that might not be understood.
- Only ask for one bit of information at a time.
- Questions should be short and simple, making sure that double meanings are avoided.
- Give clear instructions to the respondent.
- Take care to produce a clear and tidy layout of the questions that will not confuse the respondent.
- Ask questions that allow for the level of information that is required.

Structured interviews

Structured interviews, in their simplest forms, are where respondents are presently with exactly the same questions in the same chronology, or time order. To facilitate this process, often an interview schedule is used to prompt the interviewer to achieve this consistency.

The advantages of structured interviews

- Because they offer the same standardised questions again and again, they are high in reliability.

- Response rates are often very high for this technique. People are more likely to want to be interviewed than fill in a questionnaire.

- Because of the presence of the interviewer any misunderstandings or comprehension problems can be resolved before the respondent answers. This can result in greater information being gleaned from the respondent than would otherwise been the case.

- They can lead to a more representative sample than other methods as respondents who cannot read and write can be included.

The disadvantages of structured interviews

- Interviewer bias can limit responses. This may be the result of the respondent giving the answer they think the researcher wants to hear or because respondents are affected by the gender or the ethnicity of the interviewer.

- They are more costly than questionnaires, especially when a regional sample is required. It also necessitates interviewer training.

- Interactionists believe that it is insensitive to the needs of respondents who would like to express themselves, but cannot.

Research design of structured interviews

- It may be necessary to train the interviewers and pre-test questions.

- Questions should be produced that the survey is intended to answer.

- Questions need to be easy to respond to; for example, not creating too much embarrassment or undue burden on the respondent.

Official statistics or secondary data

This is pre-existing data that can be useful for a researcher, even if it not specifically collected for their purpose. Official statistics are just one source of secondary data that are produced by a myriad of government agencies. They are also produced by organisations as diverse as companies, pressure groups and charities. The largest organisation that produces statistics in the UK is the ONS: the government department responsible for collecting and publishing official statistics about the UK's society and economy.

The advantages of secondary data and official statistics

- They are often the only available resource on specific areas of research. Often this is as a consequence of the huge cost of such statistics.

- They are a cheap and available source of data that would be unobtainable without central government.

- Usually such data has been collected using statistical techniques that allow generalisations to be made.

- Because they often compare data over time, they allow analysis of trends; for example, they allow comparisons to be made before and after legislation.

The disadvantages of secondary data and official statistics

- The way data is collected may not suit the purposes of the research in hand.

- Official statistics cannot be taken at face value. Marxists, for example, believe that the government tries to 'put a gloss' on such statistics to show them in the best light possible.

- Phenomenologists suggest that statistics are merely the interpretation of the person who has collated them.

- Access to official statistics is dependent upon government believing that the statistics concerned are important.

Experiments

Experiments are used primarily by the natural sciences rather than by sociologists. The aim of experiments is to establish cause and effect, with the researcher starting with a hypothesis (a statement that can be proved or disproved) and then experimenting to establish whether can be proved or disproved.

There are two types of experiments:

1. **Laboratory experiments:** Performed under the artificial environment of the laboratory, the researcher seeks to control the variables within the setting. The researcher then changes one variable at a time (the independent variable), observing the effects on the dependent variable (what they want to measure).

. **Natural or field experiments:** These take place outside of the laboratory where it is not possible to control all the variables. However, this often results in researchers taking the opportunity to involve social actors within the experiment who they are not fully aware of their participation.

Strengths of laboratory experiments

- They have a high degree of reliability; due to the fact that conditions can easily be controlled, it is straightforward to replicate laboratory experiments.

The disadvantages of laboratory experiments

- Because a laboratory does not replicate social situations, it is likely that they will not respond in the same way as they would do in ordinary society.

- It is often highly problematic to isolate one variable within a laboratory setting. Human beings are influenced by a range of factors, rather than necessarily responding to one.

  Is it ethical to experiment with people, especially if they know that one group is to be treated differently from another? Under guidelines issued by the BSA researchers should tell all participants if they are involved in sociological research.

The comparative method

This is as it sounds: data is collected by the social researcher and then social comparisons are made between different nation states or societies. Durkheim used this method is his study of suicide, examining official statistics on suicide and postulating the causes of higher or lower suicide rates across Europe. He then compared factors as diverse as religion, weather or marital status and concluded that religious factors and social integration were key to variances in suicide rates.

Strengths of comparative sociology

- Suicide was the only method available to Durkheim. Allows comparisons over time and judgements to be made about differences between societies.

The disadvantages of comparative sociology

- However, the method relies upon statistics that can be flawed. For example, in Durkheim's study were the statistics collected in a similar way across the nation states examined?

- Additionally, how confident can we be that other factors did not influence suicide rates that were not isolated by Durkheim in his study?

Longitudinal surveys

Longitudinal surveys collect data about the same individual at different points in time, allowing sociologists to track change at the level of the individual or household. They have played an important role in developing our understanding of social change; for instance, looking at how improved educational attainment affects social mobility and the importance of the family on child development. There are several of these surveys presently being undertaken. They include the *National Child Development Study* that has been following the lives of 5000 people born between 3 and 9 March 1958, and the much more contemporary *Millennium Cohort Study* that is following a sample of nearly 19000 babies born between September and August 2001 in England and Wales. The first survey has recorded the circumstances of pregnancy and birth, the early months of life, and the social and economic background of the family into which the children have been born.

The strengths of longitudinal surveys

- Most surveys provide a snapshot of the group being surveyed; that is, a picture of a situation at a specific point in time. A longitudinal survey, on the other hand, involves surveying the same group of people over a period of time. By linking records for the same panel of respondents over time, a longitudinal survey allows the study of relationships between factors measured in one period with outcomes measured in future time periods.

- Another advantage of a longitudinal survey is that respondents are interviewed frequently and are required to recall only recent events, thus improving data quality.

The disadvantages of longitudinal surveys

- By keeping the same survey group, longitudinal surveys can find that what was originally a large sample that allowed generalisations to be made, is reduced. It therefore can become less representative. The *National Child Development Survey* started with 17000 children; however, when the study finished in 1981 the original sample had been reduced to a mere 12500. Loss of contact occurs for a number of reasons such as most obviously death, people moving abroad and respondents choosing to ignore repeated requests for participation.

- Given the time and lengths used to maintain the sample, another disadvantage of this method is the high costs of both time and money incurred.

Qualitative methods

By comparison, qualitative sociologists want to find out the meanings why social actors do things, to uncover their motivation and reasons for their actions. They therefore use the following methods:

- Unstructured interviews

- Participant and non-participant observation

Unstructured or informal interviews

With unstructured interviews, the researcher has no preset questions that they want to ask the respondent. Instead, it leaves the interviewee in primary control of the dialogue. Questions tend to be open-ended allowing for a wide range of responses.

Strengths of unstructured or informal interviews

- They offer greater reliability as respondents are able to say exactly what they think and use their own words to explain what they think about an issue. As a result a warmer and more congenial atmosphere is developed between researcher and interviewee further enhancing validity. Both **Oakley** in *From Here to Maternity* (1981), and **Kituse and Cicourel** in *The Educational Decision Makers* (1963) believed that as a consequence trust and openness was allowed to flourish with interviewees wanting to assist the researcher.

- Any difficulties in comprehension of questions can be clarified, again further assisting reliability.

- They are ideal for interviews on sensitive issues that require tact and trust. For example, interviews on criminality, sexual behaviour and domestic violence.

- Because of the dynamics of such a personal method the interviewer can make judgements to the veracity of the respondent's responses and ask further questions to either confirm or reject this view.

Weaknesses of unstructured or informal interviews

- This method is time-consuming and prohibitively expensive. As a consequence, it can lead to smaller samples which can make it difficult to make generalisations.

- Interviewer effect is far more pronounced; as Oakley found out, it is easy for both the interviewer and the interviewee to become 'too close' with each other, leading to the respondent giving the answer that they think the researcher wants to hear.

- This method relies upon the social skills of the researcher and thus unstructured interviews are almost impossible to replicate.

Participant and non-participant observation

Both these methods are favoured by non-positivists as they allow social researchers to view the world from the perspective on those they are studying. As a result they believe they can understand and empathise ('verstehen'; literally meaning 'understanding' in German) as a result of observing the group.

Participant observation involves the researcher taking an active role within the group, where by contrast with non-participant observation the researcher merely acts as an observer, and does not interact at all. This method can be covert – with the researcher not revealing the fact that the group are being observed – or overt, where the group are told from the onset of the research that they are being observed.

Strengths of participant and non-participant observation

- The researcher gains knowledge 'straight from the horse's mouth' as to how the group operates. And because the researcher blends into the background – being subsumed within the social network – data is far more valid and reliable as the group members will not change their behaviour.

- It allows the researcher to find out what they would never have suspected without going to observe the group. In **Bill Whyte**'s study of Doc, in *Street Corner Society* (1943), Bill noted that "As I sat and listened, I learned the answers to the questions that I would not even had the sense to ask if I had been getting my information solely on an interviewing basis."

- This method examines the underdog and therefore looks at those from all corners of society, who perhaps otherwise would not be observed. For example, this method has been instrumental in the process of understanding how gangs see their world and those around them. Often, participant observation is the only method available, given the difficulty of gaining access to such groups.

- This method allows the researcher to examine a group over a lengthy period of time, thereby getting to know the group and understanding whether what they are observing is typical or atypical. Consequently, validity is improved.

Weaknesses of participant and non-participant observation

- Positivists argue that the results of such a study are highly dubious. They argue that there is little chance of replicating participant observation studies because they rely so much on the observations of one social researcher.

- The mere presence of the researcher is likely to change the behaviour within the group. For example, Doc told Bill Whyte that "he had slowed me down plenty." Doc found himself actually trying to find out and answer what Bill wanted from him.

- Sometimes the researcher can become so involved with the group that they lose their objectivity and 'go native'.

- This method is both time-consuming and costly. Howard Becker spent two years observing drug users in his study. Most researchers find it very difficult to take time out from their lives to immerse themselves in such long studies.

- The ethics of covert participant observation are dubious. Guidelines issued by the BSA suggest that covert observation should be avoided for ethical reasons.

- Overt participant observation may lead to the social actors changing their behaviour, thereby compromising validity.

- It is very difficult to make generalisations from such small-scale observations. Paul Willis, for example, has been criticised for only using 12 lads in his 1977 study.

- Finally in some cases it can lead to the researcher being exposed to danger, particularly during covert observation if perhaps the cover of the researcher is blown. This happened in *A Glasgow Gang Observed* where '**James Patrick**' (not his real name) was left to quickly withdraw from the group, potentially losing years' worth of valuable research.

1. Look at the following: Are they advantages or disadvantages? What research method do they link to? (In some cases this may be a few methods.)

   • Some data, such as unemployment statistics, often has governments changing the way they collect them.

   • If people are not told they are being studied, it is unethical.

   • Participating with a group allows the researcher to see a group over time. This allows the subjects of the study to get used to the sociologist.

   • This method of going back to talk to people again and again leads to a situation where the sociologist becomes close to the group being studied.

   • This method has the advantage that you can prompt respondents to give a wider and more detailed response. These are often open-ended questions.

   • It is unlikely that social environments can be replicated within a laboratory.

   • Data gained from the media can be counted and analysed in a systematic and scientific way.

   • Closed questions have to be coded into categories which can provide problems, especially when responses are very close to each other.

2. How easy would it he to join the following groups as a participant observer? Rank them as: easy, moderately difficult and very difficult. Given the knowledge, which groups tend to he heavily observed and which are the least observed?

   • A family; a football crowd; a delinquent gang; market stallholders; prisoners; school teachers; nightclub goers; the Cabinet; a board of directors

3. Name the three types of social survey that are conducted by researchers.

4. Describe one criticism and one strength of the use of questionnaires.

5. Describe one criticism and one strength of structured interviews.

6. Explain why official statistics need to be used with caution.

7. Why are experiments rarely used in social research?

8. Isolate one method that would be advocated by qualitative researchers.

9. Explain the difference between covert and overt participant observation.

10. Give two examples of studies that used participant observation.

Key terms

Anonymity: Derived from Greek, meaning 'without name'. Personal details of the people being studied are not known.

Correlations: The measurement of the relationship between two variables.

Generalisations: Ideas taken from studying a sample of people with similar characteristics, which are then applied to the group as a whole.

Respondents: Those who respond to researchers' questions in social research.

Section summary

- Social surveys involve collecting large amounts of empirical data from a large cross-section of the population.

- Types of social survey include factual surveys, attitude surveys and exploratory surveys.

- Questionnaires are a simple and relatively cheap way to collect data on a large scale. The data that is produced is considered to be of high validity because it uses sampling procedures to allow generalisations to be made about the population being surveyed. However, their disadvantages include their inability to explore human interaction, the interviewer effect, their low response rate and how questions asked reflect the perceptions of the social researcher, whilst open-ended responses are problematic to code.

- Surveys need to ask the right questions and should be well presented. Poorly conceived questions will reduce response rates and provide inaccurate data.

- Structured interviews are, in their simplest forms, where respondents are presented with exactly the same questions in the same chronology. Because they offer the same standardised questions again and again, they are high in validity, offer high response rates and allow understands to be explained. Additionally, this method can be used for those who are illiterate, thereby ensuring a more representative sample.

- Secondary data is pre-existing data that can be useful for the social researcher. This data can be produced by government agencies (official statistics) or by other agencies (secondary data). Other agencies that produce such data include pressure groups and trade unions. They are often the only available resource on specific areas of research.

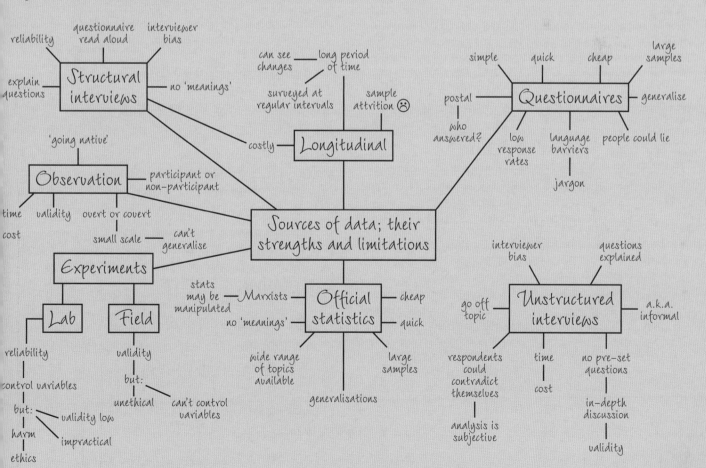

Primary and secondary data

Introduction

Although sociologists are keen to do their own research, such as conducting interviews and questionnaires, it is often far more practical to use the data that is already in the public domain. Such data is called secondary data. It comes from a wide range of different sources, such as official statistics published by the government. The government is a huge generator of statistics in areas as diverse as criminal statistics, the ten-year census, and statistics on births, marriages and deaths and examination data such as GCSE and A level results by gender and ethnicity. However, some secondary resources can be rather more personal and qualitative, such as diaries and personal documents. There is also a huge diverse range of such data that is generated by the mass media. With the advent of new technology and digital recording it is becoming easy to access television, radio and press in an ever more accessible way.

Why use secondary data?

- If the data is already out there it allows the researcher to make appropriate and apposite conclusions and save time.
- Secondary resources are far cheaper to collect than having to conduct original primary research.
- It takes far less time to search for secondary data, particularly with when using the Internet and computer-based methods.
- Quantitative theorists believe that secondary resources are more scientific and therefore more valid than using other methods. Because they have usually been collected using a large sample, they provide a far less subjective view of the world. However, as with all sociological research, there is a need to be aware of who collected the data and what the purpose of the collection was.

Marxists and feminists both believe that statistics are only a 'rough guide' and they need to be taken in context. So, whilst crime statistics give a general view of crime in the UK, it is unlikely that the government will want to reveal the full 'dark figure' of crime. Marxists argue that statistics will usually be primed to put capitalism in the best possible light, but still offer some notion of what is going on in terms of say, unemployment. Feminists believe that statistics in general underplay female experiences and that statistics fail to be collected that show how males continue to dominate society. **Bias** will always be inherent given that personal documents are written from one person's perspective. Indeed, phenomenologists, such as Maxwell Atkinson, believe that statistics are only really useful in understanding how they were collected. For example, in Atkinson's study of suicide (1968) he found that coroners had a prescribed view of what constituted a suicide. This view resulted in inaccurate statistics. Phenomenologists see statistics are merely the interpretation of those collecting them. Statistics are therefore laden with value judgements, rather than being objective as quantitative theorists would suggest.

- It is highly appropriate to use this method if a historical slant is needed in a research study. Historical data allows us to make judgements long after the death of those writing their observations.
- Statistics are the perfect starting point from which to examine social phenomena. They allow researchers to make hypothesis and to gain an insight into any area of sociology.

Examples of secondary data

The following provides a list of secondary data often used in research. It can be split into quantitative secondary resources and qualitative.

Quantitative

- Official statistics often issued by the government; for example, census data
- Content analysis
- Data archives which are available on the Internet
- Market research

Qualitative

- Previous sociological research
- Diaries and letters
- Family histories
- The media and use of content analysis
- The press
- Autobiographies
- Memoirs

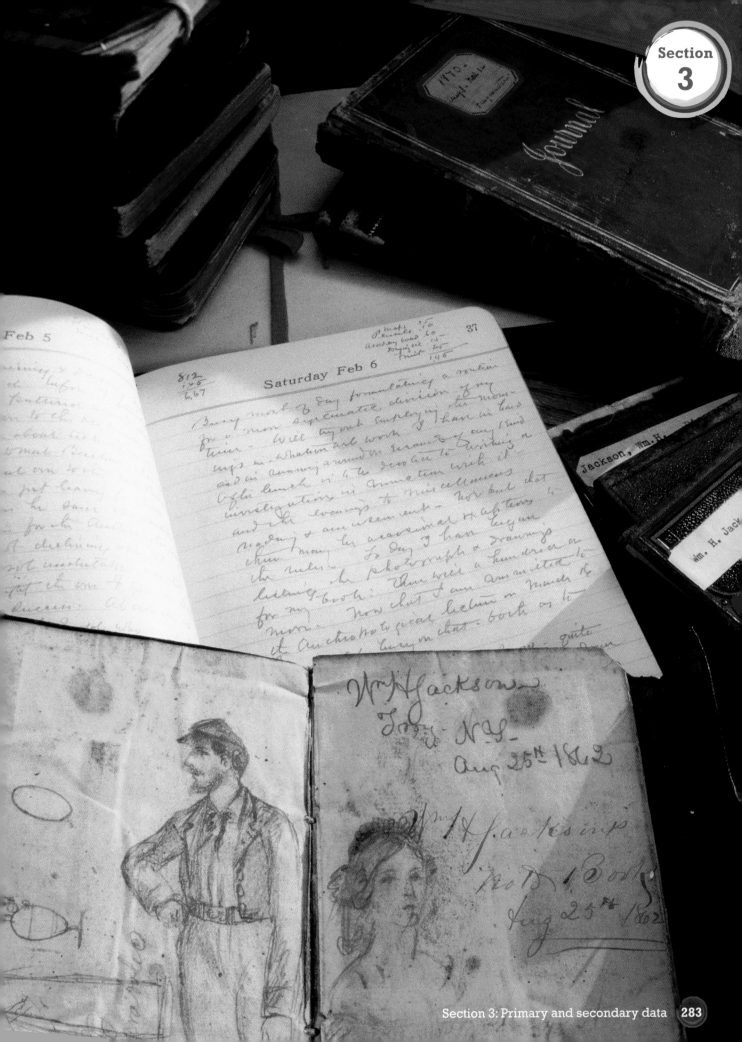

Explained examples of secondary resources

Official statistics

These are officially collected by either central or local government and are often used in research by sociologists. They importantly offer data on a wider statistical scale than could ever be achieved by an individual or a small statistical organisation. As a result they provide a cheap and accessible source of data that is reliable and **generalisable**. In the past these statistics were often hidden away in obscure expensive publications such as *Social Trends*. However, over the last ten years official statistics have become readily available from websites such as UK Statistics Authority. Secondary data is available on economy; for example, unemployment rates, inflation, gross domestic product (GDP), retail sales, the environment, health, population, society (marriage, national identity), the use of leisure time, finance (poverty and wealth distribution)and travel and tourism.

One particular advantage is that because such statistics have been collated over time, it allows sociologists to make comparisons or to look at the affect of legislation. Nonetheless, sociologists should be aware that there are problems with using this method. There is always likely to be bias; the figures that have not been included, for example. Sometimes it is also difficult to obtain figures in the area being researched. Whilst it is ok if the government sees a particular issue as being important, often interesting and challenging areas of sociology are neglected by official statistics. For example, in the research of this book it has been particularly difficult to find data on areas such as ethnicity and gender. Whilst these areas are better served with statistics than was once the case, historical data is far more difficult to find than on, say, unemployment or GDP figures. Feminists and those who examine ethnicity would naturally assume that this reflects the malestream and ethnocentric approach taken by the government and its statistical agencies.

Many also claim that statistics are used for 'spin'; perhaps those analysing them will always be suspicious of what they show. Gordon Brown promised in 2005 to hold statistical organisation at arm's length from the government; until this promise becomes reality this accusation will always remain.

Government is also responsible for issuing a myriad of reports and inquiries. These are called after extraordinary events such as the *BSE Inquiry* (1998), and 7/7. Whilst such reports often provide a useful insight as to the reasons for these events, because of the closed-door nature of them they often reveal less than is required. Additionally, the government is able to insist that those who work with 'sensitive information' must sign the Official Secrets Act 1989. The act prohibits the disclosure of confidential material from government sources by employees. It remains an offence for a member or former member of the security and intelligence services (or those working closely with them) to disclose information about their

work. There is no public-interest defence, and disclosure of information already in the public domain is still a crime. Journalists who repeat disclosures may also be prosecuted.

Content analysis

This quantitative method allows the researcher to quantify the content of a document in a scientific manner. Social researchers can classify the content of the document into categories or typologies and then count how much of the content sits in one of the categories formulated by the researcher.

Diaries and letters

Diaries and letters provide a first-hand qualitative insight into the experiences and self-perceptions of those writing them. And whilst they may be useful due to the lack of other first-hand data they can be problematic. Essentially they tend to be produced by those who do not mind revealing their thoughts. By their very nature they can be accused of being subjective, one-sided accounts that offer little objective insight. The furore over the supposed Hitler Diaries, which were authenticated by the eminent historian Lord Dacre in 1983, indicates that not all diaries and letters can be taken at face value. Additionally, their small-scale nature offer little chance to make generalisations from them.

Family histories

This qualitative method involves using the recorded histories left by those who experienced past events. Family histories can take the form of sound recordings, cine film or old photographs, which can provide a real insight into the conditions and events that occurred many years ago. However, whilst the most valid form of family history resides in the form of recorded or man-scripted interviews, the vast majority of this kind of secondary data can be said to be of poor reliability and validity. How accurate, for example, are the observations? Do they miss out the reality of the day-to-day existence of the time?

Previous research

These are a rich source of information, offering the sociologist information on what previous research has concentrated upon and the findings of these studies. A sociologist can then decide whether to replicate the study or extend the research into a new area as a result of the pervious findings. However, a critical eye is always needed when utilising the research of other social researchers. For example, is the research method reliable and representative? How far did the researcher remain objective? And most importantly, are the findings a true reflection of the research undertaken?

Novels

These can provide a real insight into the time and, although time specific, allow us to peer into a previous age. For example, Elizabeth Gaskell's novels *Mary Barton*, *North and South* and *Ruth* were based upon her observations of Manchester from the period 1832–65 on poverty in that conurbation. Gaskell visited sewing shops and refectories to gain a real understanding of what it was like to live in this industrial town. These observations were then fully articulated into her written novels, illuminating and enhancing our knowledge of that era.

The mass media

The mass media offers a multitude of sources for sociologists; for example, the press, the Internet and TV news. And whilst the mass media can provide the basis for much useful content analysis of teen magazines and bias in the press, it provides a number of challenges to the sociologist. Firstly, the huge range and type of data offers the conundrum of what material to use and which material to leave alone. If quantitative scientific methodology is to be used, the researcher needs to ensure that such material is representative; however, such judgements may be hard to make. Most importantly phenomenologists believe that the content pumped out on a daily basis by the mass media tells us far more about who produces the material rather than what actually happens in the world!

The relationship between theory and methods

Differing sociological methods are used by different theorists. On the face of it this debate can be summarised between those who want to be scientific (positivists) in comparison to interpretivists

Positivism

Positivism is a belief that the only way of explaining the social world is by using the scientific method. It was developed by Auguste Comte, who is believed to have first thought of the discipline of sociology.

Auguste Comte

- The scientific method involves replicating the methods utilised so successfully within the natural sciences to explain social phenomena.

- By using rational thought, Comte was sure that society would be able to develop faster and more efficiently and be able to move way from what Comte considered to be limiting factors religion, fate and superstition.

- Fundamental for positivism is the belief that the role of the sociologist is to only collect data that they can objectively observe, and from this gain empirical statistics that can be counted and measured. Durkheim, for example, did this by collecting data on the number of suicides in Europe and then relating these rates to religious integration.

- From gaining quantitative data, Durkheim suggested that sociologists would be able to construct social facts. Social facts would allow sociologists to predict with accuracy how society and people operate in a variety of different circumstances.

- One should remember the context that sociologists found themselves in at the time. Europe was going through profound changes with for example a revolution in France. (1789–1999). Sociology was attempting to be seen as much a rigorous scientific method as the natural sciences.

- A central belief of positivism is the use of correlation. This is where there is a strong relationship between two or more types of social phenomena. From this, positivists look for causation, which literally means 'cause or having an effect'; looking to see if there is a relationship between two social occurrences. If such a relationship was recorded this leads positivists to believe that one is causing the other.

- To avoid incorrect correlation, Durkheim suggested that positivists should use multivariate analysis. This is the simultaneous study of two variables at the same time; for example, looking at the impact of age, gender and occupation on a particular outcome.

- Positivists suggest that, armed with such data, the sociologist should take their findings are relate them to other contexts and at different times. If the same correlation is observed, then Durkheim and Comte asserted that social facts, or laws of human behaviour, could be postulated. For example, Durkheim, in his study of suicide, found that suicide rates increased either during a recession or a boom in economic activity.

In conclusion, positivists argue that laws of human behaviour can be isolated by the collection of empirical data, the analysis of this data and then by replicating the study in a variety of different cultural and time contexts. Humans, they believe, behave in prescribed ways, reacting to the environment in a regular manner. So research goes through a number of stages; with the collection of data, the statistical analysis of it, the development of theories and the testing of theories against other similar studies to see how close to the 'truth' theories are.

Positivists tend to use methods that produce statistics, so they would feel particularly comfortable using official statistics (like Durkheim) –questionnaires, structured interviews, experiments and content analysis – indeed, any method that allows them to quantify the world.

Interpretivists (anti-positivism)

By contrast some interpretivists suggest that instead of scientific methods, qualitative methods should be used. Qualitative data differs from quantitative data in that:

- Instead of data being offered in statistics, qualitative research focuses on non-numerical data, which is used to explain the reasons why social actors do things. As a result of using non-numerical data, qualitative researchers believe that their findings are far more illuminating, offering a more rich and valid image of the group or groups under investigation.

Interpretivists believe that statistics do not reveal much about human behaviour. Human beings have reactions that are far from being consistent. Asking endless questions is not the way to find out the subjective state of the individual. This subjective state is a complex mix of individual consciousness (seeing ourselves and our relationships with others) and how we relate to others. Ultimately, it is people who decide to do something; it therefore goes without saying that it is highly unlikely that individual interpretations are ever going to be the same. Therefore the notion that we can establish 'social facts' through the use of causality is a nonsense.

Fundamental to this therefore is to understand the meanings as to why people engage in particular activity. This means that for interpretivists, facts are limited to being established to individual people and circumstances. Linked to labelling theory, this means that similar deviant acts will be treated very differently depending upon the social reaction. So whilst streaking at Twickenham might be considered to be alcohol-fuelled high spirits, the same streak in a primary school would lead to an entirely different reaction.

So research methodology is straightforward for interpretivists. Instead of measuring data, they ask the actors to talk about what is happening around them from their point of view. They get inside their motives and use what Max Weber called 'verstehen'.

Anti-positivists, therefore, tend to use methods that go through this process. For example, with participant observation the researcher is able to join the group and see for themselves how they see the world and the reasons for their actions. If the researcher is unsure of what they are seeing they can ask and tease out detail that would otherwise go unrecorded with other methods.

What do you know now?

1. Decide if the following are examples of primary or secondary data and then complete the boxes to assess whether each is either quantitative or qualitative.

   - First-hand experiments
   - Participant observation by sociologist first-hand
   - Official statistics carried out by government
   - Observation by sociologist first -hand
   - Survey: questionnaires collected by previous research
   - Old diaries
   - Surveys: structured interviews carried out by a sociologist
   - Unstructured interviews done in previous research

Primary	Type of data: quantitative or qualitative
Secondary	

2. Isolate two reasons why sociologists use secondary data.

3. Explain two disadvantages of using secondary data.

4. Clarify the secondary methods that would be used by quantitative sociologists as opposed to qualitative researchers.

5. Give three examples of secondary data.

6. Explain the type of data collected by quantitative sociologists.

7. Why would they argue that this data is more scientific.

8. By contrast, explain the type of data that would be collected by qualitative researchers.

9. How would they explain the relevance of using such material?

Key terms

Bias: A one-sided view of the mind that inhibits impartial judgement.

Generalisable: Similar to the whole or wider society.

Section summary

- Although sociologists are keen to do their own research, such as conducting interviews and questionnaires, it is often far more practical to use the data that is already in the public domain. Such data is called secondary data.

- Secondary data comes from a wide range of different sources such as official statistics published by the government.

- Sociologists use secondary data because it is a cheap and easy way to obtain research material.

- It is highly appropriate to use this method if a historical slant is needed in your research study.

- Statistics are the perfect starting point from which to examine social phenomena.

- Examples of quantitative secondary data include official statistics often issued by the government.

- Examples of qualitative secondary data include previous sociological research, diaries and letters, family histories, use of content analysis, the press, autobiographies and memoirs.

- Official statistics are officially collected by either central or local government and are often used in research by sociologists.

- Diaries and letters provide a first-hand qualitative insight into the experiences and self perceptions of those writing them.

- The mass media offers a multitude of sources for sociologists for example, the press, Internet and TV news.

- Positivists believe that the only way of explaining the social world is by using the scientific method.

- Fundamental for positivism is the belief that the role of the sociologist is to only collect data that they can objectively observe and from this gain empirical statistics that count and measure.

- Anti-positivists assert that non-numerical data offers a far better way to explain the reasons why social actors do things.

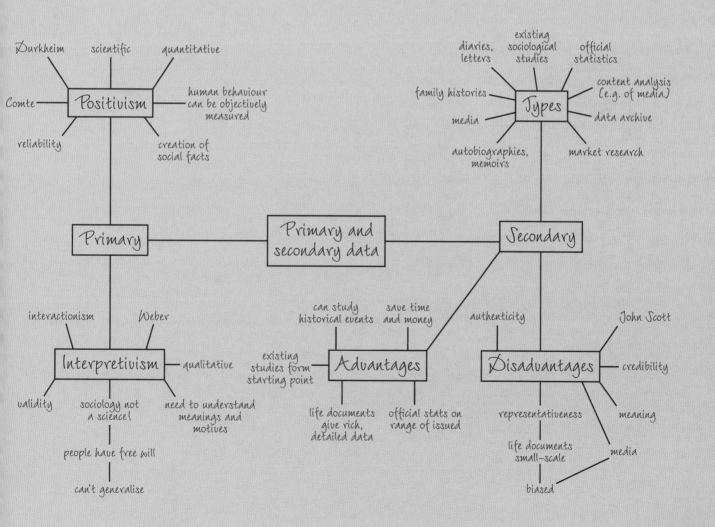

Positivism and interpretivism

Learning objectives

By the end of this section, you should be able to:

- Explain the different ways social surveys are used
- Clarify what makes a good social survey
- Make clear the problems with social surveys
- Illustrate the different ways that structured and unstructured interviews can be used, and also explain the advantages and disadvantages of this method
- Describe why some researchers favour the use of observation
- Explain the difference between participant and non-participant observation, and covert and overt observation
- Make clear the advantages and disadvantages of all types of observation
- Give details of the practical problems with all types of observation

Introduction

In this section we will examine in more detail the main methods that are used by positivism and anti-positivism. The three methods we concentrate upon are questionnaires, interviews and observation.

Questionnaires

One of the main ways that sociologists conduct research is to ask questions of their respondents through questionnaires. This method is widely used by a range of organisations, such as market-research companies. Surveys usually involve relatively large numbers of people; particularly if they are questionnaire-based surveys. Questionnaires that use interviews tend to be smaller and qualitative. If well designed with well-structured, standardised questions, questionnaires can collect a huge amount of data that can then be expertly examined.

Questionnaires can be conducted in a number of ways:

- People can be interviewed face-to-face
- The questionnaire can be completed in the presence of the researcher
- The questionnaire can be completed without supervision.

What makes a good questionnaire?

When compiling a questionnaire the following principles should be followed:

- The objectives of the survey should be carefully defined.
- The questions should be written in language and words that will make it easy for the respondent to answer.
- The minimum number of questions should be used that are needed to find out the necessary information. Long questionnaires have a notoriously low completion rate. With this in mind, brevity is vital.
- A good questionnaire should be lively and interesting to the respondent and encourage them to complete it.
- Emotionally-charged words that could influence the respondent should be avoided.

The format of responses

How questions are asked will depend upon how statistics are viewed. Quantitative sociologists like to use **closed questions** that restrict the choice of possible answers. So, for example, a question may give the options of 'Yes', 'No' or 'I don't know'. These are also sometimes known as **pre-coded questions**. The advantage of such questions is that it makes it relatively straightforward for quantification of the results to occur. From these results the sociologist can easily construct bar charts, data sets, and so on.

Open-ended questions allow for longer and more in-depth answers not limited by the the person who compiled the questionnaire. This method is most favoured by qualitative sociologists. However, most questionnaires tend to include a selection of both open and closed questions. These are called semi-structured questionnaires.

Advantages of questionnaires

- **Standardised response:** As questionnaires ask the same questions of many respondents, this leads to responses being standardised in a way that does not occur with interviews. Any differences between the respondents should therefore be real and tangible, thereby increasing objectivity.

- **It is a quick and easy way to collect information:** Questionnaires allow researchers to gain lots of data relatively quickly. It is therefore a cheap and efficient way to conduct research. However, open-ended questions may be time-consuming to interpret and categorise, so we cannot assume that questionnaires are necessarily either cheap or easy to collect.

- **Large samples can be taken:** As large samples can be surveyed, samples are much more likely to be representative of the population. This therefore allows increased validity.

Problems with questionnaires

- **Response rates:** Often questionnaires are not completed, reducing the sample size and making reliability and generalisations more difficult. Although there is no minimum response rate, it is thought that 80 per cent completion is what should be aimed for. However, it should be noted that well-designed questionnaires improve response rates and ensure that a cross-section of the population completes them. These can be improved with the use of cash-based incentives. Yu and Cooper (1983) found that the higher the value of these, the greater the response rate.

- **The inability to probe responses:** Because questionnaires are highly structured, they do not allow enough flexibility for the respondent to give their own opinion, whilst it is also impossible to explain any points that the respondent may have about any of the questions. Moreover, because of the lack of personal contact, non-verbal clues are not available. This may be a particular disadvantage when asking personal or embarrassing questions.

- **Questionnaires are not always answered by the person intended:** Because questionnaires are time-consuming they are often passed to other employees by senior managers, or within domestic households, women complete questionnaires that were meant for their husbands, for example.

- **They do not suit everyone:** Although the majority of the population is able to answer questionnaires without any problem, this is not the case for everyone. Estimates by the United Nations (2000) show that up to seven million UK citizens are **functionally illiterate**. Therefore some respondents will struggle to answer written surveys. As a consequence, reliability and generalisation is more problematic. For example, it probable that those who are illiterate may have very different issues than the rest of the population. Therefore by not eliciting their responses, validity will be compromised.

- **Respondents may not tell the truth:** Researchers can never be sure that respondents are being completely truthful, with subjective and conscious bias becoming a problem. This could be because people want to make themselves look good, want to appear to be 'normal' or be concerned about the purpose of the questionnaires. Additionally, sometimes inaccuracy may occur because the questionnaire is being answered 'after the event'.

Interviews

The phrase 'interview' refers to a situation where researchers and participants talk as normally as possible, either face-to-face, by telephone or by using other, newer technological methods, such as through video links or webcams.

When they are used

- They allow researchers in-depth knowledge of what the respondent is thinking, particularly when **open questions** are used

- As a result they often allow research to delve into areas that were not anticipated originally

- They can be used comparatively to contrast the findings of different research studies on a similar topic area

The different types of interview

There are two types of interview that are used:

1. **Structured interviews:** At their most structured such interviews are merely a verbal presentation of a questionnaire, offering standardised questions often in a multiple choice format. The advantage of this technique is that it reduces the time needed for the process, whilst offering greater reliability because standardised questions are used and so differences can be easily discovered. To assist the interviewer, structured interviews are often conducted by using an interview schedule, thereby making sure of standardisation.

2. **Unstructured interviews:** Open-ended or unstructured interviews by contrast offer only a limited amount of structure by suggesting a theme or area of discussion. The role of the interviewer is mainly to keep the respondent within the brief of the research and to help tease out what is being asked of them. The result is rich, detailed qualitative material with less bias because the answers given have been chosen by the respondent rather than being suggested by the interviewer. As with the debate between quantitative and qualitative methods, in reality most interviews use a combination of both structured questions to find out basic information at the start of the interview and open-ended questions to explore issues in greater depth towards the end of the process. It is also important to note that interviews are not necessarily one-on-one; they are often conducted in a group situation or 'focus groups' are used to examine a particular issue. Often as many as seven or eight people will participate in these; consequently a wide variety of views are expressed from all the interviewees, thereby helping reliability.

Advantages of structured interviews

- Response rates tend to be higher for structured interviews because they are less time-consuming and participants can be persuaded by the sociologist.

- **Coding** of the answers is straightforward. Quantitative data can be gained easily and then statistically analysed.

- Because no writing is involved, groups such as the dyslexic and visually impaired, can be included.

- As standardised questions are used, replication is straightforward, thereby allowing comparative studies.

- It can be argued that the structure of these interviews eliminates, or at least reduces, the effect of interviewer bias.

- Is often used in tandem with another method to explore before and after issues. This is known as formative assessment and allows the respondent to feedback their observations.

- There aren't the same problems of non-completion that occurs with questionnaires because of the presence of the researcher.

Disadvantages of structured interviews

- It is a more expensive procedure than questionnaires because the interviewer has to be paid for their time for travelling expenses.

- These costs further escalate if interviews are conducted over a wide geographical area.

- Interviewer bias can creep in. For example, the respondent may want to give the answers that they think the interviewer wants to hear.

- This method does not allow the respondent to answer questions in the detail that they might wish to.

- Structured interviews involve a great deal of preparation to make sure that questions are carefully worded and obtain the needed data from the interview. Without informative questions data obtained is often less than useful.

Advantages of unstructured interviews

- Unlike some other methods, researchers can use their interpersonal skills to create an affinity with the respondent. This is particularly vital when it comes to research into areas such as **domestic violence**, rape, and so on. For example, **Dobash and Dobash**'s study on domestic violence (1980) used interviews as it allowed this personal relationship to develop.

- Consequently data is obtained from the respondent that would remain dormant if other methods were used. This therefore increases reliability.

- Because of the presence of the researcher an assessment can be made about how far the researcher believes the respondent to be telling the truth. For example, with skilled practitioners of interviews non-verbal clues are given about the accuracy of the respondents' answers.

Disadvantages of unstructured interviews

- As a result of the small-scale nature of unstructured interviews, it is difficult to make generalisations with any certainty from them. They therefore remain unrepresentative and are low in reliability.

- They are time-consuming to conduct; this is especially the case with one-on-one interviews. For example, transcripts need to be written and then analysed.

- Interviewer bias can occur. This is when the interviewee gives the response that they think that the researcher desires.

- Because of the complexities of unstructured interviews, training can also add to the costs of the research. Given the difficulties in obtaining finance this can lead to this method being regarded as a luxury.

• There is also the issue of the impartiality of the researcher. Positivist theorists question whether researchers can avoid developing empathy with the respondents and thereby they risk losing their objectivity. **Value freedom** is always going to be difficult to achieve with this personal method.

Observation

Some sociologists believe that most effective way to do research is not to hand out questionnaires, but to go and experience the action that is taking place. An analogy of this is contrasting going to a live football match as opposed to watching it on television. Whilst watching it on television provides some of the atmosphere, the noise, the chanting of fans and the build up, it provides a sanitised version of it. When actually there, the sounds of the crowd are far louder, you get to see the reaction of all those around you, as well as the reaction of the mangers.

In the same way, some qualitative sociologists believe that quantitative data, with its over-emphasis on measurement (operationalising) concepts and classification, limits explanation of social phenomena. Their solution is to go and observe groups in situ. By doing this they argue that the researcher can gain a personal view of the life of the group or individual being studied. From these observations, the belief is that awareness can be gained of how this behaviour fits into society.

The approach itself derives from the work of anthropologists such as Lewis and Malinowski (1922) who both went to study tribal groups to gain an understanding of how their world could be linked to modern society. In doing so these writers literally went 'native' and immersed themselves in the culture of the groups to gain a real and powerful understanding of them. Whilst this approach can be criticised for lacking objectivity, it does, nonetheless, offer something very different

from quantitative methods. In particular, awareness that social lives are constantly changing. If the researcher is to understand this, they need to observe these changes on a daily basis. By doing this the researcher is less likely to impose their reality of what is going on and instead to observe the truth of the situation.

It should be noted that although students tend to assume that qualitative methods mainly revolve around observation it can also be undertaken by using other methods that peek into the lives of others; for example, video and audio recordings can also be used.

The two different types of observation

There are two main types of observation:

1. Non-participant observation is where the researcher organises the observation but does not take part in the observation itself. Instead, the researcher observes from a distance without actively participating.

2. Participant observation: By contrast here the researcher actively participates in the observational study.

The researcher then has to decide whether to inform the participants of the observation or whether to keep it a secret. So, the choice is between overt (where the participants are fully aware of the research and give '**informed consent**' and covert (where no consent has been given). Many feel uneasy about research being performed on participants who are not aware of it Ethically, the BSA believes that "Participant or non-participant observation in non-public spaces or experimental manipulation of research participants without their knowledge should be resorted to only where it is impossible to use other methods to obtain essential data."

Given this difficulty, the most commonly-used method of observation is participant observation. There are a number of key advantages to this method. This is a relatively new method of research which was only adopted when it was clear that structural explanations and methods did not fully explain the human condition. It was first used by Frank Hamilton Cushing in his study of the Zuni Indians (1879–84) and thereafter taken up by anthropologists and the Chicago School to explain the impact of migration on the USA. Its heyday, however, was in the Sixties when a succession of studies emerged on the sociology of drug taking and gangs (Becker, 1963, and Young, 1971).

The advantages of participant observation

- Qualitative theorists believe it offers rich, detailed information direct from the 'horse's mouth'.

- As a result of the researcher gaining the trust of the group concerned over time, the actors will not change their behaviour. This makes this method more reliable than others where this is not the case.

- From their observation the researcher gains a keen awareness of the norms of the group and how the workings of society influence this behaviour. By being there, the researcher is able to see the dynamics of chronology, to understand the group's reactions and to talk to them to understand them completely.

- As a consequence, new hypotheses can be generated that delve into areas of research that would never have been explored without this research methodology.

- This method allows the sociologist to be guided as to their research by the active participants. This allows them to delve into the workings of the group in a way that perhaps they would not have considered before their observation. For example, the researchers observe the group, their daily activities and their reaction to these interactions.

- It can be argued that this method is more reliable. Because of the close proximity of the researcher it is far more difficult for the actors to lie to the researcher.

The disadvantages of participant observation

- Because of the small-scale nature of participant observation it makes it very difficult to generalise findings, as each piece of research is specific.

- Participant observation relies on the interpersonal skills of the researcher, with the skills of tact and diplomacy being vital to gain entry and the trust of those they are studying. This makes replication very difficult, so reliability can be questioned.

- There is always a chance that the researcher will start to lose their objectivity. As they gain the trust and gain friendships within the group this may lead to the researcher aligning themselves and understanding the group in a less than objective manner.

- This process is very time-consuming. Often researchers are expected to take years out of their busy academic lives to undertake participant observation. This also makes it costly, both in personal and financial terms.

- Whist this method is useful, it can be argued that it leads to researchers concentrating upon groups with relatively little power and prestige. For example, there have been many studies on gangs and drug users. By contrast, observation of powerful businesses and decision making has not been undertaken. The underdog appears to be the main focus of observational studies. For Marxists, this is telling!

- The ethics of participant observation can be questioned. Is it right to observe groups without informed consent?

- In relation to the above, participant observation can be a dangerous pursuit if you are not honest with those you are studying. 'James Patrick' discovered this in his study

of Glasgow gangs (1973). Not only did he have to leave the group in haste, but waited years to publish his data because he was so afraid of the consequences.

- On occasions those performing participant observation may be asked to indulge in illegal activities. 'James Patrick' for example, was asked by the group to carry a knife.

The practicalities of participant observation

In order to perform participant observation a number of stages need to be followed:

1. **Choose the group to study:** This method is ideal for studying groups such as gangs, school groups, work groups, and so on. It is far less appropriate a method when studying those with real power, who will not want to be studied. Additionally, some other groups, such as football hooligans and cults may make entry into the group as difficult as possible.

2. **Decide how to join the group:** There are a number of ways that this can be achieved. Firstly, on occasions researchers may be in the lucky position of being part of the group anyway. This was the case with Simon Holdaway (1977) who was a serving police constable and therefore had privileged access in a way that most researchers will never have. Secondly, and the most usual way, is to become friendly with someone within the group you wish to study. This method was used by both 'James Patrick' who befriended Tim, and by Bill Whyte who became friendly with the leader of the group, 'Doc'. Finally, the researcher can be persuaded to do the research by the organisation itself.

3. **How to record data:** There are a number of problems, especially when it comes to covert participant observation. Because of the clandestine nature of this type of entry, the recording of day-to-day information can be highly problematic. Researchers are in the position of having to remember what is going on around them. Given that the human memory suffers from displacement, the accuracy of information recorded after the event might be less than accurate.

4. **How to ensure objectivity:** Watching any group and recording data is a highly subjective exercise, when positivists would claim that what is actually needed is objectivity. Whilst it may be straightforward to record what is happening, the interpretation of events is far more subjective. Moreover, researchers can find themselves becoming too involved with the group.

The ethics of participant observation

Later in this chapter we talk about the ethics of research; however, because of the particular problems thrown up by participant observation, we will briefly consider some of the issues that occur.

- For some, participant observation is inevitably unethical (Punch, 1994) because they argue it is intentionally deceitful. Should researchers always tell the group they are being studied?

- At what point does the researcher step in and breach confidentiality, especially when they are being requested to commit criminal acts?

- Will the researcher be subject to reprisals from the group they have been studying when the true intention of their research becomes apparent? For example, in *A Glasgow Gang Observed*, the researcher used the name 'James Patrick' rather than reveal his real identity (1973).

- Can those who are part of the study be recognised? If so, this could lead to them being harmed, subject to reprisals, criminalisation or derision.

Sociology and values

Is it possible for sociologists to conduct social research without letting their personal values affect their judgement? This is called value freedom. Do we think that sociologists can be personally objective? Or indeed is such objectivity actually a good thing? This really depends upon the theoretical perspective that the researcher takes. For positivists they believe that such objectivity is perfectly possible and desirable. They argue that because they deal with facts and data that are collected systematically, such objectivity is possible. This is best done by producing scientific laws on social behaviour. This is done by:

- Using logical scientific processes:
  - Observing a phenomenon and wanting to explain it
  - Suggesting a hypothesis
  - Using experiments to see if the hypothesis can be proved
  - If the hypothesis is proved then laws can be formulated that explain the phenomenon

- Scientific technique:
  - Ideally for positivists these would take place in the controlled environment of the laboratory, where one variable can be changed at a time. By doing this, the social scientist can work out what effect the variable is having. The other important reason for using this environment is that it allows experiments to be replicated. In essence, the more times the experiment is repeated and similar results are achieved, the closer to the truth it can said to be.

- The Stance:
  - Positivists contend that by adopting an objective stance to their research laws can be formulated that are not tainted by subjectivity.

The problem with social science and being 'value free'

The reality of objectivity is far more complex that the notion. Although value freedom may be possible within the natural sciences when performing experiments in the laboratory, with social science we are working with a completely different set of phenomena. Whilst bits of rock and ice can respond in a predictable manner, by contrast human beings do not. Moreover, whilst experiments in the laboratories are entirely appropriate when studying rock and ice, such an environment is not appropriate for human beings. A multitude of issues make it more difficult to use the experimental technique. For instance, is it ethical to experiment on human beings? What effect will the experiment have on the subjects? Do we really believe that social researchers social researchers are able to be dispassionate about those who they study? Evidence from previous research, such as Ann Oaklely (1974), suggests not.

This has led anti-positivists to question whether value freedom and the scientific procedure is appropriate or desirable. For anti-positivists we need not see people as robots but get into their shoes and develop verstehen. By developing an understanding of the subjective state of social actors only then can adequate explanations of the social world by made. Anti-positivists also make the point that positivist notions of objectivity, although laudable, are in reality very difficult to achieve. Science is littered with examples of where scientists have proven to be singularly unscientific in their judgements, either being influenced by money or by status. Examples of falsification include Charles Dawson and Arthur Smith Woodward, who produced fragments of the skull of the so-called Piltdown man; allegedly discovered by workmen in gravel pits in Sussex. They proposed that Piltdown man represented an evolutionary missing link between ape and man, and that it confirmed the current cutting-edge theory that a recognisably human brain developed early on in mankind's evolution. Over 40 years later, Piltdown man was shown to be a composite forgery, put together out of a medieval human skull, the 500-year-old lower jaw of an orang-utan and chimpanzee fossil teeth. The deception went unnoticed for so long because it offered the experts of the day exactly what they wanted: convincing evidence that human evolution was brain-led. Given the difficulties in science being objective, it is hardly surprising that sociology suffers similarly.

Science and the role of the researcher

Depending upon whether the researcher takes a positivist or anti-positivist approach, the role of the researcher will be fundamentally different. Positivists insist on using methods that are objective, and preferably quantitative, and easily replicable and reliable. Positivists think that this is best achieved by using **systematic** methods of data collection

that are standardised and therefore allow similar results to be achieved in a study, regardless of who is collecting the data. They also advocate the use of techniques that allow generalisations so **social facts** or laws can be made. They believe that these are best made by using data such as official statistics, whereby trends can be isolated and logic similar to that used in laboratories can be utilised. When using primary data, positivists are drawn to using experiments; however, due to this environment lacking reality and being prone to change human behaviour, they have to use other techniques that achieve similar goals. Positivists have turned to other methods that allow standardised and reliable responses that mimic the scientific enquiry used within the laboratory. These include social surveys and structured interviews that they claim offer the researcher greater objectivity and reliability through the use of standardised questions that ensure that interviewer

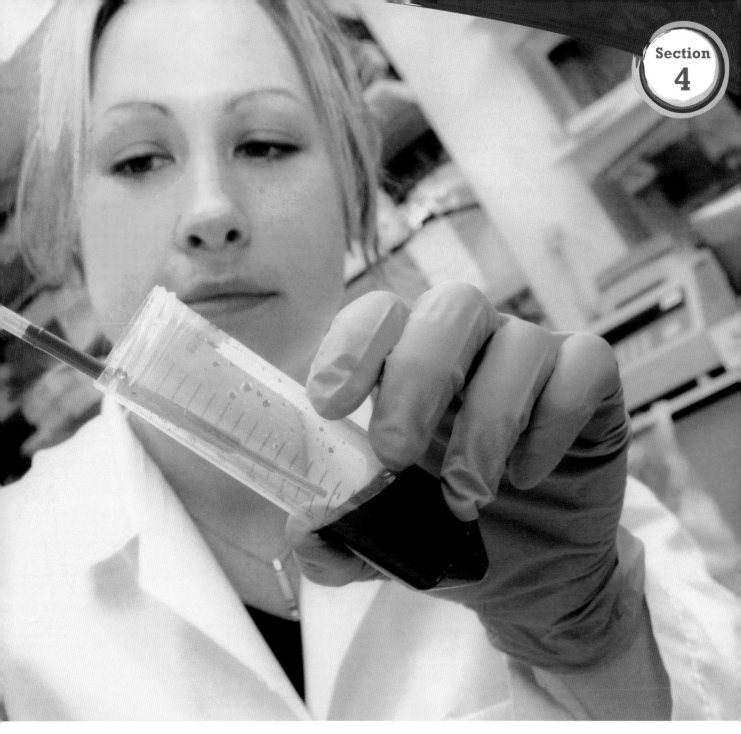

bias is kept to the very minimum. Additionally, positivists claim that through the use of statistical techniques, such as sampling, they are able to make generalisations.

Anti-positivists take a very different approach on how they see the role of the researcher. They reject the need of the researcher to be objective and argue that such a rigid stance on social research actually obscures the motivations and intentions of the social actors concerned. They therefore argue that it is the role of the researcher to look into these motivations and to uncover these so as to explain people's intentions. It therefore follows so they argue that what is needed is not scientific processes, instead, interpretativists suggest that social researchers need to develop an understanding of why people act in a certain way.

This is best done through the use of methods which allow a subjective understanding of those being studied. Anti-positivists thus want to use methods such as secondary data that explains how people see their situation. And although it can be argued that secondary data, such as diaries, books and life histories are highly subjective, they reveal the day-to-day activities of social actors in a way that social surveys fail to do. Similarly with primary data anti-positivists argue that the best place to understand how people act is in their natural environment. They therefore adopt methods such as participant observation and ethnography that allows them to ask and understand social actors' motivations. Anti-positivists, although accepting that they may not be scientific in their methods, assert that because of the close relationships developed between the social researcher and those that they are studying, reliability is actually far more likely to occur.

- Are the following strengths or weaknesses of participant observation?

  - The results are more valid and accurate. By observing people in their natural setting, the researcher can see at first-hand what they do rather than what they say they do.

  - Being accepted by the group to observe can sometimes be difficult.

  - As participant observation is carried out over time, the observer can study the process by which the meanings that people attach to their behaviour changes.

  - The researcher may find it hard to leave the group.

  - It may be the only way that some groups can be studied.

  - Observations provide a detailed, in-depth insight into naturally-occurring events or behaviour.

  - The method is expensive.

  - There is a danger that the researcher becomes too involved and therefore becomes a poor observer.

  - This observation method can he made sufficiently systematic to provide reliable valid data.

  - Because of their subjective involvement, researchers gain insight and understanding. They may learn about matters they had previously not considered.

  - For all observation, what we see and how we interpret it depends upon our values. Therefore it is hard to be objective as a researcher because of research bias.

  - As the researcher is there, it is more difficult for those being studied to mislead the researcher than in other methods.

  - There are ethical objections to this type of research.

  - It is often impossible to use recording equipment and therefore the researcher must rely on their memory.

  - Only a small group of people can be studied.

  - Researchers can understand why people behave in a particular way.

  - Covert participant observation is the best way of studying interaction because people cannot always explain their behaviour later, since much of it is instinctive.

  - Quantitative researchers would argue that the samples are too small.

  - Large numbers of people and generalisations are impossible, so comparisons cannot be made.

  - The process is very time-consuming and especially demanding on the researcher's time.

  - Positivists argue that this method is unscientific and not systematic. It cannot be checked for validity.

  - Researchers gain an understanding of the world from the point of view of the subjects of their research.

  - Studies can never be replicated. Data produced rely on the researcher's own observations.

  - Researchers may have to join in activities they disagree with.

  - The researcher may have to confront a moral dilemma if observing and participating in illegal activities whilst tying to carry out research.

Key terms

Closed questions:	Questions that only allow a limited response such as 'yes' or 'no'.
Coding:	The method of placing responses of those studied into statistical data.
Domestic violence:	Defined by the Home Office "any incident of threatening behaviour, violence or abuse between adults who are or have been in a relationship together, or between family members, regardless of gender or sexuality".
Functionally illiterate:	Having reading skills that are insufficient for modern everyday needs in contemporary Great Britain.
Informed consent:	Giving agreement to take part in a study in the knowledge that the person concerned has a knowledge of the possible facts and implications that could occur during participation.
Open questions:	These questions allow the respondent to say what they want.
Pre-coded questions:	Another name for structured questions.
Response rate:	The percentage response gained from a sociological sample.
Value freedom:	Associated with positivism. The notion that sociologists can take part in research and not let anything deflect them from the objective truth that they require.

Section summary

- One of the main ways that sociologists conduct research is to ask questions to their respondents by questionnaires.

- Questionnaires can be conducted in a number of ways: people can be interviewed face-to-face, complete a questionnaire in the presence of the researcher. or complete a questionnaire without supervision.

- When compiling a questionnaire certain principles should be followed.

- Quantitative sociologists like to use closed questions in their questionnaires, which restrict the choice of possible answers, whereas qualitative sociologists like to use open-ended questions instead.

- Questionnaires to have their problems; notably, low response rates, the inability of the researcher to probe responses, their lack of suitability with those who are illiterate, the fact that on occasions they are not answered by the required person, and finally their lack of validity.

- Interviews allow researchers in-depth knowledge of what the respondent is thinking, particularly when open questions are used.

- There are two types of interview: structured interviews offering standardised questions, often in a multiple choice format, and unstructured interviews that, by contrast, offer only a limited amount of structure by suggesting a theme or area of discussion.

- The advantage of structured interviews is that replication is straightforward as standardised questions are used, allowing comparative studies.

- The disadvantages of structured interviews are that it is a more expensive procedure than questionnaires.

- The advantages of unstructured interviews are that researchers can use their interpersonal skills to create an affinity with the respondent.

- Some sociologists believe the most effective way to do research is not to hand out questionnaires, but to go and experience the action that is taking place.

- The advantages of observation are that it offers rich, detailed information straight from the horse's mouth.

- Participant observation can be criticised for being too small-scale and therefore unreliable.

- Positivists claim that sociologists should adopt similar methods to those used by the natural sciences as they ensure high reliability and validity by using standardised methods of research.

- Anti-positivists see the social world as being a subjective and complex world that can only be understood if the researcher steps into the world of those who experience it.

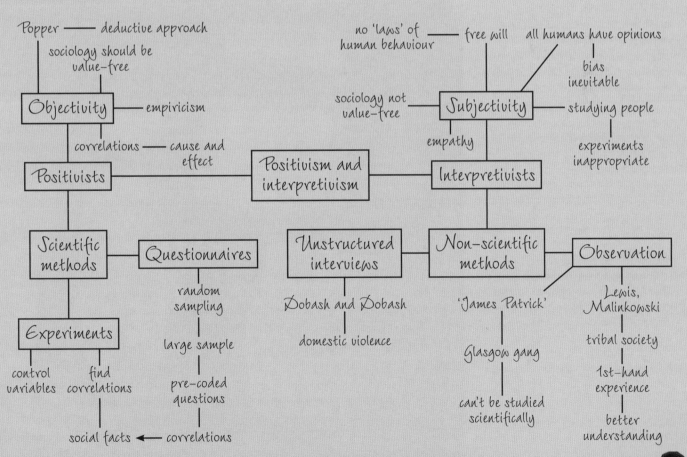

Theoretical, practical and ethical considerations

Learning objectives

By the end of this section, you should be able to:

- Understand how theory impacts on the choice of method chosen
- Comprehend how the focus of research will differ between those advocating varying sociological approaches
- Recognise how social research can be unethical
- Be aware of the issues that can lead to social research being unethical
- Realise why different perspectives tend to concentrate upon certain methods rather than others
- Understand the difference between 'top down' and 'bottom up' approaches to social research

Introduction

The role of sociology is to focus on society and come up with new insights that help both government and other agencies of social control. There are plenty of other social commentators who also like to make comments about the operation of society. However, such individuals who often appear on television news or documentaries look at the social world in terms of common-sense notions of what is going on, whether society is dysfunctional and how we can look to improve the human condition.

By contrast sociologists like to see themselves as being more intellectual and scientific about their observations. Therefore, they tend to examine and collate statistics, before revealing to society their observations. For some sociologists, such as Durkheim, from such data social facts can be asserted. Essentially, structural theorists who believe that the structure of society fundamentally affects the way we behave, suggest that social facts or laws can be made that indicate how people will consistently behave under certain conditions. Each sociologist, however, sees such behaviour as being affected by varying factors.

These lead sociologists to theorise or construct ideas on the basis of how behaviour is affected by the different ways that society is run. These theories are then organically used by others who take up the ideas of the original thinkers, such as Marx or Weber, and then formulate new ideas and draw upon the crude assumptions of the founder thinker and then expand and update them to match what is happening today.

As academic professionals sociologists need to be aware of the moral and ethical issues that might result from sociological research, and, in particular, be aware of any ethical implications of studying and publishing their findings.

Theoretical considerations

Theory plays an important role in the chosen method of research. So the macro theories of functionalism, Marxism and feminism that believe that structure of society affects the way that we behave, see the use of quantitative techniques as being most appropriate. By contrast, micro theories see the utilisation of qualitative methods as being the best way to conduct social research. For the quantitative theorists the use of **empirical** data allows for trends to be noted and

correlations and multivariate analysis to be used to assess which factors are most important. However, interpretativists do their research in an entirely different way. Instead of wanting to look at the whole of society and how it operates, they see sociology as having to look at the smaller parts that make up society. Interpretativists want to use more subjective methods, such as observation and ethnography, which although arguably less scientific, allow the researcher to uncover social interaction that is just not available to those who want to use experiments or social surveys. It should be noted that although I suggest a huge polarised view between the two camps, the reality is that most research tends to use both positivistic and interpretativist methodology in tandem with each other. This is called methodological triangulation, that is, the use of at least three methods.

What is the purpose of sociological research?

The collection of empirical data

Sociologists use systematic methods of investigation to analyse data collected from the social world. Sociologists, it has been observed, attempt to 'see the general in the particular' and the 'strange in the familiar'. To look for these they use a plethora of methods to obtain this data. Thus data concerning crime can be obtained from statistical information collected by the Home Office. However, whilst we need to remain aware that although such data can be seen to be 'facts', we should always look at who has collected it and who has paid for it. Sociologists seek to be objective in their research and attempt to cast aside moral prejudices, speaking about social life in a fair and balanced manner.

Correlations

Sociologists also wish to go beyond merely obtaining statistical information. In particular, they often use correlation to find out if a relationship exists between the two variables, and the degree of that relationship. A social researcher can use case studies, surveys, interviews and observational research to discover correlations. Correlations are either positive (to +1.0), negative (to −1.0), or nonexistent (0.0). In a positive correlation, the values of the variables increase or decrease (co-vary) together. In a negative correlation, one variable increases as the other decreases. In a nonexistent correlation, no relationship exists between the variables.

Examples of negative and postiive correlation

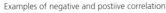

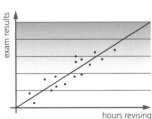

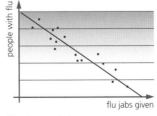

Positive correlation
• people who do more revision get higher exam results
• revising increases success.

Negative correlation
• when more jabs are given the number of people with flu falls
• flu jabs prevent flu.

Theories

Ultimately, however, the role of the sociologist comes down to either coming up with research that proves existing knowledge on a topic – perhaps refining the reasons for the correlations between variables – or refuting previous sociological research. All too often it is easy for researchers to accept the prevailing way of thinking and not look beyond the rejection of theories. Sociological research should strive to delve into new explanations of social behaviour rather than becoming tired and self-satisfied with existing **paradigms**. Researchers should remain pragmatic and flexible. Often as social research occurs, the social researcher will become aware of issues that they did not think of before. Bill Whyte found that his research moved into new areas that he just wouldn't have considered if he had not struck up such a strong friendship with the groups' leader, 'Doc'. Ultimately, though, researchers need to be mindful that the choice of topic may be linked to how interesting their topic is, either to the institution they work for or the audience for which it is intended.

Research and ethics

Researchers must be sure that their research does not have a negative impact on the lives and feelings on those who they conduct research on. They therefore need to carefully assess how they conduct their research, and consider how their actions could be harmful. The idea of ethics broadly means analysing the ideas of right and wrong. Broadly, five areas form the basis of ethical concern:

1. **What the topic research is done on**

   Even the choice of topic area under consideration may have an ethical dimension. Why, for example, has the area been chosen? Social researchers who merely concentrate upon one area of social concern may be accused of having preconceptions about an area.

2. **Who is chosen to research**

   Traditionally, social research concentrates upon the working classes and ethnic groups. In doing so, it could be argued; societal reaction will continue to link these sectors of society with crime, poverty and underachievement. What is needed is for social research to offer a full spectrum of analysis across British society, rather than a concentration upon those groups who may be easy to study.

3. **The impact the research will have on those being investigated**

   Any kind of social research can impact deeply on those being studied. Researchers need to think in advance of the possible consequences of their research and how these can be mitigated against. For instance, will the subjects be psychological harmed by the research? How might their civil rights be infringed? Social research should strive to protect the rights of those they study – their interests, sensitivities and privacy – while recognising the difficulty of balancing potentially conflicting interests.

4. **How the research will impact on others aside from the subjects**

On occasions, social researchers need to be mindful not just of how their research will impact directly on those who they conduct their research on, but also on the friends and families of the participants. How will they react to revelations about their subject being investigated? Additionally, when studying deviant individuals, it may be appropriate to think of what impact the research may have on those possibly harmed by the person under research.

5. **Legal issues**

There has been an accelerated tendency to focus on ethical and legal issues in all areas of social science including sociology. This is exemplified by the recent decision of the ESRC to require all their funded research to be approved by appropriate university-based research ethics committees (2005). This has prompted British universities to institutionalise such research ethics committees in response. However, there is little evidence that British sociologists are unethical in their research, with the ESRC itself recently stating that "almost without exception, social science research in the UK has been carried out to high ethical standards." (ESRC, 2005). Nonetheless, sociologists should ensure that they are not put into a situation where they may have to commit illegal acts or help in criminal acts or protect those who have.

How theory and methods impact on each other

Sociologists are like any other researcher: they are influenced by their values, which may result in sociologists concentrating on a certain area of sociological research: Sociologists have a huge variety of areas that they can examine; however, just as lay people like watching certain types of television, researchers also favour some topics more than others. For instance:

Marxists

This has meant for some Marxists there has been a strong predilection to studying groups who are interesting rather than powerful. Nevertheless, Marxists see the study of the powerful as fundamental and whilst they realise the importance of power, it is not always that easy to gain access to these groups. Because Marxists want to explain how the structure of society benefits capitalism, methods used by them revolve around quantitative techniques. For instance, poverty can best be explained by looking at poverty statistics, looking at trends and examining whether poverty is improving or worsening.

Feminism

For radical feminists research may be dominated by the need to uncover the way that males dominate society (patriarchy), whilst for Marxist feminists, the focus will be on how capitalism exploits women. In terms of methods used, feminism is less straightforward than Marxism and functionalism in that some feminists see the importance of explaining how patriarchy impacts on the whole of women, thereby using quantitative methods. However, others want to show how patriarchy affects individual women and want to use quantitative methodology to show this.

Functionalists

Due to the consensual way that functionalists see the world, their concentration will be on the processes that instil this agreement. This means that functionalists like to examine socialization whether it is primary socialization within the family, or secondary socialization within the workplace, the education system or when attending religious ceremonies.

Theory and method

There are two main approaches within sociology which dictate the research methodology that is used.

A 'top-down' approach

This approach emphasises that an individual is the product of a society. In essence, we are shaped by society to be conventional. Therefore it is argued by macro theorists the focus of study needs to concentrate on the way the whole of society functions.

As a consequence, the **top-down approach** uses quantitative research methodology, such as laboratory studies, comparative studies, case studies and surveys.

A 'bottom-up' approach

This approach emphasises individuals and their views of society. There is a strong inclination from a bottom-up approach for the use of qualitative research methodology such as questionnaires and interviews. Those who advocate the use of the **bottom-up approach** want to interpret the world of those around them from a first-hand perspective.

How do researchers interpret their findings?

Increasingly, sociologists now use a range of ways of interpreting their findings. With the advent of new technology, interpretation often uses statistical methods such as the use of spreadsheets For those who favour the use of quantitative methodology, the use of spreadsheets allows statistical data to be analysed and presented effectively. However, interpretation of any data will usually be affected by the ideological stance of the sociologist concerned. Although value freedom

should always be strived for, it is understandable that on occasions the world views of sociologists cloud sociological interpretation. So, those who come from alternative social backgrounds to the majority will tend to see the world in relation to their group's struggle, whilst functionalists might tend to see the world from a consensual point of view.

Are they interpreted at all?

There is a long history from both science and the social sciences of research following a ruling paradigm. By this we mean that a ruling body of thinking dominates in such a way as to limit research into alternate methods of explanation. For years, for example, it was thought that ships would drop off the top of the world, and it took the work of Copernicus to establish a new way of thinking. Research tends to follow established patterns and often stagnates due to this ruling way of thinking. It is only when visionary thinkers emerge to question the ruling way of thinking that great leaps are made, both in the natural sciences and the social sciences. Such visionaries include many of the 'greats' of science, arguably Sir Isaac Newton, Charles Darwin and Albert Einstein. Similarly within the social sciences new ruling ways of thought have emerged that have allowed sociology to delve into new areas of social research. In the 1960s, for instance, the world of interactionists emerged to explain deviant behaviour. By the 1970s the focus of research moved towards feminism. Each decade tends to see new areas of research that allow a body of work to develop in its wake.

Factors that influence the choice of method

Time

Different methods require varying amounts of time. Whilst surveys can be completed relatively quickly, participant observation can take a considerable amount of time.

The subject matter

Sociologists have to use practical methods that allow effective research. Large groups that are scattered across the UK are better suited to postal surveys, as this method allows for many surveys to be completed with the minimum amount of travel time and cost. By contrast, participant observation is a costly and time-consuming method that may not be financed easily by a research grant.

Other factors that affect research

Time

Sociologists also need to consider the amount of time that they can devote to any area. Although they might wish to spend years studying a group in an ethnographic study similar to Malinowski, reality dictates that the cost, dislocation from

family and the lost of personal liberty dictate that such studies are only undertaken by sociologists who have the inclination for such marathon research!

Funding

All research needs to be funded. In the UK a number of bodies assist with funding. Examples of organisations that help include the ESRC, which funds research and training in social and economic issues, and in the academic year 2007–8 funded 2500 researchers in academic institutions and policy research institutes throughout the UK. Another leading research funder is the Joseph Rowntree Trust which funds research and releases its findings to help influence government social policy. With both these organisations, research is only commissioned if it is considered to match the ethos and sentiments of the organisation.

To attract government funding for academic research, researchers need to carefully prepare applications for funding. Awards are usually made subject to quite specific conditions, often as binding contracts. Moreover cut-backs in public expenditure mean that academic researchers will often be competing with government researchers for government funds. There has also been a tendency to favour research that links neatly with current economic and government policy initiatives.

Funding on the face of it should be fairly straightforward. However, this ignores the difficulties that often occur. It is not uncommon, for instance, for researchers to massively underquote for funds and find that their research grant does not fully cover what they intend to research into.

Exercise

Use the Internet to go to the British Sociological Association homepage. Then navigate to:
- Studying sociology
- Equality and ethics
- Statement of ethical practice

Personal factors

Like all people, sociologists like the idea of their research being successfully published. Inevitably, this leads sociologists to look towards research that will gain prominence and importance. Research may also offer academic rewards such as a doctorate.

Practical research implications

Sociologists have to use methods that are practical and appropriate even when they would perhaps like to use more expensive methods. For those wanting to use quantitative methodology this means that the researcher is often limited to use social surveys or structured interviews.

What do you know now?

1. Explain the term 'systematic' as it relates to sociological research.
2. Clarify what the term 'correlation' means. Give an example.
3. Describe what a 'paradigm' is. Give an example of an existing paradigm in the natural sciences.
4. Give five ways that research should be ethical.
5. How does funding impact on research?
6. Isolate three organisations that fund sociological research in the UK.
7. Describe other practical considerations that a researcher might want to consider before starting their research.

Key terms

Bottom-up approach: This approach focuses on the individual and their views of society.

Empirical: Evidence that is observed via the senses. Empirical data is information that is produced by experiment or observation.

Paradigm: A set of common beliefs and agreements shared between scientists about how problems should be understood and addressed.

Social facts: Observable facts which are outside to the individual, but which act upon him or her in a restricting way.

Systematic: Characterised by order and planning. Literally using a system.

Top-down approach: Believes in looking at an overview of society.

Section summary

- Sociologists like to see themselves as being intellectual and scientific about their observations.

- Sociologists use systematic methods of investigation to analyse data collected from the social world. Sociologists, it has been observed, attempt to 'see the general in the particular' and the 'strange in the familiar'.

- Sociologists also wish to go beyond merely obtaining statistical information. In particular, they often use correlation to find out if a relationship exists between two variables, and the degree of that relationship.

- Ultimately, however, the role of the sociologist comes down to either coming up with research that proves existing knowledge on a topic – perhaps refining the reasons for the correlations between variables – or refuting previous sociological research.

- All too often it is easy for researchers to accept the prevailing way of thinking and not look beyond the rejection of theories.

- Researchers must be sure that their research does not have a negative impact on the lives and feelings on those who they conduct research on.

- Broadly, five areas form the basis of ethical concern: the topic research is done on, who is chosen as a subject, what impact the research will have on those being investigated, how the research will impact on others aside from the subjects themselves, and legal issues.

- Sociologists have a huge variety of areas that they can examine. However, some researchers can favour some topics more than others. Marxists tend to focus on power in society; feminists want to examine how men dominate society, whereas functionalists closely examine how consensus is achieved.

- There are two main approaches within sociology which dictate the research methodology which is used. The top-down approach emphasises that an individual is the product of a society. The bottom-up approach wants to interpret the world of those around them from a first-hand perspective.

- Factors that affect the use of method include the time it takes, and who is being studied.

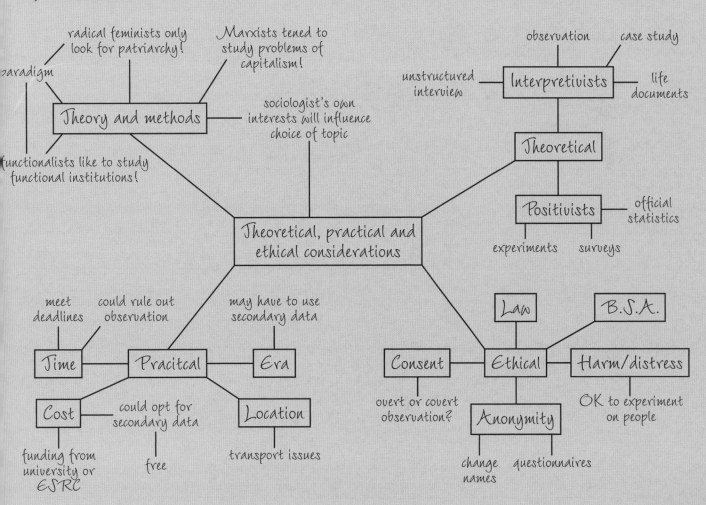

Topic summary

How to maximise your grade with AQA

Theory and methods is worth 60 per cent of the AS total mark and 30 per cent of A level. You will be expected to answer five questions on either education or health, with graduated questions with one question worth two marks and two questions worth four marks, and then the large 20 mark one. As with the previous specification the exam format is a stimulus response style question. As a result of the decision to dispense with coursework this module includes one question on sociological research methods in context and one question on research methods.

The assessment objectives for the A level are as follows:

Assessment objectives		Weighting
AO1	Knowledge and understanding of the theories, methods, concepts and various forms of evidence linked to the specification. Communication of knowledge and understanding in a clear and effective manner.	48%
AO2	Demonstration of the skills of application, analysis, interpretation and evaluation.	52%
Overall weighting		60%

AO1: You will need to know the following areas to obtain a high mark in knowledge and understanding:

- **The nature of sociological thought:** The AQA ask you to have a good knowledge of a range methods used in sociology.

  Specifically, this means knowing the difference between quantitative and qualitative research methods and knowing the strengths and weaknesses of these. You are also expected to understand the inherent difficulties in designing research. Candidates must also comprehend the different sources of data that are used by sociologists, ranging from questionnaires to official statistics. A general awareness of the difference between secondary and primary data is also required. Additionally, candidates must know about the ideas of value freedom and understand how different sociological approaches see objectivity and subjectivity. Finally candidates should be aware of the ethical and practical considerations that are needed during the process of research.

- **Methods of social enquiry:** As there is no coursework component the AQA have added a methods section to each unit. Specifically, the AQA want you to apply your knowledge of methods appropriately. You will need to apply this knowledge to show you understand how sociologists undertake research into education and health and illness and the advantages and disadvantages of these methods. Finally, students should know how theory and methods are interrelated and how this impacts on the study of education and health and illness. Overall then, a wide knowledge of primary and secondary methods is needed. It is expected that these skills will be used practically as there will be far more opportunity to undertake project work, with this new specification having few modules.

- **Themes:** You are expected to cover two themes:

- **Socialization, culture and identity:** Health and illness has long been considered as a source of identity, with many groups being labelled as being 'ill' via social construction. Health and illness offers an ideal way for students to explore how these identities are formed and self-perpetuated. Similarly education is one of the main methods of secondary Socialization, therefore this topic is ideal for exploring how the education system guides our behaviour both in school and afterwards.

- **Social differentiation, power and stratification:** There are huge differences in how illness affects and impacts on different groups within contemporary society. Factors such as class, gender and ethnicity can be explored here to achieve an understanding of these disparities. Education additionally, is an arena of huge social differentiation. These ideas can be explored by looking at how educational attainment differs between social class, ethnicity and gender.

AO2: This assessment objective asks you to be able to acquire and produce evidence and apply it to the question set. You will also be expected to be able to look at the strengths and weaknesses of each argument and come up with a reasoned conclusion. Evidence should be both from primary and secondary resources, and you will be expected to use both quantitative and qualitative data. There are a number of ways you can do this. In the study of education students need to be aware of the strengths of weaknesses of the major theories such as functionalism and Marxism and interactionism. For each theory students should know a number of criticisms. Other evaluative points can be made concerning the methodology used by each study, and how far the studies concerned can be applied to the UK educational schooling system.

When talking about health and illness, you can be critical of areas such as the methodology used, whether the study is now dated, whether the researcher is suffering from ideological bias, and so on.

It is important that you learn at least two criticisms for each major theory. However, remember that evaluation also includes strengths of theories.

There are three sections you will need to tackle for AO2:

- **Collection and recording of evidence:** Specifically you will need to evaluate the design of sociological research as it applies to education and health and illness. You must analyse and evaluate the methods used to collect data.

- **Interpretation and evaluation of evidence:** It is essential that you do the following here: show objectivity, apply a range of theories to the questions set and use appropriate concepts. When studying education, students must be able to use concepts as diverse as functionalism, Marxism, interactionism, gender, ethnicity and the ideas of genetic theorists and the New Right. When studying health and illness, you would be expected to understand what the role of doctors is and how this powerful group affects social policy. At all times, sociology students need to be aware of the highly subjective nature of sociology and apply a range of theories using their 'tool kit' of concepts to achieve this.

- **Presentation of evidence and argument:** A level examiners expect you to be able to organise your written answers so there is coherence. This means that you are expected to start with an introduction, have a number of interlinked paragraphs and a conclusion. Within this answer you must use theory that would inform the question and include any evidence that would further answer the question. You must draw conclusions and back these up with appropriate arguments.

Ideally, this means that all students should have a good overall awareness both of the British educational system and the medical profession and hospitals. It is

also suggested that students have a critical awareness of how our systems differ from those both within Europe and internationally. The recommendation is that all students should regularly read and listen to the mass media to inform their knowledge of these.

Exam practice for AQA

Although there is no individual exam paper for sociological methods, there are a few tips for students to bear in mind.

a) Question 2 tends to be asked on the strengths and weaknesses of two given methods either related to education or health and illness. Candidates must therefore know a range of evaluative points on each main method studied.

b) The short mark question (*2 Marks*) asks you to know a simple phrase in a similar way to the previous AS examination. As with all very short answers it is advised that teachers and students look at similar phrases asked in the previous AS examination. A good tip is for either the teacher to type these out or for the pupils to download these from the AQA website. Key phrases can then be learned.

c) The four mark questions again are formulaic. Candidates are expected to give two points on factors that are important in sampling and give two reasons why a sociologist might want to use a particular method. Popular methods that have questions asked on them include participant observation, interviews, and questionnaires. Questions on official statistics are also prevalent.

d) The last question is the 20 mark question. This is invariably on a particular method.

Bibliography

Abbas, T., 'British South Asians and pathways into Selective Schooling: Social Class, Culture and Ethnicity', *British Education Research Journal*, Vol. 33 (1), (February 2007), pp. 75–90.

Abbott, D., *Teachers and failing black boys*, The Observer (6 January 2002).

Abel-Smith, B., and Townsend, P., *The Poor and the Poorest* (London: G. Bell & Sons, 1966).

Abraham, J., *Divide and school: gender and class dynamics in comprehensive education* (London: Falmer Press, 1995).

Acheson, D., *Independent Inquiry into Inequalities in Health Report*, The Stationery Office (London, 1998).

Allan, G., and Crowe, G., 'Family Diversity and Change in Britain and Western Europe', *Journal of Family Issues*, Vol. 22 (7), (2001), pp. 819–837.

Allan, G., and Crowe, G., *Families, Households and Society* (Basingstoke, UK: Palgrave, 2001).

Allen, H., 'Using participant observation to immerse oneself in the field', *Journal in Research in Nursing*, Vol. 11 (5) (Sage publications, 2006), pp. 397–407

Althusser, L., *For Marx* (Allen Lane, The Penguin Press, 1969).

Anderson, E., *The Three Worlds of Welfare Capitalism* (New Jersey: Princeton University Press, 1990).

Anderson, M., *Approaches to the History of the Western Family* (London: Cambridge University Press, 1971).

Anderson, M., *Family, Household and the Industrial Revolution* (Penguin, 1971).

Archer, L., *The impossibility of girls' educational 'success': entanglements of gender, 'race', class and sexuality in the production and problematisation of educational femininities* (Centre for Public Policy Research, 2005).

Arkwright, P. D., and David, T. J., *Past mortality from infectious diseases and current burden of allergic diseases in England and Wales* (Cambridge University Press, 2005).

Arnot, M., 'Gendered Citizenry: new feminist perspectives on education and citizenship', *British Educational Research Journal*, 23 (3), (1997).

Arnot, M., *Citizenship Education and Gender* in *Education for Democratic Citizenship – Issues of Theory and Practice*, Lockyer, A., Crick, B., Annette, J., eds. (Aldershot, 2004), pp. 103–119.

Arnot, M., *Gender Inequality in the Classroom*, paper presented at *Beyond Access: Pedagogic Strategies for Gender Equality and Quality Basic Education in Schools*, Nairobi (2–3 February 2004).

Asthana, A., *Why single-sex education is not the route to better results*, The Observer, (25 June 2006), (Accessed 14 November 2007).

Atkinson, M., *Discovering Suicide* (London: Macmillan, 1968).

Autletta, K., *The Underclass* (Random House, 1982).

Avico, U., Kaplan, C., Korczak, D., and Van Meter, K., *Cocaine epidemiology in three European Community cities: a pilot study using a snowball sampling methodology* (European Communities Health Directorate: Brussels, 1988).

Baggini, J., National Centre for Social Research, *Welcome to Everytown* (Granta Books, 2007).

Ball, S. J., *Beachside Comprehensive: A Case Study of Secondary Schooling* (Cambridge University Press, 1986).

Ball, S., *Education for Sale, The Commodification of Everything* (Institute of Education, University of London, 2004).

Ball, S., *Sociology in Focus* (Longmans, 1986).

Barker, E., *The Making of a Moonie: Choice or Brainwashing* (Blackwell, 1984).

Barlow, A., Duncan, S., James, G., and Park, A., *Just a Piece of Paper? Marriage and Cohabitation in Britain* in *British Social Attitudes: The 18th Report*, Park, A., Curtice, J., Thomson, K., Jarvis, L., and Bromley, C., eds. (London: Sage, 2001), pp. 29–57.

Barlow, A., Duncan, S., James, G., Park, A., *Cohabitation, Marriage and the Law* (Hart Publishing, 2005).

Barnes, C., Mercer, G., and Shakespeare, T., *Exploring Disability: A Sociological Introduction* (Polity, 1999).

Basil, Bernstein, 'Class, Codes and Control', First Edition (London: Paladin, 1971)

Bates, D.G., and Plog, F., *Cultural Anthropology*, 3rd edition, (New York: McGraw-Hill, 1990).

Baudrillard, J,. *Screened Out* (New York: Verso Books, 2002), p. 174.

Baudrillard, J., *The Gulf War did not happen* (Blookington: Indiana Press, 1995), p. 85.

Baudrillard, J., *The System of Objects* (Verso Books, 2005).

BBC News, *Divorce rate lowest since 2000*, http://news.bbc.co.uk/1/hi/uk/5301270.stm (31 August 2006), (Accessed June 2007).

BBC News, *Record Number of New Minority MPs*, http://news.bbc.co.uk/1/hi/uk_politics/4530293.stm (Accessed 20 January 2008).

BBC, 'Shocking' racism in jobs market (BBC News, 12 July 2004).

BBC, *1995 The Future is Female* (Panorama, 1994).

BBC, *Broken home linked to psychosis*, http://news.bbc.co.uk/1/hi/health/6169120.stm (Accessed 2 January 2008).

BBC, *Divorce rates lowest since 2000*, http://news.bbc.co.uk/1/hi/uk/5301270.stm (Accessed. 4 July 2007).

BBC, *The Real Cost of Divorce*, http://news.bbc.co.uk/1/hi/business/6083814.stm (October 2006), (Accessed 1 July 2007).

BBC, *Women make men's GP appointments*, http://news.bbc.co.uk/1/hi/health/3646811.stm (2004), (Accessed 21 December 2007).

Beck U., and Beck-Gernsheim, E., *The Normal Chaos of Love* (Cambridge: Polity Press, 1995).

Becker, H. S., 'Social-Class Variations in the Teacher-Pupil Relationship', *Journal of Educational Society*, 25 (American Sociological Association, April 1952), pp. 451–65.

Becker, H., *Outsiders* (New York: The Free Press, 1963).

Beck-Gernsheim, E., *Reinventing the family: in search of new lifestyles*, Camiller, P., tr. (Oxford: Polity Press, 2002).

Bell, N. W., and Vogel, E. F., *The Emotionally Disturbed Child as a family Scapegoat* in *A modern introduction to the family*, Bell, N. W., and Vogel, E. F., eds. (New York: Free Press, 1968), pp. 382–97.

Berger, J., *Ways of Seeing* (Penguin Books, 1972).

Bernstein, B., *Social Class and Linguistic Development: a theory of social learning (a theory of social learning)* in *Education, economy and society: a reader in the sociology of education*, Halsey, A. H., Floud, J., and Anderson, C. A., eds. (New York,1961), p. 288.

Berrington, A., and Diamond, I., 'Marriage or cohabitation: a competing risks analysis of first-partnership formation among the 1958 British birth cohort', *Journal of the Royal Statistical Society*: Series A (Statistics in Society), Vol. 163 (2), (2000).

Berthoud, R., *Family Formation in Multi-Cultural Britain* (ISER, Institute for Social and Economic Research Working Paper: University of Essex, 2000).

Berthoud, R., *Family Formation in Multicultural Britain*, Institute for Social and Economic Research (Essex University, 2000).

Berthoud, R., *Family Formation in Multicultural Britain: Three Patterns of Diversity* (Institute for Social and Economic Research, 2000).

Berthoud, R., *The Incomes of the Ethnic Minorities*, (Colchester: University of Essex, Institute for Social and Economic Research, 1988).

Beveridge, W., *Social Insurance and Allied Services (Report on Social Security)* (London, HMSO, 1942).

Black, R. E., Morris, S. S., Bryce, J., 'Where and Why are 10 Million Children Dying Every Year?' *The Lancet*, Vol. 362. (London: Lynhurst Press Ltd., 19 July 2003)

Blacksacademy.net, *Family and Social Structure: The Changing Functions of the Family*, http://www.blacks.veriovps.co.uk/content/3274.html (Accessed 30 January 2008).

Blair, M., *Getting it: The challenge of raising black pupils' achievement in schools and local authorities*, Department for Children, Schools and Families (2007).

Blair, M., *Why Pick on Me? School Exclusions and Black Youth* (Stoke on Trent: Trentham Books, 2001).

Blane et al., *Social selection: what does it contribute to social class differences in health? Sociology of Health and Illness 1993* (1993), pp. 15:1–15.

Blaxter, M., and Paterson, E., *Mothers and Daughters: A Three-generational Study of Health Attitudes and Behavior* (London: Heinemann Educational Books, 1982).

Blaxter, M., *Health* (Cambridge: Polity Press, 2004).

Blaxter, M., *Health and Lifestyles* (London: Tavistock/Routledge, 1990).

Bly, R., *The Sibling Society* (Vintage Books, 1997).

Boardman, B., *Home Truths: A low Carbon Strategy to Reduce UK Housing Emissions by 80% by 2050*, University of Oxford's Environmental Change Institute. A research report for the Cooperative Bank and Friends of the Earth. (2007)

Boseley, S., *Social class key to child's success, Guardian*, http://www.guardian.co.uk/uk/2002/aug/09/socialsciences.artsandhumanities (Accessed 25 July 2007).

Bourdieu, P and Passeron, J.C. *Reproduction in Education, Society and Culture* (London: Sage, 1977).

Bowles, S., and Gintis, H., *Schooling in Capitalist America*, (New York: Basic Books, 1976).

Bradley, H., *Fractured Identities: Changing Patterns of Inequality* (Polity Press: Cambridge, 1997).

Brand, R. C., and Claiborn, W. L., 'Employer attitudes and practices toward rehabilitated convicts, mental and tuberculosis patients', *Community Mental Health Journal* 12 (1976), pp. 168–75.

Brand, R. C., and Claiborn, W. L., 'Two studies of comparative stigma. Employer attitudes and practices toward rehabilitated convicts, mental and tuberculosis patients', *Community Mental Health Journal* (1976), pp. 12: 168–175.

Brewer, M., Goodman, A., Muriel, A., and Sibieta, L., *Poverty and Inequality in the UK* (Institute for Fiscal Studies, 2007).

Brewer, M., Goodman, A., Muriel, A., Sibieta, L., *Poverty and Inequality in Great Britain*, Institute for Fiscal Studies (2007).

British Crime Survey, *Crime in England and Wales 04/05 Report, The Home Office* (2007).

Brown, S., *Private Health Care issues explained, Guardian*, (19 March 2001).

Bryman, A., *The Disneyization of Society* (Sage publications, 2004).

Bundy, R., *Mutual Benefits* in Health Service Journal, 111 (2001), p. 34.

Butler, I., Robinson, M., and Scanlan, L., *Children and decision making*, National Children's Bureau, *Understanding Children's Lives* (2005).

Byrne, L., *Forethought Britain in 2020*, The Labour Party (2003).

Carrington, B., 'The recruitment of new teachers from minority ethnic groups', *International Studies in Sociology of Education*, 10 (1), (2000), pp. 3–22.

Chamberlain, M., and Goulbourne, H., *The family as model and metaphor in Caribbean migration*, Journal of Ethnic and Migration Studies 25 (2), (London: Pluto, 1999), pp.319–29.

Chan, S., 'Oxford's South Asians as the entrepreneurial middle class', *Asian Pacific Business Review*, Vol. 4 (1), (October 1997), pp. 97–102.

Chesler, P., *Women and madness* (New York: Four Wall Eight Windows, 1997).

Childline, *A Childline Information Sheet: Step Families* (2007).

Coard, B., *How the West Indian Child is Made Educationally Sub-Normal in the British School System: The Scandal of the Black Child in Schools in Britain* (New Beacon Books, 1971).

Cole, M., *Racism, History and Educational Policy: from the origins of the Welfare State to the rise of the Radical Right*, unpublished Ph.D. thesis (University of Essex, 1992).

Collison, D., Dey, C., Hannah, G., Stevenson, L., 'Income inequality and child mortality in wealthy nations', *Journal of Public Health*, Vol. 29 (2), (10 October 1993), pp. 114–7.

Commission for Health Improvements, http://ratings2003.healthcarecommission.org.uk/ratings/ (Accessed 5 January 2008).

Commission for Healthcare Audit and Inspection, *Count me in* (2005).

Commission for Racial Equality, *Ethnic Minorities in Great Britain*, factfile 2, (London, March 2004).

Connolly, P. *Researching Racism in Education: Politics, Theory and Practice* (Buckingham: Open University Press, 1998).

Connolly, P., *Boys and Schooling in the Early Years* (London, Routledge, 2004).

Coombes, R., *Professor Ian Kennedy, the chairman of the Healthcare Commission Watchdog criticises unequal distribution of NHS funding* in British Medical Journal, (17 July 2004), pp. 329:130.

Couprie, H., *Time Allocation in the Family* (GREMAQ: Toulouse University, 2006).

Dahl, R., *Who Governs? Democracy and power in an American city*, (New Haven: Yale University Press, 1961).

Davis, K., and Moore, W., 'Some Principles of Stratification', *American Sociological Review*, Vol. 10 (2) 1944 Annual Meeting Papers (April 1945), pp. 242–9.

De Beauvoir, S., *The Second Sex* (Vintage Books, 1973).

Deal, M., *Attitudes of disabled people toward other disabled people and impairment groups* (City University, 2007).

Deitch, J., *Post Human* (New York: Distributed Art Publishers, 1991,

Delamont, S., *Sex roles and the school* (London: Routledge, 1990).

Delphy, C., *Familiar Exploitation: New Analysis of Marriage in Contemporary Western Societies*, Feminist Perspectives (Polity Press, 1992).

Dennis, N., and Erdos, G., *Families Without Fatherhood*, (London: Institute for the Study of Civil Society, 2000).

Department for Children, Schools and Families, *Aiming High: Raising the Achievement of Minority Ethnic Pupils* (2003).

Department for Children, Schools and Families, *Annual Statistical First Releases (2003/2004) Permanent and Fixed Period Exclusions from Schools and Exclusion Appeals in England*, Pupil Level Annual School Census (PLASC, 2004).

Department for Children, Schools and Families, *Ethnicity and Education: The Evidence on Minority Ethnic Pupils* (2006).

Department for Children, Schools and Families, *Exclusion of Black Pupils "Getting it. Getting it right"* (2006).

Department for Children, Schools and Families, *Five Year Strategy for Children and Learners* (2004).

Department for Children, Schools and Families, *Higher Standards, Better Schools for All: More choice for parents and pupils* (2005).

Department for children, schools and families, *Youth Cohort Study: Activities and Experiences of 17 Year Olds: England and Wales*, http://www.dcsf.gov.uk/rsgateway/DB/SFR/s000619/index.shtml (2005), (Accessed 12 September 2007).

Department for Work and Pensions, *Households below Average Income* (2007).

Department for Work and Pensions, *Making a Difference* (2007).

Department for Work and Pensions, *Pathways to Work: Helping people into employment* (2002).

Department of Health and Social Security, *The Black Report* (1990).

Department of Health, *Delivering Race Equality in Mental Health Care* (2005).

Department of Health, *Health Survey for England* (2005).

Department of Health, *Health Survey for England* (2007).

Department of Health, *The Health Survey for England* (2005).

Department of Transport, *Travel to Work Personal Factsheet*, (July 2007).

Derran, M. *McDonald and Tipton's oral history study Belfast in the 1930s*, www.sociology.org.uk/lbppmeth.ppt (1970), (Accessed 14 February 2008).

Dixon, A., and Le Grand, J., *Tackling Social Class Inequalities: Status Report on the Programme for Action* in *Is the NHS Equitable?* (Department of Health, 2003).

Dizaei, A., *Face up to the Figures*, The *Guardian* (18 September 2006), (Accessed 4 June 2007).

Dobash, E., and Dobash, R., *Violence against Wives, a Case study Against the Patriarchy* (Open books, 1980).

Dobson, B., Beardsworth, A., Keil, T., and Walker, R., *Diet, choice and poverty: Social cultural and nutritional aspects of food consumption among low-income families* (The Family's Policy Study Centre, 1994).

Doran, T., *Is there a north-south divide in social class inequalities in health in Great Britain? Cross sectional study using data from the 2001 census* in *British Medical Journal* (London, 2001).

Dorling, D., and Thomas, B., *People and places: A 2001 Census atlas of the UK* (The Policy Press, 2001).

Dorling, D., *Death in Britain: How Mortality Rates have changed 1950s to 1990s* (Joseph Rowntree Foundation, 1997).

Dorling, D., Rigby, J., Wheeler, B., Ballas, D., Thomas, B., Fahmy, E., Gordon, D., and Lupton, R., *Poverty, wealth and place in Britain 1968 to 2005* (Joseph Rowntree Foundation: Policy Press, 2007).

Dorling, D., Rigby, J., Wheeler, B., Ballas, D., Thomas, B., Fahmy, E., Gordon, D., and Lupton, R., *Poverty and Wealth across Britain 1968–2005* (Joseph Rowntree Foundation, 2007).

Douglas, J. W. B., *The Home and School* (MacGibbon and Kee, 1964).

Doyle, L., *Sex, Gender and Heath* in *British Medical Journal* 061 (2001) 323, pp. 1061–3.

Drew, D., and Munn, S., *Researching Discrimination in Employment, Department for Work and Pensions* (DWP, 2007).

Drew, J., *Cultural Tourism and the Commodified Other: Reclaiming Difference in the Multicultural Classroom*, The Review of Education, 19 (1997).

Dunscombe, J., and Marsden, D., *Love and intimacy: The gender division of emotion and emotion work*, Sociology, 27 (2), (1993), pp. 221–42.

Durex, *Give and Receive 2005 Global Survey Results*, http://www.durex.com/cm/gss2005result.pdf (2005), (Accessed 12 June 2007).

Durkheim, E., *Moral education* (Glencoe: The Free Press, 1961).

Durkheim, E., *Suicide* (New York: Free Press, 1951).

Durkheim, E., *The Division of Labour in Society*, Simpson, G., tr. (New York: The Free Press, 1893).

Eastwood, S. L., and Harrison, P. J., *Hippocampal synaptic pathology in schizophrenia, bipolar disorder and major depression: a study of complexion mRNAs*, Departments of Psychiatry and Clinical Neurology (Neuropathology) (University of Oxford, UK, 1998).

Economic and Social Research Council, *Changing Households and Family Structures and Complex Living Arrangements*, ESRC Seminar Series, *Mapping the Public Policy Landscape* (2006).

Economic and Social Research Council, *Research Ethics Framework* (2005).

Edgell, S., *Middle Class Couples* (London: Allen and Unwin, 1980).

Edleson, J., *Children's Witnessing of Adult Violence*, Journal of Interpersonal Violence 14 (8) (1999).

Edwards, R., *Parenting and Step-parenting after divorce/separation: issues and negotiations* (2004). London, South Bank University.

Eliot, L., *Inequality at the same level as under Thatcher*, The *Guardian* (18 May 2007).

Elliott, J., Hufton, N., Illushin, L., and Willis, W., *The kids are doing all right*, Cambridge Journal of Education, 31, (2002), pp. 179–204.

Elwood, J., *Gender and achievement: What Have Exams Got to Do with It*, Oxford Review for Education (2005).

Elwood, J., Gipps, C., *How effective is single sex teaching?* www.literacytrust.org.uk/Research/ressinglesex.html, National Literacy Trust (1999), (Accessed) last accessed October 5th 2007.

Engels, F., *The Origin of the Family, Private Property, and the State* (London: Lawrence & Wishart, 1940).

Equal Opportunities Commission, *Overview of the Gender Equality* (February 2007), (Accessed 3 February 2007).

Equal Opportunities Commission, *Sex and Power: Who Runs Britain?* http://www.equalityhumanrights.com/Documents/EOC/PDF/Unpublished/Sex%20and%20power%20who%20runs%20Britain%202007.pdf (2007), (Accessed 10 October 2007).

Equal Opportunities Commission, *The Gender Agenda*, http://www.gender-agenda.co.uk/ (Accessed 3 July 2007).

Erens B., McManus S., Field J., Korovessis C., Johnson A. M., Fenton K. A., *National Survey of Sexual Attitudes and Lifestyles II: Technical Report*, National Centre for Social Research, (2001).

Erickson, R. J. *Reconceptualising family work: The effect of emotion work on perceptions of marital quality 1993*, The Journal of Marriage (1997).

Family Planning Association, *Teenage Pregnancy*, http://www.fpa.org.uk/information/factsheets/documents_and_pdfs/detail.cfm?contentid=113 p.196 – UNICEF (December 2007), (Accessed 28 May 2008).

Fawcett Society, *One in Four* (Age Concern England: London, 2003).

Feinstein, L., Hearn, B. and Renton, Z., *Reducing Inequalities: Realising the talents of all*, National Children's Bureau (2007).

Feinstein, L., Wyse, B., Leslie, C., *Fade or Flourish*, Institute of Education (2007).

Figueroa, P., *Education and The Social Construct of Race*, (Routledge, 1991).

Fletcher, R., *The Family and Marriage in Britain*, (Harmondsworth: Penguin, 1966).

Forde, C., *Tackling Gender Inequality: Raising Pupil Achievement*, (Edinburgh: Dunedin Press, 2006).

Foster, J., *Villains: Crime and the Community in the Inner City* (Routledge, 1990).

Foster, P., *Cases not proven: an evaluation of two studies of teacher racism*, British Educational Research Journal, 16 (1990), pp. 335–49.

Foster, P., *Policy and Practice in Multicultural and Anti-Racist Education: a case study of a multi-ethnic comprehensive school* (Routledge, 1990).

Foucault, M., *Civilisation and Health* (Vintage, 1988).

Foucault, M., *The History of Sexuality* (Harmandsworth: Penguin, 1976).

Francis, J., *Step Families*, http://www.channel4.com/health/microsites/F/family/21st/stepfamilies.html (June 2005), (Accessed 5 July 2007).

Freidson, E., *Profession of Medicine: A Study of the Sociology of Applied Knowledge* (Dodd Mead, 1970).

Furlong, A., and Forsyth, A., *Losing out? Socioeconomic disadvantage and experience in further and higher education* (Joseph Rowntree Foundation: Policy Press, 2003).

Gallagher, M., and Waite, L. J., *The Case for Marriage: Why Married People Are Happier, Healthier, and Better Off Financially* in Journal of Marriage and the Family (New York: Doubleday, 1990).

Gane, M., *Auguste Comte* (Routledge, 2006).

Garner, R., *Black pupils 'failing under pressure from peers'*, Independent (9 December 2002).

Gaskell, E., *Mary Barton*, Oxford World Classics (Oxford University Press, 2006).

Gaskell, E., *North and South* (Wodsworth Editions, 1993).

Gaskell, E., *Ruth* (Penguin Classics, 1988).

Gaunlett, D., *Media, Gender and Identity* (London, Routledge, 2002).

Giddens, A., *Modernity and Self-Identity: Self and Society in the Late Modern Age* (Stanford: Stanford University Press, 1991), pp. 187–201.

Gillborn, D., and Mirza, H., *Educational Inequality: Mapping Race, Class and Gender*, www.ofsted.com (OFSTED, 2000). Last accessed November 7th 2007.

Gillborn, D., *Written Evidence on the Education White Paper (2005): race inequality, 'gifted & talented' students and the increased use of 'setting by ability'* (University of London, 2005).

Gillborn, D., Youdell, D., *Rationing Education: policy, practice, reform and equity* (Open University Press, 2000).

Gilroy, P., *There Ain't No Black in the Union Jack* (Routledge, 2002).

Gingerbread, *Lone Parents and Employment*, http://www.gingerbread.org.uk/information-and-advice/LoneParentsEmployment.htm (Accessed 23 December 2007).

Gittens, D., *Is Childhood Socially Constructed?* (New York: St Martins Press, 1998).

Gittens, D., *The Child In Question* (Macmillan Press, 1998).

Goffman, E., *Asylums: Essays on the Condition of the Social Situation of Mental Patients and Other Inmates* (New York: Doubleday, 1961)

Goffman, E., *Stigma: Notes on the Management of Spoiled Identity* (Spectrum, 1963).

Goffman, E., *The Presentation of the Self in Everyday Life* (University of Edinburgh, Social Sciences Research Centre, 1959).

Goode, W. J., *World Revolution and Family Patterns* (New York: Free Press, 1963).

Gordon, D., and Townsend, P., *Child Poverty in the Developing World* (Policy Press, 2003).

Gornick, V., *The Daily Illini* (Urbana, 1981).

Goss, D., Goss, F., and Smith, D. A., *Disability and employment: a comparative critique of UK legislation*, International Journal of Human Resource Management, 11, (2000), pp. 807–21.

Gove, W. L., 'The Family and Delinquency', *The Sociological Quarterly* 23, 301-319 (1982).

Graham, H., *Women, Health and the Family* (Brighton: Wheatsheaf Books, 1984).

Gray, A., 'We want good jobs and more pay': The new dealers who still have no jobs, Local Economy Policy Unit (South Bank University, March 2000).

Greater London Authority, Black teachers in London (2006).

Green, J.,ed., Zuni: The Selective writing of Frank Hamilton Cushing (University of Nebraska Press, December 1981).

Griffin, C., Typical girls? Young women from school to job market … Constructing female identities (London: Routledge and Kegan Paul, 1985).

Griffiths, P., Gossop, M., Powis, B., and Strang, J., 'Reaching hidden populations of drug users by privileged access interviewers: methodological and practical issues', Addiction, Vol. 88 (1993), pp. 1617–26.

Grundy, E., 'Reciprocity in relationships: socio-economic and health influences on intergenerational exchanges between Third Age parents and their adult children in Great Britain' in British Journal of Sociology, 56 (2), (2005) pp. 233–55.

Gurshunny, J., Lader, D., and Short, S., The Time Use Survey: How we spend our Time, Office for National Statistics, 2005).

Hammersley, M. Constructing Educational Inequality (London: Falmer, 1996).

Hansen, K., and Joshi, H., eds., National Child Development Study, Millennium Cohort Study, Centre for Longitudinal Studies (2007).

Haralambos, M., and Holborn, M., Sociology, Themes and Perspectives (Collins, 2004).

Haralambos, M., Sociology Themes and Perspectives (Collins, 2004).

Hardill, I., A tale of two nations? Juggling work and home in the new economy in The Economic and Social Research Council Seminar Series, 2003,

Hargreaves, D. H, Social Relation in a Secondary School (London: Routledge and Kegan Paul, 1967).

Hargreaves, D. H., Social Relations in a Secondary School (Humanities Press, 1967).

Harris, A., Handicapped and Impaired in Great Britain (Her Majesty's Stationery Office, 1971).

Harris, A., Wood International Classification of Impairments, Disabilities and Handicaps (International Classification of Impairments, Disabilities and Handicaps, 1971).

Harris, J., and Grace, S., A question of evidence? Investigating and prosecuting rape in the 1990s (Home Office: London, 1999).

Harrison, G., and Eaton W., Migration and the Social Epidemiology of Schizophrenia, Hafner, H., ed. (Steinkopff Darmstadt, 2002).

Hart, J. T., 'The inverse care law', The Lancet. 1971; 1 (7696) pp. 405–12.

Health and Safety Executive, Health and Safety Statistics, http://www.hse.gov.uk/statistics/overpic.htm (Accessed 6 December 2007).

Health Knowledge, Lay Health Beliefs and Illness Behaviour, http://www.healthknowledge.org.uk/Medical%20Sociology/HK%204a%20section%204.htm (1984), (Accessed 9 November 2007).

Heather, N., Radical perspectives in psychology (London: Methuen, 1976).

Held, D., Models of Democracy, fully revised, second edition (Polity Press, 1996).

Helman, C., Culture, Health and Illness: an introduction for health professional (Hodder Arnold, 2000).

Hendrick, H., Children, childhood, and English society, 1880–1990, Economic History Society (Cambridge, England, 1997).

Her Majesty's Stationery Office, Children and their Primary Schools, The Plowden Report: A Report of the Central Advisory Council for Education (London, 1967).

Her Majesty's Stationery Office, The British Crime Survey (2007).

Hester, M, Pearson, C, Harwin, N, Making an Impact: Children and Domestic Violence (2000, London: Jessica Kingsley).

Higher Education Funding Council for England, Participation of Lower income Groups (DFES, 2001).

Himmelweit, H., Humphreys, P., and Jaeger, M., How Voters Decide, revised edition (Open University Press, 1985).

Hochschild, A., The Second Shift, (Viking Adult, 1989).

Hock, R. R., Forty Studies That Changed Psychology: Explorations Into the History of Psychological Research 4th Edition (Upper Saddle River, NJ: Prentice-Hall. 2002), pp. 221–9.

Holdaway, S., 'Changes in Urban Policing', British Journal of Sociology 28 (2), (1977), pp. 119–37.

Home Office, Crime and Victims, http://www.homeoffice.gov.uk/crime-victims/reducing-crime/domestic-violence/ (Accessed 24 July 2007).

Home Office, Crime in England and Wales 2002–3, http://www.homeoffice.gov.uk/rds/crimeew0203.html (Crown Copyright, 2004), (Accessed 8 July 2007).

Home Office, Crime in England and Wales 2004/2005, http://www.homeoffice.gov.uk/rds/crimeew0405.html (Crown Copyright, 2005), (Accessed 8 October 2007).

Home Office, Crime in England and Wales 2006/2007, http://www.homeoffice.gov.uk/rds/crimeew0607.html (Crown Copyright, 2006), (Accessed 10 October 2007).

Home Security Action, Domestic Violence…Accounts for 17% Of All Violent Crime In The UK, http://www.home-security-action.co.uk/domestic-violence.html (Accessed 25 July 2007).

Howe, C., Gender and classroom interaction: a research review (Edinburgh: Scottish Council for Research in Education, 1997).

Human Rights Watch, World Report 2007, http://www.hrw.org/wr2k7/ (Accessed 5 November 2007).

Humphreys, C., and Thiara, R., Routes to Safety, Women's Aid, (Bristol, 2002).

Hunt, K., and Ford, G., Are women more ready to consult than men? Gender differences in general practitioner consultation for common chronic conditions in Journal of Health Services Research and Policy (1999), pp. 4:96–100.

Hunte, C., 'Inequality, Achievement and African-Caribbean Pupils', Race Equality Teaching, Vol. 22 (3), (Summer 2004).

Huxley P, and Rogers, A, 'State-event relations among indicators of susceptibility to mental distress in Wythenshawe in the UK', Social Science and Medicine, 55 (6) (2001), pp. 921–35.

Huxley, P., and Rogers, A., 'Evaluating the impact of a locality based social policy intervention on mental health: conceptual and methodological issues' in International Journal Of Social Psychiatry, Vol. 47 (4) (2001).

Iezzoni, L., Towards Universal Design in Assessing Health Care Experiences, Medical Care 40 (2002).

Illich, I., Medical Nemesis: Cultural Iatrogenesis (Pantheon Books, 1976).

Inciardi, J. A., *In search of the class canon: a field study of professional pickpockets* in *Street Ethnography: Selected Studies of Crime and Drug Use in Natural Settings*, Weppner, R. S., ed. (Beverley Hills: Sage, 1977).

Institute for Public Policy Research, The *Guardian* (7 September 2002).

Iversen, L., Andersen, O., Andersen, P. K., Christoffersen, K., and Keiding, N., *Unemployment and mortality in Denmark, 1970–80* in *British Medical Journal* (1987), pp. 295:879–84.

Jackson, B., and Marsden, D., *Education and the Working Class* (Penguin History, 1999).

Jackson, D., *Masculine identities* in *Failing Boys*, Epstein, D., Elwood, J., Hey, V., and Maw, J., (Oxford University Press, 1998).

Jackson, P., *Life in Classrooms*, (Peter Lang Publishing, 1988).

Jamous, H., and Peloille, B., *Changes in the French university hospital system* in *Professions and Professionalisation*, Jackson, J.A., ed. (Cambridge University Press, 1970).

Jamous, H., and Peloille, B., *The mystification of medical knowledge* in *Professions or Self Perpetuating System, Changes in the French University Hospital System* (Cambridge University Press, 1970).

Jary, D., and Jary J., *Collins Dictionary of Sociology* (Glasgow: HarperCollins, 1991)

Jayatilaka, G., and Rake, K., *Home Truths an Analysis of Financial Decision Making in the Home* (Fawcett Society, 2002).

Jefferies , B. J. M. H., Power, C., and Hertzman, C., *Birth weight, childhood socioeconomic environment, and cognitive development in the 1958 British birth cohort study* in *British Medical Journal* (10 August 2002), pp. 325:305.

Jesson D, and Crossley, D, *Educational Outcomes and Value Added by Specialist Schools* (Specialist Schools and Academies Trust, 2004).

Johnstone, D., *An Introduction to Disability Studies*, second edition (London: David Fulton Publishers, 2001).

Kaplan, C. D., Korf, D., and Sterk, C., 'Temporal and social contexts of heroin-using populations: an illustration of the snowball sampling technique', *Journal of Mental and Nervous Disorders*, Vol. 175 (9) (1987), pp. 566–74.

Keddie, N., *Classroom Knowledge* in *Knowledge and Control*, Young, M. F. D., ed. (London: Collier-Macmillan, 1971).

Kegan, P., *Black Girls in a London Comprehensive School* in *Schooling for Women's Work*, Deem, R., ed. (Routledge, 1980).

Kelly, A., *Science for Girls* (Milton Keynes: Open University Press, 1987).

Kenway, P., and Palmer, G., *Poverty among ethnic groups: how and why does it differ?* (New Policy Institute, 2007).

Kenway, P., Parsons, N., Carr, J., and Palmer, G., *Monitoring Poverty and Social Exclusion* (The Joseph Rowntree Foundation, 2005).

King's College, *The Blofeld Report*, (London, 2003).

Kings Fund, *Access to health care and minority ethnic groups* (2006). http://www.kingsfund.org.uk/publications/briefings/access_to_health.html

Kitsuse, J., and Cicourel, A., 'A Note in the Use of Official Statistics', *Social Problems*, 11, (1963), pp. 131–9.

Kituse and Cicourel, *The Educational Decision Makers* (The Bobbs Merrill Company, 1963).

Kleinman, A., *Patients and healers in the context of culture: an exploration of the borderland between anthropology, medicine, and psychiatry* (Los Angeles: University of California Press, 1980).

Krause, I, B, *Sinking heart: a Punjabi communication of distress, Social Science and Medicine*, 29 (4), (1989), pp. 563–75.

Krause, I, B, *Therapy Across Culture* (London: Sage Publications, 1989).

Krueger, R, Casey, M. A, *Focus groups: A practical guide for applied research*, 3rd edition, Thousand Oaks (Sage, 2000).

Kruger, D. J., 'Integrating quantitative and qualitative methods in community research', *The Community Psychologist*, 36 (2003), pp. 18–9.

Lacey, C., 'Hightown Grammar: The School as a Social System', *British Journal of Educational Studies*, Vol. 19 (1), (February 1971).

Laing, R. D., and Esterton, A., *Sanity, Madness and the Family* (Penguin, 1970).

Lampl, P., *Educational Opportunities Declining in Modern Britain*, (*Eastern Daily Press*, 20 December 2005).

Landman J., Cruickshank J. K., 'A review of ethnicity, health and nutrition-related diseases in relation to migration in the United Kingdom', *Public Health Nutrition*, 4 (2B) (2001), pp. 647–57.

Laslett, P., *The World we have lost* (Methuen & Co, 1972).

Le Grand, J., and Dixon, A., 'Is the NHS Equitable? A Review of the Evidence', *Health and Social Care Discussion Paper Series*, London School of Economics and Political Science, 11 (2003).

Le Grand, J., *Can we afford the Welfare State?* in *British Medical Journal* 307 (1993), pp. 1018-19.

Leach, E., *A Runaway World*, BBC (1968).

Lewis, O, *Five Families: Mexican Case Studies in the Culture of Poverty*, (Perseus Books, 1959).

Lewis, O, *The Children of Sanchez, Autobiography Of A Mexican Family*, (New York: Random House, 1961).

Lewis, O., *Life in a Mexican Village: Tepoztlan Restudied* (University of Illinois Press, 1951).

Lewis, O., *The Sexual life of Savages in Northwest Melanesia* (New York: Liveright, 1929).

Liamputtong, P., and Douglas, E., *Qualitative research methods* (Oxford University Press, 2005) p.45.

Licht, B., and Dwect, C., *Some Differences in Achievement Orientations* in *Sex differentiation and schooling*, Marland, M., ed. (London:Heinemann, 1983).

Link, B. G., 'A Modified Labelling Theory Approach to Mental Disorders: An Empirical Assessment', *American Sociological Review* pp. 54:400–23, 1987

Link, B. G., 'Understanding Labeling Effects in Mental Disorders: An Assessment of Expectations of Rejection', *American Sociological Review* (1987), pp. 52:96–112.

Link, B. G., Cullen, F., Frank, J., and Wozniak, J., 'The Social Rejection of Ex-Mental Patients: Understanding Why Labels Matter', *American Journal of Sociology*, 92 (1989), pp. 1461–500.

Link, B. G., Struening, E, Rahav, M, Phelan, J.C and Nuttbrock, L 'On Stigma and Its Consequences: Evidence from a Longitudinal Study of Men with Dual Diagnoses of Mental Illness and Substance Abuse', *Journal of Health and Social Behavior* (1977), pp. 38:117–90.

Littlewood, R., and Lipsedge, M., *Aliens and Alienists: Ethnic Minorities and Psychiatry* (London: Routledge, 1997).

Lupton, D., *Medicine as Culture: illness, disease and the body in Western societies* (London: Sage, 1994).

Lyon, N., Barnes, M., and Sweiry, D., *Families with Children in Britain: Findings from the 2004 Families and Children Survey* (Department of Work and Pensions, 2006).

Lyotard, J. F., *The Post Modern Condition* (Manchester University Press, 2004).

Mac an Ghaill, M., *The Making of Men: Masculinities, Sexualities and Schooling* (Buckingham: Open University Press, 1994).

Mac an Ghaill, M., *Young, Gifted and Black* (Open University Press, 1988).

Macalister, F., *Marital Breakdown and the Health of the Nation*, 2nd Edition, (One plus One, 1995).

Macalister, F., *Marital Breakdown and the Health of the Nation*, 2nd Edition, www.oneplusone.org.uk *last accessed January 6th 2008*.

Machin, S., and McNally, S., *Gender and Student Achievement in English Schools*, Oxford Review of Economic Policy (2005).

Macy, R. J., Nurius, P. S., Norris, J., 'Responding in her best interests: Contextualizing women's coping with acquaintance sexual aggression', *Violence Against* Women,12 (5) (2006), pp. 478–500.

Malinowski, B., *Argonauts of the Western Pacific* (New York: E.P. Dutton & Co. Inc, 1922).

Marmot, M. G., Shipley, M. J., Rose, G., 'Inequalities in death – Specific explanations of a general pattern?' *The Lancet* (1984), pp. 1003–6.

Marmot, M., et al., 'Health Inequalities amongst British Civil Servants', *The Lancet* 337 (1991), pp. 1387–93.

Marmot, M., *Scientific Reference Group of Health Inequalities study* (Department of Health, 2005).

Martikainen, P., and Valkonen, T., 'Excess mortality of unemployed men and women during a period of rapidly increasing unemployment', *The Lancet* (1996), pp. 348:208–213.

McCreith, S., Ross, A., and Hutchings, M., *Teacher Supply and Retention 2001: A study of twenty two Local Education Authorities* (London: Teacher Training Agency, 2001).

McKeown, *The Role of Medicine* (Blackwell publishers, 1979).

McRobbie, A., and Garber, J., *Girls and Subcultures* in *The Subcultures Reader*, Gelder, K., and Thornton, S. (Routledge, 1975).

McRobbie, A., *Girls and Subcultures* (Hutchinson, 1975).

McRobbie, A., *Girls and Subcultures*, in *Resistance through rituals: youth subcultures in post-war Britain*, Hall, S., and Jefferson, T., eds. (Hutchinson, 1976).

Meltzer, B., *The Social Psychology of George Herbert Mead* in *Symbolic Interaction: A Reader in Social Psychology* (Allyn & Bacon, 1978).

Meltzer, H., and Jenkins, R., 'The national survey of psychiatric morbidity in Great Britain', *Social Psychiatry Psychiatric Epidemiology* 30 (1995), pp.1–4.

Mental Health Foundation, *Statistics on Mental Health*. http://www.mentalhealth.org.uk/information/mental-health-overview/statistics/ (Accessed 14 December 2007).

Mental Health Foundation, *The Fundamental Facts* (London: Pavillion, 1999).

Merton, R. K, *Social Theory and Social Structure* (New York: Free Press, 1968).

Merton, R. K., 'Social Structure and Anomie', *American Sociological Review* 3 (1938) pp. 672–82.

Millband, R., *The State in Capitalist Society* (Quartet Books Ltd, 1968).

Miller, W., *Lower Class Subculture as a Generating Milieu of Gang Delinquency*, *Journal of Social Issues*. Vol. 14 (1958), pp. 5–20.

Millett, K., *Sexual Politics*, (Doubleday: New York, 1970).

Miniwatts Marketing Group, *Internet Usage Statistics: The Internet Big Picture*, http://www.internetworldstats.com/stats.htm (2007), (Accessed 6 June 2007).

Mirza, H. S., *Young, Female and Black* (London: Routledge, 1992).

Mitsos, E., and Browne, K., 'Gender differences in education: The underachievement of boys', *Sociology Review*, 18 (1) (1998), pp. 27–31.

Morgan, C., 'Raised incidence of schizophrenia and other psychoses in ethnic minority groups in three English cities', *Psychological Medicine*, 36 (2006), pp. 1541–50.

Morgan, P., *Family Policy, Family Changes: Sweden, Italy and Britain Compared* (Civitas, 2006).

Morris, E., *Boys will be Boys* (Policy Press, 1996).

Morris, E., *Boys will be Boys* (The Labour Party, 1976).

Morris, J.K., Cook, D. G., Shaper, A. G., *Loss of employment and mortality* in *British Medical Journal* (1994), pp. 308:1135–9.

Moser, K. A., Fox A. J., and Jones D. R., 'Unemployment and mortality', OPCS longitudinal study, *The Lancet* (1984), pp. ii:1324–8.

Moynihan, R., *Who pays for the pizza? Redefining the relationships between doctors and drug companies* in *British Medical Journal* 326 (2003), pp. 1189–92.

Murdock, G., *Sociology, themes and perspectives*, 6th edition (London: Collins, 2004), p. 466.

Myers, J. K., *Life Events, Social Integration and Psychiatric Symptomatology* in *Journal of Health and Social Behaviour*, Vol. 16 (4), (special issue on 'Recent Developments in the "Sociology of Mental Illness"') (December 1975), pp. 421–7.

Myers, J. K., *Suicide Attempts and Recent Life Events: A Controlled Comparison*, Arch Gen Psychiatry (1975), pp. 32:327–37.

National Centre for Social Research, *British Social Attitude Survey*, http://www.data-archive.ac.uk/findingData/snDescription.asp?sn = 5823 (2006), (Accessed 14 February 2008).

National Centre for Social Research, *The British Social Attitudes Survey*, http://www.data-archive.ac.uk/findingData/snDescription.asp?sn = 4615 (2001), (Accessed 14 February 2008).

National Society for the Prevention of Cruelty to Children, *Facts and Figures about Child Abuse*, http://www.nspcc.org.uk/WhatWeDo/MediaCentre/MediaResources/facts_and_figures_wda33295.html (Accessed 23 July 2007).

Navarro, V., *Class Struggle, the State and Medicine: An historical and contemporary analysis of the medical sector in Great Britain* (Medicine in society series), (London: Martin Robertson, 1978).

Navarro, V., *Medicine Under Capitalism* (Croom Helm, 1979).

Nazroo, J., *Ethnicity and Mental Health* (Policy Studies Institute, 1997).

Nelson, W., Future Foundation, *Middle Britain*, http://www. futurefoundation.net/publications.php?disp = 236 (Accessed 2 June 2007).

NHS Information Centre, *Hospital Episode Statistics*. http://www. ic.nhs.uk/statistics-and-data-collections/hospital-care/hospital-activity-hes/hospital-episode-statistics-admitted-patient-care-england-2006-07 (Accessed 7 March 2008).

Norman, F., et al., *Look Jane, look: anti-sexist initiatives in primary schools* (Open University Press, 1988).

Norris, J., George, W. H., Stoner, S. A., Masters, N. T., Zawacki, T., and Davis, K. C., *Women's responses to sexual aggression: The effects of child trauma, alcohol and prior relationship. Experimental and Clinical Psychopharmacology*, 14 (2006), pp. 402–11.

O'Connor, J. *Accumulation Crisis* (New York: Blackwell, 1984).

O'Donnell, M., *A New Introduction to Sociology* (London: Nelson, 1992).

O'Neill, O., A Question of Trust, Reith Lectures (2002).

Oakley, A., *Becoming a Mother* (Oxford: Martin Robertson), under the title *From Here to Maternity* (Harmondsworth: Penguin, 1979).

Oakley, A., *Subject Woman*, (Oxford: Martin Robertson, 1981).

Oakley, A., *The Captured Womb: A history of the medical care of pregnant women* (Oxford: Basil Blackwell, 1984).

Oakley, A., *The Sociology of Housework* (London: Martin Robertson, 1974).

Office for National Statistics, *2001 Census*, http://www.statistics. gov.uk/census2001/census2001.asp (Accessed 8 December 2007).

Office for National Statistics, Department for Education and Skills, *National Curriculum Assessment, GCSE and Equivalent Attainment and Post-16 Attainment by Pupil Characteristics in England 2004, Statistical First Release*, http://www.dcsf.gov.uk/ rsgateway/DB/SFR/s000640/SFR09_2006.pdf (2005), (Accessed 9 December 2007).

Office for National Statistics, *General Household Survey, Living in Britain*, (Crown, 2005).

Office for National Statistics, *Labour Force Survey* (ESDS, 2002).

Office for National Statistics, *Labour Force Survey* (ESDS, 2004).

Office for National Statistics, *Labour Force Survey* (ESDS, 2006).

Office for National Statistics, *Labour Force Survey*, (ESDS, 2003).

Office for National Statistics, *Labour Force Survey*, (ESDS, 2005).

Office for National Statistics, *Labour Market Review* (2006).

Office for National Statistics, *Live births outside marriage: age of mother and type of registration, 1971 onwards*, Population Trends, 132, (2004).

Office for National Statistics, *Living in Britain, General Household Survey* (Crown, 2002).

Office for National Statistics, *Living in Britain, General Household Survey* (Crown, 2004).

Office for National Statistics, *Low Pay Estimates* (2006).

Office for National Statistics, *Marriage, Divorce and Adoption Statistics* (Crown, 2008).

Office for National Statistics, *Mortality Statistics, child, infant and Perinatal*, http://www.statistics.gov.uk/STATBASE/Product. asp?vlnk = 6305 (2007), (Accessed 25 February 2008).

Office for National Statistics, *Mortality statistics: Review of the Registrar General on deaths by cause, sex and age, in England and Wales* (London, 2005).

Office for National Statistics, *Pupil Level Annual Schools Census and Termly Exclusions Survey, Department for Education and Skills; Annual Population Survey, January 2004 to December 2004*, http://www.statistics.gov.uk/cci/nugget.asp?id = 461 (Accessed 29 December 2007).

Office for National Statistics, *Social Trends*, 37 http://www. statistics.gov.uk/socialtrends37/ (2007), (Accessed 7 October 2007).

Ofsted, *The Gender Divide*, Equal Opportunities Commission, Her Majesty's Stationery Office (1996).

Oliver, M., *The Politics of Disablement*, (Basingstoke: Palgrave Macmillan, 2000).

Oliver, M., *Understanding Disability from Theory to Practice* (Macmillan Press, 1996).

Orton, M., and Rowlington, K., *Public attitudes to economic inequality* (Joseph Rowntree Foundation, 2007).

Osler, A and Starkey, H eds., *Citizenship and Democracy in Real Schools: Diversity, Identity, Equality* (Trentham Books, 2000).

Ots, T, The angry liver, the anxious heart and the melancholy spleen: the phenomenology of perceptions', *Chinese culture, Culture, Medicine and Psychiatry* 14 (1990), pp. 21–58.

Pahl, J., and Vogler, C., *Social and economic change and the organisation of money within marriage*, Work, Employment and Society, 7, (1) (1993), pp. 71–95.

Palmer, G., Howarth C., Kenway, P., and Miorelli, R., *Monitoring poverty and social exclusion* (Joseph Rowntree Foundation, 1999).

Palmer, G., MacInnes, T., and Kenway P., *Monitoring poverty and social exclusion* (Joseph Rowntree Foundation, 2006).

Parentline Plus, *Being a Stepfamily* (2005).

Parliamentary Office of Science and Technology, *Ethnicity and Health*, http://www.parliament.uk/documents/upload/ postpn276.pdf (2007), (Accessed 8 March 2008).

Parsons, T., and Bales, R. F., 'Socialization and Interaction Process', *American Anthropologist*, New Series, Vol. 58 (6), (Dec. 1956).

Patrick, J., *A Glasgow Gang Observed* (London: Methuen, 1973).

Patton, G. C., Coffey, C., Posterino, M., et al., 'Life events and early onset depression: cause or consequence?', *Psychological Medicine*, 33 (2003), pp. 1203–10.

Patton. G.C, Coffey, C and Posterino, M. *Life events and early onset depression: cause or consequence* (University of Melbourne, 2003).

Pease, K., and Farrell, G., *Crime in England and Wales: More Violence and More Chronic Victims*, CIVITAS (2007).

Peck, S., *NHS superbugs on the rise*, http://www.telegraph. co.uk/news/uknews/1549722/NHS-superbugs-on-the-rise.html (Accessed 21 January 2008).

Penn, R., and Soothill, K., *Ethical Issues in Social Inquiry: the Enemy Within?* (Lancaster University, 2006).

Philippe, A., *Centuries of Childhood* (Vintage books, 1962).

Piachaud, D., *Peter Townsend and the Holy Grail*, New Society (10 September, 1981), pp.419–21.

Pill, R. M., and Stott, N. C. H., *Concepts of illness causation and responsibility* (London: Heineman, 1982).

PLAN, *Growing up in Asia* (2005).

Platt, L., 'Making Education Count: the effects of ethnicity and qualifications on intergenerational social class mobility', *The Sociological Review*, Vol. 55 (3), (Blackwell Publishing, August 2007).

Platt, L., *Poverty and Ethnicity in the UK* (Policy Press, 2007).

Platt, L., *The intergenerational social mobility of minority ethnic groups*, Working Paper 2003–24 of the Institute for Social and Economic Research, Poverty and Ethnicity in the UK (Colchester: University of Essex, 2003).

Policy Studies Institute, *Caribbeans at no greater risk of severe mental illness*, press release (1997).

Pollok, M., and Schlitz, M. A., *Does voluntary testing matter? How it influences homosexual safer sex*, paper presented at the Fourth International Conference on AIDs (Stockholm, Sweden, 13 June 1998).

Postman, N., *Amusing ourselves to Death* (Methuen, 1985).

Prior, P. M., *Gender and mental health* (Basingstoke: Macmillan Press, 1999).

Pulp Fiction

Punch, M., *Rotten Barrels: Systemic origins of corruption* in *Strategieen voor corruptie-beheersing bij de polei.t Arnhem: Gouda Quint*, E.W. Kolthoff, ed. (1994).

Rahkonen, O., Arber, S., and Lahelma, E., *Health-related social mobility: a comparison of currently employed men and women in Britain and Finland* in *Scandinavian Journal of Social Medicine*, 25 (1997), pp. 83–92.

Raja, F., and Thandi, R., *The Impact of Domestic Violence*, EACH specialist counselling & support service (2007).

Ramos, X., *Housework and Paid Work: Continuing Contrasts in the Time Spent by Husbands and Wives*, Institute for Social and Economic Research, (Essex University, 2003).

Reay, D., 'Useful Extension of Bourdieu's Conceptual Framework? Emotional capital as a way of understanding mothers' involvement in their children's education', *The Sociological Review*, Vol. 4 (2004) pp. 568–85.

Reay, D., et al., *Cultural Reproduction: mothers' involvement in their children's primary schooling*, in *Bourdieu and Education: acts of practical theory*, Grenfell, M., and James, D., eds. (London: Falmer Press, 1998), pp. 55–71.

Redfield, R., *Tepoztlán: A Mexican Village* (Chicago: University of Chicago Press, 1930).

Revill, J., *Britain Shamed by NHS Death Rates*, The Observer (7 September 2003).

Riddell, S. *Gender and Politics of the Curriculum* (London: Routledge, 1992).

Rigg , J.A and Sefton, T. A, *Income Dynamics and Lifecycle* (Cambridge University Press, 2006).

Ritzer, G., *The McDonaldization of Society* (Forge Press, 2000).

Robert R. Alford, *Health Care Politics* (University of Chicago Press, 1975).

Rogers, A., and Nicolaas, G., 'Understanding the patterns and processes of Primary Care use: A combined quantitative and qualitative approach', *Sociological Research online*, Vol. 3, (4), http://www.socresonline.org.uk/3/4/5.html (1998), (Accessed 12 February 2008).

Rogers, A., and Pilgrim, D., *Mental Health and Inequality* (Palgrave Macmillan, 2003).

Rohrer, F., *Mirror not first to be duped*, BBC, http://news.bbc.co.uk/1/hi/uk/3716013.stm (15 May 2004).

Rosenblatt, G., and Rake, K., *Gender and Poverty*, (Fawcett Society, 2003).

Rosenhan, D., 'On being sane in insane places', *Science*, 179 (1973), pp. 250–258.

Rowntree, J., *Poverty a Study of Town Life* (Macmillan, 1901).

Rudat, K., *The Manchester Inner City Survey. Health and Lifestyles: Black and Minority Ethnic Groups in England*, Health Education Authority (London, 1994).

Ruhm, C., 'Are Recessions Good for your Health?' *The Quarterly Journal of Economics*, MIT Press, Vol. 115 (2), (2000).

Russell, M., *The Piltdown faker*, BBC, http://news.bbc.co.uk/1/hi/sci/tech/3285163.stm (Accessed 7 July 2007).

Sefton, T., and Burchardt, T., *Case Annual Report* (London School of Economics, 2005).

Sewell, T., *Black Pupils Failing Under Pressure from Peers*, *Independent* (2002), (Accessed 2 June 2007).

Shain, F., *The Schooling and Identity of Asian Girls* (Trentham, 2003).

Sharpe, S., *Just Like a Girl: How Girls learn to be Women* (Penguin, 1994).

Sir Peto, R., 'Smoking and inequalities', *The Lancet* 368 (*2006*), pp. 341–342

Slater, L., *Opening Skinner's Box: Great Psychological Experiments of the Twentieth Century* (W. W. Norton & Company, 2004), pp. 64–94.

Smart, C., and Stevens, P., *Cohabitation and Breakdown* (Family Policy Studies Centre, 2000).

Smart, C., *Changing Aspects of Family Life: Parents, Children and Divorce* (paper given at the National Council for One Parent Families Annual Conference (London.2003).

Smith, V. D., *Are you Married? If not, Why not?* http://www.thefword.org.uk/features/2004/03/are_you_married_if_not_why_not (The F Word, 2007). (Accessed 30 July 2007).

Spilsbury, K., and Meyer, J., 'The use, misuse and non-use of health care assistants: understanding the work of health care assistants in a hospital setting', *Journal of Nursing Management*, 12 (2004), pp. 411–8.

Spitzer, R. L, *On pseudoscience in science, logic in remission, and psychiatric diagnosis: a critique of Rosenhan's 'On being sane in insane places'* in *Journal of Abnormal Psychology*, 84 (5), (1975), pp. 442–52.

Sport England, *Driving up Participation: The Challenge for Sport* (2004).

Stand, S., *The educational progress of African heritage pupils in Lambeth schools* in *The achievement of African heritage pupils: Good practice in Lambeth schools*, Demie, F., McLean, C., and Lewis, K., eds. (Lambeth: Lambeth Children and Young People's Service, 2006), pp. 24–44.

Stationery Office, *BSE Inquiry* (Crown, 1998).

Stationery Office, *Independent Inquiry into Inequalities in Health Report* (London, 1998).

Stobbart, G., Elwood, J., and Quinlan, M., 'Gender Bias in Examinations: How Equal are the Opportunities?' *British Educational Research Journal*, Vol. 18 (3), (1992), pp. 261–76.

Stobbart, G., Elwood, J., and Quinlan, M., *Gender bias in Examinations* (Whitehouse and Sullivan, 1992).

Sudman, S., and Freeman, H., 'The Use of Network Sampling for Locating the Seriously Ill', *Medical Care*, Vol. 26 (10) (1988), pp. 992–9.

Swain, J., Finkelstein, V., French, S., and Oliver, M., eds., *Disability: A social challenge or an administrative responsibility?* In *Disabling Barriers – Enabling Environments* (Open University Press, 1993).

Syeandle, S., Escott, K., Grant, L., and Batty, E., *Women and Men Talking About Poverty*, Equal Opportunities Commission (2003).

Taylor, M., *It's official: class does matter*, Guardian (28 February 2006).

The British Sociological Association, *Statement of Ethical Practice for the British Sociological Association*, http://www.britsoc. co.uk/equality/Statement + Ethical + Practice.htm (March 2002). Last accessed April 3rd 2008.

The Institute of Fiscal Studies, *English Longitudinal Study of Ageing* (2007).

The Observer, *The Uncovered Poll*, http://observer.guardian.co.uk/ drugs/story/0,,686454,00.html (21 April 2002). Last accessed August 7th 2007.

The Potteries, *Key dates in Working Conditions, Factory Acts Great Britain 1300–1899*, http://www.thepotteries.org/dates/work. htm (Accessed 4 June 2007).

The Poverty Site, *Low Income and Disability*, New Policy Institute 2007, http://www.poverty.org.uk/24/index.shtml (Accessed 7 August 2007).

The Poverty Site, *Low pay by ethnicity*, http://www.poverty.org. uk/31c/index.shtml (Accessed 31 January 2008).

The Poverty Site, *Numbers in low income*, http://www.poverty. org.uk/01/index.shtml (2006), (Accessed 4 July 2007).

The Poverty Site, *United Kingdom – Premature Death*, http:// www.poverty.org.uk/35/index.shtml (Accessed 8 December 2007).

Thomas, W. I., and Thomas D. S., *The Child in America* (New York: Alfred A. Knopf, 1929).

Times, *Times Hospital Consultants' Guide* (Times Group, 2003).

TNS Media Intelligence, *Flu pandemic could kill 750,000, chief medical officer warns*, http://presswatch.com/health/print. php?searchterm = donaldson&archive_year (Accessed 9 January 2008).

Twenty-07, *Research Findings*, http://www.sphsu.mrc.ac.uk/ studies//2007_study/index.php?Page = 96&mitem96 = 1 (Accessed 17 December 2007).

UK Statistics Authority, *2006 Annual Survey of Hours and Earnings*, http://www.statistics.gov.uk/pdfdir/ashe1006.pdf (2006), (Accessed 8 January 2007).

Unicopli, I. C., *Gender socialization within the family: A study on adolescents and their parents in Great Britain* (Milano, 2003).

United Kingdom's Disabled People's Council, http://www.bcodp. org.uk/ (Accessed 5 December 2007).

University of Cambridge, *The Health and Lifestyle Survey*, Department of Community Medicine (1984).

Van de Gaer, E., Pustjens, H., Van Damme, J., and De Munter, A., 'Effects of single-sex versus co-educational classes and schools on gender differences in progress in language and mathematics achievement', *British Journal of Sociology of Education*, 25 (2004), pp. 307–22.

Verkaik, R., *Who Owns Britain?*, *The Independent* (9 April 2007).

Wadsworth, M. E. J., 'Follow-up of the first British National birth cohort: findings from the MRC National Survey of Health and Development', *Paediatric and Perinatal Epidemiology* 1, (1987), pp. 95–117.

Walby, S., *The Cost of Domestic Violence*, The Women's Equality Unit (September 2004).

Wanless, D., *Securing Our Future Health: Taking a Long-Term View*, Her Majesty's Treasury (2002).

Watson, D., *He Never Really Understood Us*, Guardian (11 May 2007), (Accessed 4 December 2007).

Watt, G., *Policies to Tackle Social Exclusion* in *British Medical Journal* (28 July 2001), p. 323.

Weber, M., *Essays in Sociology by Max Weber* (New York: Oxford University Press, 1958).

Weber, M., *Max Weber: Essays in Sociology*, (Oxford University Press, 1946).

Weber, M., *The Theory of Economic and Social Organisation'* (New York: Free Press, 1947).

Weiner, G., *Education Reforms and Gender Equality in Schools* (Equal Opportunities Commission, 1997).

Weiner, G., *Learning from Feminism: Education, Pedagogy and Practice* (Sweden: Umeå University, 1997).

West, A., Hind, A., and Pennell, H., *Secondary Schools in London: admissions criteria and cream skimming*, (Centre for Educational Research, September 2003).

Westergaard, J., and Ressler, H., *Class in Capitalist Society* (London, 1976).

Wharton, A.S., and Erickson, R., *The Consequences of Caring: Exploring the Links between Women's Job and Family Emotion Work*, Sociological Quarterly 36 (2) (Spring 1995), pp. 273–96.

Whyte, W. F., *Street Corner Society* (Chicago: University Press, 1943).

Wilkinson, H., *No Turning Back, Generations and the Genderquake* (Demos, 1994).

Wilkinson, R., *Income inequality and population health: a review and explanation of the evidence*. Social Science and Medicine 62 (Elsevier Ltd. 2006), pp. 1768–84.

Wilkinson, R., *The Impact of Inequality: empirical evidence* in *Renewal*, 14 (1) (London, 2006), pp. 20–6.

Williams, J. H., *Patriarchy for Children: On the Stability of Power Relations in Children's Lives*, in *Children, Youth and Social Change: A Comparative Perspective*, Chisholm, L., Buchner, P., Kruger, H. H., and Brown, P., eds. (London: Falmer Hood, 1990).

Williams, R., *Lay understandings of health and illness*, http:// www.soc.surrey.ac.uk/pdfs/Lecture%207%20-%20Lay%20un derstandings%20of%20health%20and%20illness.pdf (1983), (Accessed December 2007).

Willis, P., *Learning to Labour* (Aldershot: Gower, 1977).

Willmott, P., and Young, M., *Family and Kinship in East London* (Routledge and Kegan Paul Ltd, 1957).

Wilson, A., *Northern Soul Music, Drugs and Subcultural Identity* (Willan Publishing, 2007).

Wilson, C., M., and Oswald, A. J., *How Does Marriage Affect Physical and Psychological Health? A Survey of the Longitudinal Evidence,* http://www2.warwick.ac.uk/fac/soc/economics/staff/faculty/oswald/healthlong2005.pdf (The Warwick Economics Research Paper Series, 2005), (Accessed 24 June 2007).

Winlow, S., *Badfellas: Crime Tradition and New Masculinities* (New York: Berg, 2001).

Wittenberg, R., Comas-Herrera, A., Pickard, L., and Hancock, R., *Future demand for long-term care in the UK* (Joseph Rowntree Foundation, 2004).

Witz, A., *Professions and Patriarchy* (London: Routledge, 1992).

Womack, S., *Cost of raising a child 'has soared',* http://www.telegraph.co.uk/news/uknews/1571820/Cost-of-raising-a-child-%27has-soared%27.html, *Telegraph,* (Accessed 7 December 2007).

Women and Equality Unit, *Gender Pay Gap,* http://www.equalities.gov.uk/women_work/pay.htm (2006), (Accessed July 2007).

Women's Aid, *British Crime Survey underestimates domestic violence statistics,* http://www.womensaid.org.uk/page.asp?section=0001000100050013 (Accessed 23 July 2007).

Women's Aid, *What is domestic violence?* http://www.womensaid.org.uk/domestic-violence-articles.asp?section=00010001002200410001&itemid=1272 (Accessed 23 July 2007).

Women's Health Council, *Women, Disadvantage and Health* http://www.whc.ie/documents/40_women_disadvantage.pdf (Accessed February 17th 2008)

Women's Resource Centre, *Statistics about Women in the UK 2006* http://www.wrc.org.uk/resources/facts_and_statistics_on_womens_inequality_in_the_uk.aspx (2006), (Accessed 10 October 2007).

Women's Resource Centre, *Uncovering Women's Inequality in the UK: Statistics,* http://www.whywomen.org.uk/Downloads/Statistics.pdf (April 2007), (Accessed 12th October 2007.).

Women's Resource Centre, www.wrc.org.uk (Accessed 3 November 2007).

Wood, P., *International Classification of Impairment, Disability and Handicap* (World Health Organization: Geneva, 1981).

Woods, P., *Sociology and the School* (London: Routledge and Kegan Paul, 1983).

Woods, P., *The Divided School* (London: Routledge and Kegan Paul, 1979).

World Health Organisation, *Gender Equality: Work and Health, A Review of the Evidence* (2001).

World Health Organisation, *Investing in mental health* (Geneva, 2003).

Wright, C., Eggleston, S. J., Dunn, D. K., and Madju, A., *Education for Some* (Trentham Press, 1986).

Wright, C., *School Processes – an ethnographic study* in *Education for Some,* Eggleston, S., Dunn, D., and Anjali, M., (Stoke-on-Trent: Trentham Books, 1986).

Wright, C., Weekes, D., and McGlaughlin, A., *'Race', Class and Gender in Exclusion from School* (Falmer Press, 2000).

Young, J., *The Drugtakers: the Social Meaning of Drug Use* (London: McGibbon and Kee, 1971).

Younger, M., Warrington, M., Gray, J., Rudduck, J., McLellan, R., Bearne, E., Kershner, R., and Bricheno, P., *Raising Boys' Achievement*, Department for Children, Schools and Families (University of Cambridge Faculty of Education (2003).

Yu, J., and Cooper, H., 'A quantitative review of research design effects on response rates to mail questionnaires', *Journal of Marketing Research*, Vol. 20 (1983), pp.36–44.

Zajdow, G., *Caring and Nurturing of Women Married to Alcoholics*, Women's International Studies Forum, 18 (1995).

There are instances where we have been unable to trace or contact the copyright holder. If notified the publisher will be pleased to rectify any errors or omissions at the earliest opportunity.